Communication in Business

2nd edition

s. bernard rosenblatt
salisbury state university

t. richard cheatham
southwest texas state university

james t. watt
corpus christi state university

Library of Congress Cataloging in Publication Data

ROSENBLATT, S. BERNARD.
  Communication in business.

  Includes bibliographies and index.
  1. Communication in management.   I. Cheatham, Thomas
Richard.   II. Watt, James T.   III. Title.
HF5718.467 1982   658.4'5   81-15418
ISBN 0-13-153478-5   AACR2

editorial production / supervision
  and interior design: barbara kelly
cover design: infield / d'astolfo assoc.
manufacturing buyer: edmund w. leone

Printed in the United States of America

10 9 8 7 6 5 4 3 2

ISBN 0-13-153478-5

Prentice-Hall International, Inc., *London*
Prentice-Hall of Australia Pty. Limited, *Sydney*
Prentice-Hall of Canada, Ltd., *Toronto*
Prentice-Hall of India Private Limited, *New Delhi*
Prentice-Hall of Japan, Inc., *Tokyo*
Prentice-Hall of Southeast Asia Pte. Ltd., *Singapore*
Whitehall Books Limited, *Wellington, New Zealand*

To Julia, Donna, Michael, and Sam;
Juan Nell, Tina and Ricky;
Margaret and Helen

Contents

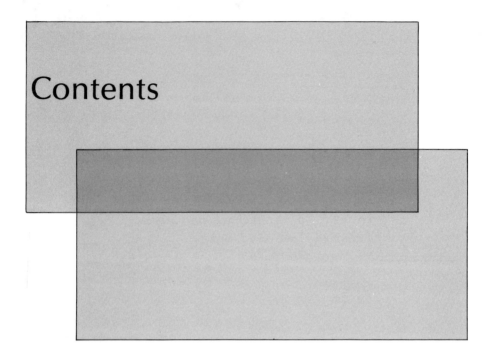

6   Listening: A Neglected Art,   110

7   The Process of Persuasion,   125

8   Nonverbal Communication,   144

3   Business Communication Systems in Action,   38

II   business communication: processes   55

4   Understanding the Communication Process,   57

5   Communication Variables,   85

9   Visual Communication in Business,   159

III   business communication: applications   189

10   Communication With One: Interviewing,   191

11   Communicating With Groups: Discussion and Conference,   219

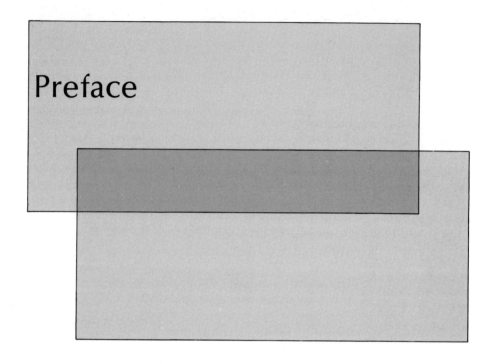

Preface

In the five years that have transpired since the first edition of this book was published, little has happened to diminish the initial statements made in the first preface. In fact, time and history now show them to understate and underemphasize the importance of communication in business today.

It is by communication, still faster and using more sophisticated technology, that a business receives and conveys information, transmits instructions and suggestions, practices motivation and persuasion. Communication is the life-blood of the organization and the means by which management gets things done. The greater emphasis on worldwide competition, depletion of natural resources, social inequities, pollution, quality of life, energy shortages, and government control points to a still greater importance for business to com-municate more effectively with all its publics in the future.

This book is designed as an introductory overview—a survey of communica-tion used in business today *with* some foundation in organizational and com-munication theory. By taking this approach, we have provided source material for understanding how, where, when, and why communicaton serves business. This allows us to include many important areas of business communication ignored or briefly touched on in other books. Several changes have been incorporated into this edition in an effort to make it more viable as a learning tool. Materials considered relatively unimportant now have been deleted and other materials have been condensed. A new chapter on listening has been added and the applied writing section has been expanded. Admittedly, we leave gaps in our presentation, but we hope that exposure will stimulate readers to seek out more specific information about the varied and interesting communication areas.

Communication is something practiced by all, regardless of occupation or level of authority and responsibility. We all need to improve on this very vital skill, and for this reason, we felt that the inclusion of pragmatic guidelines was needed. In effect, this book was a pioneering effort to merge theory and practice, not only in speech and written communication, but also in such areas as nonverbal, visual, and mass communication as found in modern business activity.

Our reviewers, friends, and critics recommended that the organization employed in the first edition be retained, and so it has. To accomplish our objectives of presenting business communication in a logical, informative, and interesting manner, we have organized the book as follows:

Part I describes how communication is employed in business and the processes and systems employed. The topics and areas are management-oriented and provide the setting and understanding required to introduce the theoretical overlays.

Part II introduces and explores different communication theories, explaining their ramifications and applications to business needs. Understanding the theoretical bases of communication should be of great value in the self-improvement of communicative skills. The materials digested in this section are not usually found in a business communication text, but in an array of highly useful but specialized areas.

Part III focuses on the application of theory to practice. Presented is a useful survey and evaluation of oral and speech communication forms. While traditional presentation speech is included, emphasis is placed on the extensively employed one-to-one and small group interpersonal communication process. Written communication is next treated in the same manner. Included are aids to improve the effectiveness of letters, reports, and other commonly used written communiques. The section concludes with discussion and explanation of the mass communication process and business applications, advertising, and public relations.

At the end of each chapter, you will find discussion questions, projects and problems, suggested additional reading materials, and a list of periodicals pertaining to the subject matter. Lively discussion will put your communication skills to the test and should amplify your knowledge of the area. The projects have been designed to reinforce the reading material. They should prove both interesting and enlightening. A final word about the periodicals.

Read these from time to time to stay alert to the latest happenings and findings in the respective area. New research findings and developments occur daily and the periodicals are your best avenues to this information.

The Appendix includes suggestions on how you can better employ your communicative abilities when seeking or changing a position.

We are indebted to the many who have contributed ideas and suggestions in the formulation and the implementation of this book, including John C. Tootle, Eric S. Stein, James M. Lahiff, John D. Pettit, Jr., Larry L. Barker, Robert L. Kibler, Doug Andrews, Ted Arnold, Brian Walker, Bob Wesley, Mac McClure, and Marina Harrison. We wish to express our gratitude to those who have provided the many illustrations used and to those who have granted us permission to reproduce their efforts. We, of course, are solely responsible for what appears.

S. BERNARD ROSENBLATT
T. RICHARD CHEATHAM
JAMES T. WATT

Business Communication: Environment

Communication
in
business

1

key points to learn

Why it is important to view a business firm as a system.

What business communication is.

How the communication process works.

The purposes for which managers use communication.

The various forms of business communications.

Why communication in business will become increasingly important.

"The business of communicating has become as important as finding more oil," said a former president of a major oil company recently. This remark came, I am sure, after some frustrating efforts to communicate with the many publics of a modern business organization—especially one caught up in controversy and dramatic change.

Business organizations in general have had to adapt to numerous conflicting pressures coming from many sources. During the seventies there was a general growing barrage of anti-business criticism; employees were seeking more challenging and rewarding work; consumer interest groups exerted greater pressures on pricing and marketing strategy; and the government, through its ubiquitous agencies, reshaped many aspects of business operations previously thought beyond its scope of providence.

One characteristic of a healthy organization is its ability to adapt to pressures and change. Lahiff and Hatfield conducted a study to examine the changes in communication policies and practices in business organizations between the years 1973 and 1978. One hundred and eighty-three firms responded to the survey. These firms represented a broad spectrum of manufacturing and service industries. A summary of the significant changes in communication policies and practices revealed:

I. Internal Communication
   A. Organizations are placing higher priorities on downward communication and attempting to improve on this practice. Employees, on the other hand, appear generally more inclined to question the contents of management's communication.
   B. The flow of upward communication in organizations has greatly improved during the five study years. Upper management has shown a high degree of willingness to listen to lower management and in turn, there appears to be a dramatic increase in the willingness among employees to speak their minds.
   C. A changing emphasis on communication formats appears to be emerging. Signs of this stem from:
      1. Important decisions are made more frequently by groups rather than by individuals.
      2. Employment interviews are playing more important roles in selection decisions.
      3. Greater emphasis is being placed on written communication with increased opportunity for communication training.
II. External Communication
   A. Organizations are much more concerned about enhancing their public image than they were five years ago.
   B. In efforts to enhance their images, organizations are more receptive to communication from the public, are placing greater emphasis on truthfulness, and are having their executives increase their public speaking activities.[1]

The complexity of the communication problem, in both society and business, grows daily. Over a decade ago, John Platt estimated that the speed of communication in 1965 was ten million times faster than it was in 1865.[2] It may have doubled that since 1965.

These problems are not just those of small businesses but of all organizations. The world's largest communication organization, the American Telephone and Telegraph Co. (AT&T), has its share. With all of its technical know-how, its vast financial resources, its equipment and paraphernalia, the Bell Telephone division of AT&T has communication problems. In the March–April 1971 issue of the *Bell Telephone Magazine*, one article begins:

Within the greatest communication organization in the world we are hurt and puzzled by a seeming communications failure—the problem of talking with our employees. The fact that we are perhaps no worse off than any other comparable organization (perhaps even better) is small comfort. In a corporation of more than 1,000,000 population, such a gap can be destructive. We should perhaps replace the omnipresent safety plaque with one that reads,

COMMUNICATE OR PERISH

[1]James M. Lahiff and John D. Hatfield, "The Winds of Change and Managerial Practices," *Journal of Business Communication*, Vol. 15, No. 4, Summer, 1978, pp. 19–28.
[2]John Platt, "What We Must Do," *Science*, No. 28, Nov. 1968, pp. 115–121.

a systems approach
════════to business communication

Regardless of size, of products and services produced, and of geographical location, communications are the vital link holding organizations together. Communications provide the means by which business managers perform their functions. Organization and communication are interdependent. Recognition of this interdependency gave rise to what is called the "systems approach."

Visualize a business firm as an organization or system of related parts and also as a part of a larger system of organizations within a total environment. Like a pebble thrown into a pool, a change in any part of the system will have a "ripple effect" and eventually will be felt in some magnitude throughout the total system. The greater the change, the more powerful the waves.

Wroe Alderson viewed the business firm as having to find equilibrium or a state of balance with its proximate environment and its ultimate environment. Starting at the core, a business firm must first find balance within itself. There must be a harmonious relationship among ownership, management, and labor. Moving out into the proximate environment, the business must be in equilibrium with its customers, suppliers, distributors, competition, and regulatory agencies in order to maintain profitable operations. Attaining balance with the ultimate environment is essential. The social, political, technological, and economical factors must also be seriously considered as guidelines to the future for failure to eventually be in balance with this overall environment can spell the end of the business firm. Examples of failure to provide balance are seen every day. A strike is evidence that management and labor have failed to reach agreement. A failure to produce profits may force a business to liquidate. A firm unable to meet customer demands may be forced to quit. A business or industry that is unable to withstand economic or technological pressures, but that is vitally needed, may be subsidized by the government. Communication is often the key to the maintenance of balance and therefore to survival. The signals are often there, but a failure on the part of those responsible for communication prevents the interaction needed to foresee and avoid the consequences. What then do we mean by business communication?

───────Business Communications Defined

The words communicate and communications are used loosely in everyday conversation. We hear, read, and talk about, "the communications gap," or, "communications, or the lack of them being a major cause for many of today's problems." What do we consider "business communications" to be?

Business communications are *purposive interchanges of ideas, opinions, information, instructions, and the like,* presented *personally or impersonally by symbol or signal* as to *attain the goals of the organization.*
Let's examine the meaning of the six major points:

1. purposive: must have predetermined objective in line with attaining the goals of the organization. May be formal or informal but not social, unless in line with ultimate firm goals.

2. interchanges: always involves at least two or more people including the sender and the receiver. An old parable asks, "If a great tree in a forest falls, is there a noise?" The answer would have to be, "Only if there were someone to hear it fall."

3. ideas, opinions, information, instructions, and the like: content of the message will vary depending on purpose and circumstance.

4. personally or impersonally: the channel may be direct, eyeball-to-eyeball, or via television to millions of persons simultaneously.

5. symbol or signal: any device or method that can be coded to convey a message or bring about an interchange may be employed. Symbols may be positive or abstract; signals may be verbal or nonverbal, the key is how well the intended message is understood.

6. attain the goals of the organization: one of the distinguishing characteristics of any formal organization is a set of goals or purposes determined by the management. Bettinghaus named two major kinds: a) productivity goals, and b) maintenance goals. As the success of a business firm is measured by profits, productivity goals establish levels of operation, and maintenance goals are set for the continuity of these levels.

Before discussing further the importance and the role of communication in business, let us examine a simple communication model and identify its parts. Part II will elaborate on the many other forms the model may take.

A Communication Model

A communication or interchange requires as few as two people, a sender and a receiver, but because of the complexity of the problem, many others may be involved. Regardless of the number the process is somewhat as follows:

The sender, or the source, decides upon the nature of the message and to whom the message will be directed. Next the message is encoded or put into the language or meaning that would be most acceptable or useful to the receiver. The encoding or message creation may be performed by the source or entrusted to others. The channel is the means or method for delivering the message. It could be direct or face-to-face between sender and receiver or one of the many indirect channels such as advertising media. Decoding is performed by the receiver and is a selecting process. A receiver decodes and accepts what is desired of the message and rejects what is undesired. Feedback

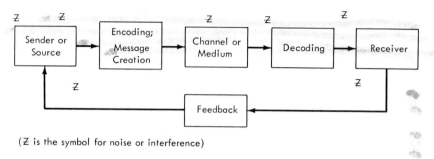

(Z is the symbol for noise or interference)

Figure 1–1 A basic communication model.

is the response to the message and may take many forms such as stimuli for another message, the following of an instruction, the request for samples or more information, a vote, purchase of a good, etc. Noise or intereference surrounding the steps of the process represent all physical and psychological conditions that could cause interference.

══════════communications and efficient operations

Bavelas and Barrett view the concept of organization as an elaborate system for gathering, recording, and disseminating information. They correlate the effectiveness of an organization with that of its communications.[3]

The concept of communication efficiency and organization efficiency is not a new one:

THE POWER OF COMMUNICATION

And the whole earth was of one language, and of one speech.

And it came to pass, as they journeyed from the east, that they found a plain in the land of Shi-nar; and they dwelt there.

And they said to one another, Go to, let us make brick, and burn them thoroughly. And they had brick for stone, and slime they had for mortar.

And they said, Go to, let us build us a city and a tower, whose top *may reach* unto heaven; and let us make us a name, lest we be scattered abroad upon the face of the whole earth.

And the LORD came down to see the city and the tower, which the children of men builded.

And the LORD said, Behold, the people *is* one, and they have all one language; and this they begin to do; and now nothing will be restrained from them, which they have imagined to do.

---

[3]Alex Bavelas and Dermot Barrett, "An Experimental Approach to Organizational Communication," *Personnel*, **27**:5 (March 1951) pp. 366–371.

Go to, let us down, and there confound their language, that they may not understand one another's speech.

So the LORD scattered them abroad from hence upon the face of all the earth: and they left off to build the city.

Therefore is the name of it called Babel; because the LORD did there confound the language of all the earth: and from thence did the LORD scatter them abroad upon the face of all the earth.

—GENESIS 11:1–9

Using Communication

Communication situations involving managers span a wide range of settings. These can be viewed as a continuum ranging from the most interpersonal setting through mass communication as shown in Figure 1–2.[4]

Managers of a business depend upon communication for:

1. Information
   a. Decision making
   b. Control
2. Influence
   a. Motivation
   b. Persuasion
   c. Control

Information[5]

Communication and information are totally different, *but* information presupposes communication as it must be received and transmitted to manifest value.

Communication involves an interpersonal exchange while information is

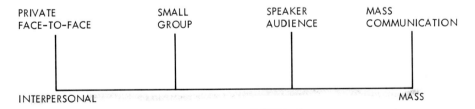

| PRIVATE FACE-TO-FACE | SMALL GROUP | SPEAKER AUDIENCE | MASS COMMUNICATION |

INTERPERSONAL   MASS

Figure 1–2   The full range of a manager's communication responsibilities.

[4]Richard K. Allen, *Organizational Management through Communication*, New York: Harper & Row, Pub., 1977, p. 56.

[5]Note: the terms data and information are used interchangeably in common usage, but technically, they have different meanings. Data refers to raw bits of knowledge entering a system as an input. When data has been processed or transformed in some structured form for a specific purpose, it becomes information.

impersonal or neutral. As humans, we do more than receive a raw message, we perceive it in light of our experience or expectations. Information is logical, factual, and must be interpreted. Information is also concrete and oriented to a specific topic, while communication takes the form of a pattern.

A business manager makes decisions based on the way information is interpreted. The information may be received from internal or external sources; transformed or adjusted to meet the needs of the decision-maker, and then in turn transmitted to enable others to act. To be received and used, the information must be encoded and the code known and understood by the receiver. A series of numbers, 103, 407, 32, and 519, is useless unless one knows what the series means. These numbers could refer to inventory, styles, addresses, etc. They are of no value without the code or meaning. The speed and capacity of computers have created a data explosion and a busy manager cannot afford the time to determine what is of importance and what is not by screening all that is available. Codes identify what should be considered in the solution of specific problems.

Information is also required as a control device. Production requires equipment, manpower, materials, and supplies. Adequate stocks must be maintained for smooth and continuous operations, but on the other hand, if goods are not selling, finished inventory will build up. When a certain level of inventory is reached, production is stopped. This is but one example of how the need for information operates in the control situation.

Business also receives and provides information from and to external organizations. Government agencies, trade associations, chambers of commerce, universities, and other organizations supply valuable information as well as collect it.

A business today depends upon a continuous supply of information, and a dependable distribution or communication system for both the receiving and delivering of the information messages to those responsible for making decisions and controlling operations.

_____ Influence

Communication is employed to influence individuals and groups personally and impersonally, directly or indirectly, internally or externally. By "influence," we mean to motivate, persuade, or control behavior in a predetermined direction. A manager could order a subordinate to perform a task but a more effective means of getting the job done would be to motivate the individual to willingly and eagerly do what was needed, and do it with the feeling that it was in the subordinate's best interest.

A highly visible form of business persuasion is advertising. American business spends over $50 billion annually to motivate and persuade viewers, readers, listeners, and shoppers to purchase its goods and services.

Image-building, conditioning, and visual representation are all devices used to convey the idea that "this is the firm to do business with." By using verbal and nonverbal messages, the business firm attempts to present, promote, and persuade prospects to accept their ideas and products.

Motivation and persuasion are influential devices. Employing these techniques, the communicator more effectively may achieve goals than by attempting to order or coerce.

forms of business communication

Forms vary from person to person, from company to company, from situation to situation. Confidential matters may be discussed face-to-face or transmitted in written form with an appropriate label such as "Personal," "Private," "Confidential," or "Secret." Some communications require a two-way flow in order to answer any questions that might arise while others can be transmitted in just one direction. Nonverbal cues can be very informative, for instance visual symbols used by business. Some of the different forms of communication include:

oral:

Interviews	Assignment giving	Work place meetings
Appraisals	Sales meetings	Formal addresses
Staff meetings	Sales presentations	Grievance handling
Conferences	Radio commercials	Public address systems
Orientations	Sound tapes	Training sessions
Counselling	Report meetings	Union negotiations

written communications:

Announcements	Pay envelope inserts	Magazines and News-
Reports	Advertisements	papers
Letters	Manuals	Bulletins
Newsletters	Signs	Booklets
Posters	Memos	Publicity
	Speechwriting	Statements

combining oral and written (audio-visual):

Films	Slide presentations	Videotape
Television	Film strips	Closed circuit TV

visual communications:

Illustration	Photography	Architectural style
Trademarks	Packaging	Type design
Color	Symbols	Signs

| Trade characters | Brandmarks | Shape |
| Dress or attire | Size | Contrast |

nonverbal:

| Facial expression | Feel | Time |
| Body movement | Space | Odor |

importance of business communication
══════════════in the future

Business communicates in many ways and for many reasons. Wiley categorizes the reasons as:

1. Employee recruitment and training.
2. Employee relations.
3. Sales and promotion.
4. Reporting to management.
5. Reporting to stockholders.[6]

As important as these functions are, the process and practice of communication in business is one of the least understood facets of business, and it needs the most improvement. Peter Drucker wrote in *The Effective Executive*:

Communications have been in the center of managerial attention these last twenty years or more. In business, in public administration, in armed services, in hospitals, in all major institutions of modern society, there has been great concern with communications. Results to date have been meager. Communications are by and large just as poor today as they were twenty or thirty years ago when we first became aware of the need for, and lack of adequate communications in modern organizations.[7]

Not only will the manager of the future be concerned with interpersonal and mass communication but also with person-to-machine interface. Computers and electronic data processing will continue to grow in importance as will the need for better communication between the machine and man.

In addition to the many information input devices for instructing computers, cards, tapes, discs, and other equipment, we will soon be able to address computers directly through our voices. According to Charles Brown, the Bell Labs of AT&T are working on this difficult problem "to get computers to recognize spoken words and convert them into data the computer can use."

---

[6]J. Barron Wiley, *Communication for Modern Management*, Elmhurst, Ill.: The Business Press, 1966, pp. 1–6.

[7]Drucker, Peter F., *The Effective Executive*, New York: Harper & Row, Pub., 1967, p. 65.

Bell Labs is currently working on a direct voice interface for airline reservations. You would call for reservations, tell the computer what city you wished to visit, and a schedule would be presented to you in computer voice. When further directed, the computer would print your ticket and mail it to you.[8] Imagine what doors this will open.

It should be obvious that effective communication is essential in all organizations and that the corps of managers, business executives, supervisors, and other communicators will have to improve their communicative abilities to meet the challenges of today, let alone of tomorrow. That American businesses, including the giant AT&T, recognize an inability to communicate efficiently within, should illustrate the difficulty and enormousness of the task. To compound matters, the problems of business communication will increase because of such factors as:

1. Attitudes and needs of employees are changing.
2. Business is growing larger.
3. Business organization is growing more complex.
4. The quantity of data and information is exploding.
5. Competitive pressures are increasing.
6. Society is demanding improvement of the "quality of life."
7. Governmental regulations are increasing.
8. Others.

Changing Attitudes and Needs of Employees

According to E.B. Weiss, "Employees, blue collar and white collar, will no longer tolerate merely being numbers. They want to be more fully informed about company policies and programs."[9] Recent articles and studies point out the dissatisfactions of the work force, especially the young. Unions are now bargaining for more participation on the part of the workers in issues and policies that directly affect them. New lines of communication will have to be established using innovative methods. The pattern is becoming increasingly apparent that managers and supervisors who are prone to secrecy are replaced by superior communicators.

Business Is Growing Larger

Growth, expansion, merger, consolidation, amalgamation, multinational development, along with product diversification have increased and will continue to increase the problems of communication. Once the man-

---

[8]"The Phone in Your Future," *U.S. News and World Report*, Feb. 12, 1979, pp. 63–64.

[9]E.B. Weiss, "There's Revolution Brewing in Internal Communications," *Advertising Age*, Aug. 16, 1971, pp. 51–52.

ager of the small factory or office could call all of his or her employees together for a meeting. Today, a top executive knows only a few people on the upper managerial levels and has little or no contact with the vast number of employees.

As the business firm grows, so do the distances between plants and people. The "communication chain" illustrated in Figure 1–3 shows only one level between the supervisor and the employee but the distances increase between levels of middle and top management. With the development of international and multinational business enterprises, the barriers of language and cultural differences also will have to be overcome in communicating effectively.

_____Business Is Growing More Complex

Technology, problems of environment and pollution, international competition, and the effects of foreign government regulations and policies have contributed to the need for complex organizations to cope with all possible situations. As doing business becomes more demanding, the need for coordination through communication becomes more critical.

Technology has added to the problem of employee morale and communication. With work simplification and automation, the operatives feel little challenge and almost no identification with their employer or the products they help make. Specialization has added to this problem of boredom and frustration. As a result, the rate of productivity suffers.

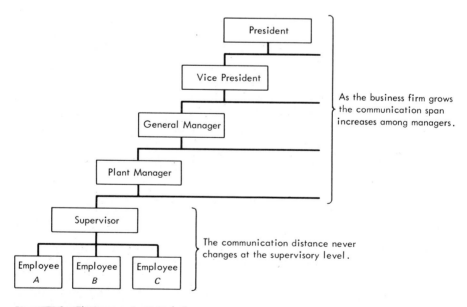

Figure 1–3 The communication chain.

The Data and Information Explosion

The increased amount of available data resulting from the ability of the computer to process and store has created a veritable information explosion. This in turn places greater-than-ever burdens on the communication system to see that information is retrieved and distributed to those needing such material. Improved data processing systems are being created, adding to the existing dilemma.

The Increase of Competition

Not only is business faced with domestic competition, it is faced with that of big-scale and widespread international competition. To compete internationally, business will have to become more efficient in manufacturing and in marketing. Accurate and rapid communication is vital in this endeavor.

Society's Demand to Improve the Quality of Life

While business once operated in a laissez-faire, or unregulated and almost irresponsible manner, it can no longer do so. Business must be responsive to the demands of society and both listen and respond to critics. In the future, there will be greater need for continuous dialogue between the business firms and the general populace. Witness the many institutional advertisements explaining what business firms are doing to curb pollution, maintain ecological balance, conserve resources, eliminate social problems and the like. Business must communicate what it is doing or else face censure and possible litigation and regulation forced by an uninformed population.

Government Regulation

A composite of the above six factors has brought about increased regulation of business. Regulation and control require vast amounts of raw data and detailed reports. Witness substantiation of advertising claims which call for very detailed write-ups of tests and results. To lessen regulation, business must be more responsive to the needs and desires of society and practice self-regulation and self-discipline. Doing is not enough, business must also inform through communication what has been done, what is being done, and what is planned for the future.

Other factors indicating the continued importance of communication in business include increased organizational specialization, changes in organizational structures, decentralization, international as well as domestic anti-business sentiment, and enlightened and sophisticated research.

summary

With all of its communication know-how, America's largest business, the American Telephone and Telegraph Company, has difficulty in communicating.

A business must be able to maintain open lines of communication within itself but also with the proximate and ultimate environments in order to be in equilibrium and to survive. Managers use communication for information and for influence. The information that managers base their decisions on must be transmitted via a dependable communication system. Information is logical, impersonal, and specific, while communication is personal, subject to human perception, and patterned. Influencing also involves motivating and persuading. It has been proposed that the efficiency of an organization is proportionate to the efficiency of its communication system.

The business manager uses information for decision making. This is received from both internal and external sources. An almost continuous supply of information is required as decision-making and control activities are continuous.

Business managers also exert influence both inside and outside the business. Employees are motivated to increase their productivity, and prospects are persuaded to purchase products and services. The firm has many forms of communication available and most use a combination of oral, written, visual, and nonverbal in their operation.

As important as communication is to business today, this importance will grow in the future because of a number of factors. These include: changing employee attitudes; growth of the business enterprise; increased complexity of the organization; data and information explosion; pressure of competition; demands of society; and, increased government regulation.

Discussion Questions

1. An AT&T executive suggested that the ever-present safety plaques be replaced with ones reading, "Communicate or Perish." Explain the suggestion.
2. Why must a business firm find equilibrium with its proximate and ultimate environments?
3. In your own words, explain the reasons underlying the definition of "business communication" given in this book.

4. Using examples, explain the two basic purposes of business communications.
5. Comment on "information presupposes communication."
6. How do communication and information differ?
7. How do data and information differ?
8. Assume that you are a business executive. How could society's demands for improvement in the quality of life affect your firm's communication policies and practices?
9. Mention some recent governmental laws or regulations that could affect business communication in the future.

Project

1. Secure a recent copy of *Newsweek* or *Business Week*. Go through it and analyze the advertisements in terms of their communication purposes as you see them. Pay particular attention to the institutional or nonproduct advertising seeking to convey the image of a "concerned company." Describe the different approaches taken in these "image" ads.
2. Select an organization that you are familiar with: a business, school, hospital, religious or governmental agency. Conduct a brief study of its communication system and write a report based on your evaluation of its effectiveness.

Additional Reading

DeMare, George, *Communicating for Leadership: A Guide for Executives.* New York: Ronald Press, 1968.

Drucker, Peter F., *Technology, Management and Society.* New York: Harper & Row, Pub., 1970.

_____ *The Effective Executive.* New York: Harper & Row, Pub., 1967.

Haney, William V., *Communication and Interpersonal Relations,* 4th ed. Homewood, Ill.: Richard D. Irwin, 1979.

Mayerson, Evelyn W., *Shoptalk.* Philadelphia: W.B. Saunders Co., 1979.

Peterson, Brent D., Gerald M. Goldhaber, and **R. Wayne Pace,** *Communication Probes,* 2nd ed. Chicago: Science Research Associates, 1977.

Scholz, William, *Communications in the Business Organization.* Englewood Cliffs, N.J.: Prentice-Hall, 1962.

Vardaman, George T., *Effective Communication of Ideas.* New York: Van Nostrand Reinhold, 1970.

Some Periodicals to Read:
Business Week
Dun's Review
The Wall Street Journal

Communication and management

2

key points to learn

The different types of systems found in business organizations.

What the functions of management are.

The characteristics and forms of organizations found in business.

Differences between the formal and informal organization.

How organization overlays work.

Theorists' ideas about motivation.

An organization is a systematically arranged whole of independent parts, each having a special function or relationship to the whole. This definition, extended to business or to any other human enterprise, describes an organization of people who, through cooperation, can achieve goals which were formerly unavailable to the individual.

For cooperation to exist, a process of interaction between people must be discovered or developed. This interaction process is communication. To organize is to imply a goal. Authority and responsibility must be accepted by organization members if they are to act as one in reaching their goal. Communication is required to transmit the directives of authority and to achieve cooperation and coordination of the parts.

the business organization as a system

One of the major barriers to people communicating with one another is language or the meaning of words. In fact, "word" is listed sixteen different ways in *The American Collegiate Dictionary*. According to Charles C. Fries and the *Thorndike Word Book*, the 500 most-used words have 14,070 separate meanings in *The Oxford Dictionary*. Various systems exist in business and so, to overcome this initial communication barrier, let's examine some of these systems and how they operate.

What Is a System?[1]

In its simplest form, a system consists of two or more elements and a relationship among them. Systems can range from the very simple to highly complex structures such as the solar system. A systems approach to the study of business communication is a method of identifying and ordering the elements; simplifying the problem in order that it may be examined conveniently. As simple as Figure 2–1 is, it is useful in that each of the elements can be further divided, and each part, in turn, can be more closely examined and analyzed. All problems can be examined using the systems approach. This will become more apparent as we become more involved. Systems can be classified in order of complexity:

Framework. Unchanging, simple, and predetermined structures fall into this category. Static or unmoving communicating systems would be road maps, airline schedules, blueprints, etc. Simple moving devices would be pendulums or levers.

Cybernetic or Closed. The classic example is a house or room kept at a predetermined temperature by a thermostatic device. Everything in the system is self-contained or closed. The thermostat is set at the desired temperature and then, regardless of season, will automatically turn on the furnace or air-conditioning unit to maintain the preset temperature.

In a retail business, the inventory level for certain items may be set and reordering will be automatic when the level is reached. Many other similar examples are found in the business world.

Open. This system goes further than the cybernetic or closed structure by having interchange with its environment. The open system depends on feedback for control, and this is obtained from many sources depending upon the

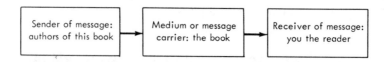

Figure 2–1   A very simple communication model. This is an example of a one-way communication system in that there is no feedback or response from the receiver back to the sender.

---

[1]Much of the systems material in this section was based on S. Bernard Rosenblatt, Robert L. Bonnington, and Belverd E. Needle, *Modern Business: A Systems Approach*, 2nd ed. Boston: Houghton Mifflin, 1977, Chap. 3, pp. 53–71.

circumstances. The business firm is of this order, receiving materials and information from outside. After processing the material and information, a product is supplied back to the market. A combination cybernetic system would look like the diagram in Figure 2–2.

Inputs or forces are received from the environment and then processed in the closed business system. The objectives of the firm serve as a controlling device or a feedback mechanism.

Social. The most complex is the one that deals with the interaction of people in groups. Within the business organization, we find groups that voluntarily choose to interact and those that must cooperate and coordinate their efforts.

A business enterprise is first and foremost a social system; a grouping of people who, through joint efforts, may achieve goals that would be unattainable to the individuals. As an organization, these people will be functionally assigned. Within every area, the members will divide further into social subsystems in order to meet their individual goals.

Table 2–1 sums up the characteristics of the systems discussed:

As can be realized, the business firm is a composite of the various systems. Regardless of classification, communication is the means by which the parts interrelate. The parable of Babel in Chapter 1 was a good example. When communications fail there is lack of coordination and the system fails. Communication is a tool of management; it is the means by which the organization comes into being and functions.

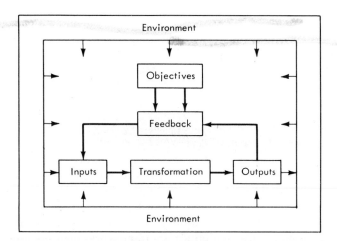

Figure 2–2 A simplified systems diagram of a business enterprise. In this illustration we see a combination open and cybernetic (closed) system: information and materials entering the closed system from the environment and products and services going back into the external surroundings. Each portion or component of this diagram may be dissected, examined, and analyzed in depth.

TABLE 2-1 types of systems arranged by complexity

Type	Description	General Examples	Business Examples
Framework	A static or simple dynamic system with predetermined necessary motions.	Maps, arrangement of atoms in a crystal, solar system, simple machines.	Blueprint, organization chart, balance sheet, laws of economics.
Cybernetic or Closed	Controls by monitoring an essential variable through feedback.	Body temperature, human adjustment of radio sound volume, heat system.	Internal control of cost, inventory, sales, credit; control of computer.
Open	Self-maintaining through environmental feedback.	Flame, river, living organisms: human, plant, animal.	Production and marketing systems, national economy.
Social	Interrelates human activity, formation of groups.	Families, clubs, neighborhood organizations.	Departments, committees, informal groups, labor unions.

From S. Bernard Rosenblatt, Robert L. Bonnington, and Belverd E. Needles, Jr., *Modern Business: A Systems Approach*, Boston: Houghton Mifflin, 1973. p. 39.

the managerial functions

Management is the process by which individual and group effort is coordinated toward group goals. Inherent in all of the definitions of management are what one writer has called "the essence of management, the process of integration and coordination." Management can also be defined in terms of the functions performed.

The Functions of Management

Regardless of size, scope, or the nature of the problems involved, the managers of any enterprise perform such functions as planning, organizing, actuating, directing, coordinating, and controlling. Understanding the role of the manager and the functions performed will enable you to understand the value of communications in a business and the use of communications for operations. In a communication framework, management operates as shown in Figure 2-3.

Planning. Planning, the first and most important of the functions, has been called "a rational approach to the future." Planning depends on the availability and quality of information, and on how well the manager can interpret and convert this into action.

Planning starts with awareness of opportunity. If an opportunity is found, then objectives and goals are defined. These are given time and priority ranking, then structured to show how the components of the system must be coordinated. Information must constantly be sought as business operates in an open system and a changing environment may alter plans.

The budget is a financial plan and a key to how well the monetary arrangements were perceived. The budget is also a guide or control device as to how money is being spent and the objectives met. Budgets and plans are often based on forecasts, which are predictions of economic conditions and the firm's marketing expectations.

Policy-making is still another of the planning activities. It is through policies that management directs the overall actions of the enterprise. Policy consists of statements that reflect the basic thinking of the planners and provide guidelines for action throughout the firm.

Organizing. The design of a *framework* for the performance of all activities necessary to efficiently attain predetermined goals. An organization is a device to hold the parts together in a related and integrated manner and to establish the lines of authority and responsibility.

Rensis Likert lists the following as the important characteristics and processes of an organization:[2]

1. It has a structure.
2. It has observational and measurement processes that collect information about the internal state of the organization, the environment in which the organization is functioning, and the relationship of the organization to this environment.
3. It has communication processes through which information flows.
4. It has decision-making processes.
5. It has action resources to carry out decisions regarding such matters as personnel of the organization—skilled and unskilled—and the machinery, equipment, and energy sources used by them.

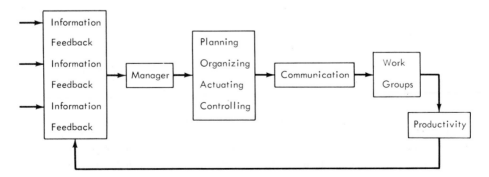

Figure 2–3 Functions of management in a communication framework.

[2]Rensis Likert, *New Patterns of Management.* New York: McGraw-Hill, 1967, p. 50.

6. It has influence processes.

7. It has attitudinal dimensions and motivational characteristics such as the basic motivational forces it seeks to draw upon in using the efforts of its members and the degree of favorableness of attitudes and loyalties toward the organization, its component parts, and its members.

Reading this list, you will note the prominent role that communication plays. Tracing the communication network of a business often provides a better understanding of the organization than examining a descriptive organization chart.

Organizational Design.   There are two kinds of organization, the formal organization and the informal organization. The formal organization is one established by management with a clearly defined hierarchy of authority and areas of responsibility. An organization chart is a static framework system showing the component parts and their relationships. The other organizational form almost defies charting for, as the name implies, it is informal. This informal organization is a social system that develops when the formal order does not satisfy the individuals involved. The informal organization often develops because the formal organization communication system fails to provide information to those desiring it. Often, the only evidence of its existence is the "grapevine," or that chain of communication that holds the parts of this organization together. Informal organizations develop within almost all formal organizations, the degree depends on how well individual needs are met within the formal structure.

The earliest form of organization was the highly authoritarian structure which had only one direction: down! Examples would be a king and his subjects; a master and slaves. The tasks performed in these early line organizations were simple and repetitious. Preindustrial tasks were undifferentiated and allowed a leader to supervise a large number of people. Communications were all downward: from the leader to the subjects or subordinates. None could question the authority of the orders.

As technologies developed and as distances increased between the central authority and those to be supervised, layers were added to the organization. Eventually, advisors or counselors were added to the organizational scheme, and these were the forerunners of what are now known as "line and staff" organizations.

Figure 2–4 shows two forms of a line and staff organization. The one at the top has three scales or levels to supervise twenty-four subordinates, while the one below is more decentralized and shorter with only two levels or scales for the same number of subordinates. Also note that in both illustrations there is a staff advisor to the president and supervisors. The staff positions are advisory with no authority. Authority may be delegated to the staff by the superior.

The formal structure in Figure 2–4 embodies the concepts of Mooney and Reiley and of Weber's idea of a "bureaucracy." Basic in their ideas of an organization were:

1. Coordination: unity of action in pursuit of a common purpose.
2. Scales: levels of hierarchy.
3. Functionalism: the idea of specialization.
4. Staff and line: the staff providing ideas and advice, the line representing authority.

The Mooney and the Weber models of organization are often called the classic form. It is more than a description, it is a philosophy of managerial thought. The classicists were concerned with form. They sought a general body of principles that could guide a manager in almost every situation. During the 1950s, a new philosophy of management began to emerge. It was based on human relations, and researchers such as Douglas McGregor and Rensis Likert led the field seeking better and more efficient ways to manage.

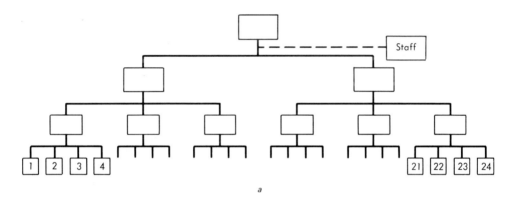

a

Tall and narrow structure with three levels of management. Usually found in highly centralized organization.

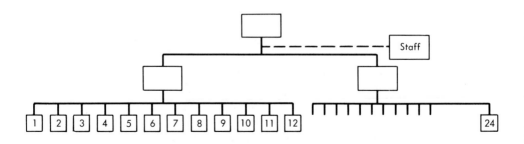

b

Short and wide organization with two levels of management. Typically found in decentralized enterprise.

Figure 2–4 Typical organization charts illustrating the classic line and staff structure.

In seeking information about managerial effectiveness, Likert found that greater output resulted when there was greater interaction within the organization. He developed what then was called the "linking pin" organization, now called "Systems 4." Shown in Figure 2–5, Likert said that an organization will be optimally effective to the extent that its processes insure the maximum potential of interactions in all possible relationships, and that each individual will view such experiences as supportive, building and maintaining a sense of personal worth. The overlap in the chart recognized that managers may belong to more than one work group.

Organizational theorists have suggested other models to overcome the weaknesses in the classical model or to incorporate the strengths of the model in a modern communicative and participative framework. The Glacier theory is one of these efforts. One of the interesting innovations in this organization is the inclusion of a grievance system and worker representation to sit in council with the managers. This provides a "linking pin" situation or linkage through participation in different groups.[3]

Others, including Warren Bennis, advocate a more situational approach. Bennis suggests temporary systems organized around problems to be solved; others suggest different departmental organizations that would best solve each work group's needs. An outgrowth of contingency or situational management has been the matrix organization concept. The easiest way to explain the matrix idea is by an example. Imagine a modern high technology business organized into various engineering areas as in the case of a vertically organized line firm. Each engineer would report to his or her supervisor; that is, electronic engineers would report to the Director of the Electronic Engineering Department, and mechanical engineers would report to the Director of the Mechani-

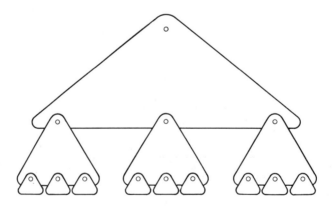

Figure 2–5   The linking pin or "Systems 4" organization chart as visualized by Rensis Likert. (Adapted from Rensis Likert, *The Human Organization*. New York: McGraw-Hill, 1967, p. 50.)

---

[3]Rensis Likert, *The Human Organization*. New York: McGraw-Hill, 1967, p. 50.

cal Engineering Department. This is the classical or traditional line or line-and-staff firm.

Now, this business has many research and development projects underway or under consideration. Each is complex, requiring a team effort by people of different scientific specialties. Each project is directed by a Project Manager. This director secures the needed staff for the project by requesting specialists from the different departments. The project team is vertical in that it cuts laterally across all of the department lines. The various engineers are borrowed from the departments for the duration of the project and returned when the project has been completed. This is shown in Figure 2–6:

Regardless of organizational form or framework, there is clear consensus that more involvement, participation, and understanding need be incorpo-

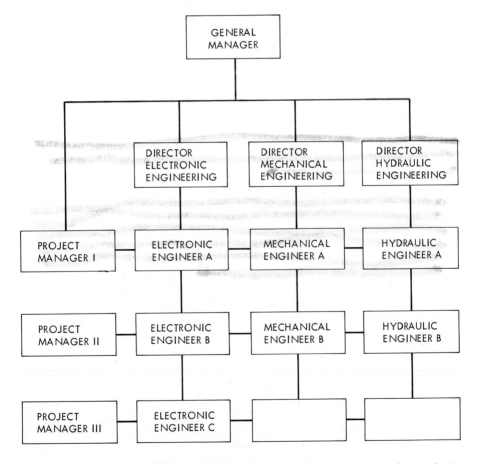

Figure 2–6 A matrix organization chart. The matrix has become increasingly popular in applicable organizations. It does present some problems of coordination and communication as the people involved have both vertical and horizontal relationships with their superiors.

rated into the design, and that this interaction can come about only with upward, diagonal, and horizontal communication added to the existing downward direction of the classical organizational model.

_____ Informal Organizations

Keith Davis saw the development of the informal organization as inevitable because of the complexity of business and industry. The informal organization is often born out of the need that the firm cannot provide adequately for social and emotional satisfactions. The feeling of belonging and being accepted draws employees together at every level. People unite on the basis of common interests, shared attitudes, or simply the need to be accepted by their work groups. What formal organization charts don't show are the results of how individuals adjust themselves to the behavior patterns of others by seeking out informal or subsystems to meet various circumstances. One way to conceptualize this behavior is to think in terms of overlays; patterns of behavior that fit over the formal organization scheme but do not conform to the rules of bureaucracy or classical theory.

Shown in Figure 2–7 are some examples of overlays with captions to imply the circumstances:

Actuating (Staffing, Directing, and Coordinating). With planning and organizing accomplished, the manager must next "get the ball rolling." Leonard Sayles sees the role of a manager:

> like a symphony orchestra conductor, endeavoring to maintain a melodious performance in which the contributions of the various instruments are coordinated and sequenced, patterned and paced, while the orchestra members are having personal difficulties, stage hands are moving music stands, alternating heat and cold are creating audience and instrument problems, and the sponsor of the concert is insisting on irrational changes in the program.[4]

In addition to knowing the score, the manager-conductor must be able to select the right musicians, cope with people and equipment problems, withstand the pressure of a schedule, resolve conflicts, and somehow manage to hold things together and keep the organization moving in the right direction.

Actuating has been described as, "getting all members of the group to want to achieve and strive to achieve the objectives the manager wants them to achieve because *they* want to achieve them." Staffing is one of the keys to actuating. If a manager staffs his or her organization with the right people, able to carry out their roles, then the problems of directing are minimized. Once staffed, the manager must give the subordinates direction. Directing involves the issuance of orders, directives, instructions, and assignments along with the overseeing and guidance that might be required. In reality, it is much more

_____

[4]Leonard Sayles, *Managerial Behavior.* New York: Harper & Row, Pub., 1964, p. 162.

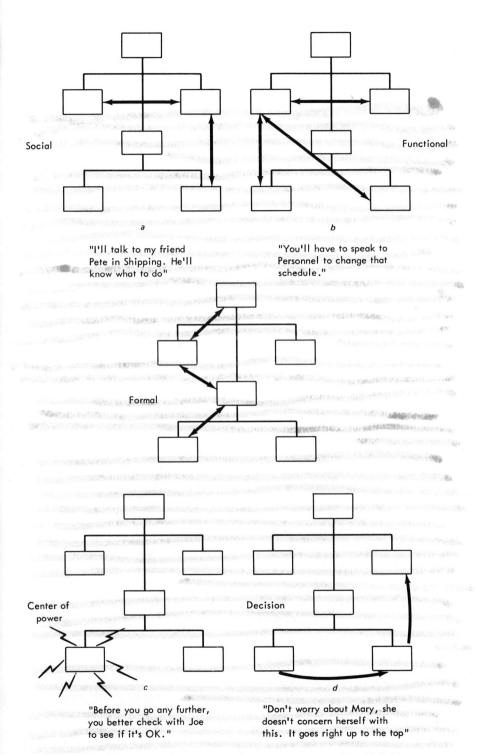

Social

Functional

"I'll talk to my friend
Pete in Shipping. He'll
know what to do"

"You'll have to speak to
Personnel to change that
schedule."

Formal

Center of
power

Decision

"Before you go any further,
you better check with Joe
to see if it's OK."

"Don't worry about Mary, she
doesn't concern herself with
this. It goes right up to the top"

Figure 2–7 Examples of organizational overlays: adjustments to the formal organization by
seeking out the informal organization or subsystems to meet various circumstances.

than this. It is building a motivated work force that will perform willingly and enthusiastically at high levels of productivity toward the accomplishment of objectives.

In building such a work force, the communicator or manager in this case must recognize and be able to deal with a multitude of different employee types. Robert Presthus describes three types of employees as (a) the upward mobile, (b) the indifferent, and (c) the ambivalent.

The upward-mobile employee is motivated by a desire to achieve and wants to move up the organization ladder. This person places the organization above all and is willing to pay the price, or play the game required for advancement. Supervision of the organization man or woman is relatively easy if the manager remembers that the upward mobile person is motivated by achievement.

The indifferent employee is another matter. This employee is motivated by a desire to have satisfactory interpersonal relationships usually off, rather than on the job. While they are not committed to organizational goals, they don't dislike the organization. It serves as a means rather than an end to their personal goals. These employees usually want a clear and understandable set of job standards, an acceptable wage, and the mental freedom to pursue their nonwork interests.

The ambivalent personality requires a manager with astute listening and counseling skills. This employee wants the fruits of achievement but is unwilling to give up the personal freedoms, as is required of the upward mobile.

Paul Preston further refines these three personality types into six subtypes: (1) tribalistic, (2) egocentric, (3) conformist, (4) manipulative, (5) sociocentric, and (6) existential.

Tribalistic people are most comfortable with an established ritual. They take pride in working for a prominent company and see this as being a member of a strong tribe. They have little or no ambition to rise out of their group and interpret most of their job in terms of whether they have a good or bad boss.

This group works best in an environment of easily understood and precise rules administered by a benevolently autocratic manager. Improved working conditions to the tribalistic are indications that management cares about them. They are short-run thinkers and are concerned with monetary compensation rather than retirement or deferred payments.

Egocentric employees have no conception of company loyalty and are likely to walk out on a job or fail to show up. Usually malcontent and suspicious, they need hard rules and will respond to firmness and threats of demotion or loss of pay.

Conformists believe they should do their jobs as the company asks. They appreciate good working conditions but will not complain if they are bad. They are reluctant to bend or break company rules.

Manipulative employees are self-achievers and "wheeler-dealers," who play angles and reap rewards. Sometimes aggressive and overbearing, they are often loose in their ethics. This individual demands treatment as an individual and wants to be included in any process involving his or her personal goals.

Sociocentric employees are concerned with the welfare of mankind, preventing strife, and generally keeping the peace. They respond to an agreeable boss who gets people working together in a spirit of friendship. They have little or no desire to move into management, are not motivated by money, do not like to make decisions, and are likely to be motivated by group job-enrichment programs.

The sociocentric values group identification and wants to be considered part of a group. Each will cooperate in group decision-making and will respond to open and friendly communication.

Existential people are usually members of the new breed of managers who bring high levels of creativity to their jobs. As workers, the existentials are indifferent to physical conditions but chafe under restriction and regimentation. They work best alone and when given the freedom of action they desire.[5]

Planning and organizing are key activities, but they are often performed with a minimum of interpersonal relationships. Directing takes on new communication dimensions. Directing requires two-way, face-to-face dialogue. Many managers fail in their ability to actuate, not from lack of knowledge or judgment but from inability to communicate.

Leadership, Motivation—Ingredients of Actuating.   To be able to direct requires an understanding of human relations. Formally, one may be appointed a manager and leader, but in reality leadership comes from below, not from above. Leading involves showing rather than threatening; inspiring rather than driving; assuming responsibility rather than passing the buck. Likert and others have found that productivity in work groups is higher for employee-centered supervisors than for job-centered ones.

Leadership takes on more meaning in the informal organization where the leader is selected by peer group members. They are chosen for their understanding of the group needs and their commitment to satisfy them. Unlike the formal organization, a leader who fails the group can be quickly replaced without ceremony. This concept of leadership is evident also in democratic organizations, but here formal procedures are followed. Don't we elect those who govern us? The officers of our clubs, unions, etc.? A business firm is not democratically organized nor are the military services nor many religious congregations. The ideal business manager-actuator is the person delegated authority in the formal organization and accorded leadership from the work group.

The ability to motivate is a highly desirable quality in a director-leader-communicator. Motivation requires an understanding of human behavior and the components that form such behavior: perception, attitude, personality, etc. Motivation is an understanding of why we behave as we do and motivating is the process of persuading or influencing someone to perform some behavior with the thought that the instrumental behavior will satisfy a need.

---

[5]This section adopted from Paul Preston, *Communication for Managers.* Englewood Cliffs, N.J.: Prentice-Hall, Inc., 1979, pp. 208–220.

Psychologists generally believe that all behavior is motivated and that people have reasons for doing what they do and how they do it. Abraham Maslow developed a "hierarchy of needs" that will help explain this concept.[6] At the lowest level are those required for survival or to fulfill our basic needs. All people, regardless of environment, have these. The next group of needs are learned or products of our environments. While these needs may also be universal and shared by all people, the means of satisfying them will differ greatly. In Figure 2–8, we see the organization of needs in the hierarchy.

While the above needs are set in broad categories, they can be subdivided and various appeals can be associated with each. For example, safety and security could mean job security and be obtained by many routes: being the hardest and best worker, staying on friendly terms with the supervisor, gaining seniority, etc. To another person, safety and security could be social rather than economic and the motivation could be "You want to be a member of the group, don't you?"

Patterned after McGregor's positive attitude approach toward employees (Theory X) and incorporating Maslow's "hierarchy of needs," Kafka and Schaefer have developed a management system they call the Open Management System (OMS). Central to their approach is the circle-of-reference made up of self-image, human symbols, and human needs. OMS suggests that empathy and knowledge of the individual enables the manager to create an environment in which open understanding can grow between people on the job. This atmosphere contributes to individual need satisfaction resulting in organizational gain.[7]

When communicating, it is necessary to motivate a receiver to listen to your message. This is done by telling the receiver how he or she will benefit by listening or doing what you request. Gaining attention through motivation or

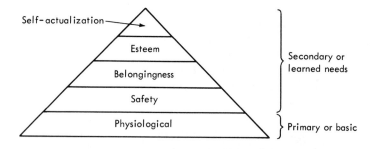

Figure 2–8   Maslow's Hierarchy of needs. Data (for diagram) based on Hierarchy of Needs in "A Theory of Human Motivation," in Motivation and Personality, 2nd ed., by Abraham H. Maslow (Harper & Row, Pub., 1970).

---

[6]Abraham H. Maslow, *Motivation and Personality*. New York: Harper & Row, Pub., 1954, Chap. 5.

[7]Vincent W. Kafka and John H. Schaefer, *Open Management*. New York: Peter W. Wyden, 1975.

the use of need-satisfaction is a far stronger method of gaining cooperation than such devices as fear-arousal, coercion, etc.

Herzberg, as a result of his research, identified the following six factors or satisfiers in the work situation:

1. Achievement
2. Recognition
3. Advancement
4. The work itself
5. The possibility of growth
6. Responsibility.[8]

In his study of automobile assembly line workers, Neal Q. Herrick found dissatisfaction with work resulting from what he called "satisfaction gaps." These were measured in terms of what the workers felt most important to them yet were least possible of the jobs that they had. He included such factors as: opportunity for promotion; good pay; opportunity to develop special abilities; adequacy of fringe benefits; interesting work; and, the help and equipment to get a job done. These are the type of problems a supervisor must cope with and communication is the tool to be used.

Controlling. The management process is continuous, acting in a circular form. The function of control is the means by which the manager can gauge whether objectives are being met, and if they are not, set in action corrective plans. Control always involves three steps:

1. Establishment of standards.
2. Information and measurements against established standards.
3. Action to correct deviations from the standards.

Control is the feedback system that informs the manager how well plans are being carried out.

Control may be highly mechanistic and involve little more than resetting some dials to correct a closed or cybernetic mishap. On the other hand, in an open and social system, such problems as energy or material shortages, legislative acts, social reform, could necessitate a reexamination of the enterprise and result in sweeping changes.

The control function is one of information and, if indicated, action. The communication channels permit the flow of information and if choked or misdirected, would inhibit the operation of the control system. Today's enterprise—large or small, public or private—cannot operate in a vacuum and is highly dependent upon ready access to the information vital to its existence.

---

[8]Frederick Herzberg, B. Mausner, and B. Synderman, *The Motivation to Work.* New York: John Wiley, 1959.

Frederick Herzberg, *Work and the Nature of Man.* Cleveland: World Books, 1966.

MBO: A Case in Point.   Management by objectives (MBO), is a concept first introduced by Peter Drucker in the early 1950s. He saw this approach as a means by which an organization could motivate its employees, especially at the managerial level, through genuine involvement. It has been widely accepted and considered to be almost universally applicable.[9]

Odirorne describes MBO as a process whereby superior and subordinate managers of an organization jointly identify its common goals, define each individual's major area of responsibility in terms of expected results, and use these measures as guides for operating the unit and assessing the contribution of each of its members. Three guidelines for MBO provide further understanding:

1. Superiors and subordinates meet and mutually discuss goals or results which are in line with overall organizational goals.
2. They then jointly establish attainable goals for subordinates.
3. They meet again after initial goals are established and evaluate the subordinates' performance in terms of the goals. The essential feature is the feedback on performance provided subordinates. The subordinates know where they stand with regard to their contributions to their organizational unit and the firm.

As seen in the guidelines, the success of MBO, or formal goal setting and review, will depend largely on the abilities of those involved to effectively communicate. MBO implies a series of meetings in which first goals are set, actions are planned, progress is reviewed, and performance is evaluated.

Although this explanation of MBO is simplified, it does provide an overview of the concept in general and illustrates the importance of interpersonal communication in making it work.

Summary

A business firm is a system in itself with numerous intrarelationships as well as interrelationships with its environment. The business firm is a composite of the framework, closed or cybernetic, open and social systems. Each of these play a part in the total. To operate the business system, management is required and those who manage use four functions in the process.

The manager accomplishes his or her tasks by: planning, organizing, actuating, and directing. Planning is "a rational approach to the future" and is concerned with obtaining and relating information in such a way as to form goals and objectives for the emerging enterprise. Goals are assigned priorities, structured, and given an organizational form.

---

[9]Dallas T. DeFee, "Management by Objectives: When and How Does it Work?" *Personnel Journal*, January 1977, Vol. 56, No. 1. pp. 37–39, 42.

The organization structure is the means by which materials and human resources are coordinated through the design of a task and authority framework. The framework holds the parts together in an integrated manner with established lines of authority and responsibility. Communications are the means by which these interrelationships are kept informed and guided. As in any human organization, there is an accompanying social system. If the formal organization fails to meet the social needs of its members, they form an informal organization that has a unique communication system known as the "grapevine."

Once organized, the structure must be staffed and directed to obtain the predetermined goals. Staffing and directing have been called actuating or "putting the organization into motion." The ability to communicate is inherent in directing as this function, above all, requires face-to-face dialogue and exchange of ideas, opinions, views, etc., as well as giving orders and directives. The effective manager-communicator must be aware of, and use the principles of, motivation to achieve individual and organizational goals in as simultaneous a manner as possible. The inherent quality of leadership is a great advantage to the manager faced with directing the cooperative efforts of peers and subordinates. While authority may be delegated from above, leadership is bestowed from those that are led. Ideally, a manager has leadership qualities along with authority.

The final function is that of control which often sets the process of management in a cycle. Control is the feedback system that informs management as to how well plans are working out. Controls are established wherever standards may be set and measurements are available. An information system is required to convey messages to those responsible and to implement action to correct deviations from the standards when and if they occur.

The purpose of this chapter has been to provide you with an understanding of the functions of management and the need for maximum communication efficiency. In the next chapter, we shall examine some of the communication networks found in an organization with which a manager must work.

=============== **Discussion Questions**

1. What is the value of using a systems approach as an analytic tool?
2. Illustrate why a business is usually a composite of the four systems models discussed.
3. Which of the functions of management are the most demanding of communications?
4. Explain the process of planning and why it is known as "a rational approach to the future?"
5. Under what conditions does an informal organization and the need for a "grapevine" arise?

6. Compare the formal line and staff organization structure to a more situational "linking pin" structure.
7. What is the difference between authority and leadership?
8. How can a communicator use knowledge of motivation?
9. Discuss the steps needed in the establishment of a control system.
10. Would you agree or disagree with the statement, "Management *IS* communication."?

══════════ Problem

1. If you were the supervisor of a work group, how would you handle the following problems using a motivation approach:
   a. A member of the group has been late three times this week.
   b. Production for the group fell below normal standards last week.
   c. Asking one of your subordinates to be your assistant without any increase in pay.
Outline the appeal you would use in each case to seek desired behavior.

══════════ Project

1. Visit the personnel manager or an administrator of a local business or institution. Obtain or draw an organization chart of the enterprise. Ask whether the formal organization chart really shows how the enterprise operates. Use overlays or colored pencils to show the deviations. Also ask about the presence of an informal organization and how that operates within the question.
2. Role play a situation in which one student attempts to guide the other in establishing goals for performance in class. As an MBO example, reverse the superior-subordinate roles.

══════════ Additional Reading

Allen, Richard K., *Organizational Management Through Communication*. New York: Harper & Row, Pub., 1978.

Bradford, J. Allyn, and Guberman, Rueben, *TA, Transactional Analysis*. Reading, Mass.: Addison-Wesley, 1978.

Gibson, James L., John M. Ivancevich, and James H. Connelly, Jr., *Organization: Structure, Processes, Behavior*. Dallas: Business Publications, 1973.

Haimann, Theo, William G. Scott, and Patrick E. Connor, *Managing in the Modern Organization*, 3rd ed. Boston: Houghton Mifflin, 1978.

Likert, Rensis, *New Patterns of Management*. New York: McGraw-Hill, 1961.

McGregor, Douglas, *The Human Side of Enterprise*. New York: McGraw-Hill, 1960.

Merrihue, Willard V., *Managing by Communication*. New York: McGraw-Hill, 1960.

Preston, Paul, *Communication for Managers*. Englewood Cliffs, N.J.: Prentice-Hall, 1979.

Rosenblatt, S. Bernard, Robert L. Bonnington, and Belverd E. Needles, *Modern Business: A Systems Approach.* 2nd ed. Boston: Houghton Mifflin, 1977.

Senn, James A., *Information Systems in Management.* Belmont, Calif.: Wadsworth, 1979.

Towsend, Robert, *Up the Organization.* New York: Alfred A. Knopf, 1970.

Some Periodicals to Read:

Forbes
Journal of Management
Michigan State Business Topics

Business communication systems in action

3

key points to learn

The information needs of managers.

The different patterns of communication flow.

How the grapevine works.

The barriers to organizational communication.

The methods of communication training.

Walk from an industrial shop into the adjacent offices and notice the difference. You move from noise to quiet, from heavy electric cables to slim telephone lines, from a machine-dominant to a people-dominant environment. You have moved from a section of the business system in which energetic exchange is the first priority and information exchange the second to a section where the priorities are reversed. The closer you get to the decision-making and control center of an organization, the more pronounced is the information emphasis.

the management information system

As discussed in Chapter 2, business managers use communications (1) to receive and disseminate information; and (2) to exercise influence. A reliable communication system to attain and transmit information is essential to the management process of planning, organizing, actuating, and controlling. In this chapter we will examine an information system, communication systems, and some of the problems of communicating in business organizations.

The management process requires continuous decision-making. Since information is necessary for the decision-making process, the quality and quantity of information influences the correctness of management decisions. To ensure accurate information for its manager, a business firm will want to establish an information system that has the ability to:

1. Measure events and attributes.
2. Store data for retrieval when needed.
3. Communicate information to decision-makers.

Figure 3–1 shows an open system with both internal and external information sources. The "information sources" at the left include internal information

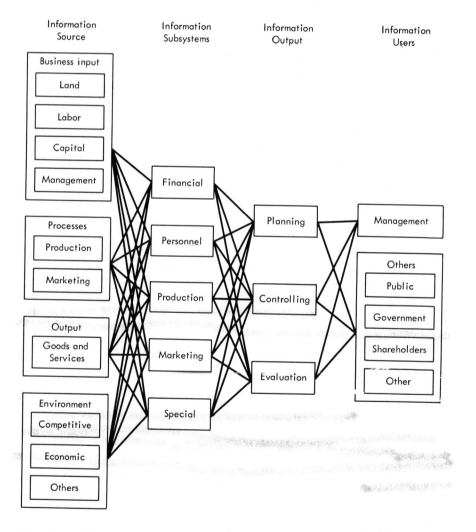

Figure 3–1   Management information system with internal and external information sources. (From S. Bernard Rosenblatt, Robert L. Bonnington, and Belverd E. Needles, Jr., *Modern Business: A Systems Approach.* Boston: Houghton Mifflin, 1973, p. 345.)

as a "transaction data base" and external information from the environment. This information enters the "information subsystems" of the various functional areas of the business. The information output column refers to the transformation of the data into useful information. In this case, the information users are management and various members of the public outside the firm. Based on this model, the information and communication networks can become very complex for even a small business enterprise.

_____ Information Needs At All Levels

Upper-level managers are not the only group in the firm needing and seeking information; first-level managers (supervisors), and operating employees also have informational needs. Although the supervisors or operatives will not be involved in policy-making decisions, they require information to effectively perform their jobs. Some of the desired information will be for personal needs, whereas other information will be directly linked to the work situation. The following lists detail information line employees want:

information about the job and personal needs:

1. Opportunities for advancement.
2. Information on job security.
3. Opportunities for training.
4. Future employment prospects.
5. Facts about wages.
6. Benefit programs.
7. Service programs.
8. Department performance results.

information about the company:

1. History.
2. Position in the industry.
3. Organizational structure.
4. Sales trend, earnings, growth.
5. Financial position.
6. Research activities.
7. Advertising program.
8. Current, new, and proposed products.
9. Relationship with union.
10. Names and something about executives.
11. Shifts of management personnel.
12. Company policies.
13. Expansion plans.
14. Community relations.
15. Official stand on current issues.

Supervisors form the next level in the organization. In addition to the information needs listed above, these people are usually interested in:

1. Supervisory responsibilities.
2. Limits of their supervisory authority.
3. Relationship and policies dealing with unions and the grievance procedure.
4. Function in relation to higher management and other departments.

Upper-level management, in turn, should be aware of additional employee needs. Those at a distance from the line would want to know:

1. Employee attitude toward the company.
2. How well understood and received are company rules, policies, and programs.
3. How employees can contribute to greater operational efficiency.
4. The "gripes" and complaints of individual workers before they develop into full-sized grievances.

In addition to those involved internally with the business organization, some people who are outside the organization are concerned and desirous of information. Stockholders, suppliers, distributors, customers, and neighbors are but a few of the parties interested in the operation of a business. Communication among all these parties is what this book is all about. In the next section, we will examine the structure and operation of some communication patterns of business organizations.

patterns of communication

Communications should flow smoothly and directly through the organization to accomplish stated goals. In this section we will examine the patterns of communication that tend to emerge from different organizational situations.

Bettinghaus suggests that communication patterns can be described in terms of:

1. Direction—the vertical, horizontal, and diagonal flow.
2. Nature—the type of communications carried such as reports, summaries, orders, directions, social conversation, etc.
3. Formality—how closely communications follow the lines of authority.[1]

The formal organization structure tends to be highly authoritarian because the expression and communication of ideas are limited to the formal lines of authority and responsibility. Communications follow the vertical, au-

---

[1]Erwin Bettinghaus, *Persuasive Communication*. New York: Holt, Rinehart and Winston, 1968, p. 242.

thoritarian structure of the organization. Each level reports to the level directly above. Major decision-making power is vested in the person at the top.

There is no communication between people on the same levels or between people on different levels in different groups, unless specified by policy. In this type of organization, there is a tendency to favor downward communication and discourage upward movement.

Decentralization is a systematic means of delegating authority to subordinates, while maintaining upper-management's right to overrule lower management. An organization may be decentralized for many reasons; growth, distance, diversity of products, available managerial talent, or communication problems.

Although still formal in nature, there is more likelihood for horizontal and diagonal communication in the decentralized organization than in the authoritarian model. This is due to the prevailing management philosophy of decision-making at lower-levels of the organization and freedom of exchange of ideas.

The "rumor-mill" or "grapevine" is the informal or social communication network present within every organization and at every level. Messages transmitted along the "grapevine" may be highly accurate when containing data but questionable when dealing with decisions. Rumors often start from persons with high communication centrality but not necessarily in a high organizational position. An elevator operator or a secretary may overhear a conversation; a janitor may be aware of a high-level meeting lasting late into the night; a cleaning person may see a portion of a discarded message.

No organization is immune to the "grapevine" since it furnishes social satisfaction as well as otherwise unavailable information. Management can use knowledge of the "grapevine" as a communication tool to reach informal group members not included in the path of the formal communication network.

_____ Mixed Patterns of Communication Flow in an Organization

As mentioned above, a "grapevine" exists in every organization regardless of how structured. This network represents a means of communication for the informal organization and may be thought of as an overlay to the formal communication network. This mixed pattern is a natural development of any social organization where members develop their own small group affiliations.

_____ Communication Patterns and Small Group Performance

Figure 3–2 shows the patterns of small group organization developed by Harold J. Leavitt to evaluate the effects of communication on work performance.[2]

_____

[2]Harold J. Leavitt, "Some Effects of Certain Communication Patterns of Group Performance," *Journal of Abnormal and Social Psychology*, Jan. 1951, pp. 38–50.

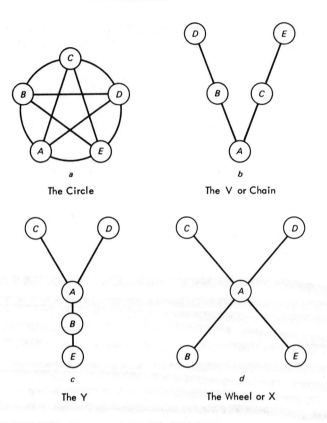

Figure 3–2   Patterns of small group communication. (From Harold J. Leavitt, "Some Effects of Certain Communication Patterns on Group Performance," *Journal of Abnormal and Social Psychology,* Jan. 1951, pp. 38–50. Copyright 1951 by the American Psychological Association. Reprinted by permission.)

Each pattern depicts the form of communication that could take place in the group. In the circular pattern (a), all members can talk with each other. In the V or chain pattern (b), each member can communicate only with the next member in line, A having direct access to B or C but not to D or E. The Y pattern (c), shows limited direct access similar to the V pattern, but here E can communicate only with B, B with E or A, and A with C and D. In the X or wheel pattern (d), A can communicate with all members, but B, C, D, and E cannot talk directly with one another.

Leavitt found that the circle arrangement, with communication possible among all members, provided the most group satisfaction and the Y pattern provided the least. The wheel pattern was judged fastest and most accurate in solving the problems that Leavitt used in his study.

Each pattern in Figure 3–2, except the circle is considered centralized because all communication is routed through one member. The circle pattern is decentralized. Others have studied patterns and problems of centralization and they acknowledge that the problem used in the experiment is the critical factor in determining the effectiveness of these communication patterns. Studies other than Leavitt's show that the circle of decentralized patterns is, in general, faster and more accurate in solving complicated problems than are the centralized ones.

A Rumor Mill: Study of a Grapevine. Keith Davis examined the communication patterns of a manufacturing company located in a rural town of approximately 10,000 people.[3] The plant employed 67 in its management group and about 600 nonmanagers. Davis interviewed employees to learn how they receive a given bit of information and from where it came.

He found that the four most significant characteristics of the grapevine in this company were:

1. The grapevine was fast in its speed of transmission.
2. The grapevine was selective in terms of what it carried.
3. The grapevine did fill gaps left by ineffective formal communications.
4. The grapevine of company news was confined to the place of work.

Davis identified four types of patterns in the spreading of information via the grapevine. These can be seen in Figure 3–3. They are: (a) the single strand in

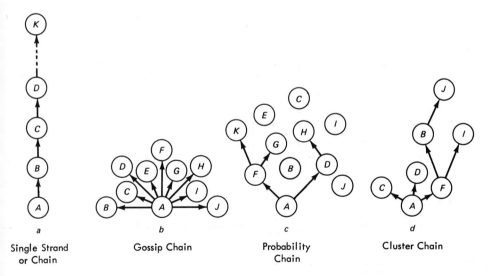

a

Single Strand
or Chain

b

Gossip Chain

c

Probability
Chain

d

Cluster Chain

Figure 3–3 Patterns of informal or rumor networks. (From Keith Davis, "Management Communication and the Grapevine," *Harvard Business Review,* Jan.-Feb. 1953, pp. 31, 43–49.)

---

[3]Keith Davis, "Management Communication and the Grapevine," *Harvard Business Review,* Jan.-Feb. 1953, pp. 31, 43–49.

which information passes in a line where much distortion can occur; (b) the gossip chain in which everyone communicates with everyone else; (c) the probability chain in which communication takes place randomly; and (d) a cluster chain in which there is selectivity in how the message is passed.

The study also disclosed that there was an active minority transmitting information in the grapevine. This group operated within the cluster pattern. Certain liaison individuals connected the clusters together. Others were isolated and received or transmitted little. In one case, although 68 percent of the managers knew about a certain situation, only 20 percent passed it on. In another case, 81 percent knew but only 11 percent passed the information along.

A Closed Communication System.   Communication subsystems are established to exchange specialized information among business departments or individuals. The advantage of such a system is that it can reduce errors, oversights, and personality problems in the transfer of routine information.

Figure 3–4 shows a closed (cybernetic) system drawn in flow-chart fashion. Use of such a chart as a communication device helps prevent errors and misunderstanding among individuals involved in communication systems. Responsibility is clearly indicated at each step of the process.

In the flow-chart, the sales department sends a copy of an order to the production-planning department (Step 1). Material requirements are esti-

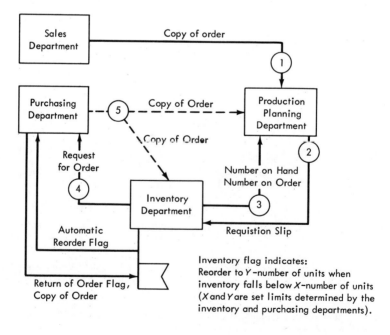

Figure 3–4   Flow-chart of a closed system for inventory reorder.

mated and a requisition slip is sent (2) to the inventory department which then advises production planning (3) of the quantities of material on hand and on order. Inventory also requests the purchasing department to order what is needed (4). The purchasing agent does so and sends copies of the order to the inventory and production-planning departments (5). An automatic "inventory flag," a warning that stock has fallen below a certain level, is sent from the inventory department to the purchasing department when inventory falls below a certain set minimum. The flag is returned to inventory with a copy of the order when material has been ordered per standard specifications.

The system illustrated in Figure 3–4 is one that is actually used in a small manufacturing company. Many other such systems can be devised to reduce the chances of error in day-to-day routine business operations. In addition, more complex patterns and systems can be designed to cover nonroutine events in which communication plays a vital role and speed is of the essence. Plans for closed communication networks can cover such things as a fire, a power failure, or any disaster threatening the operations of an enterprise.

some barriers to effective
organization communication

Barriers to effective communication may exist between departments in a business, between managers and subordinates, or between individuals at the same level of operations anywhere in the organization scheme. Barriers to effective communications between people and units of organizations are of three broad types:

1. Physical: Environmental factors can reduce or prevent the sending and receiving of messages. Such physical interferences include distance, distracting noise, and the breakdown or elimination of communication media such as telephones and interoffice memoranda.
2. Personal: Differences in the personal and psychological makeup of individuals may create barriers between people.
3. Semantic: The idiosyncracies of language, such as multiple meanings of words and differences in connotations, and interpretations of language from individual experience may cause communication breakdowns.

Among these three broad types, there can be many specific barriers. Business consultant William Scholz listed forty items in his *partial* list of "Obstacles to Communication."[4] Many of these dealt with general communication or interpersonal communication obstacles. Five specific organizational barriers will be discussed here. They are:

---

[4]William Scholz, *Communications in the Business Organization.* Englewood Cliffs, N.J.: Prentice-Hall, 1962.

1. Lack of a communication policy.
2. Authoritarian attitude of management.
3. Poorly defined authority and responsibility.
4. Too many levels of management, resulting in loss of detail and accompanying distortion.
5. Insufficient communication training.

_____ Lack of a Communication Policy

Few companies, including those that are largest and most "progressive," have clean-cut and stated policies dealing with intra- or interorganizational communication. Charles B. McCoy, former President and Chairman of the Board of DuPont, stated in an issue of DuPont's employee magazine:

> Communication has a high priority at DuPont. Employees have the right to be informed. They should be told important news immediately, good or bad.
>
> The people who work for DuPont want to know what the enterprise is all about. They want a sense of involvement, want to be a part of the organization, therefore, they need to know about current business problems, the company's stand on such important matters as imports and pollution control, and its views on issues of public importance. Employees want straight-forward, honest, balanced information, not propaganda.
>
> Informed employees are better, more productive employees. They get more out of their work, and they do a better job for the company.

Harold Zelko and Harold O'Brien have made several suggestions as to how a communication policy can create a climate conducive to organizational transactions.[5] They suggest that all levels of management be made "communication conscious," that management provide adequate proof that it is earnest in wanting to improve communication, and that all communication channels be employed to provide whatever information is needed and wanted. Management must show that upward communication is desired and that it will listen to what is transmitted.

For such a policy to be effective, there must be a climate conducive to communication within the organization. There must be free and permissive attitudes for the exchange of ideas and information in all directions. This will be possible when the organization is shown to be:

1. People-centered rather than production-centered.
2. Open with clear indications that effective communication will be practiced.
3. Sincerely interested in listening at every level of management.

_____

[5]Harold P. Zelko, and Harold J. O'Brien, *Management, Employee Communication in Action.* Cleveland: Howard Allen, 1957.

Other suggestions for establishing communication policies include: keeping employees informed of company goals, objectives, and plans about the marketplace and about negative, sensitive, and controversial issues; providing information fast; encouraging or requiring every supervisor to meet on a frequent and regular basis for honest two-way discussions of job-related situations; requiring meetings be held to discuss the subordinate's progress and position in the firm; and, establishing a climate where innovation and creativity are encouraged and employees rewarded for trying and succeeding but not penalized for trying and failing.

Authoritarian Attitude of Management

Without a clear-cut policy encouraging upward communication, Zelko and O'Brien observed an attitude of "I give the orders, you carry them out," prevalent among many managers and supervisors.[6]

Upward communication is important to management as it reveals how well ideas, policies, and work rules have been accepted. Free and honest talk often contributes ideas of value and makes known possible problem areas before trouble develops.

Scholz lists five important contributions of upward communication:

1. Provides management with information.
2. Helps relieve work pressures and frustrations.
3. Serves as a measure of downward communication effectiveness.
4. Enhances employees' sense of participation.
5. Suggests more rewarding uses of future downward communication.

Not all of the upward communication problems are those of management. Circumstances and inabilities on the part of subordinates can contribute to the problem. The most difficult subordinate barriers to upward communication are:

1. Freedom to contact supervisors.
2. Lack of ability to articulate or get the message across.
3. Unfamiliarity with the supervisor's job.

In firms that are unionized or have adopted a Glacier approach to organization, there is a formal grievance procedure to provide an upward flow of communication. Union contracts usually spell out the formal procedure for handling a grievance. The advantage of such a policy is that the employee need not fear recrimination for expressing a complaint or alleged violation of a right.

---

[6]Earl Planty and William Machaver, "Upward Communication: A Project in Executive Development," *Personnel Journal*, Jan. 1952.

Business firms use a number of techniques to encourage upward communication. Some of these are: employee attitude surveys, panels, comments and question columns in company publications, employee counselors, direct meetings, exit interviews, performance-appraisal interviews, suggestion boxes, and contests.

Poorly Defined Authority and Responsibility

The organization chart may not show where the true authority and responsibility is vested. Communications may bypass individuals or levels by design or through lack of understanding. Individuals often become communication or power-centers as a result of their technical knowledge, their access to information, or their leadership abilities.

Too Many Levels of Organization Result in Message Loss or Distortion

The more levels of management through which a message must be transmitted, the more chances for distortion, delays, or total failure of the message to reach its destination.

The greater distance a message has to travel, the greater the danger that it will be changed, modified, shortened, amended, interpreted, etc., to a point where it would not be recognized by the original sender.

Insufficient Communication Training

Although some firms have a formal communication training program, or lectures dealing with the subject as part of management or supervisory training, it is a sorely neglected area. Recently, such important areas as listening and nonverbal communication have been added to the more traditional written and verbal programs. Exposure to communicating problems may be provided through human relations programs or exercises such as sensitivity training, T-group sessions, or transactional analysis. For the most part, communication training has been a trivial portion of another program.

Not only is communication training important for managerial purposes, it is also morale-building. A study indicated that where communication training was employed, attitudes of the employees were twice as favorable to the company as compared to businesses where no training was given. Some of the results are given in the table on the following page.

The implications are clear that communication training could lead to both direct and indirect increases in the efficiency of management and in turn, the attainment of organizational goals.

Question	Communication Training	
	Company with	Company without
Employees felt they knew what was planned.	55%	18%
Employees felt a part of the company.	62%	29%
Employees felt that company was one of the best to work for.	45%	20%

communicating with outside groups

Most of this chapter has been concerned with internal communication and internal networks. As discussed in the management information system, business managers have a great need for internal information to plan and control operations but must also have a continuous supply of relevant information from outside the firm. This is necessary for long-range planning and for those decisions that could be affected by environmental changes.

Business requires information from the market place about competition and the availability of materials, parts, and equipment. Business must know about government rules and regulations and about the supply and cost of future money and labor. In turn, business supplies information to government agencies, to stockholders, to banks, and credit-rating agencies.

With all of today's pressing environmental, economic, and social problems, business must go beyond the usual communications which the public required in the past. The future will require even more disclosure and openness with the general public on the part of business. Supplying information through advertising and public relations is not enough. With some members of the public, the business firm must engage in two-way dialogue, working closely in order that needs be understood and problems worked out mutually. Listening becomes essential to cope with the new problems of the times.

What are some of the ways business is communicating with its new responsibilities in mind? It is doing so by listening to the community, by participating in community organizations, and by keeping abreast of local happenings and developing an awareness to community problems.

With the many problems facing society today, it will be imperative that business finds more efficient ways and means of communicating with its many audiences. To fail to do this could mean the end of a free enterprise, capitalistic system of profit and private ownership.

Summary

Information is the basis for managerial decision-making. Every business firm has some sort of information system for this purpose. The system should be able to measure, store, retrieve, and communicate internal and external information as needed.

Information needs vary with the firm and within groups of employees. Various communication networks, formal and informal, exist in every organization. The patterns can be discussed and analyzed in terms of direction, nature, and formality with mixed formal and informal patterns the rule.

Different small group communicating patterns affect the speed, accuracy, and group satisfaction in problem solving. Informal communication or the "grapevine" was found to be of a cluster type and faster than formal lines in a study by Keith Davis.

The major barriers to communication are physical, personal, and semantic. In addition to these general barriers are those that affect organization communication. Five of the more important ones are: lack of communication policy, authoritarian attitude of management, poorly defined lines of authority and responsibility, too many levels of management, and lack of communication training.

To have efficient organizational communications, there must be upward as well as downward channels. Some barriers to this are lack of freedom to contact superiors, inability to communicate ideas with superiors, and failure to understand the role of the superior's job. Today, business executives have new roles and responsibilities to communicate with the many external public groups affected by their organizations.

Discussion Questions

1. What are some of the problems you see in the organization and operation of a management information system?
2. To what extent should a company keep employees aware of future plans? Are there areas where information should be held back?
3. What reasons do you see for management limiting the bypassing or diagonal flow of communication?
4. Why should a "wheel" pattern of group organization be faster and more accurate in solving a problem than a "circle" pattern?
5. Explain the "cluster" pattern of grapevine communication.
6. Discuss, with examples, the three broad types of personal and organizational communication barriers
7. Why do you think the lack of a formal communication policy would be an organizational communication barrier?
8. What suggestions would you have to a manager for improving upward communication?
9. Why should "unfamiliarity with the supervisor's role," be a barrier to upward communication?

========= **Project**

1. Select an organization that you are familiar with and develop a formal communication policy for the enterprise.
2. Outline a presentation to the president of a business concern stating the importance of establishing a formal communication training program.

========= **Additional Reading**

Brennan, John, *The Conscious Communicator*. Reading, Mass.: Addison-Wesley, 1974.

Connelly, J. Campbell, *A Manager's Guide to Speaking and Listening*. New York: American Management Association, 1967.

DeVito, Joseph A., *Communication: Concept and Processes*. Englewood Cliffs, N.J.: Prentice-Hall, 1971.

Huseman, Richard D., Ca. M. Logue, and Dwight L. Freshly, *Readings in Interpersonal and Organizational Communication*, 2nd ed. Boston: Holbrook Press, 1973.

Leavitt, Harold J., *Managerial Psychology*, 2nd ed. Chicago: University of Chicago Press, 1964.

Murphy, Dennis, *Better Business Communication*. New York: McGraw-Hill, 1957.

Some Periodicals To Read:
Administrative Review
Fortune
Harvard Business Review

Business
Communication:
Processes

II

Understanding the communication process

4

key points to learn

The relationship between sound theory and effective practice.

The components of the intrapersonal communication process.

The components of the interpersonal communication process.

The manner in which vocabulary deficiencies result in communication breakdown.

The relationships between word symbols and the objects or thoughts that they represent.

How to maintain attention on message rather than competing stimuli.

The proper use of feedback.

The manner in which "bypassing" and "the tendency to evaluate" affect the communication process.

In the first three chapters you were introduced to the role and significance of communication in contemporary business transactions. It is hoped that the materials presented in those chapters in conjunction with your own observations have led you to the conclusion that effective business transactions cannot be realized apart from effective communication. You are probably thinking one of two thoughts as you begin reading this theoretical discussion of the communication process:

1. "All right, I agree. Communication is vital to efficient business and industrial activity. But, either you have it or you don't! With as much time as we spend talking and listening, if we aren't pretty good at it by now, there's nothing we can read in a textbook that will change our behaviour."
2. "O.K., so communication is important. Give me a list of techniques appropriate for each situation. I'm sure not willing to waste my time reading about theories of communication. Just tell me how to do it."

If your thoughts are represented by statement 1, we say you are both right and wrong. You are right when you say that we spend an incredible amount of time talking and listening. Paul Rankin's research led him to the conclusion that three-fourths of our waking hours are spent in some form of communication.[1] Think of it! Seventy-five percent of the time that we are conscious and awake, we are either listening, speaking, reading, or writing. More recently, a survey of communication behaviors of 700 executives yielded data indicating an average of 80 percent of an executive's day is spent talking and listening.[2] However, we must not confuse the *prevalence* of communication with *effectiveness* of communication. Familiarity in some cases may breed contempt, but it may also breed complacency. Practice does not necessarily make *perfect*. Practice does tend to make *permanent!* Conscientious rehearsal of desirable behaviors will result in predispositions that are desirable. Frequent repetition of undesirable behaviors will also result in predispositions, but of an undesirable nature. Most of you who are familiar with participation sports know the danger of frequent repetition of a poor delivery in bowling, a faulty golf swing, or a tendency toward arm tackling in football. Sure, you've been talking and listening since you were less than two years of age. But much of your success may be due to nothing more than chance, and many of your communication habits may be bad habits in need of correction.

If you are anxious to move on to the study of practical rather than theoretical aspects of communication, you need to realize that good practice is built upon sound theory. More and more we are being reminded that education is a life-long venture, rather than an achievement such as the acquisition of a degree or even several degrees from academic institutions. We feel that an understanding of theoretical elements involved in the communication process will prepare you to face communication problems of the future—problems which as of this moment are unanticipated—and develop your own solutions to those problems. Pragmatic applications of theoretical concepts are the focus of Part III of this text.

In this chapter you will be introduced to the *intrapersonal* and *interpersonal* communication processes through (1) definitions and (2) discussions of communication models. After you have gained a basic understanding of the communication process in the first half of this chapter, you will be introduced to the major barriers to effective communication.

the intrapersonal communication process

You may remember the old vaudeville routine which developed somewhat like the following:

---

[1]Paul T. Rankin, "Listening Ability: Its Importance, Measurement and Development," *Chicago Schools Journal*, 12 (June 1930), pp. 177–179, 417–420.

[2]*Nation's Business*, June 1967, p. 8.

Dick: "I'm worried! I can't seem to stop talking to myself!"
Dan: "Aw, that's natural; everybody does it."
Dick: "Yeah, but lately myself's been talking back!"

In a very real sense all of us talk to ourselves from time to time. To some extent the classic Shakespearean soliloquy behavior as exemplified in Hamlet's "To be, or not to be" is a vital segment of our communication behavior. At this very moment many of you are talking to yourselves about the necessity of reading this chapter. "To read, or not to read . . . that is the question." You say to yourself: "I need to study for that management test." Almost immediately, the stimulus *management test* evokes responses ranging from extreme apprehensiveness to a calm complacency. It is hoped that eventually you convince yourself that you will have time to read this chapter and *then* study for your management examination. As you proceed with your reading, however, another debate shapes up inside you. "Should I ask Susan for a date this weekend, or should I ask Carol? I always have a good time with Susan; she's loads of fun. But Carol . . . what a girl!" Well, if you are still with us and haven't moved to the telephone to line up your dates for the weekend, you are beginning to comprehend *intrapersonal* communication in its most elementary form—talking to one's self.

Internal Stimuli—Internal Responses

Intrapersonal communication at its most basic level—talking to one's self—involves stimuli and responses that are exclusively *within* the individual. Every day we make decisions and evaluations as a result of such intrapersonal communication activity. Without intrapersonal communication—carefully thinking through a matter while considering the pros and cons of alternatives—our decisions would be considerably less valid. Although he never referred to his decision-making approach as intrapersonal communication, John Dewey's "Reflective Thinking" process could be employed as a means of structuring our intrapersonal decision making. Dewey's system consists of a five-step process:

1. *A Felt Difficulty*—Recognition of the existence of a problem which has no obvious solution.
2. *Location and Definition of the Difficulty*—What are the causes of the problem? What are the nature and scope of the problem?
3. *Suggestions of Possible Solutions*—What are my alternatives? How many courses of action are possible and plausible?
4. *Exploration and Elaboration of Alternative Hypothesized Solutions*—What are the advantages? Which solution seems most desirable?
5. *Further Observation or Experimentation*—If the solution is implemented, how

can its effectiveness be tested? What observable effects will vindicate the decision?[3]

If time permits, a busy manager or executive might use an adaptation of Graham Wallas' "Creative Thinking" approach in structuring intrapersonal communications. The Wallas approach consists of four steps:

1. *Step One: Preparation*—After collecting and digesting all available materials pertinent to the problem at hand, carefully go over all facets of the problem in your mind. Try to evaluate the pros and cons of all facets.
2. *Step Two: Incubation*—Let your mind turn to some other problem, totally unrelated to the issue at hand. Give your mind a rest from the problem which you are most interested in solving. Remember, this is not a period of procrastination. Incubation will yield little of value unless careful preparation has preceded.
3. *Step Three: Illumination*—At times a sudden new revelation will come to us after a few days or even weeks of incubation. We may even be amazed at the obvious nature of the solution and wonder how it could have taken so long to cross our cortical centers. The solution may materialize in the middle of a coffee break, while driving to work, or even while taking a shower. Wallas called the illumination step the "Aha Phenomenon."
4. *Verification*—The suddenly-discovered solution is carefully compared with other possible solutions. Is the solution as workable as it first seemed? Does it really provide the best answer to the problem under consideration?[4]

_____ **External Stimuli—Internal Responses**

The process of carefully thinking out problems and solutions—of playing the role of Devil's Advocate with yourself—is only one form of intrapersonal communication. Consider the following situations:

You have been looking forward to your Saturday morning golf match since the middle of the week. On Friday a cold front passes through, resulting in light rains during the afternoon. You tell yourself that the rains are so light that they will actually be good for your game. After all, the greens and the fairways are usually watered each Friday preceding the usual heavy weekend traffic on the course. You anxiously await the late evening weather forecast. Just as the weatherforecaster predicts a 50 percent chance of showers continuing through the weekend, your phone rings. A member of your anticipated foursome informs you that it looks like the match should be canceled. You go to the window and observe that the rain is barely falling. "Let's give it a try," you say to your caller. Despite the light rain that greets you as you walk out the door on Saturday morning, you notice a few bright spots in the clouds and conclude that the rains will dissipate shortly.

_____

[3]John Dewey, *How We Think*. Lexington, Mass.: D.C. Heath, 1910.
[4]Graham Wallas, *The Art of Thought*. New York: Harcourt Brace Jovanovich, 1926.

Upon entering the classroom on the first day of a new semester, you observe that you are the only female in a class of twenty-eight students. "Oh well," you think, "I'm here to study advanced management, and that's what the men are here for. Just as long as they refrain from their chauvinism, I can stand it." Your thoughts turn to the course and to how difficult the instructor will be. As the instructor enters the room, he glances only briefly around the room, sizing up his new students before beginning his lecture. "So you *men* want to become managers, do you?" he begins. Your impulse is to raise your hand, gain recognition, and inform the old coot that the class is composed of more than *men*. But, then you think it over. You notice that the professor is getting on in years. He hasn't called the roll yet, so maybe he didn't see you as he hastily glanced around the room. Maybe it would be better to approach him at the end of class in a less threatening manner.

In each of the preceding situations *reception* of external stimuli and *interpretation and evaluation of those stimuli* constitute intrapersonal communication. Intrapersonal communication *receivers* are the same as interpersonal communication receivers: sight, sound, touch, taste, and smell. The function of the central nervous system is information processing that results in interpretation and evaluation of stimuli received by any one or any combination of our five senses. It is beyond the scope of our treatment here to provide a detailed analysis of the neurological aspects of intrapersonal communication. However, the following summary by George Borden should prove an ample introduction to the process:

> We receive a message through one or a combination of our senses. Our sense receptors transform this message into neural impulses and send it toward the brain. As it passes from neuron to neuron, our nervous system may block or modify it. Thus we have no guarantee that the message our senses received is the one our brain receives. If the reticular formation arouses our brain to receive the incoming signals, it receives, decodes, conceives, and experiences. Our cybernetic, which is innate, governs the storage and subsequent processing of this information.
>
> Over the years our cybernetic directs our brain in the development of many mental states, e.g., fears, desires, beliefs. The total effect of these mental states is to form a basic attitudinal frame of reference. Then, as the cybernetic directs the processing of information, it is evaluated against the present state of our attitudinal frame of reference with the constant goal of obtaining and maintaining mental balance. As this new information is processed, associations are established between its memory traces and those of previous information that has some substantive connection with it. The addition of this new information to our mental states changes them to some degree. Thus, our attitudinal frame of reference is a dynamic system, and we should take this fact into consideration when communicating. The conscious processing of information we call thinking; it involves the recall of previously stored data, their extrapolation, and correlation. How one recalls information is still a mystery, but we know that one's ability to do this is directly proportional to his ability to communicate.[5]

---

[5]George A. Borden, Richard B. Gregg, and Theodore G. Grove, *Speech Behavior and Human Interaction*. Englewood Cliffs, N.J.: Prentice-Hall, 1969, pp. 69–70.

Intrapersonal communication is communication within an individual. Internalized responses result from internal stimuli (talking with one's self) and external stimuli (perception, interpretation, and evaluation of signals received through one or more of the five senses).

_____ Intrapersonal Communication: A Verbal-Pictorial Description

In an effort to further acquaint you with the basic process of intrapersonal communication, we have included the Barker-Wiseman verbal-pictorial model. This model is designed to describe the communication system of an *individual* from the reception of stimuli to the transmission of coded messages along a selected medium. In Figure 4–1 the bold-lined rectangle represents the individual communicator. The intrapersonal communication process is set in motion by internal and external stimuli. *Internal stimuli* may be physiological (muscle cramps, headaches, drowsiness, hunger) or psychological (fear, happiness, anticipation, worry). Although internal stimuli alone are sufficient to initiate intrapersonal communication, these stimuli are frequently accompanied by and even supplanted by *external stimuli*, stimuli received from sources outside the communicator's body. External stimuli

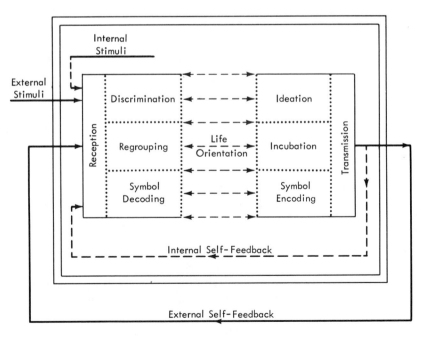

Figure 4–1 The Barker-Wiseman Communication Model. From Gordon Wiseman and Larry Barker, *Speech Interpersonal Communication,* 2nd ed. New York: Thomas Y. Crowell Company, Inc., Chandler Publishing Company, 1974, p. 24. Reprinted by permission of the publisher.

include both *overt* and *covert* stimuli received by one or more of the five senses: sight, sound, touch, taste, and smell. Overt stimuli, those received at the conscious level, include such stimuli as the aroma of a particularly pleasing perfume, the taste of liver and onions, the sound of an ambulance siren, flashing red lights at a railroad crossing, and having a door slammed on one's fingers. Covert stimuli, those received at a preconscious or subconscious level, include such stimuli as background music in an office, thinking of something else while reading, and all forms of subliminal stimulation.

All available internal and external stimuli are *received* by the communicator in the *reception* process, the process of converting received stimuli into nerve impulses and transmitting those impulses to the central nervous system. Although all stimuli within range are received, relatively few are *perceived* sufficiently to initiate continued intrapersonal communication. The process of *discrimination* determines which stimuli shall be allowed to stimulate thought. In your classroom you will find hundreds of competing stimuli, ranging from the hum of the fluorescent lights to the sound of your professor's voice. You have the capacity of shutting out most of the competing stimuli and of focusing on those which you deem most salient. Operating almost simultaneously with discrimination is the *regrouping* or ordering process. In the classroom, your professor hopes that you will place the class discussion at the top of your perceptual field, while forcing your other internal and external stimuli to a lower level of consciousness.

Stimuli that have survived the weeding out process of discrimination and are perceived as higher order stimuli as a result of the regrouping process are then *symbol decoded*. In other words, raw stimuli are changed into thought symbols. Once these electrochemical impulses we call thoughts materialize, we move into the *ideation* phase of intrapersonal communication. This is the process of thinking, planning, and organizing your thoughts. During an *incubation* phase our ideas "jell" in our minds and pick up additional strength from previous relationships already imprinted on our brains. This incubation period may range from a few days or weeks to a fraction of a second.

Following incubation, thought symbols are *encoded*. The *symbol encoding* process is one of translating thought symbols into words and gestures that can be transmitted. The *transmission* process involves sending coded messages along a selected medium. The selected medium may be either external (air and light waves) or internal (brain cells or nerve impulses).

You will note that *life orientation* occupies a central position in the Barker-Wiseman model. Life orientation includes a communicator's socio-economic value systems, basic personality factors, political and religious value systems, as well as hereditary traits, all of which make the communicator a unique individual. The arrows are intended to suggest that life orientation influences *every* phase of the intrapersonal communication process.

Two types of feedback are suggested in the Barker-Wiseman model. *Internal self-feedback* is felt through bone conduction and muscular movement (sensing the movement of our jaws, our eyes, etc.). *External self-feedback* is that portion of the message which we can hear through the airwaves while we are talking. For example, we know when we have mispronounced a word. We sense whether our volume level is too loud or too soft.

interpersonal communication

Up to this point we have been discussing the communication process as it pertains to *one* communicator. However, human beings are social animals, and twentieth-century life styles demand frequent interactions with other human beings. We hope that the model and the discussions of the intrapersonal process have convinced you that communication within a single individual is immensely complex. When even one additional communication agent is added to the communication act, the complexity of the process is increased significantly. Intrapersonal communication becomes a component of interpersonal communication. In fact, effective interpersonal communication between two communicators can result only from effective intrapersonal communication within each of the communicators.

Let us imagine a typical situation in everyday business experience. A junior executive by the name of Linda has an innovative advertising campaign that she wants to sell to the chairperson of the board. Prior to entering the chairperson's office, Linda has no doubt engaged in a great deal of intrapersonal communication activity. Let's assume, however, that the intrapersonal activity has now reached the transmission stage. How does Linda get her ideas across to her boss? Well, if both Linda and her boss were skilled mental telepathists, transmission of the innovative advertising campaign plans would be effected with ease and accuracy. Linda could simply *think* through the various phases of the campaign, while her boss closed her eyes, allowing Linda's thoughts to pass through the air waves and into the brain. We are not skilled telepathists, however, and like Linda in our illustration, we must *encode* stimuli which can be transmitted outside our intrapersonal communication system—stimuli that can pass through a channel of communication and, it is hoped, be received by another communication agent, who can *decode* those stimuli within his or her own intrapersonal system.

Interpersonal Communication: A Verbal Definition

Interpersonal communication occurs when two or more persons interact through encoding and decoding auditory and visual stimuli. Although some theorists reserve the term "interpersonal" for communication on a one-to-one level and within small groups of people, our definition is intended to include presentations to large groups as well.

Each significant component of the interpersonal communication process will be discussed and defined as we progress through an explanation of several models. From among the many excellent verbal-pictorial models now available, we have chosen for presentation here an adaption of the Shannon-Weaver model.

A Modified Shannon-Weaver Model. *The Mathematical Theory of Communication,* first published in 1949, includes a verbal-pictorial model of information transmission. This model has influenced more than a generation of communication students. It grew out of Claude Shannon's research in the Bell Telephone Laboratories. Shannon's basic concern was to determine what happens to information contained in a given message from the time it is transmitted by a source until it is finally received at a predetermined destination. Although Shannon's interests were exclusively confined to telecommunicated messages, his research associate, Warren Weaver, expanded the findings to other forms of communication. Specifically, Weaver suggested that their research isolated three levels of communication problems:

1. *The Technical Level*—"How accurately can symbols be transmitted from a source to a receiver?"
2. *The Semantic Level*—"How accurately can meaning be transmitted from a source to a receiver?"

Figure 4–2 If all human beings were capable of transmitting their thoughts by means of mental telepathy, communication would be an easy task. (Photo by A. Borodulin, from De Wys, Inc.)

3. *The Strategic Level*—"How can desired communication effects be achieved?"

The original Shannon-Weaver model as diagramed in Figure 4–3 illustrates a typical telephoned message. The *source* (calling party) has a *message* to communicate. The message is *transmitted* by means of the telephone speaker. The transmitted message travels through a noise-infested *channel* (telephone wires) until it reaches the speaker in the *receiver* telephone. The message emerging from the receiver then reaches its final *destination*.

In its original form the Shannon-Weaver model includes no provision for feedback and lacks clarity in illustrating such significant processes as encoding and decoding. Figure 4–4 illustrates the interpersonal communication process by means of our modifications of the Shannon-Weaver model. The key concepts of this modified model include *idea, encoder, transmitter, channel, receiver, decoder, idea X, feedback,* and *communication noise.*

In our modified model, the source has an *idea* in the form of thought symbols. The idea in the mind of the source may be the result of external or internal stimuli (see the discussion of the Barker-Wiseman intrapersonal communication model on p. 63). If thought transmission were a viable option for the source and the receiver, the mere thinking of the idea would result in reception of that idea by the receiver. Since we are unable to transmit thought symbols to our listeners, we must translate those symbols into transmittable stimuli.

The translation process involves *encoding*, the process of selecting verbal and nonverbal codes suitable for transmission. In other words, we may select words (verbal stimuli) and gestures (nonverbal stimuli) which most accurately express the idea which we wish to communicate. Although vocabulary limitations significantly reduce the number of available alternatives into which a given idea may be encoded, most of us are constantly faced with a split-second choice of determining the best word to express our thoughts. This is the psychological phase of translation.

Our original idea is further translated when the language and gestures selected in the encoding process are reduced to transmittable stimuli. In interpersonal communication the *transmission* phase involves the translation of untransmittable thought symbols into vibrations of the sound waves (audible stimuli created by the vibrations of the vocal cords) and disturbances of the light waves (visual stimuli created by facial expressions, gestures, movements, etc.). This is the physiological phase of translation.

The original idea, not reduced to vibrations of the sound waves and disturbances of the light waves, is transmitted into the communication channel, which is the medium through which the stimuli are sent. In telephone conversations the channel might be a telephone wire. In face-to-face communication the channel would consist of the light waves and sound waves within the perceptual field of the communicators.

Receivers may be a combination of one or more of the five senses. However,

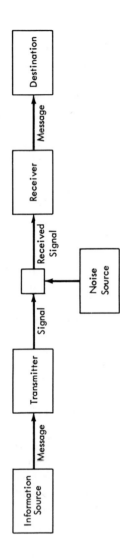

Figure 4–3 (top) The Shannon-Weaver model of communication. (From C. E. Shannon and W. Weaver, *The Mathematical Theory of Communication*. Urbana: University of Illinois Press, 1949, p. 98. By permission of the publisher.)

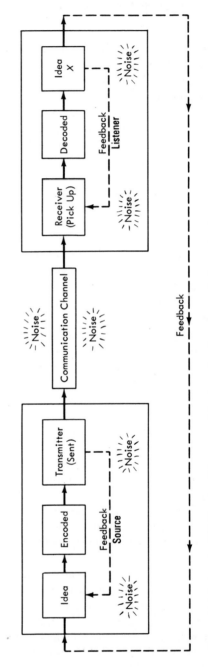

Figure 4–4 (bottom) The Shannon-Weaver model adapted to interpersonal communication.

interpersonal communication relies most heavily upon the eyes and the ears to pick up the stimuli transmitted through the channel.

Once the auditory and visual stimuli are picked up by the receivers, they are *decoded*, i.e., translated back into language symbols and finally back into some type of "meaning" for the listener. The decoding process is the reverse of the psychological translation process earlier defined as encoding.

Since the original image in the mind of the source has been translated several times by the time it reaches the mind of the listener, we label the image in the mind of the listener *idea X*. Such labeling is intended to suggest that the idea perceived by the listener is not necessarily the same as the original image in the mind of the communication source.

Feedback is the concept making interpersonal communication a circular process rather than a static or linear act. We use the term to describe several phenomena. Any verbal or nonverbal reactions by listeners that are intended to provide the source with indications of confusion, understanding, approval, or disapproval are defined as feedback. Skilled communicators will constantly be aware of such reactions and will modify their messages in light of listener feedback. You will recall from our discussion of intrapersonal communication, however, that feedback may also be *internal*. Sources receive feedback during the encoding process as they select language symbols. We react positively and negatively to the use of potential words and phrases. Such feedback probably comes from prior favorable and unfavorable experiences in communication. The source also receives feedback once stimuli are transmitted. When you speak, you know if you have mispronounced a word, if you are talking too loudly, or if your voice has cracked. You have the option of making adjustments as a result.

Internal receiver feedback is so significant that we are treating it in a major subsection under communication breakdowns. For now, we shall simply stress that ideas perceived as a result of decoding one portion of a message will influence the decoding of future portions of a message. Indeed, receivers may become so "turned off" by an interpretation of a portion of a message that their sensory receivers actually tune out the incoming stimuli.

Communication noise may be defined as any distortion or distraction preventing perfect transmission of the idea in the mind of the source to the mind of the listener. Communication noise may result from cultural differences, physical sounds, nonverbal distractions, and physical defects. In the remaining pages of this chapter, seven barriers to effective communication will be discussed. Each of these barriers may be viewed as a type of communication noise.

barriers to effective communication

"What we have here is a failure to communicate!" You probably have heard that phrase so many times and in so many contexts that you are somewhat suspicious of its validity. Indeed, many people are too eager to suggest "communication breakdown" as the cause of their problems, both personal and professional; "faulty communication" is overused as a simple explanation for complex problems. However, the fact remains that we are not as effective in our communication abilities as we think we are, and our lack of effectiveness is *at least one contributing factor* in many of our problems.

Why are we not better communicators? Why is it that people sometimes cannot understand *plain* English? The reasons are many and complex. By the time you have finished reading this section, you will be at least familiar enough with a few of the barriers to effective communication to spot them in your own experience.

═══════════════vocabulary deficiencies

Control over *words* is often an index to a person's education, culture, and general intelligence. It is related to the degree of control an individual is able to exert over the ideas that words represent. Most of us are *familiar* with 30,000 to 40,000 of the more than 600,000 words in the English language, but we *use* only around 10,000 of them. This fact would not present a problem if all of us were familiar with and used the *same* 10,000 to 40,000 words. However, the range of available words is so great that the *use vocabulary* of a communicator may include a large number of words not within the *recognition vocabulary* of the listener. Such vocabulary deficiencies are magnified by the ever-increasing use of jargon.

Communication breakdown occurs when we *assume* that we understand the meaning of a word that in reality is outside our recognition vocabulary. Rather than admit that we do not know what a particular word means, we frequently try to deduce a meaning from an examination of the context in which the word occurred and from nonverbal clues such as intonation. To illustrate the point, consider the example of George Smathers' campaign speech. In his campaign for the U.S. Senate seat held by incumbent Claude Pepper, Smathers supposedly developed a speech specifically adapted to the mentality of cracker-box voters who would not know what many of the words meant but would assume that they meant something bad:

> Are you aware that Claude Pepper is known all over Washington as a shameless extrovert? Not only that, but this man is reliably reported to practice nepotism with his sister-in-law, and he has a sister who was once a thespian in wicked New York. Worst of all it is an established fact that Mr. Pepper before his marriage habitually practiced celibacy.
>
> Furthermore, Claude Pepper had the audacity to matriculate at our home state university in full view of a major portion of the student body.[6]

---

[6]"Florida—Anything Goes," *Time*, **55** (Apr. 17, 1950), p. 38.

Although vocabulary deficiencies may account for relatively few misunderstandings such as those that were intended to result from the above message, increasing our vocabularies would enhance our communicative effectiveness both as senders and receivers of messages.

word-thought-thing relationships

"The word is not the thing. It is but a symbol of the thing." "Words don't mean. People mean." Suppose for a moment that two people are engaged in a communicative transaction. Suppose further that each of the individuals is familiar with the dictionary definitions of all the more than 600,000 words in the English language. Even then, individual differences in perception and individualized experiences with the *things* that *words* represent would render precisely accurate communication impossible. Two types of semantic noise would interfere in the communication process: (1) noise that prevents the sender from expressing *thoughts* accurately by means of verbal and nonverbal language symbols; and (2) noise that prevents the sender and the receiver from attaching the same meaning to verbal and nonverbal language symbols.

No matter how perfect an individual's vocabulary might be, some meaning may be lost in the translation processes of encoding and decoding. The *word* chosen in the encoding process, and it is hoped recognized in the decoding process, constitutes only a *representation* of reality as *perceived* in the minds of the communicators. An illustration of a map and territory is useful in demonstrating this point. We are all willing to admit that a map is not actual territory; rather, a map represents territory. Some maps may be more accurate representations than others, but no map becomes so accurate that it assumes all the properties of the territory it represents. Imagine the vocabulary development of an individual as an analogue of the map-territory example.

Assume that you are attempting to use language to describe the Chase Manhattan Bank to an individual who has no concept of what the bank is like. First, you must realize that the images of the bank in your mind are not necessarily accurate representations of the bank. Rather, those images are of the bank *as you perceive it.* For our purposes, however, let us assume that your perceptions are reasonably complete and accurate. Comparing your ability to verbalize your perceptions with the specificity of map drawing should bring you to the conclusion that language symbols are as incapable of conveying all your thought as a map is of presenting all of a given territory.

If you were armed with only an elementary-school vocabulary, your language symbols might be compared to a globe of the world. You would be able to do little more than spin the globe around to the North American continent and point to the tiny circle labeled New York City as the location of the headquarters of the Chase Manhattan Bank. The puzzled look on the face of your listener would let you know that you need to be more specific in your description. After several years have passed you return with a junior high school vocabulary—a large map of the United States of America. This time you are able to point with pride to a specific point labeled Manhattan within the area designated as New York City. However, your ability to locate Manhattan still does not fully describe the bank to your auditor. "Can you be more specific?" he asks. Three years later, having acquired a high school vocabulary, you return with a map of New York State. As further evidence of your vocabulary refinement, you are able to fold the map to an insert drawing of the greater New York City area, so detailed that you are able to pinpoint the city block on which the headquarters building is located. Still, your friend is unsatisfied and asks for additional description.

After four years of college, you return with a college level vocabulary—a map of New York City, with a special section devoted to the island of Manhattan. With specificity you are able to point to the precise location of the central headquarters of the Chase Manhattan Bank and discuss the location of the bank in relation to key points of interest such as Central Park, Madison Square Garden, and the Empire State Building. "I'm beginning to understand," replies your friend, "but I would appreciate a little more description." With years of additional study you obtain a postgraduate vocabulary, returning to your friend with plot maps obtained from the city tax assessor's office. These maps are so exact that you are able to determine the exact portion of the block occupied by the Chase Manhattan headquarters. When your listener replies that an even more exact description would be appreciated, you turn away in disgust, vowing never again to talk to such an imbecile. However, in the course of your imaginary conversation, you could have obtained blueprints of the Chase Manhattan Bank and still lacked symbols capable of *fully* representing reality.

There is no way that language symbols can become so explicit that they convey all the image or thought within our minds. There is no way that the image or thought within our minds can become so accurate that all properties of the object as it exists in reality can be accounted for in our perceptions. Communication between individuals would be more accurate if we fully realized the relationships between language, reality, and our thoughts. Perhaps we would, at the minimum, expect less of the language that we use and become more tolerant of those who fail to understand exactly what we *mean*.

Even if language were so precise that complex thoughts could be encoded accurately, experience differences among our listeners and between us and our listeners would result in a degree of distortion. Occasionally someone suggests that a common language for all peoples of the world would result in significant improvements in ability to communicate. Such would be true only at the *denotative*, or dictionary meaning, level of comprehension; we would still have to contend with differences in *connotative* meaning—differences in meaning that result from experiences with the objects that the language cues symbolize.

A child bitten by a rattlesnake cannot respond to the word *snake* without consciously or subconsciously interpreting the language symbol in terms of pain, a hospital stay, and so forth. Such an interpretation would differ markedly from that of a child whose only experience with snakes involved harmless green creatures less than ten inches long.

Connotative language meanings are more of a problem in the communication process when we fail to realize and accept their existence. As a communication *source*, you should realize from the outset that your receivers will interpret your language cues within an experiential frame of reference that will be different from yours. Consequently, you must use all the available means of communication—facial expressions, gestures, intonation—as additional cues to the meaning that you attach to the language symbols. As a *receiver* of messages, you should realize that your experiences will be different from those of the communicator. Therefore, it makes sense to give the communicator the benefit of the doubt until you are absolutely sure of the *intended* message meaning. It makes little sense for us to allow a *word*—a symbol for perceived reality—to so emotionally disturb us that we lose the entire message. The next time a speaker uses words that arouse your emotions to the extent that you are ready to walk out of the room, take a moment to consider that your reactions may be the unique result of experiences that the speaker had no control over and of which the speaker had no knowledge.

selective attention

At any given moment we are being bombarded by physical and psychological stimuli competing for our attention. Although our eyes are capable of handling more than five million bits of data per second, our brains are capable of interpreting only about five hundred bits per second. With similar disparities between each of the other senses and the brain, it is easy to see that we must *select* the visual, audible, or tactile stimuli that we wish to compute at any specific time. The modified Barnlund communication model shown in Figure 4–5 is useful in explaining the phenomenon of selective attention. As the drawing indicates, both participants in the communication process are able to choose from among positive, negative, or neutral private cues, public cues, and verbal and nonverbal behavioral cues in determining to what they shall attend. At the same time, each participant transmits numerous nonmessage cues (nervous movements, physical appearance, clothing, and so forth) which may be attended to in lieu of message cues. To the extent that nonmessage cues capture the attention of a receiver, message information will be lost or distorted.

"Your actions are speaking so loudly that I can't hear a word you're saying!" The preceding statement is an example of a receiver focusing on nonverbal,

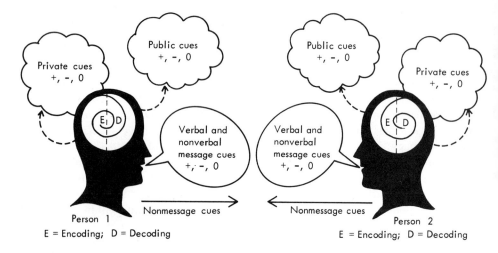

Person 1
E = Encoding; D = Decoding

Person 2
E = Encoding; D = Decoding

Figure 4–5 A modified Barnlund model. (Adapted from Dean C. Barnlund, "A Transactional Model of Communication," from Johnnye Akin, Alvin Goldberg, Gail Myers, and Joseph Stewart, ed., *Language Behavior: A Book of Readings*, p. 59. By permission of Mouton Publishers, The Hague, © 1970.

nonmessage behavioral cues to the extent that the verbal message is lost. As a communication source, you need to concern yourself with your facial expressions, gestures, general body movement, and vocal expressiveness, taking care that the nonverbal cues reinforce rather than compete with or contradict the verbal cues. Both of the following extremes result in communication breakdown:

"How was the lecture?"

"Who knows? Old Bumgardner mumbled and coughed his way through the whole thing. I don't think I understood a word he said! When he wasn't coughing and mumbling, he was reading in that awful monotone!"

"How was the speech?"

"Fantastic! I've never seen anyone with such a command of words. Such a melodious voice! Such sweeping gestures! Honestly, it was the best speech I've ever heard!"

"What was it about?"

"What was what about?"

"The speech. What was the speech about?"

"Well, . . . actually it was about . . . just a minute now . . . let me think. . . . What *was* it concerned with?"

In the first conversation, the communicator obviously was so inept in his communication abilities that negative nonverbal behavioral cues won the battle for receiver attention. In the second example, the source's nonverbal behavioral cues were so powerful (even in a positive sense) that they, too, overshadowed the message.

What can receivers do to overcome selective attention problems? For one thing, we need to realize that a speaker's individual mannerisms, no matter how obtrusive, are not worthy of distracting our attention from the message. One favorite American indoor pastime is criticizing the mannerisms of speakers; we seem trained to zero in on gestures. However, this should not be the case. The message should be the most important object of our attention— much more important than delivery mannerisms. We need to approach communication situations with determination to focus on messages, no matter how difficult that task may be. If you were attending a sales meeting in a crowded room and a janitor rushed through the door yelling in broken, profane English, "Get da hell outa here! Da building's on fire!" you hardly would sit back thinking, "Such pronunciation! I'm not going to move until he rephrases that statement in a more acceptable manner." You would rush out of the room at the first warning, because obviously you would be more concerned about the message (the fire) than the distracting mannerisms of the source. Many communication breakdowns could be avoided if we could focus on the potential urgency of the messages to the extent that delivery problems would be minimized in our minds.

Unfortunately, receivers must contend with many competing stimuli in addition to the source's nonverbal cues. There are internal physiological stimuli (headaches, sore backs, hunger, sleepiness) as well as psychological stimuli (anxiety, happiness, anticipation, anger) that compete for our attention.

Figure 4–6 At any given moment we are bombarded with more stimuli than we can possibly attend to. We must select from among those audible and visual stimuli. (Photo by Sybil Shelton)

It is estimated that most of us can think at a rate of 400 to 500 words per minute, although most people with whom we communicate speak at a rate of only 100 to 125 words per minute. This means that we can think at a rate at least five times faster than most people can talk. Because of this difference between thought speed and speech speed, most of us are lured into a false sense of security. We listen to the message of a speaker for a few seconds, pick up the basic concept being discussed, and proceed to think of something else for several seconds. After a few seconds of "daydreaming," we check back in with the speaker for a second or two and then wander off into our pursuits of other mental stimuli. It would not be so bad if we always managed to check back in with the speaker. However, eventually one of those other mental stimulus sources becomes attractive to the degree that we lose mental contact with the communication source altogether. The stimulus that finally wins the battle for attention may be either the backache or extreme anxiety about a coming business deal; whatever type of stimulus—physiological or psychological—it may exert a great deal of influence on the total effectiveness of our attention to communication.

Here are four suggestions that may help you keep your attention on a communication message rather than on the competing stimuli.

1. Realize that maintenance of attention is hard work. Attention might best be defined as a series of tensions; therefore, you cannot sit back, relax, place your mind in neutral, and expect to concentrate on message stimuli.
2. Anticipate the communicator's next point. Try to guess what will be said next. If you guess right, you think the concept twice—once when you anticipated it, and once when the communicator expressed it. If you guess wrong, compare what you thought would be said with what was actually spoken. One of the oldest laws of learning concerns learning through comparison and contrast.
3. Analyze the message in terms of supporting materials. Not only will this mental exercise keep your mind on the topic, it will expose the charlatan who asserts much but supports few of those assertions.
4. From time to time briefly summarize what the speaker has said up to that point. A few brief mental summaries will help you maintain a perspective of the theme that the speaker is developing.

failure to react properly to feedback

Two types of improper feedback reactions adversely affect the communication process. On the one hand is the temptation to overlook feedback, whether internal or external. On the other hand is the tendency to overreact to feedback.

Whether engaged in an interview, a small group discussion, or a presentation to a group of listeners, the communicator who fails to look for verbal and nonverbal cues of message effect upon listeners is short-circuiting the entire communication process. Such a failure to become concerned with listener reactions can result in bored listeners remaining bored, confused listeners remaining confused, and angry listeners becoming even more angry. Failure to consider listener feedback reduces what ideally should be two-way sharing to a mere recital of the message.

Some communicators overreact to feedback, regardless of whether that feedback is of a positive or a negative nature. In an interview, for instance, feedback is so immediate and so massive that participants may attach too much significance to rather unintentional nonverbal reactions. Participants in small group discussions frequently find it difficult to keep their deliberations on the idea level because of overreactions to perceived ego threats. Speakers presenting messages to groups of listeners sometimes allow one or two negative responses to adversely affect the entire communication attempt. If you are presenting a message to a group of listeners, you should avoid the temptation to talk only to those listeners who seem to agree with you; at the same time, you must remain rational enough to realize that some listeners may not approve of your message and so avoid exaggerated attempts to win over one or two "sour grapes" in the audience.

In summary, effective communicators are able to use feedback constructively without allowing the feedback to enslave them.

bipolar thinking

In a complex world we constantly must fight the impulse to create order out of chaos through illogical oversimplification. *Bipolar thinking* is one illogical oversimplification that frequently interferes with effective communication. It is the reduction of complex phenomena to simple, either-or, good-or-bad conceptualizations. The world is not simple enough to allow reduction to a two-value system. We must learn to be tolerant of those who refuse to accept an idea exactly as we propose it, and we must recognize that refusal to accept and outright rejection are two different things. Countless mistakes have resulted from employees' fears that questioning a policy might be interpreted as total rejection of that policy. A good manager will encourage feedback, even negative feedback, so long as it is constructive. A poor manager may stifle considerable communication because of an attitude of "he who is not for me is against me."

bypassing

In his essay, "They Talk Past Each Other," Irving J. Lee defined bypassing as talking *past* rather than talking *with* people. Lee continued his discussion with a listing of several bypassing instances:

A foreman told a machine operator he was passing: "Better clean up around here." It was ten minutes later when the foreman's assistant phoned: "Say, boss, isn't that bearing Sipert is working on due up in engineering pronto?"

"You bet your sweet life it is. Why?"

"He says you told him to drop it and sweep the place up. I thought I'd better make sure."

"Listen," the foreman flared into the phone, "get him right back on that job. It's got to be ready in 20 minutes."

What the foreman had in mind was for Sipert to gather up the oily waste, which was a fire and accident hazard. This would not have taken more than a couple of minutes, and there would have been plenty of time to finish the bearing. Sipert, of course, should have been able to figure this out for himself—except that something in the foreman's tone of voice, or in his own mental state at the time, made him misunderstand the foreman's intent. He wasn't geared to what the foreman had said.[7]

A lady recently ordered some writing paper at a department store and asked to have her initials engraved thereon. The salesgirl suggested placing them in the upper right-hand corner or the upper left-hand corner, but the customer said no, put them in the center. Well, the stationery has arrived, every sheet marked with her initials equidistant from right and left and from top and bottom.[8]

I remember a worrisome young man who, one day, came back from the X-ray room wringing his hands and trembling with fear. "It is all up with me," he said. "The X-ray man said I have a hopeless cancer of the stomach." Knowing that the roentgenologist would never have said such a thing, I asked, "Just what did he say?" and the answer was on dismissing him, the roentgenologist said to an assistant, "N.P." In Mayo clinic cipher this meant "no plates," and indicated that the X-ray man was so satisfied with the normal appearance of the stomach on the X-ray screen that he did not see any use in making films. But to the patient, watching in agony of fear for some portent disaster, it meant "nothing possible": in other words that the situation was hopeless![9]

Although the bypassing incidents listed by Irving Lee probably are adequate to illustrate the problem, we cannot resist the temptation to add one additional breakdown that recently came to our attention. A young lady just had turned 16 and was preparing to attend a major high school prom for the first time in her life. She had purchased a new dress for the special occasion, but on the evening of the prom, the young lady announced that she was not going after all. Her mother, after careful questioning, discovered the reason. The daughter had decided at the last minute that the dress tended to further flatten her somewhat underdeveloped chest. Quickly, the mother came up with a couple of appropriate solutions: (1) She suggested a bit of padding in the places where it was most needed, and (2) she placed a string of pearls around her daughter's

---

[7]From *The Foreman's Letter*, Feb. 8, 1950, p. 3. Reprinted by permission of National Foreman's Institute, Waterford, Conn.

[8]"As per Instructions," from "The Talk of the Town," *The New Yorker*, January 28, 1950. Used by permission.

[9]Walter C. Alvarez, *Nervousness, Indigestion, and Pain*. Hagerstown, Md.: Harper & Row, Pub. Copyright 1943 by Paul B. Hoeber, Inc. Copyright 1954 by Harper & Row, Pub. Used with permission.

neck in an attempt to distract from any apparent deficiencies. At any rate, the solutions pleased the daughter, and after a few hours she was out the door and on her way to the prom. Only 45 minutes later she was back in the house. She ran to her room, threw herself across her bed, and began weeping uncontrollably. In a flash her mother was in the room inquiring as to what had happened. "That beast," screamed the girl, "I'll never go out with him again as long as I live!" "What on earth did he do?" questioned the mother. Trying unsuccessfully to hold back the tears, the daughter replied, "Just after we began our first dance, he looked at me and said, 'Are *those* real?' " "I certainly hope you told him they are," countered the indignant mother. "Those pearls belonged to your great grandmother Hester."

In all of these bypassing incidents one simple question would have eliminated much of the misunderstanding. Before overreacting to an assumed meaning, the offended party could merely have asked, "What do you mean by that?"

the tendency to evaluate

Although a large number of other communication barriers have been identified and are worthy of discussion, we have chosen to conclude our discussion with what Carl Rogers called "the tendency to evaluate."[10] This tendency, which Rogers claims is the major barrier to mutual interpersonal communication, may be defined as "our very natural tendency to judge, to evaluate, to approve (or disapprove) the statement of the other person or the other group . . . from *your* point of view, your own frame of reference."[11]

A number of years ago a young black man stood up on a stump in a southern state, raised his clenched fist toward the heavens, and shouted "Black Power! Black Power!" Television crews from each of the major networks were on hand, and by evening millions of Americans experienced difficulty digesting their dinners as they viewed the "black power" incident in the privacy of their homes. Without stopping to think the matter through, a large number of whites ran to their bedrooms, ripped the sheet off the bed, cut out three holes, and prepared to wear the sheet during the black uprising that they believed was sure to come. Visions of civil war appeared in the minds of many. It mattered little that the young black man was referring to "political" power and "monetary" power for blacks. Millions of Americans assumed that he meant the raw power of physical force, and that assumption at least in part accounted for a portion of the transracial communication barriers that we have experienced during the past decade.

---

[10]Carl R. Rogers, "Barriers and Gateways to Communication," *Harvard Business Review*, **30** (July–Aug. 1952), pp. 46–52.
[11]Ibid., p. 47.

The tendency to evaluate would be bad enough if it occurred only in isolation. However, one negative response builds upon another, until finally even positive statements are interpreted negatively. How many times have we heard something with which we did not agree very early in a speech? Immediately, we began to prepare some type of argument or some embarrassing question to hurl at the speaker. Upon stating our argument or asking our question, we realize that the speaker is staring at us in bewilderment and asks "Didn't you hear me when I said that theory sixteen was also true?" Of course we didn't hear that; we were too busy preparing our little rebuttal speech.

Rogers suggests that the tendency to evaluate may be overcome at least in part through empathic understanding—by mentally placing yourself in the position of the other person. We never can become the other individual in fact, but we can attempt to imagine the reasons that individuals say what they say and talk as they talk. Perhaps the old Indian proverb was more correct than most of us have realized: "Never criticize a man until you have walked ten miles in his moccasins"!

A marriage counselor in Indiana has put Rogers' advice into practice. When a couple comes to him for counseling, he agrees to work with them under two conditions: (1) They will allow each other to say *anything*, no matter how negative, without interrupting; and (2) they will summarize what their partner has said before attempting a refutation. The ground rules appear harmless enough, so most couples agree. As an example, let us assume that in a particular case the wife begins with the argument "He doesn't take out the trash." The minute that the husband hears the word trash, his blood begins to boil. "Trash,

Figure 4–7 Negotiations between labor and management would be enhanced if both sides attempted to listen with empathy. Our tendency to judge, to evaluate, to approve or disapprove from our biased, selfish point of view, is a very real cause of communication breakdown during contract negotiations. (Courtesy of Wide World Photos.)

trash, trash!" he thinks to himself. "That's all I ever hear from her." The husband immediately begins to think of ten good reasons why the wife should carry out the trash herself. Meanwhile, the wife has gotten down to more serious business. She is discussing her feelings of alienation, of not being involved in her husband's career. Finally, it is the husband's chance to talk. "Why don't you take out the garbage yourself?" he asks. "Wait a minute," interjects the counselor, "you must summarize what your wife said before you proceed with your own arguments." "Aw, she said she didn't like me cause I don't take out the garbage," mutters the husband. "What else?" asks the counselor. Actually, the husband heard nothing beyond the mention of taking out the garbage because he had stopped listening and begun evaluating.

A large number of misunderstandings might be avoided during interviews, small group discussions, and casual conversations if we would summarize in the form of a question what we *think* someone said. "Oh, you are saying . . .?" Asking these kinds of questions will insure that you are on the same mental track as your co-communicators. In a public speaking situation where you would be reluctant to stop the speaker in order to ascertain whether or not you are understanding from his or her point of view, try to wait patiently, giving the speaker the benefit of the doubt until the message is completed. One university that sponsors a listening improvement training program installed a sign over its blackboard that reads: "Withhold evaluation until comprehension is complete." In case someone's vocabulary is inadequate to interpret the message, another sign hangs below: "Hear the man out before you judge him!"

========= *Summary*

Although communication is something which we are involved in 75 percent of our waking hours, we frequently lack an understanding of the complexity of the process. Through the use of verbal-pictoral models, you have been introduced to the basic components of intrapersonal and interpersonal communication.

Intrapersonal communication is communication that takes place within an individual. Interpersonal communication occurs when two or more persons interact through encoding and decoding auditory and visual stimuli. The basic components of intrapersonal communication include reception, information processing, and transmission. The basic components of interpersonal communication include encoding, decoding, channel, feedback, and communication noise.

You may engage in intrapersonal communication without being involved in interpersonal communication, but effective interpersonal communication demands effective intrapersonal communication within each participant in the communication transaction.

Communication breakdown occurs for many reasons. At times the breakdown results from vocabulary deficiencies. Some of us simply lack similar enough recognition vocabularies to effectively communicate. Breakdowns also occur during the encoding and decoding processes—when perceptions must be translated into language symbols and back again to perceptions. No matter how precise the language symbol, that symbol may never become the perception in the mind of the sender. Therefore, some meaning is lost in translation. In addition, the uniqueness of connotative meanings insures a degree of communication breakdown in almost every communication transaction. Words mean different things to different people, because people's experiences with the objects that words symbolize are dissimilar. Because our brains are not capable of computing the thousands of bits of information picked up by our five senses, the phenomenon of selective perception frequently becomes another source of communication breakdown. We simply choose nonmessage stimuli rather than message stimuli as the focal point of our attention. Some individuals short-circuit the communication process by ignoring feedback from their listeners. Others lose communicative effectiveness by overreacting to either positive or negative feedback. Oversimplification of complex phenomena into simple bipolar conceptualizations also significantly reduced the options available to participants in a communication transaction. At other times our breakdowns result from bypassing—talking past one another. Finally, the tendency to evaluate, to interpret incoming message stimuli strictly from our own frame of reference without regard to the speaker's perspective, is a barrier that may be overcome, at least in part, by empathic understanding—by putting oneself in the other person's shoes.

Discussion Questions

1. Compare and contrast the role of feedback in interpersonal and intrapersonal communication contexts.
2. What is meant by the term "communication noise?" List as many different types of noise as you can categorize.
3. Compare and contrast the kinds of feedback available to the source in interpersonal communication. In what situations have you experienced feedback as a receiver in communication?
4. List several situations in which structuring our intrapersonal communication by means of "reflective thinking" or "creative thinking" might improve our decision-making abilities.
5. If all peoples of the world spoke a common language, which barriers to communication would be overcome? Which ones still would exist?
6. Select several common words. Write out definitions of what you think the words mean. Now, look up the dictionary definitions and compare dictionary definitions with your own definitions. What are the similarities? What are the differences? How do you account for the differences?
7. Explain the statement, "Words don't mean. People mean."

8. Discuss ways in which selective attention affects communication encounters that you face daily.
9. Discuss ways that you have reacted or overreacted to feedback received from your listeners.
10. In many respects bypassing is similar to what Carl Rogers called the "tendency to evaluate." In what ways are the concepts similar? In what ways are they different?

===================== Study Probes

1. A number of cartoons and jokes are based on the premise of communication breakdown. Clip out some cartoons related to communication breakdown, and write down jokes you hear that involve communication failure. Share these with your friends. Ask if they know of additional examples. Try to label the kind of communication breakdown involved in each of your examples.

2. Ask a friend to help you develop your understanding of communication barriers by assisting you in a project. Choose two controversial subjects on which you suspect that you and your friend will disagree. Discuss the first subject. Try to convince your friend to adopt your point of view. After your discussion ask your friend to write down your major arguments, while you write down the arguments of your friend. Compare notes. Do you feel that your friend accurately perceived your arguments? Did you accurately perceive the arguments of your friend? Move on to the next topic. This time enforce the rule that arguments advanced by one party must be *summarized* by the other party *prior* to any rebuttal statement. After the discussion is concluded follow the same procedures that you followed after the first discussion. Was the accuracy of perceptions improved?

3. Attend a lecture with two of your friends. At the conclusion of the lecture, ask your friends to write down the most important idea expressed by the speaker, the things that impressed them most about the entire communication event, and the things that impressed them least. How do the lists differ? What does this tell you about the phenomenon of selective perception?

===================== Additional Reading

Alexander, Herbert G., *Meaning in Language.* Chicago: Scott, Foresman, 1969.

Barker, Larry L., and Robert J. Kibler, (eds.), *Speech Communication Behavior: Perspectives and Principles*, Englewood Cliffs, N.J.: Prentice-Hall, 1971.

Berlo, David, *The Process of Communication.* New York: Holt, Rinehart and Winston, 1960.

Bois, J. Samuel, *The Art of Awareness.* Dubuque, Iowa: Wm. C. Brown, 1966.

Borden, George A., Richard B. Gregg, and Theodore G. Grove, *Speech Behavior and Human Interaction.* Englewood Cliffs, N.J.: Prentice-Hall, 1969.

Daniel, Robert S. (ed.), *Contemporary Readings in General Psychology.* Boston: Houghton Mifflin, 1959.

Johnson, Wendell, *People in Quandaries.* New York: Harper & Row, Pub., 1946

Katz, Daniel, "Psychological Barriers to Communication," *The Annals of the American Academy of Political and Social Science,* **250** (Mar. 1947), pp. 17–25.

Lee, Irving, *How to Talk With People.* New York: Harper & Row, Pub., 1952.

Nichols, Ralph G. and Leonard A. Stevens, *Are You Listening?* New York: McGraw-Hill, 1957.

Rogers, Carl R. "Barriers and Gateways to Communication," *Harvard Business Review,* **30** (July–Aug. 1952), pp. 46–52.

Communication
variables

5

key points to learn

The impact of status, power, and source credibility on the communication process.

The impact of message content and message structure on the communication process.

The impact of demographic and personality variables on listener reception of messages.

The impact of the physical and psychological contexts on the communication process.

The impact of the communication channel on the communication process.

The potential effects of a communication transaction.

In the late 1940s, Harold Lasswell developed a five-question verbal model of communication.[1] Primarily intended to reflect factors influencing the effectiveness of mass communications (newspapers, radio, and television), the model includes the following questions: Who? Says What? To Whom? Through What Channel? With What Effect? After taking the liberty of adding one additional question to Lasswell's original five, we employed the Lasswell model as the organizational framework for our discussion of the variables that you will encounter in your communication transactions. Our modified Lasswell's model of communication variables includes:

1. Source Variables (Who?).
2. Message Variables (Says What?).
3. Receiver Variables (To Whom?).
4. Context Variables (In What Context?).
5. Channel Variables (Through What Channel?).
6. Effect Variables (With What Effect?).

---

[1]Harold Lasswell, "The Structure and Function of Communication in Society," in *The Communication of Ideas*, L. Bryson (ed), New York: Harper & Row, Pub., 1948, p. 37.

source variables (who?)

Although we have fabricated the following dialogues for illustrative purposes, it is likely that similar conversations occur daily in most business organizations.

"That bonus is gonna be great, huh?"

"What bonus?"

"You mean you haven't heard about the 10 percent bonus we're getting along with our December checks?"

"Where on earth did you hear that?"

"Mason, over in accounting, told me."

"It figures! Every year about this time that old buzzard starts talking about year-end bonuses. He's just dreaming. After you've been here a while, you'll learn to take what he says with a grain of salt."

"You look like you've been raked over the coals!"

"Man, I feel like it. Just had a conference with Greenbaum. To listen to him, you would think I didn't have sense enough to come in out of the rain. Honestly, I don't think he likes the way I do anything around here!"

"Aw, consider the source! The old boy's getting a little senile. They're gonna put him out to pasture in a couple more years. Just let him have his say, and go on about your business."

"Consider the source!" Whether we realize it or not, we do indeed *consider the source* in just about every communication transaction in which we participate. Frequently, our acceptance or rejection of a message is vitally correlated with our like/dislike, trust/distrust, or respect/disrespect of the message sender. Our openness to a communication effort may correspond proportionately to the *status* or *power* of the communicator. What are the factors which determine the credibility of a communication source? How do the variables of status and power affect the communication process?

Source Credibility

Both ancient and modern theorists have attested to the impact of the source upon the communication process. Twenty-five centuries ago, Aristotle pinpointed the *ethos* or credibility of the speaker as the singularly most persuasive element in rhetorical communication. Several hundred years later Quintillian emphasized source credibility in his definition of oratory as "a *good* man speaking well." For the most part, empirical research results of twentieth-century psychologists and social scientists have validated the subjective judgments of the ancients. Encouraged by the results of research conducted in the early 1950s by Carl Hovland, I. L. Janis, and H. H. Kelley, during the past two decades social scientists have redoubled their efforts to isolate factors influencing source credibility.[2]

Components of Credibility.   Each of us could make a list of people we like and people we dislike; of magazines, newspapers, and professional journals that we are willing to read and those that we feel are unworthy of the paper on which they are printed. What causes us to prefer one source over another? Why do we believe what we read in one news magazine, while raising an eyebrow at the content of another? In short, what causes a source to be perceived as credible?

Just how many components are actually involved in the total makeup of source credibility is a debatable matter. Researchers tend to concur that *expertness* or *competence* and *trustworthiness* or *safety* are two of those components, and there is general acceptance of a third component—*dynamism* or *extroversion*.[3] Although other researchers in addition list *personality, intention of the source*, and *composure*, we feel that those components are better considered as subpoints of trustworthiness and dynamism.

The *expertness* or *competence* factor is an evaluation of perceived qualifications. A source rated high in the competency dimension will be perceived as informed, skilled, experienced, trained, etc. A source rated low in the competency dimension will be perceived as uninformed, unskilled, inexperienced, and untrained. Up until the ideological revolutions of the 1960s which resulted in the shattering of many stereotyped assumptions of competency for people in powerful positions, it was safe to say that many people confused status with qualification. Today's communicators are not nearly as safe as they might have been prior to the "credibility gaps" of the 1960s in assuming that listeners will blindly accept the expertness of political, industrial, academic, and religious leaders.

The *trustworthiness* or *safety* factor focuses on the basic character of the communicator. Is the source honest, kind, decent, just, friendly, and ethical? If so, we perceive the individual as trustworthy. If we perceive the source as dishonest, unkind, indecent, unjust, unfriendly, and unethical, we have doubts as to the extent to which we should trust the communicator. The trustworthiness factor is a major part of the Aristotelian concept of ethos. In his *Rhetoric*, Aristotle advised speakers to be "of good moral character" and to "exhibit goodwill" as a means of building their ethos. Certainly, we are concerned today with the *motives* of those who communicate with us. We are turned off by those whom we suspect of Machiavellianism. We do not wish to be manipulated or used as stepping stones by a source in pursuit of power or position.

---

[2]Kenneth Anderson and Ted Clevenger, "A Summary of Experimental Research in Ethos," *Speech Monographs*, **30**: (1963), pp. 59–78.

[3]D.K. Berlo, J.B. Lemert, and R.J. Mertz, "Dimensions for Evaluating the Acceptability of Message Sources." Research Monograph, Department of Communication, Michigan State University, 1966.

The *dynamism* or *extroversion* is a measure of the source's vitality and/or energy. Credibility derived from dynamism results from a source being perceived as aggressive, emphatic, forceful, bold, active, and energetic. Sources lacking this credibility component are perceived as timid, passive, lethargic, indecisive, and defensive and are rated low in dynamism. Much of our stereotyped perception of "the junior executive" is based on the dynamism factor of credibility.

We have defined and illustrated the three dimensions of credibility as if those factors were separate and discrete categories. In reality, the lines separating trustworthiness, competence, and dynamism are nonexistent. An individual source may be perceived so highly in the trustworthiness dimension that a resulting halo effect causes us to assume competency and overlook a lack of dynamism. Individuals who blindly trust a syndicated columnist are frequently willing to assume competency for their source on topics ranging from headaches to heartbreaks. Receivers must reach some kind of balance in their perceptions of a source's trustworthiness and dynamism. We suspect the "fast talker" and the salesperson who employs the "hard sell."

Source Credibility: A Dynamic Phenomenon.   The mammoth credibility losses experienced by Lyndon Johnson and Richard Nixon illustrate the dynamic or ever-changing nature of personal credibility. Both of these presidents rode the crest of popularity during election-year landslide victories, only to face constantly declining popularity ratings in the major polls. During the fall of 1979, President Jimmy Carter's credibility with the American people had slipped so low that it appeared that almost *any* Democratic or Republican challenger could defeat him. However, his handling of the early months of the Iranian embassy hostage crisis resulted in an almost unbelievable reversal of public opinion. By late December of 1979, the American people had rallied behind their President and expressed confidence in his abilities as their leader. As the hostage crisis extended on into 1980, however, the American people began to concentrate more and more on economic and other domestic issues, and Jimmy Carter suffered a landslide defeat at the hands of Ronald Reagan in the November general election. Credibility must not only be gained; it must be maintained.

A source's credibility will also be subject to change as different audiences are confronted. A popular source among one ethnic group may be very unpopular among another. The heroes of the under-thirty generation may be perceived as villains by the over-fifty set. There is even something to the old adage, "familiarity breeds contempt." You may find that your credibility rating goes up when you are working on a consultancy basis with an organization where you are relatively unknown. Indeed, someone defined an expert as "one who is at least seventy-five miles from home."

Finally, source credibility may change if the field changes. We tend to resent the world-renowned economist who dares to pose as an expert on child-rearing, or the popular evangelist who speaks on the communist conspiracy. If you try to pose as an expert in too many fields, you will likely gain the stigma of "Jack-of-all-trades, master of none."

Increasing Your Credibility as a Source. We have been emphasizing the importance of source credibility in the communication process. By now you should be convinced that credibility is a complex, multidimensional phenomenon, subject to constant change. Is there anything which you as a communicator can do to improve your credibility as perceived by those with whom you communicate?

First, let's stress the fact that credibility is *perceived*. Just being good may not be enough. Your boss or business associates must *perceive* your competencies. Consequently, without making an outright nuisance of yourself, avail yourself of opportunities to be seen and heard by those whose approval you desire. To an extent you must constantly serve as your own public relations person.

In any communication situation, bring into the conversation speech sources that you know enjoy high credibility ratings from your listeners. This involves much more than "name-dropping." It's a matter of "borrowing" credibility for your ideas.

In a formal presentation context, arrange to have a formal introduction delivered by someone whom your audience perceives as highly credible. The formal introduction should concentrate on your qualifications and possibly include statements pertinent to outstanding public service or civic work (trustworthiness). In this situation, you will also enjoy a degree of credibility transfer from the individual who introduces you. With what we now know about source credibility, you should do all you can to avoid being introduced by an inept speaker, who is willing to say little more than "I present to you an individual who needs no introduction."

Finally, you can affect your own dynamism rating by preparing a presentation that is coherent—one that moves! Not only should your message be dynamic, but your vocal and nonvocal presentation should also. The speaker who exhibits perceived nonfluencies such as "Uh." . . . "And, uh," and who generally mumbles throughout the presentation will not enjoy a high dynamism rating from auditors.

-------------------- **Status And Power**

Source *status* and source *power* are interrelated variables affecting our communication behavior. We use the term *status* to designate a source's societal *role* (usually determined by a configuration of rights and responsibilities) as *perceived* by those with whom the source interacts. *Power* is the degree of control vested in a source (capacity to satisfy basic needs) as *perceived* by those with whom the source interacts. Note that in each case we are concerned with perceived status and perceived power, rather than with the legalistic aspects of the terms.

Source Status.   Perceived status often dictates the frequency of communication contacts as well as our evaluation of those contacts. Societal conventions dictate that we communicate more frequently with those of *similar* status; empirical evidence coupled with our own observations suggests that we communicate more accurately with individuals of similar status. [4] The military-like chain of command characteristic of most formal business organizations creates status barriers to communication contacts between individuals of dissimilar status, resulting in vice-presidents who talk only with the chairperson of the board, and a chairperson of the board who talks only with God!

Although we communicate more frequently and with greater accuracy with sources of similar status, we tend to assume greater credibility for sources of higher status. The first of the fictitious dialogues at the beginning of this chapter provides an illustration of the point. Suppose the initiator of the dialogue could have named the chairperson of the board, or even the general manager, rather than an accountant named Mason, as the source of the promise of a year-end bonus? We can surmise that the reaction of the skeptical co-worker would have been very different.

Source Power.   As with status, the power that we perceive a source to possess will influence our responses to messages. Since power is so frequently derived from status, it may seem inappropriate to discuss the concepts separately. However, the impact of power on the communication process appears so significant that, with a reminder that status and power are interrelated variables, we shall briefly explore the *dimensions of power* and the *types of power* as they relate to our communication transactions.

The *dimensions of power* have been identified as *perceived control, perceived concern*, and *perceived scrutiny*. [5] Perceived control involves the degree to which we perceive the source capable of providing rewards (if we comply with the source's request) or assessing punishments (if we fail to comply). Perceived concern is our perception of whether or not the source *really* cares if we comply with the request. Perceived scrutiny concerns the degree to which we perceive the source as capable of monitoring our behavior in determining whether or not we have complied with the request. As in the case of the dimensions of credibility, the power dimensions are not separate, discrete categories. For example, a manager (perceived as having the capacity of firing noncomplying employees) may be assigned by his or her supervisor the task of informing employees that anyone caught applying for unjustifiable sick leave will be summarily dismissed. However, the manager's prior reputation as an understanding, empathetic, and forgiving person may lead employees to receive the communication with the underlying assumption that the manager is

---

[4]Ronald L. Appelbaum and Karl W.E. Anatol, *Strategies for Persuasive Communication.* Columbus, Ohio: Charles E. Merrill, 1974, pp. 78–82.

[5]William T. McGuire, "The Nature of Attitudes and Attitude Change," in *The Handbook of Social Psychology,* 2nd ed., Vol. 3, Gardner Lindsey and Elliott Aronson (eds.). Reading, Mass.: Addison-Wesley, 1969, pp. 194–196.

just following orders in relaying the message, and that compliance to so rigid a demand is really not expected (perceived unconcern). This, coupled with the conviction that it would be impossible for anyone to prove that you really weren't sick on the day of the deciding World Series Game (perceived lack of scrutiny), would more than compensate for the manager's actual power to hire and fire employees.

Although their list is by no means exhaustive, John French and Bertram Raven have identified five *types of power* which affect our social transactions.[6] *Reward power* applied to business communication would include the ability to grant promotions, salary increases, better office space, and extra vacations with pay. *Coercive power* includes the ability to fire, to deny promotions, or to employ any one of a number of negative sanctions. *Referent power* includes use of appeals to "do this for me." Such power can exist only if workers respect the source to a degree that they want to be like this person, or to a degree that they

Figure 5–1 A top executive's status is frequently indicated by the quantity and quality of office space he or she occupies. His or her power over company personnel may be based upon his or her ability to grant rewards, to impose negative sanctions, and employees' desires to be liked by their supervisor, as well as expertise, or what French and Raven identified as *legitimate* power. (Photo by Sybil Shelton.)

---

[6]John R.P. French, Jr. and Bertram Raven, "The Bases of Social Power," in *Group Dynamics*, D. Cartwright and A. Zander (eds.), New York: Harper & Row, Pub., 1968, pp. 259–268.

have a compelling desire to satisfy this person. *Expert power* is derived from a source's qualifications and competencies. The willingness of a junior executive to follow the advice of a successful, self-made vice-president is an example of expert power. *Legitimate power* exists when a source is perceived as having a "right" to require compliance with requests. In the business world we are all familiar with the quip: "The boss isn't always right, but he's always the boss." When willingness to comply with demands is based on the loyalty concept of not biting the hand that feeds, workers are attributing legitimate power to their boss. It is almost impossible to distinguish between recognition of *status* or position and perception of legitimate power.

message variables (says what?)

In the preceding chapter we noted that messages are transmitted interpersonally by means of *verbal* and *nonverbal* message cues. Although a later chapter will treat the subject of nonverbal communication in considerably more detail, we shall briefly consider nonverbal aspects of the message signal before turning our attention to variables related to message content and structure.

Nonverbal Message Variables

Depending upon the channel used in message transmission, nonverbal message cues may range from paper quality and the impressiveness of the letterhead (written correspondence) to vocal quality, pitch, loudness, and rate of speech (oral communication). Since written communication is treated in Part III of this text, we shall focus our attention on oral communication nonverbal clues.

Effective use of nonverbal message cues will result in communication that: (1) *is easier to decode and comprehend*, and (2) *is more attention-demanding*. That is, variety in vocal and body behavior will assist your listener in determining what it is that you are saying, while at the same time make your message a more appealing set of stimuli within the perceptual field of your listener.

Nonverbal Message Variables Facilitate Understanding. At least a few of the difficulties resulting from the imprecision of our language code may be overcome through effective use of vocal cues and gestures in message communication. You may remember the "George-Marsha" recording in which the male speaker would say "Marsha," followed by the female speaker's reply, "George." That was the entire record: George. . . . Marsha. . . . George. . . . Marsha. . . . George. . . . etc. However, considerably more was communicated nonverbally. Through variations in *pitch* (frequency of sound vibrations; especially rising and falling inflection), variations in *force* (loudness), variations in *rate* (speed of speaking; length of time spent on particular syllables and length of time between syllables), and variations in *quality* (clear, husky, warm, whisper-like, hard, or soft vocal tones) George and Marsha communicated messages so suggestive as to cause some radio stations to ban the airing of their recording. In addition to variations in vocal cues, *demonstrative gestures* (holding hands apart to demonstrate height or depth) and *emphatic gestures* (hand, arm, or body movements to emphasize a point) may be used to aid the understanding of your message by your listeners. Remember, in oral communication, variations in the use of your voice and your body must accomplish the kinds of emphasis communicated by writers through the use of commas, paragraphs, italicized or underlined words and phrases, quotation marks, and boldfaced headings.

Nonverbal Message Variables Help Maintain Listener Attention.   You have heard it said that the human eye will tend to follow a moving object. Similarly, the human ear tends to be receptive to stimuli that vary in rate, force, pitch, and quality. Consequently, the communicator who uses meaningful gestures and avoids speaking in a monotone will find the task of obtaining and maintaining audience attention more manageable.

─────────── Message Content

In constructing a message, should you try to present both pros and cons? Which kinds of message appeals have the greatest impact on listeners? What is the relationship between evidence and message effectiveness?

One-Sided Versus Two-Sided Messages.   In various communication encounters, you will be faced with the problem of determining whether you should withhold arguments that tend to run counter to your proposal or include those counterarguments in your presentation. At the risk of oversimplification, we offer the following advice as a summary of research findings to date:

> *One-sided presentations* are more effective when the receiver is generally favorable toward the source and/or his topic; when the receiver is unlikely to be exposed to future counter-arguments; when the receiver is aware of the communicator's intention to persuade; and when temporary opinion change is the extent of the source's desired receiver response.
>
> *Two-sided presentations* are more effective when the receiver is highly educated; when the receiver is generally unfavorable toward the source and/or his topic; when the receiver is likely to be exposed to arguments countering the source's stand on the topic; when the receiver is unaware of the communicator's intention to persuade; and when the source desires that his receiver perceive him as fair and unbiased.[7]

───────────

[7]Carl I. Hovland, A.A. Lumsdaine, and F.D. Sheffield, *Studies in Social Psychology in World War II*, Vol. 3. Princeton, N.J.: Princeton University Press, 1949, pp. 201–227.

Message Appeals.   Erwin Bettinghaus has identified four types of appeals that may be incorporated into the source's message: *fear appeals, emotional appeals, reward appeals,* and *motivational appeals.* [8] *Fear appeals* may be low, moderate, or high in intensity. Exactly which type of fear appeal is most effective is a controversial issue. However, the following conclusions regarding the use of fear appeals seem warranted:

1. If a strong fear appeal is used, that appeal must be balanced with a specific, definitive plan of action that will enable the receiver to escape the threatened calamity.
2. High-credibility sources are more effective in the use of strong fear appeals, while sources with questionable credibility are more effective when they use low-level fear appeals.
3. Strong fear appeals are more effective when receivers perceive the topic as extremely important to them personally. As you sense a decline in the personal importance of your message to your receivers, you should reduce the intensity of your fear appeals.
4. Finally, there seems to be a correlation between personality types and the effectiveness of fear appeals. "Copers" are more responsive to high-level fear appeals, while "avoiders" are significantly less responsive.

Emotional appeals include the use of "loaded language," the association of your topic with either popular or unpopular ideas, the association of your topic with emotion-laden visual aids (picture of child on crutches to support a Red Cross speech), and finally, physical display of emotions by the source during a communication transaction.

Reward appeals and *motivational appeals* are very similar. The only distinction made by Bettinghaus would appear to be the location of each type of appeal on a selfishness-unselfishness continuum. Reward appeals are based upon the promise of money, status, or power in exchange for compliance. Motivational appeals rely on a receiver's sense of fair play, humanity, religious or political convictions, and basic human drives for their impact.

Evidence.   The incorporation of evidence into a message at times will increase the effectiveness of the message. By evidence we mean the citing of outside sources to support message issues. The impact of evidence on receivers is influenced by the following factors:

1. The ability of the source to deliver the message; poor delivery lowers the impact of the evidence.
2. The credibility of the communicator; generally, the higher the credibility of a source, the less the impact of evidence in the messages.
3. The subject of the message; we are willing to grant assertions regarding familiar topics, but we require documentation for other topics.

---

[8]Edwin P. Bettinghaus, *Persuasive Communication*, 2nd ed. New York: Holt, Rinehart and Winston, 1973, pp. 158–163.

4. The perceived soundness of the evidence; to be effective the evidence must be relevant, recent, and adequate.
5. The intelligence level of the audience; the higher the intelligence level, the more effective the impact of evidence.[9]

_____ Message Structure

Investigations of the effects of message structure on receiver retention and receiver attitudes have resulted in contradictory conclusions. For the most part, however, we feel that the following premises will prepare you to approach the problem of message structure:

1. Some kind of message structure is needed. Orderly presentations of messages most likely will result in increased comprehension and retention of your messages. It may also enhance the persuasiveness of your messages.
2. If your message includes three or more points, place the most impressive points at the beginning and at the end of your presentation and your weakest point in the middle. Whether you place your strongest point first or last depends on your assessment of probable audience response. If you think your audience will be favorable, the *climax* order (strongest point last) would seem appropriate. If on the other hand, you suspect unfavorable audience attitudes, the *anticlimax* (strongest point first) is probably best.
3. In a two-point, problem-solution presentation, you will generally want to establish the problem (need area) first, and then proceed with a discussion of your solution to the problem.
4. In two-sided presentations of both pros and cons, you should first present the positive side (the argument that you personally favor) and then present the negative side. You will, of course, be more effective if you are able to refute the negative points.
5. If your message will include ideas that your receiver will find undesirable, as well as ideas that will be perceived as desirable, present the desirable ideas *first*.
6. In most cases you will want to include an explicitly drawn conclusion at the end of your message. Implied conclusions may be better, however, for counseling interviews, and in other situations in which you feel it essential for the receiver to be a participant in decision making.
7. If you cite the source of a particular piece of evidence used in your message, it is usually best to cite the source *following* the evidence. Cite the source *first* only if you know that your receiver perceives the cited source as highly credible.
8. Finally, if your intention is to persuade your receiver through your message, it is best not to state your intention early in the message. Such statements tend to build up resistance in the minds of receivers.

_____

[9] These conclusions are drawn from J.C. McCroskey, "A Summary of Experimental Research on the Effects of Evidence in Persuasive Communication," *Quarterly Journal of Speech*, **55** (1969), pp. 169–176; and Robert S. Cathcart, "An Experimental Study of the Relative Effectiveness of Four Methods of Presenting Evidence," *Speech Monographs*, **22** (1955), pp. 227–233.

════════════receiver variables (to whom?)

An advertising campaign of the Equitable Life Insurance Company was based on the theme, "There's Nobody Else Exactly Like You." After screening a series of very different personality types engaged in a similar activity (bowling, for example), company spokespeople insist that Equitable is aware of individual differences and willing to tailor their policies in an effort to meet individual needs.

The philosophy behind the Equitable Life Insurance advertisement might well be applied to receivers in the communication process. No communication audience will be *exactly* like another communication audience. In addition to the obvious difference created by the *number* of receivers as you progress from interviews to large group presentations, you will be wise to consider other physical characteristics as well as the psychological aspects that *make each audience unique.* Since we now know that physiological and psychological receiver characteristics influence the reception, interpretation, and evaluation of messages, it is vitally important that we take those characteristics into account in each communication transaction.

_____ Demographic Variables

Many years ago John Donne wrote "no man is an island, apart from the main." In our complex twentieth-century society we are constantly being influenced by those with whom we frequently interact. Such factors as age, sex, religion, race, political affiliation, intelligence level, and socioeconomic status are *demographic* variables affecting both the frequency of communication contacts and the receptivity to communication contacts. By demographic variables we mean factors over which the individual has little or no control. Although some authorities might wish to object to the inclusion of 'religion, political affiliation, and socioeconomic status as demographic variables, we feel that the evidence is overwhelming that the vast majority of individuals never escape the environmental hold of family influence in these three factors.

Age. "You can't teach an old dog new tricks." While empirical evidence pertaining to the relationships between age and persuasibility is not yet overly convincing, there is some support for the hypothesis that as age increases, susceptibility to persuasive messages decreases.[10] There are many possible explanations for this phenomenon. The most plausible, however, is that age

---

[10]Clare Marple. "The Comparative Susceptibility of Three Age Levels to the Suggestion of Group versus Expert Opinion," *Journal of Social Psychology.* 4 (1933), pp. 176–186.

brings with it increased experiences, many of which may run counter to the suggestion made by the would be persuader.

Sex.   Several years ago speakers were advised that female audiences would be more susceptible to persuasive messages than would male audiences.[11] Experts theorized that female susceptibility to persuasion could be accounted for in light of one or more of the following qualifiers:

1. The difference in susceptibility to persuasive messages appears to be a result of social conditioning. Previously women were urged by societal mores to be nonaggressive and agreeable, while aggressiveness and even disagreeableness was tolerated in men.
2. Women are more verbal than men. Hence, they may simply be receiving more of the persuasive message than men do. (Note: Girls almost always learn to talk and read before boys do.)
3. The difference in susceptibility to persuasive messages may be topic bound. Most of the evidence suggesting that men are more difficult to persuade has come from experiments that involved male-oriented topics.

More recent investigations have brought earlier generalizations about female susceptibility to persuasion into serious question, however. Dramatic changes in societal norms during the 1970s have resulted in a serious questioning of traditional sex roles by both men and women. There are now men who readily embrace behavioral characteristics that were once considered exclusively in the feminine domain, and there are females who work in traditional male jobs and are comfortable with traditional male behavioral characteristics. It is no longer safe to assume that females would not be interested in speeches about automobile racing or that males would not be interested in a speech concerning needlepoint techniques. Research by Sandra Bem resulted in the introduction of a new classification entirely for individuals who possess *both* masculine and feminine attributes—*androgynous*. Bem has estimated that approximately 35 percent of our population could be correctly typed as androgynous, rather than feminine or masculine.[12]

Following Bem's procedures for typing individual audience members as feminine, masculine, or androgynous, researchers have recently concluded that feminine individuals (those identified as feminine by means of Bem's Sex Role Inventory questionnaire) were more susceptible to persuasion than were individuals typed as masculine.[13] The fact that androgynous individuals were neither easily changeable nor extremely resistant to persuasion may partially

[11]Thomas M. Scheidel, "Sex and Persuasibility," *Speech Monographs*, **30** (1963), pp. 353–358.

[12]Sandra Lipsitz Bem, "Androgyny vs. the Tight Little Lives of Fluffy Women and Chesty Men," *Psychology Today*, **9** (September 1975), p. 58.

[13]Charles L. Montgomery and Michael Burgoon, "An Experimental Study of the Interactive Effects of Sex and Androgyny on Attitude Change," *Communication Monographs*, **44** (June 1977), pp. 130–135.

explain why inconsistent conclusions have been reached by researchers who did not take the androgynous variable into account.

Religious and Political Affiliations.   Without doubt affiliation with a particular religious or political group is not as influential a frame of reference as it was in years past. Today, a democrat is not a democrat is not a democrat, and a Roman Catholic is not a Roman Catholic is not a Roman Catholic. By this we simply mean that individuals today tend to do more of their own thinking as it pertains to religion and politics, and they are unwilling to allow either political or religious leaders to dictate to them.

Race.   There is no evidence that any one race of individuals is any more susceptible to persuasive messages than any other race. However, differences in socioeconomic status and environmental backgrounds common to certain ethnic groups may result in differences in persuasibility *on certain topics.* Communicators who face the task of frequent transracial communication would be wise to prepare by reading newspapers published by the ethnic group with which they plan to communicate. Listening to related radio or television programs might also aid in the preparation of messages. Such advance preparation at least might enable communicators to avoid the obvious ethnic insults. In addition, the communicators will have some idea of the stand of that ethnic group on the issues they are likely to discuss, and even more importantly, they may discover the reasons for that stand.

Intelligence.   While we have determined that individuals of higher intelligence may be more responsive to certain kinds of message treatment (two-sided presentations, for example), there is no concrete evidence supporting the premise that intelligence correlates either positively or negatively with persuasibility. Again, common sense tells us that the more educated an individual is, the more alternatives available to that individual. For that reason, you might find more resistance to persuasion among the highly educated, inasmuch as they are more equipped with counterarguments.

Socioeconomic Background.   Cutting across the cultural gaps created by social conditioning and economic restrictions can become especially difficult. We have ample evidence to conclude that socioeconomic backgrounds play a vital role in determining an individual's willingness to listen to a message, as well as that individual's willingness to believe the message. Indeed, it would be unwise for a high-level management representative to drive a Lincoln Continental into an impoverished neighborhood, and begin a message with "I know just what you're facing."

_____ **Personality Variables**

Up to this point we have been discussing receiver variables that *may* influence the effectiveness of the communication process in certain situations. The personality variables of self-esteem, dogmatism, authoritarianism, Machiavellianism, and anxiety interact to form a unique personality, and they influence receiver response to communication in just about every conceivable situation.

Self-Esteem. Receivers who are confident, optimistic, and experience few feelings of inadequacy are said to be *high in self-esteem.* Those who lack confidence in themselves, experience frequent feelings of inadequacy, and are generally pessimistic are often classified as *low in self-esteem.* As a general rule, we know now that receivers with *low self-esteem* are more susceptible to persuasive messages than are *high self-esteem receivers.* High self-esteem receivers require more order and more support in persuasive messages than do low self-esteem receivers. Low self-esteem receivers are particularly susceptible to persuasive messages from high self-esteem sources, and they generally respond more favorably to appeals linked to authority figures and majority support. Low self-esteem receivers prefer messages that are simple and clear-cut, and they tend to resist messages that are complex and difficult to follow. [14]

Dogmatism. Receivers who are closed-minded (dogmatic) tend to view the world in very narrow terms. Their right is always right, their wrong is always wrong, and their authorities are always authorities. Dogmatic receivers are generally reluctant to allow their various beliefs to come under comparison and contrast scrutiny. Instead they tend to pigeon-hole or compartmentalize their beliefs to the degree that contradictions in cognitions rarely are perceived. Receivers who are high on the dogmatism scale experience difficulty in separating sources of messages from the content of those messages. Consequently, persuasive messages from positive sources (especially high authorities) effect opinion change among dogmatic receivers, while messages from negative sources are so distrusted that dogmatic receivers tend to view even positive messages as negative. Receivers low in dogmatism tend to be able to incorporate new ideas into their existing frames of reference and adjust those reference frames accordingly. For that reason the open-minded receiver (low dogmatism) will respond more willingly to recommendations for sweeping social change or massive innovation. The very opposite can be said for dogmatic receivers. [15]

Authoritarianism. Receivers who rate high in authoritarianism are those who are extremely conscious of status and power possessed by others. They will tend to exhibit great respect for individuals with high status and power, while slighting those with low status and power. Authoritarian receivers tend to cling to middle-class value systems in making their judgments—judgments that are absolute and doctrinaire. You will find authoritarian receivers less susceptible

---

[14]Irving L. Janis and Peter B. Field, "A Behavioral Assessment of Persuasibility," in *Personality and Persuasibility,* Hovland and Janis (eds.). New Haven: Yale University Press, 1959, pp. 29–54.
[15]Milton Rokeach, "The Nature and Meaning of Dogmatism," *Psychological Review,* **61**:3 (1954), p. 195.

to messages based on logic and evidence, but more susceptible to messages that come from powerful, prestigious, and high-status sources. There is some evidence that receivers low in authoritarianism are better able to recall points made by persuasive messages than are receivers high in authoritarianism.[16]

Machiavellianism. This term is used to describe the personality of individuals who are manipulative of others without regard for the morality of their manipulations. Since high-Machiavellian individuals tend to be constantly suspicious of the methods and motives of other people, it is easy to see why they present special problems for a would-be communicator when they are cast in the role of receivers. Before high Machiavellian receivers will manifest opinion change, they must be provided with an exceptionally high reward or justification. Receivers low in Machiavellian traits are more willing to manifest opinion change as a result of face-to-face communication than are receivers high in these traits. Low-Machiavellian receivers are more susceptible to persuasive messages based on opinion data than are high Machiavellians. High Machiavellian receivers demand messages based on factual, scientifically demonstrable information.[17]

Anxiety. Psychologists have identified two types of anxiety affecting individuals: neurotic and situational. Neurotic anxiety is indicated by feelings of apprehension, uncertainty, and even panic when confronted with everyday situations and events. Situational anxiety can be defined as a reaction of mild apprehension about a specific event or a specific decision that must be reached. Neurotically anxious receivers tend to become so defensive about the world around them that they react negatively to persuasive attempts. Situational anxiety in a receiver may actually increase readiness to respond to a message. Many of the best sales presentations (ranging from presentations for vacuum cleaners to life insurance) owe their success to the creation of mild anxiety in the mind of the customer—anxiety which can be eliminated through the purchase of a particular product.[18]

_____ Prior Commitment

Before we move on to a discussion of channel variables, we will touch briefly on one additional factor influencing a receiver's reception of a message. Has your receiver either publicly or privately taken a stand on the issue that you plan to discuss? If so, research results indicate that such _prior commitment_ will either help you or hinder you in your efforts to influence that

[16]T.W. Adorno, E. Frenkel-Brunswik, D.J. Levinson, and R.N. Sanford, _The Authoritarian Personality_. New York: Harper & Row, Pub., 1950.

[17]R. Christie and F. Geis, _Studies in Machiavellianism_. New York: Academic Press, 1970.

[18]J. Nunnally and H. Bobren, "Variables Governing the Willingness to Receive Communications on Mental Health," _Journal of Personality_, **23** (1954), pp. 154–166.

receiver's position. Since none of us wants to "lose face" with our associates, we are particularly reluctant to modify a publicly made position. We are, however, somewhat more willing to modify private commitments, providing that counterarguments appear sufficiently valid.[19]

===context variables (in what context?)

Up until a few years ago it was common practice among motion picture promoters to lift bits and pieces of critical reviews out of context. For example, a *New York Times* reviewer might have written: "The producer, actors, designers, and directors accomplished the near impossible in *Twenty-second Century*. Together, they have managed to reduce a truly suspenseful and imaginative plot to a series of cheap shocks and third-rate sensationalism." By the time the promoters "edited" the review, they were able to say: "Truly suspenseful and imaginative plot. . . N. Y. Times."

We should all be aware of the problems involved in lifting an isolated comment out of the context of an entire message. We recall frustrations created by misunderstandings when only a small portion of one of our messages reached the ears of some receiver—that late night phone conversation that began with an icy "I just want you to know that I heard what you said about my idea." While we are aware of contextual significance as it pertains to individual messages, we sometimes overlook the fact that the *entire message* (indeed, all phases of a communication transaction) is contextually bound. In order to fully comprehend any communication effort, physical and psychological aspects of the communication context must be considered.

Physical Context

Does the communication transaction occur in a plush-carpeted, paneled office with one communicator sitting behind a massive executive desk? Or, does it occur over coffee during a hurried 15-minute break? Is the message communicated in an elevator and in the office lobby area as the communicators exit at the end of a hard day on the job? Or, does it occur over a leisurely dinner at one of the town's nicest restaurants? Depending on the specific location where the communication occurs, there will be varying degrees of competing stimuli as well as varying degrees of "openness" on the part of the communication participants.

Within the general location of the communication transaction, studies have indicated that specific arrangement of seating affects the communication proc-

---

[19]Ronald Appelbaum, and others, *Fundamental Concepts in Human Communication.* San Francisco: Canfield Press, 1973, p. 155.

ess. In large group meetings, rows of seats facing a single podium will create a very different context than concentric circle seating with a speaker standing in the center of the circle. Contextual implications of possible seating arrangements for committee or board meetings and for interviews will be discussed in later chapters.

The total number of receivers involved in the communication transaction must be considered. In general, interaction both verbally and nonverbally decreases as the number of receivers increases. We must adjust from a transaction with maximum interaction and feedback (the interview) to transactions with minimum interaction and feedback (a presentation to 500 or more employees).

Does the communication occur in the morning, in the afternoon, or in the evening? If the communication occurs too early in the morning, receivers may not be as alert as they will be later in the day. On the other hand, communication very late in the day may be influenced by listeners who are simply too exhausted to accurately receive and decode the message. Adolph Hitler suggested evening meetings for his rallies, because he felt the people would be so tired that they would "succumb more easily to the dominating force of a stronger will."

Psychological Context

In reality it is difficult to separate the physical context from the psychological context, for they operate interdependently. For example, the number of receivers influence the psychological as well as the physical communication context. If only fifteen people attend a meeting for which over a hundred were anticipated, interaction between speaker and audience may increase, but the effectiveness of that interaction may be negated by the psychological impact of the low attendance. On the other hand, if many more people attend a meeting than were anticipated, a feeling of excitement and satisfaction about the excellent response may enable communicators to more than compensate for problems created by the physically crowded conditions.

Peer pressure being what it is, we are generally affected psychologically by the reactions of other receivers. The term *social facilitation* refers to the effects that receivers have on one another as a result of their physical and emotional proximity. Psychologically, we will perceive a good speech as a great speech if reactions of other receivers are sufficiently positive. On the other hand, we may perceive a great speech as a poor speech if other audience members are extremely negative and unreceptive.

Timing may be psychological as well as physical. For example, in a conversation with an individual whom you have just met, you may be able to say things just before you part company that would be inappropriate during the first few minutes of your communication transaction.

Figure 5–2 Social facilitation refers to the effects that receivers have on one another. We will psychologically perceive a good speech as a great speech, if reactions of other receivers are sufficiently positive. (Photo by Catherine Ursillo, courtesy of De Wys, Inc.)

In summary, we may safely say that the number of people involved, the physical setting (place and space available), seating arrangement, expectations of communicators, along with general attitudes (favorable, negative, or apathetic) operate interdependently to create a unique context for *each* communication transaction.

channel variables (through what ═══════════ channel?)

For many years leaders in the business community exhibited a basic distrust of the oral communication channel through such slogans as "Never Say it–Write it." However, as it became apparent that employees were being swamped with letters, memos, and reports—many of which were not read at all, much less read carefully—one giant corporation replaced this slogan with "Talk it over—Jot it down." They had come to the realization that really important messages could be communicated better by using two- rather than one-channel communication.

Many years ago Adolph Hitler explained why he preferred oral communication to written communication. In a chapter of *Mein Kampf* entitled "The Significance of the Spoken Word," Hitler outlined his reasons for using the oral channel:

1. He felt that the oral channel availed the speaker with an opportunity to receive "continuous correction" from his audience, i.e., *feedback.*
2. He felt that the mass of people were unwilling to expose themselves to written material "not in agreement with what they themselves believe," i.e., written material allows too much selective exposure.
3. He felt that the oral channel allowed more specific adaptation to listeners. Written messages may be above or below the intelligence level of the reader.
4. He felt that the oral channel was better suited for effecting attitude change. The value of written communication lay in reinforcing or deepening a point of view already held.[20]

The advantages which Hitler noted of using the oral channel are essentially as valid today as they were in the 1930s. However, the physical impossibility of face-to-face communication with extremely large groups of people necessitates the use of writing from to time. In addition, there is considerable evidence that the written channel is superior to the oral channel for the communication of difficult materials, since the written channel allows the receiver to proceed at an individual pace allowing maximum comprehension. Still to be contended with, however, are the facts that the vast majority of Americans are unwilling to take the time to read all the information directed toward them through the written channel. The message source may have to decide between accuracy of transmission through the written medium (transmissions that may not be received, however) and somewhat inaccurate transmissions through the oral channel (transmissions that at least will be minimally received).

The best advice we can offer is based upon a doctoral dissertation completed at Purdue University. In that study the oral communication, written communication, and bulletin board were evaluated individually and compared in various combinations. Best results were obtained with a *combination* of oral and written communication channels. Whenever possible, it appears desirable to "Talk it over—Jot it down."

_____ Visual Plus Oral Communication?

One picture is not necessarily worth a thousand words during a communication transaction. A flashy, multimedia presentation may be impressive, but actually may *reduce* receiver retention of the message. There is

---

[20]Adolf Hitler, *Mein Kampf,* Ralph Manheim (trans.). Boston: Houghton Mifflin, 1943.

considerable evidence that the human nervous system can assimilate multichannel messages much better if those messages are presented sequentially rather than simultaneously. Brightly-colored visual aids may be effective in gaining and focusing audience attention, but there is the danger that such aids will detract from *what you are saying* unless they are used with great care. It is always best to cover visual displays at all times when you are not directly using them. In other words, we are suggesting the use of visual aids *only* if those visuals do aid in the sense of clarifying complex concepts, and *only* if they are brought into the presentation at a point when you are willing to have maximum audience attention focused on the aids rather than on what you are saying.

Mass Media

So great is the impact of the mass media on our lives today that an entire chapter of this text is devoted to effective use of those channels. You will find in Chapter 17 a discussion of "interposed communication" and "opinion leaders" along with additional implications of mass media for the communication process.

effect variables (with what effect?)

Our communication contacts are designed to result in some kind of behavior, attitude change, information gain, or perhaps just "positive vibrations" among our listeners. Our purpose in communicating may range from enabling our listeners to "feel good about us and about themselves" to convincing them to purchase a product or to buy an idea. Some communication effects are immediate, while others require the passage of time before emerging.

Types of Effects

Hovland and Janis have suggested four kinds of effects which may result from varying degrees of attitude change. Those effects include *opinion* change, *perception* change, *affect* change, and *action* change.[21]

Opinion Change. An opinion is a verbalized evaluation of an object, individual, or concept. "I like Ike," "I don't trust Harry," "I think this new policy will really be good for us," or "In my opinion, this company discriminates in its hiring practices" are all examples of opinions. At the conclusion of your message you have achieved opinion change effects if your receiver is willing to verbalize agreement with your stand.

---

[21]Hovland and Janis (eds.), *Personality and Persuasibility*, pp. 1–28.

Perception Change. Perception involves the way we see things. Consequently, a perception change would imply that our receiver had experienced adequate attitude change to warrant the visualization of new images. An individual may perceive all "long-hairs" as societal misfits until some personal experience or a message relating the experiences of others changes that perception.

Affect Change. The affect change is sometimes called the "gut" reaction. How do you feel when you hear a particular concept discussed? Does the discussion make you feel "warm" inside, or does it send "chills" down your back? When a message results in a change of these basic feelings, we say that the communicator has obtained an affect change in the receiver.

Action Change. Action changes are changes in overt, physical behavior. They may range from giving a pint of blood during a company blood drive to voting to ratify a new union-approved contract. Anytime that a source asks for a specific behavior in a message, and the receiver exhibits that behavior, we may conclude that action change has been effected.

Retroversive Effects

Each of the effects discussed in the preceding section are effects over which the source may exercise considerable control. None of us can anticipate all the possible effects which our messages will create, however. We must be prepared to face the possibility that at times we will obtain results that are unanticipated and even opposite to those sought. Thomas Scheidel discusses four retroversive or retroactive effects that may occur as a result of your message. His list of retroversive effects includes *boomerang* effect, *regression* effect, *sleeper* effect, and *focusing* effect.[22]

Boomerang Effect. When listeners react in the opposite direction of that which the speaker advocates, we say that a boomerang effect has occurred. The source has doubly failed. Not only have the listeners refused to adopt the proposed stand, they are more negative than they were before the attempted persuasion!

Regression Effect. Suppose a group of workers upon hearing a speech advocating new safety precautions immediately begin to follow the new safety standards. However, in the weeks that follow the workers revert back to their usual job behavior. This reverting back to original ideas or behaviors after an initial change is known as the regression effect. A degree of regression occurs following all successful persuasion attempts (probably caused in part by the forgetting phenomenon). At other times, however, the regression may be total.

---

[22]Thomas M. Scheidel, *Speech Communication and Human Interaction.* Glenview, Ill.: Scott, Foresman, 1972, pp. 118–124.

Sleeper Effect.   Consider the following situations. A speaker whom you highly regard advocates a position which you somewhat reluctantly adopt. Two weeks later you have abandoned that position. A speaker whom you dislike advocates a position which you mildly favor, but because of your dislike of the speaker, you decide to reject it. Two weeks later you discover that you are supporting that position. In each of the above cases, a sleeper effect has occurred. In the case of sleeper effects the message and the source become disassociated over a period of time, allowing the message impact to determine the ultimate effect (without regard for the credibility of the source).

Focusing Effect.   If you have ever peered through a screened window at some object outside, you may have noticed the ease with which you could bring the screen in and out of focus. You had to choose, however, between the screen and the outside scene. You were unable to focus on both simultaneously. A similar phenomenon operates in a communication transaction. During the communication of a message, our receivers may be focusing so intently on our evidence that they temporarily block out counterarguments. When the stimulus of the message is removed, however, the receivers may again focus on the counterarguments to the extent that any gains realized immediately following the message presentation are negated.

Summary

Using the Lasswell model as the framework for our discussion we have examined the variables influencing the communication process. Factors relating to the communication source were discussed as source credibility dimensions, status, and power variables. Message variables considered included nonverbal message cues, message content, and message structure. Receivers were discussed in relationship to age, sex, religious and political affiliations, race, intelligence, socio-economic background, self-esteem, dogmatism, authoritarianism, Machiavellianism, anxiety, and prior commitment. Consideration was afforded both psychological and physical contextual variables. Communication channels were considered in light of written versus oral channels and one channel versus two channel use. Basic effects discussed included opinion change, perception change, affect change, action change, boomerang effect, regression effect, sleeper effect, and focusing effect.

Discussion Questions

1. Distinguish between status and power. Can you think of sources who possess one without the other?
2. Which of the three dimensions of credibility (competency, trustworthiness, and dynamism) do you feel is most critical in the business community?

3. Do you feel that you are more susceptible to high or low fear appeals? Why?
4. Is it unethical to present only one side of an issue in a persuasive speech? Why?
5. Do today's youth tend to accept the political and religious affiliations of their parents to the same degree that they did a generation ago? What differences have you noted?
6. Define Machiavellianism. What is the origin of the term?
7. On p. 105 several advantages of the oral channel of communication are listed. Can you think of additional advantages? Disadvantages?
8. Distinguish between regression effects and focusing effects.

=========== **Study Probes**

1. List three people whom you perceive as highly credible. Try to determine in which of the credibility dimensions they are strongest? Weakest? Characterize each of the three people according to status, power, and the personality types discussed in the section on receiver variables.
2. Collect at least ten advertisements from newspapers and magazines. Analyze those advertisements in light of the message variables discussed in this chapter.
3. Conduct a self-inventory using the receiver characteristics discussed in this chapter. Categorize yourself according to each characteristic. Try to remember various attempts of others to persuade you. Were your reactions similar to the predicted reactions for that personality type?
4. Conduct a survey among several of your acquaintances. Try to determine why they prefer either written or oral communication. In your survey, ask about attitudes toward the use of visual aids? Do your friends think the use of visuals help or hinder a speaker?

=========== **Additional Reading**

Anderson, K., *Persuasion: Theory and Practice*. Boston: Allyn & Bacon, 1971.

Anderson, K., and T. Clevenger, "A Summary of Experimental Research in Ethos," *Speech Monographs*, 30 (1963) pp. 59–78.

Hovland, C. and I. Janis, *Personality and Persuasibility*. New Haven: Yale University Press, 1959.

Hovland, C., I. Janis, and H. Kelley, *Communication and Persuasion*. New Haven: Yale University Press, 1953.

Karlins, M. and H.I. Abelson, *Persuasion: How Opinions Are Changed*. New York: Springer Verlag, 1970.

Listening: a neglected act

6

key points to learn

What listening is.

The difference between active listening and passive listening.

The importance of being a good listener.

General and specific rewards of active listening.

The components of active listening.

What the barriers are to active listening.

How to develop a "third ear" ability.

Ways to improve your listening ability.

An ancient philosopher wrote, "We have been given two ears and but a single mouth in order that we may hear more and talk less." More recently, Stuart Chase said, "Americans are not good listeners. In general, they talk more than they listen. Competition in our culture has put a premium on self-expression, even if the individual has nothing to express."[1]

In the over 2,000 years between the above observations, not much has seemed to change. People are still anxious to talk but reluctant or unable to pay the attention necessary for listening.

═══════════what is listening?

Zeno of Citium used the word "hear," and Stuart Chase employed "listen" as synonymous in meaning, but do they really mean the same thing? In a communication sense, these words mean two entirely different activities. Hearing is thought to be passive. One definition of hearing is the act or process of perceiving sounds through the stimulation of auditory nerves in the ear through sound waves.

---

[1]Stuart Chase, "Are You Listening," *Reader's Digest*, Dec. 1962, p. 83.

Unless our physical auditory system is damaged or there are distractions or interferences, we should be able to hear (without further effort) any sound waves within our range of capability.

Listening goes beyond hearing. According to the dictionary, it involves making a conscious effort to hear; to give heed; take advice. Lundsteen suggests that listening is "the process by which spoken language is converted to meaning in the mind."[2] Applying listening to business, Keefe describes it as "the conscious, active process of eliciting information, ideas, attitudes, and emotions in interpersonal, oral exchange for the purpose of increasing the listener's capacity for planning and decision making."[3]

_____ Active Listening: Importance

Listening and reading have been compared as they are our major sources of learning and they have strong similarities. Both involve decoding or intake and both involve a "thinking base," but a listener can use verbal and nonverbal data to interpret meaning. In a face-to-face situation a listener can interrupt and ask questions while the reader must decipher the printed word as best he or she can.

On the other hand, listening must be far more active, as the listener is "caught in the flow of time." He or she must be alert to the message and its meaning. While a speaker can be questioned, the listener cannot go back into time as a reader can turn back pages or read something over and over until the meaning is clarified.

William Foote Whyte called listening "action research."[4] Action was the encouragement for others to talk and make idea contributions: research was the seeking of useful information and guidance from others. The facilitation of such information, ideas, and guidance is not an accidental process. Active listening requires that the listener be active, not passive.

Active listening requires a concentration on what is being said, not for sound but for meaning. The pitch, the timbre, the rhythm and pace of words are telling us things the words in themselves do not betray. When people talk, the words uttered are only a part of the communication. Heading the list of the top-forty some 400 years ago was a song by Ben Johnson, "Drink to me only with thine eyes," and this love song has been sung ever since. Not only do the eyes communicate but also our mouths, facial expressions, arms, and other body movements. Even body temperature and skin color convey meanings well apart from words. How communicative dead silence can be!

---

[2]Thomas G. Devine, "Listening: What Do We Know After Fifty Years of Research and Theorizing," *Journal of Reading*, Jan. 1978, p. 297.

[3]William F. Keefe, *Listen Management!* New York: McGraw-Hill, 1971, p. 4.

[4]*Ibid.* Attributed to William Foote Whyte, p. 25.

As a manager or supervisor, we should be able to recognize the importance of being an active listener. On an elementary basis, listening is important in the everyday communication of information: Did they order four or forty? Should I stop for the pickup first or last? Remember, the blueprints are to be flopped. Simple instructions are frequently confused by an uninvolved listener.

On a more complex level, a recent newspaper story told of a food processing plant going out on strike as the result of a breakdown in contract negotiations. When interviewed as to the reason for a walkout, one picketer answered, "If you only knew! No one in there ever listens to us." How often have you seen, read, heard, or experienced a similar situation?

Formal interest in listening dates back only a half-century or so. Paul T. Rankin, supervising director of the Detroit Public School System's research department, conducted a landmark study in 1929. He selected 68 adults of different occupations and asked them to keep a record of the time they spent talking, reading, writing, and listening (apart from radio).

The survey was conducted over approximately two months with the following results:

Seven out of every ten minutes awake was spent in some form of communication activity. Of these seven minutes—or 70 percent of waking time:

9 percent was spent writing;
16 percent was spent reading;
30 percent was spent talking; and
45 percent was spent LISTENING[5]
(and this was 20 years before popular TV).

Other studies have yielded similar results.

The sales manager of a major electronics manufacturer kept tab of his time and discovered that 70 to 80 percent was spent on the phone. Half of this time—35 to 40 percent of his total working time—was spent listening on the phone. A survey of dieticians revealed that 63 percent ranked listening as the most important skill in communication, and that they spent about three times as much time listening as they did reading. Managers and supervisors, in another study, were found to spend 1,200 to 1,500 hours a year meeting and talking with subordinates and in a normal year spent 55 to 80 percent of their time communicating.[6]

"Throughout all areas of endeavor and daily routines, the amount devoted to listening far exceeds, in almost all cases, other human activity." Nichols and Stevens go on to say that their research indicates that 40 percent of the average

---

[5]Paul T. Ranking, "Listening Ability: Its Importance, Measurement and Development," *Chicago School Journal*, *12* (June 1930), pp. 177–79, 417–420.

[6]Ralph G. Nichols and Leonard A. Stevens. *Are You Listening?* New York: McGraw-Hill, 1957. pp. 6–10.

business person's salary is earned listening, and for an executive, this can increase to 80 percent.[7]

With this much time and money being expended on listening, we had better be concerned with the results. Lyman Steil[8] reports that half the content of a ten-minute presentation is lost immediately following the message. Retesting 48 hours later results in a further drop of 50 percent or half the retained material. The net remembrance would then be 25 percent of the original message.

These tests usually measure the retention of the explicit data contained in the message but there are two kinds of data in a verbal message: the explicit and the implicit. Explicit data is what is actually verbalized but sometimes more important in interpersonal communication are the implicit or implied messages. Much of what we mean or want the listener to hear remains unsaid. A nonresponse to a question or statement is often more effective than any words we might utter. A good listener must therefore hear the explicit data and also "hear" the implicit data to make the most accurate inference of the message.

Major research since the 1950s has reaffirmed the importance of listening as a communication tool. Whereas the importance of reading to the learning process had never been challenged, now listening has begun to receive increased attention. Generally agreed among language art experts are these five points:

1. Most of us are poor listeners
2. Training could improve our listening abilities
3. Schools should provide such training
4. To be an effective listener one must be active and dynamic
5. Effective listening is sure to be richly rewarded.[9]

_____ Toward Becoming an Active Listener

It should now be immediately apparent that if managers are going to improve their efficiency and effectiveness they must become better listeners. "The cost of wasted time, wasted productivity, broken down relationships, injury, death, and lawsuits all come about because Party A sends a message to Party B and Party B may not respond to it or interpret it."[10]

Listening is the most frequently used form of verbal communication; it is a critical skill in learning: and, it helps us develop other language skills. Whether

_____

[7]Ibid.

[8]Associated Press, *Salisbury Daily Times*, Jan. 5, 1980, p. 3.

[9]Ernest Borman, et al., *Interpersonal Communication in the Modern Organization*. Englewood Cliffs, N.J.: Prentice-Hall, 1969, pp. 171–72.

[10]Associated Press, *Salisbury Daily Times*, p. 3.

we are in a serious role, listening to comprehend, understand, evaluate, or criticize—or in a social role, listening for entertainment, more effective listening has its rewards.

Barker delineates both general and specific bonuses for the serious listener:

General Rewards: helps expand knowledge through new information; develops language facility and vocabulary; and enables evaluation of strong and weak points in a message.

Specific Rewards: saves time and money through learning more efficient ways of doing business; short-cut to knowledge. When an expert on a given subject is available, more and better questions may be asked for immediate answers; and helps gain promotions and pay increases in salary by being in tune with what is expected.

Social listening improvement can provide rewards to the individual of direct value in "quality of life" and indirect benefits to one's business career. Benefits include increased enjoyment of aural stimuli, expanded interests, aids in social maturity, improved image, increased self-confidence, broadened awareness of cultural and ethnic influences, and decreased tensions.[11]

_____ Components of Active Listening

Active listening is a two-way device. Not only does the active listener gain more from what has been said, he or she encourages elaboration of the message. There is then more data from which to glean the message. Evelyn M. Mayerson lists four components required for active listening:

1. *Willingness:* The active listeners keep their own pearls of wisdom to themselves and allow others to express theirs. Listeners often tend to stereotype messages as well as people. This placing like things in a category helps provide quick and easy processing, but when we deal with someone who reminds us of someone else, we expect the same behavior from them. We have closed the door to openness and willingness.

2. *Time:* The act of listening requires time. Both the quantity and the quality of the time set aside are important. If active listening is taken seriously and the manager recognizes the payoff involved, that person will make the time to listen to a subordinate.

3. *Space:* Once a time to listen is arranged, so must a suitable location and the allocation of space. If a superior indicates that an employee can choose rather than be assigned a chair or if a manager moves out from behind an imposing and separating desk discourse may be encouraged. If privacy and quiet are available at the subordinate's work area this will offer some sense of security, and comfort and conversation will be encouraged.

4. *Attention:* Good listening will be created if the subordinate is given attention. Focusing on the speaker with both ears and eyes causes that person to be

---

[11]Larry Barker, *Listening Behavior*. Englewood Cliffs, N.J.: Prentice-Hall, 1971, pp. 7–9.

spotlighted. The manager should eliminate or minimize all distractions such as receiving incoming calls, visitors to the office, and the like.[12]

The factors needed for improved interpersonal listening also extend to larger groups. A room must be large enough to comfortably house the size audience involved. Listening will be affected by the room's temperature, ventilation, and external disturbances, such as noise, light, or movement. The comfort of the chairs and other variables will also affect the manner in which an audience will listen—all apart from the ability of the communicator and the nature and content of the message.[13]

Are You an Effective Listener?

Morris proposes the following self-administered test to help you determine if you are a good listener or not. Answer the following questions and analyze whether your listening can be improved upon:

1. Does your mind wander off on mental excursions while you are listening?
2. Does something you hear turn you off so that your listening stops?
3. Do you stop listening because you feel the speaker has nothing to say?
4. Do you puzzle over the meaning of the speaker's words as you listen?
5. Do you concentrate on facts rather than structure?
6. Do you stop listening if the speaker is difficult to understand?
7. Do you fake attention while your mind wanders?
8. Are you easily distracted by the speaker's appearance or actions?
9. Are you easily distracted by outside sights or sounds?
10. Are you an elaborate note taker?[14]

Now, with a little understanding of our own approach to listening, let us examine some of the obstructive forces barring the way to more productive listening.

barriers to active and effective listening

There are a number of reasons explaining why listening has not been given the importance and emphasis it deserves. A very basic barrier to better listening in our society, is the lack of attention received in our formal

---

[12]Evelyn M. Mayerson, *Shoptalk: Foundations of Managerial Conversation*. Philadelphia: W.B. Saunders Co., 1979, pp. 102–109.

[13]*Ibid*, p. 109.

[14]John O. Morris, *Make Yourself Clear*. New York: McGraw-Hill, 1972, pp. 206–207.

educational process. It is of late that the subject of listening has been incorporated into language arts units and programs at the elementary level and still later, added to the college curriculum.

General barriers to more active listening can be classified as:

Conceptual. Until recently, listening has been considered a passive and natural activity. As a result, it has not been given its intellectual due, and therefore, has lacked attention. Listening has not been considered an important tool, and effective listening in itself cannot achieve miracles overnight. Many successful managers, executives, and entrepreneurs have reached their goals without being effective listeners, or for that matter, effective communicators. Others view listening merely as a device for "letting others talk it out."

Organizational. Both organizationally and procedurally, managers have often treated listening as inconsequential to the success of their organization, at least as part of upward communication. Superiors expect subordinates to listen (a condition perpetuating the superior/subordinate roles), and therefore do not reciprocate. In many organizations, top management may be committed to more open communication but fail to convey this to middle management and supervisory personnel. Often the physical opportunity is neither available or conducive to open dialogue. It frequently becomes apparent that management listens because they have been told to listen, but in reality they hear nothing. This results in lack of action. This failure to follow through soon discourages any further attempts or efforts at communication. Management has failed to realize that good listening creates good listening in turn.

Procedural. Management may block effective communication by listening to the right person or people—but at the wrong time. An example would be listening to union representatives at contract negotiation time but not paying any attention to grievances or requests during earlier periods. The result of not listening often creates an eventual hostile environment where simple problems escalate to monumental proportion.

Attitudinal. Psychotherapist Carl Rogers believes the major barrier to mutual interpersonal communication is our natural tendency to judge, evaluate, approve, or disapprove the statement of the other person or the other group. Listening with understanding is Rogers' solution to this barrier.[15]

Other attitudinal barriers include the "superiority of role" associated with the speaker and the "inferiority" with the listener. The more aggressive the party (usually the manager), the more anxious he or she will be to control or speak rather than listen.

Closely related is an organizational/managerial hang-up exemplified by a "you think you have a problem" attitude. How can a manager, with a multitude

---

[15]Carl R. Rogers, *On Becoming a Person.* Boston: Houghton Mifflin, 1961, pp. 330–331.

of monumental and earth-shaking problems, listen with patience and understanding, to an underling having a squabble with a computer operator in the data processing center?

Language. A final barrier to effective listening is that of language itself. Here we encounter a difficulty or inability to communicate or listen due to different levels of language. A manager or executive with one perspective may encounter difficulties conversing with a subordinate of a different educational attainment level, set of expectations, and experiences.

Another language barrier is that of words and their emotional quality. Nichols and Stevens cite the following example:

> The firm's accountant drops in to see the general manager and says, "I have just heard from the Bureau of Internal Revenue, and . . . . " The general manager suddenly breathes harder and thinks, "That blasted Bureau! Can't they leave me alone?" Red in the face, he whirls and stares out of the window. The label, "Bureau of Internal Revenue" cuts loose emotions that stop the general manager's listening. In the meantime, the accountant is going on to say that "there's a chance to save $3,000 a year if the firm will take the proper steps," but the fuming manager doesn't hear. [16]

Specifically, most managers simply have not been properly prepared to be good listeners. They have not had the training or the encouragement to develop the skill of active learning. Organizationally, they do not have the time necessary to listen with attention or the authority to follow through after such listening. On the personal side, managers resist listening as it is a blow to the ego. Along the same line, listening requires a manager to reverse the usual role of authority and initiative.

Signs point to a change. More and more business firms and other organizations are realizing the importance of listening to the success of their endeavors. Recently the Sperry Company launched a series of advertisements telling of their efforts in this direction. A slogan used by a national advertiser was "We listen better." Listening training has become a part of managerial training as the importance of the function increases.

improving listening ability

Theodor Reik proposed a unique approach to active listening with his "third ear listening" concept. This is an analytical approach in which the "central core" of the listener's mind is allowed to "float free," or to range from the conscious to the subconscious and back pulling together pertinent evidence and suggesting innovative additions to what is being said.

In developing "third ear listening," the listener is not bound by experience

[16]Nichols and Stevens, p. 100.

or what has been heard or learned, but allows for creativity. Reik claims the following advantages for this technique:

1. Important messages or points may be winnowed from the unimportant.
2. Different backgrounds, environments of the speaker and listener are considered.
3. Connotative and denotative meanings are analyzed.
4. The context of delivery is examined for meaning.
5. Words, ideas are tested against group and/or individual norms, values, biases, and ambitions.

Other claims for "third ear listening" are that it separates facts from feelings, promotes an empathetic view, and makes the listener aware of "kinesics," or the whole lexicon of nonverbal communication. "Third ear listening" according to Reik, allows the listener to relate the individual to the group or environment from which he comes. This helps determine loyalties and other social and organizational relationships.[17]

Less theoretical and more immediately apparent are Keith Davis' "Ten Commandments of Good Listening":

1. *Stop talking.* You cannot listen if you are talking.
2. *Put the talker at ease.* Help him or her to feel free to talk.
3. *Show that you want to listen.* Look and act interested; listen to understand rather than oppose.
4. *Remove distractions.* Eliminate or limit the possibilities of interference as best you can.
5. *Empathize.* Try placing yourself in the speaker's shoes; feel as they do.
6. *Be patient.* Allow time and don't interrupt.
7. *Hold your temper.* Be in control of your emotions; listen to meaning, not words or statements.
8. *Go easy on arguments and criticisms.* Hear the person out.
9. *Ask questions.* Show your interest and attention; keep them pertinent to the speaker's frame, not yours.
10. *Stop talking.* First and last, because all other communication depends on it.[18]

George de Mare suggests some of the points made by Davis and adds a few:

1. Establish an agreeable atmosphere.
2. Hear others through on their terms, not yours.
3. Be prepared on the subject to be discussed.
4. Evaluate the speaker and make whatever allowances for his or her circumstances.
5. Avoid getting mentally sidetracked.

---

[17]Theodor Reik, *Listening with the Third Ear.* New York: Farrar, Straus & Giroux, 1964.
[18]Keith Davis, *Organization Behavior*, 6th. ed. New York: McGraw-Hill, 1981, p. 413.

6. Listen for and summarize basic ideas.

7. Restate the substance of what you heard to the speaker for clarification.[19]

Some additional ideas that will lend to be better listening and comprehension include finding an area of interest: "What is being said that I can use?" "What worthwhile ideas or information does he or she have?" "How can I use the information to produce more goods, or improve morale?" Listen to content, not delivery. Overcome the tendency to evaluate the communicator and method or style of delivery. Base your listening on the content of the message. Let the speaker finish. If you are thinking about what you are going to say in defense or attack of the speaker's words, you are not listening to the message. Listen for the central idea. Focus on the main ideas rather than try to memorize facts. When memorizing, you are not listening. Be flexible in how you listen. Take notes, make an outline, use whatever helps you but remember that note taking can be a distraction. Work at listening. It is hard work that requires concentration and effort. Fight distractions. Keep an open and exercised mind so that you can accept challenges. Too often any ideas that require effort are rejected. Finally, capitalize on thought speed. We have the ability to listen about four times as fast as we can talk; to hear about 500 words a minute, while we speak at about 125 words per minute. This leaves 375 words of thinking to spare during every minute of listening. A good listener uses this time to advantage by anticipating what is coming next, summarizing what has been said, weighing evidence as it is presented, and listening "between the lines" for the nonverbal clues and cues.

Banville offers some advice to improve listening following slightly different directions: in being empathetic, be aware of another's expectations of you as a listener. How you will act toward the speaker? Will you be hostile, friendly, remote, accepting, rejecting, open? What are you showing? Recognize how you see the speaker. Do you see this person as active or passive, sharing or withholding, accepting or rejecting? Your perception of the speaker and his or her perception of you as listener will most certainly affect the outcome of your communication transaction.

Banville suggests cues available to you that will give indication of feelings. Some of these are:

1. *Voice:* overbearing or loud; soft; used as an instrument of aggression; indicating great vitality; flat, unspirited and characterless; light or relaxed; rapid or measured and deliberate.

2. *Body Language:* posture; facial expressions; gestures.

3. *Idiosyncratic Expressions:* phrases or expressions; ending a sentence with "OK," "Did you get what I mean?" or "I want to make this crystal clear."

4. *Message Value:* defensive behavior; story telling, past episodes. How you interpret such cues will again affect the quality of the communication as will your

---

[19]George de Mare, *Communication for Leadership: A Guide for Executives.* New York: The Ronald Press, 1968, pp. 232–233.

response style. Banville elaborates on five of these: 1) advice giving, which may tend to be judgmental, making the speaker defensive; 2) interpretive, which may not reflect the speaker's reality but your feelings and often tends to eliminate openness and sharing; 3) cross examination responses, which may change direction and also shift from feelings to content; 4) reassurance responses, which may say "you're making too much of it," and minimize the speaker's feelings; and 5) paraphrasing, which allows you to let the speaker know whether you heard what you were supposed to hear and that you are sensitive to the message.[20]

William Rogers discusses twelve listening styles and identifies the "understanding" and the "focusing" listener to be most effective. These styles closely resemble the paraphrasing style mentioned above. The understanding listener shows a capacity to empathize with the central feelings being expressed while the focusing style aids in identifying the deeper reaches of experience and in "getting handles" on an experience.[21]

Note Taking: An Aid to Listening

Employ whatever device or technique that enables you to learn more through listening. Many people take notes, which may be more of a distraction than a learning aid. Whatever auxiliary devices you do use, remember that they are aids and not substitutes for attentive and empathetic listening. They should be an aid and not an end in themselves.

Reik sees positive value in note taking, as it can:

1. enhance attentiveness
2. simplify review
3. make learning easier
4. make forgetting more difficult.

He goes on to suggest that notes be clear, brief and to the point, classified, and legible.[22]

In note taking, there may also be a positive effect on the speaker. Your taking notes shows an interest in the subject and this may be a motivating factor. Speakers may summarize their points as a result.

There is also a danger. In a one-to-one or small group interview, the speaker may become distracted by the note taking, thus influencing the information flow. You will have to be the judge.

Nichols and Stevens offer two techniques for note taking:[23]

---

[20]Thomas G. Banville, *How to Listen-How to Be Heard*. Chicago: Nelson-Hall, 1978, pp. 160–166.
[21]William R. Rogers, "Twelve Styles of Listening," in *Project Listening, A Training Package*. Boston: Unitarian Universalist Association, 1974.
[22]Reik, pp. 127–128.
[23]Nichols and Stevens, pp. 117–123.

Précis Writing.   Using this method, the note taker or listener writes only at widely spaced times. The listener sits back, listens for several minutes and then writes a brief paragraph or a one-sentence abstract summarizing the main point of what has been heard. Practice in précis writing will also help develop a keener awareness, an acuteness for organizing the main points in a presentation.

Fact versus Principle.   This method is particularly effective when listening to a disorganized speech or message. If one took "straight" notes, the end results would be as disorganized as the presentation was.

Using this method, you would head up a two column page with *Fact* over one column, and *Principle* over the other. As you listened, you would jot down what seem to be facts under the appropriate column and principles under the other. Principles may be thought of as the "essence" of things: laws, doctrines, rules, and themes. They are concepts or core ideas. Principles control or give system to many facts. A principle helps explain facts. On the other hand, a fact is evidence or support for a principle. Descriptions of acts, statistics, and explicit examples would all fall into this category.

As in the case of any note taking, review your facts and principles as soon as possible after the speaking experience. Look for explanations and relationships. Organize your information to create meaning. Often the principles may be reclassified into fewer categories. A disorganized speech is difficult to follow in the first place; the fact and principle approach may aid you in giving it some logical structure and meaning.

Having now scratched the surface of how one may improve his or her ability to actively listen, we see what a difficult task it is. The complexity is enormous and must be approached with a great deal of patience and openness. Listening is hard work calling for the concentration of all of our senses if we are to "hear" the totality of a message.

Summary

Research since the 1950s indicates that while most of us are poor listeners, training could improve this ability. Some of the rewards of being a better listener include our expanded knowledge through gaining more information, saving time and effort in work leading to financial and promotional gain.

Listening is more than hearing. It is the process by which the spoken language is given meaning in the mind. Listening has been called action research as it involves action in the form of seeking information from others and encouraging such activity. Listening is active rather than passive. It involves more than listening for sound but utilizing all senses to receive meaning as well.

The manager must develop into a better listener in order to receive information and to perceive problems and correct them before they erupt into major issues. As a manager spends some 40 to 80 percent of his or her time listening, any increase in efficiency will be highly beneficial to the organization.

To be a more effective listener, a manager must exhibit a willingness to listen, the time, the place, and the attention to encourage subordinates to speak out. There are many barriers to free and open dialogue. Some of the barriers to active listening are conceptual, organizational, procedural, and attitudinal.

Managers have difficulty listening to others as there is role ego connected with speaking. Often a manager is overcome with his or her problems and this serves as a barrier. Levels of language and the emotional quality of words often serve to prevent conversation.

"Third ear listening" is a technique for more active and penetrating listening activity. This technique is creative and attempts to aid in a deeper understanding of the message, deeper than just the meaning of the words. Many suggestions are offered as to how one may become a better listener. For the most part, these techniques urge attention and focusing to allow the speaker latitude and encouragement. The listener is urged to listen beyond the words to the feelings and needs of the speaker. Nonverbal cues must also be seen and heard in the context of the message.

Discussion Questions

1. Why aren't Americans good listeners?
2. What are the differences between hearing and listening?
3. How does listening resemble reading? How are they different?
4. Explain why William Foote Whyte called listening "action research."
5. Has the need to be a good listener increased or decreased since the 1950s?
6. How are we rewarded by being better and more active listeners?
7. Discuss the importance of "willingness" to being a good listener.
8. In what ways can a business organization provide a better framework for "active listening"?
9. Carl Rogers claims that understanding is the key to better listening. Explain that point.
10. Discuss nonverbal communication as a variable of listening.

Problem

1. You are the manager of the Sporting Goods Department of a local department store. The manager of the store has requested a report on your department and it is due at 2:00 P.M. You are almost finished with it. It is now 1:30 P.M., when there is a knock on your door. In walks Pete Steel, who is a very good and dependable salesman. He says, "Mr. Mack, I have to talk to you about a very serious and immediate problem. Am I in trouble."

    a. What would you do?

    b. Discuss your alternatives.

Project

1. Carl Rogers proposed an experiment which you can try to test the quality of your understanding. He claims the major barrier to mutual interpersonal communication is to judge or evaluate, to approve or disapprove the statement of others. To perform this experiment set up a discussion over a controversial subject. The following rule must apply:

Each person can speak up for themselves only after they have first restated the ideas and feelings of the previous speaker accurately and to that speaker's satisfaction.

See how well all the participants listen in order that they may speak.

Additional Reading

Banville, Thomas G., *How to Listen—How to Be Heard.* Chicago: Nelson-Hall, 1978.

Barker, Larry, *Listening Behavior.* Englewood Cliffs, N.J.: Prentice-Hall, 1971.

Merrihue, Willard V., *Managing by Communication.* New York: McGraw-Hill, 1960.

Reik, Theodor, *Listening with the Third Ear.* New York: Farrar, Straus & Giroux, 1964.

Weaver, Carl H., *Human Listening.* Indianapolis: Bobbs-Merrill, 1972.

Some Periodicals to Read:

    Journal of Business Communication

    Journal of Communication

    Journal of Reading

The process
of
persuasion

7

key points to learn

The relationships among attitudes, beliefs, and motivation factors.

The distinctions among facts, inferences, and judgments.

The role of terminal and instrumental values in determining individual motivation.

The impact of goals and needs in determining an individual's susceptibility to persuasion.

Several methods of demonstrating relationships between an individual's motivation factors and the communicator's persuasive objective.

Howell's "blockbuster formulas" for successful persuasion.

Seven perspectives on ethics in persuasion.

Every day of our lives we are faced with the task of selling our ideas, ourselves, or our products to other human beings. While we are trying to cause others to "see things our way," we are being bombarded with hundreds of stimuli designed to effect changes in *our* attitudes and behaviors. In attempting to persuade others you have no doubt experienced failures at times when you were certain of success and success at times when you anticipated failure. How can we account for our successes and failures in persuasive efforts? On the receiving end of persuasive attempts you are probably able to recall times when you were eager to follow the advice of some persuader and other times when you were totally unmoved by persuasive messages. Why do some messages evoke a willingness to respond while others "leave us cold?" In this chapter we will discuss the bases of attitudes and suggest the most effective means of achieving attitude change. Our discussion should prove helpful both in your attempts to persuade others and in your ability to understand why you respond as you do to persuasive stimuli.

=============== **the bases of our attitudes**

In this section you will become familiar with attitudes, beliefs, opinions, attitude objects, and motivation. You will discover how motivation influences the beliefs determining our attitudes toward people, places, concepts, and things.

_____ Attitudes and Attitude Objects

For our purposes here we shall use a paraphrase of Martin Fishbein's definition of attitude.[1] *An attitude is a predisposition to react favorably, unfavorably, or neutrally toward an object or a group of objects.* The use of the terms object and objects at first may be misleading. Most of us are accustomed to thinking of objects as *things* that can be seen and touched. However, our use of the term is much broader. We are using it in an inclusive sense to indicate people, places, things, concepts, etc. Our attitudes may be directed toward the president of a company, a new policy on sick leave, open marriage, the two-party political system, unemployment, inflation, Chicago, etc. In each of these examples we are dealing with *attitude objects,* i.e., *any object toward which attitudes are directed.*

The major term in our definition of attitude is *predisposition.* Once we have formed an attitude toward an object, we react to that object automatically in a favorable, unfavorable, or neutral manner. We are conditioned or predisposed to respond. There is no need to stop and think about how we should respond—to ask "do I like this object, or do I dislike this object?"

_____ Beliefs

We develop our predispositions to respond as a result of our beliefs in and beliefs about the attitude object. Again, paraphrasing Martin Fishbein's definition, we consider beliefs as *hypotheses that an object exists and that relationships exist between the object under consideration and other objects.*[2] In other words, there are two kinds of beliefs: beliefs *in* objects and beliefs *about* objects. The following are examples of beliefs *in* objects:

We are in a recession.
We are experiencing a shortage of crude oil.
Chicago is in Illinois.
This book is concerned with communication.

In addition to our existing beliefs *in* objects, we develop many beliefs *about* objects. The following are examples of beliefs *about* objects:

---

[1]Martin Fishbein, "An Investigation of the Relationships Between Beliefs About an Object and the Attitude Toward That Object," *Human Relations,* 4 (Aug. 1963), p. 233.
[2]Ibid.

This recession will not last long.

Our crude oil shortage is caused by a worldwide conspiracy on the part of the major oil companies.

Chicago is a windy city.

This book is not as difficult to read as I thought it would be.

Beliefs differ in their degree of influence in determining a particular attitude. Assume that an attitude is formed on the basis of fourteen separate beliefs. We cannot predict a positive attitude simply on the determination that ten of the fourteen beliefs are positive. The strength of the remaining four beliefs may indeed be such that the overall attitude toward the object will be negative. For example, workers may perceive a supervisor as extremely competent, hardworking, intelligent, energetic, friendly, etc., and yet dislike that supervisor intensely on the basis of one belief—that the supervisor takes credit for workers' accomplishments.

People may share the same attitude toward an object and yet have very different beliefs about that object. If this were not the case, no politician would ever get elected. On the national level several million voters may support a Presidential candidate with relatively equal intensity, and yet they may have widely divergent beliefs about the candidate. Some support may result from "the lesser of two evils" philosophy. Other people may infer a relationship between the candidate and support for education, a tax cut, reduction of inflation, increased social security benefits, amnesty for draft evaders, or clean air and water. We should never *assume* common beliefs on the basis of common attitudes.

Why do we hold certain beliefs about a particular object? Our beliefs result from a complex mixture of observations, experiences, second-hand evidence, and *motivation*. We now believe that the world is round rather than flat. That belief is partially the result of second-hand evidence (textbooks, parental and teacher testimony over a period of many years), partially of our own observations (flying around the world, viewing televised pictures of the earth as transmitted from the moon, etc.), and at least partially of social pressure to believe what *everyone* believes. We tend to think of our own observations and experiences of trusted sources as *facts*, and we like to think that most of our beliefs are based on factual data. However, many of the perceptions that we regard as facts are really *inferences* or *judgments*. For example, you walk into an executive's office and notice a set of golf clubs in the corner. The *fact* that the clubs are in the office may lead you to *infer* that the executive is an avid golfer and even to make *judgments* about the dedication and professionalism of a person who "takes off in the middle of the afternoon to play golf!" Indeed, you may leave the office with a negative attitude toward the executive, thinking that your attitude is based on *facts*, when, in reality, the attitude has resulted from your *inferences* and *judgments*. In this example we are using the term inference in sense of "an educated or uneducated guess," and the term judgment as "an evaluation or conclusion based on facts *or* inferences." A few moments of introspection will make us aware of instances where we have adopted beliefs on the basis of inferences and judgments when we *thought* we were basing those beliefs on factual data. Why do we readily adopt beliefs on the basis of inferential and judgmental data? William McGuire would attribute such inferential "leaps" to *wishful thinking*. Indeed, McGuire's thesis is sobering. He suggests that we believe what we believe to a large extent *because we want to believe it*—because we *wish* it were true. [3]

_____ Motivation

We wish certain beliefs to be true because we sense relationships between those beliefs and factors that motivate us. The term motivation is used here to include *goals* (short term and long term), *values* (social, political, moral, economic, and religious), and *needs* (physical and psychological).

Goals. Either as a result of our own choosing or as a result of societal or peer pressures we all have a number of *goals* that we are seeking to attain. Such aims or objectives may be short-term (finishing this chapter, completing work on a contract, finding summer employment) or long-term (becoming a senior executive in a prestigious company, obtaining a comfortable retirement income, buying a cabin in the mountains). We are more willing to believe whatever will help us make progress in the attainment of our goals and less willing to believe whatever will hinder goal attainment.

Values. When a belief becomes an abstract ideal about "how one ought or ought not to behave, or about some end-state of existence worth or not worth attaining," that belief ceases to be attached to any one specific attitude and thus becomes a part of the individual's *value* system. [4] Broadly speaking, our values may be social, political, moral, economic, religious, etc. More specifically, Milton Rokeach and Seymour Parker have identified two types of values —*terminal* and *instrumental*. [5] Terminal values are defined as "end-states of existence," while instrumental values are "preferred modes of behavior." Rokeach and Parker list a comfortable life, a world at peace, family security, social recognition, self-respect, and wisdom as examples of *terminal values*. A listing of instrumental values would include such "preferred modes of be-

_____

[3]William J. McGuire, "A Syllogistic Analysis of Cognitive Relationships," *Attitude Organization and Change*, M.J. Rosenberg and others, (eds.). New Haven: Yale University Press, 1960.

[4]Edward D. Steel and W. Charles Redding, "The American Value System: Premises for Persuasion," *Western Speech*, **26** (Spring, 1962), pp. 83–91.

[5]Milton Rokeach and Seymour Parker, "Values as Social Indicators of Poverty and Race in America," *Annals of the American Academy of Political and Social Sciences*, **388** (Mar. 1970), pp. 101–102.

havior" as broad-minded, clean, courageous, helpful, honest, polite, and self-controlled.

Needs. Abraham Maslow's often-mentioned "Pyramid of Needs" is an attempt to identify and order the basic need levels of human beings:[6]

Maslow's need pyramid is designed to illustrate the relative importance of the five levels of needs. Beginning with the foundation of the pyramid, we encounter the basic needs for physiological well-being. The needs for food, water, air, sleep, sex, and so on compromise our basic needs. Until these needs are minimally satisfied, an individual cannot be very concerned about higher-order needs.

Safety needs include our desires for a smoothly functioning, orderly world in which we are settled and at ease rather than unsettled and threatened. The desire for a job with a promising future, a good retirement plan, a home in a low-crime neighborhood, and financial security are all examples of safety needs.

Once an individual's physiological and safety needs are met, the need to belong—to be a part of something—becomes significant. While some people are able to satisfy the need to belong within their family and job reference groups, others appear to be habitual "joiners," sensing a need to be a part of just about every group that appears important. Indeed, some people are unable to carry all of their membership cards on their person.

After the need to belong has been met at least partially, Maslow predicts that we will begin sensing a higher-order need—the need to feel that members of our reference group *love* us or consider us a valuable member of the team. Workers need to feel that their work is important and that they are appreciated for their contributions. Members of families need reinforcement as to their importance within the family unit. In business organizations this higher-order need is often met through promotions, recognition or testimonial dinners, and other forms of public compliments.

At the top of Maslow's need pyramid is self-actualization. When all the other needs have been satisfied, Maslow predicts a drive toward personal self-fulfillment. Most of us have known wealthy individuals who at least temporarily abandoned their business interests to run for public office. Many such people are seeking self-actualization. They are seeking to become everything that they *could* become. Nelson Rockefeller's compelling desire to hold high political office may have been one example of this.

The Interrelationships of Goals, Values, and Needs.   At this point it should be clear to you that no distinct lines can be drawn between goals, values, and needs. What one individual calls a need may be viewed as a value by another. We have discussed goals, values, and needs separately because you will frequently hear them mentioned as though they were distinct, unrelated

---

[6]A. H. Maslow, *Motivation and Personality.* New York: Harper & Row, Pub., 1954.

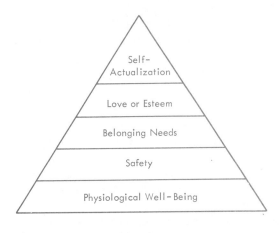

Figure 7–1   Maslow's hierarchy of needs.

Figure 7–2   In addition to a sense of belonging to a company or organization, most employees need reassurance that their contributions are important—that they are held in high esteem by their supervisors. (Photo by John V. Dunigan, courtesy of Design Photographers International, Inc.)

phenomena. Regardless of what we call them, however, the phenomena discussed in this section comprise the bases of our motivation.

_____ Opinions

An opinion is a verbalized attitude. Obviously, we have no means of entering a person's mind and determining the precise nature and intensity of an attitude. Therefore, we must rely on what an individual says or writes as the attitude index. Such statements as "I don't like Paris," "I wouldn't take that job for love or money," "What a lousy meeting," and "I'm going to vote for the policy change" are all opinion statements.

The Attitude-Belief Structure

Though admittedly oversimplified, the model in Figure 7–3 may be useful in demonstrating the relationships between opinions, attitudes, beliefs, attitude objects, and motivational factors. According to our model, an individual's attitude is directed toward the attitude object (people, places, things, and concepts). That attitude may be favorable (+), unfavorable (−), or neutral (0). Our attitudes are based on our beliefs pertaining to both the existence and nature of the attitude object and the attitude object's relationships with other attitude objects. We develop our beliefs from two sources: (1) our experiences and observations pertinent to the attitude object, and (2) our perceptions that the attitude object is related in a positive or negative way to our goals, values, and needs (motivational factors).

Although most of our attitude change results from changes in our beliefs (arrows from beliefs to attitude), we must leave room for the possibility that sudden changes in attitude may effect changes in our beliefs (arrows from attitudes to beliefs). Beliefs are formed on the basis of experiences, observations, facts, inferences, judgments, and motivational factors (arrows from motivational factors to beliefs and from experience observation elements to beliefs). The attitude object is perceived as being related to motivational factors positively or negatively (dotted line from attitude object to motivational factors). Finally, motivational factors exert a direct influence on our attitudes (dotted line from motivational factors to attitude), and in some cases sudden

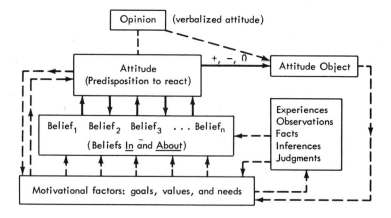

Figure 7–3   Relationships between opinions, attitudes, beliefs, attitude objects, and motivational factors.

changes in attitude may require a reordering of our motivational factors (dotted line from attitude to motivational factors).

If you carefully examine Figure 7–3, you will notice that it forms a pyramid with the verbalized attitude (opinion) at the top and motivational factors at the bottom. We have drawn the model in this way to illustrate the importance of motivational factors in the formation of our attitudes. Such factors are indeed the *foundation* of the attitude-belief structure. Would-be persuaders can come into communication situations armed with more evidence supporting their positions than they could possibly deliver, but they still would be unsuccessful if they fail to relate their messages (the attitude object) to the motivational factors in their listeners.

In most cases you will be more successful if you approach the persuasion task from a belief-attack perspective. In other words, try to effect belief changes by relating your arguments to the factors motivating your listener. You may not change enough beliefs to accomplish radical conversion of attitude during one persuasive attempt. As a matter of fact, *several* efforts at persuasion may be required before enough beliefs are modified to cause detectable attitude change. Direct attacks on a listener's attitude or a listener's goals, values, and need perceptions may at times succeed, but, for the most part are doomed to failure. Most of us can recall the resentment which we felt when someone sternly requested, "You better change your attitude." We also may remember our bitterness resulting from some person's ridiculing retort: "You mean you believe in such Puritanical standards?"

connecting messages with motivation

A number of years ago the Russian scientist Pavlov conducted an experiment that illustrates what we feel is the essence of effective persuasion. Pavlov noticed that blowing food powder into a dog's mouth resulted in salivation. Repeatedly, he blew food powder into the dog's mouth while simultaneously ringing a bell. After many repetitions of this practice, he rang the bell without blowing food powder into the dog's mouth. The dog salivated. Somewhere in the inner reaches of that dog's brain a connection had been established between food powder and the bell. Insofar as the dog was concerned, the two stimuli were equally rewarding. Pavlov had taken a neutral stimulus (the bell) and repeatedly related it to a positive stimulus (food powder). After several repetitions the neutral stimulus (the bell) was received by the dog as a positive stimulus. This is the essence of persuasion. You must connect your message with motivating factors in the minds of your receivers. If you desire a negative attitude toward an object stimulus, relate that object to unfulfilled needs, unrealized goals, and breakdowns in value systems. If you desire a positive attitude toward an object stimulus, relate that object to need satisfactions, goal realizations, and expressions of basic values.

Effective persuasion can be explained by use of a relatively simple model:[7]

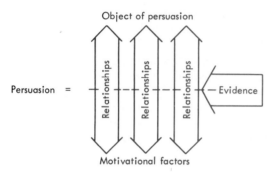

Figure 7–4   A model of persuasion.

In this model the object of persuasion may be a belief, a person, an action, etc. Your objective may be to receive a salary increase or promotion, to convince your listener of a new production plan, or to secure votes in an upcoming election. Regardless of what the objective is, you must establish in the mind of your listener *relationships* between the objective and your listener's motivational factors (goals, needs, and values). Simply asserting a relationship is not enough. The assertion must be supported with evidence. Evidence may be in the form of expert testimony, factual illustrations, statistics, etc.

Making the Connection

Gary Cronkhite has identified five kinds of arguments that tend to establish relationships between motivation factors and objects of persuasion.[8] Those relationships include *contingency* (cause-effect arguments), *categorization* (parts-of-the-whole arguments), *similarity* (arguments by analogy), *approval* (arguments based on testimony), and *coincidental* (perceived relationship derived from common context).

Contingency Relationship.   Whenever you suggest that your idea will, if adopted, result in increased profits for the company, you are using the contingency relationship. Persuasion accomplished by means of contingency relationships is based on the premise that the right response toward the object of persuasion will result in satisfaction of needs, attainment of goals, or expression

---

[7]Our model is an adapted version of Gary Cronkhite's "paradigm of persuasion." See *Persuasion Speech and Behavioral Change.* Indianapolis: Bobbs-Merrill, 1969, p. 75. Used by permission.
[8]Ibid., pp. 80–84.

of values. If politicians did not use the contingency relationship to cement themselves to our motivation factors, neither dogcatchers nor presidents could ever get elected. Next time you find yourself in the midst of a local, state, or national election, just try to count the promises of better highways, lower taxes, world peace, breaking the back of inflation, increased social security benefits, and economic reform associated with the various candidates.

Commercial advertising has long recognized the value of cause-effect relationships. We have been assured that drinking decaffeinated coffee will make us less nervous and irritable, and that driving a particular car will result in many dollars saved at the gas pumps. The use of a certain underarm deodorant is sure to keep your friends by your side, while proper denture cream will allow you to stop babying yourself by eating soup when your business associates are eating steak and corn-on-the-cob.

The cause-effect association may be negative as well as positive. "Caution: The Surgeon General Has Determined That Cigarette Smoking May Be Hazardous to Your Health." "Don't be caught dead sitting on your seat belts." The American Medical Association warned that national health insurance plans, such as the one advocated by Senator Edward Kennedy in 1979, would result in long lines at hospitals and clinics and a reduction in the quality of medical care. Anytime that you use evidence to establish a causal link between your persuasive objective and your listener's motivational factors, you are using the contingency relationship.

Categorization.   Let's suppose that you have come up with a new idea, and that your supervisor is hesitant to accept it. In addition to discussing the positive results which the company will realize by adopting your idea, you might also wish to argue that the idea is consistent with stated company policies and past practice. Anytime that you preface an argument with "How can we say that we believe . . ." and continue with "if we don't . . ." you are employing a categorization relationship between your persuasive objective and motivational factors. Any continuing organization has maintenance goals and productivity goals. Arguments of a cause-effect nature seem well-suited for associating your cause with productive goals (increased sales, better working conditions, increased production). Categorization arguments are especially useful when associating your cause with maintenance goals (public image, self-concept, etc.).

"How can we say that we are concerned about the environment, if we continue to ignore pollution standards?" "If you're a red-blooded American, you will follow the President's voluntary energy conservation suggestions." "How can we claim to believe in equal rights with our long history of suppression of women?"

.   If you are thinking that there is a degree of similarity between cause-effect reasoning and categorization, you are not mistaken. At times, the two argument types are difficult to distinguish. To assist you in determining which argument you should use, we offer the following guidelines:

1. When you wish to demonstrate that the proper response toward your persuasive objective will *result in* the attainment of some motivational factor, use the contingency relationship.

2. When you wish to demonstrate that the proper response toward your persuasive object is consistent or inconsistent with motivational factors, a part of or not a part of an individual's goals, values, or needs, employ the categorization relationship.

Similarity.   Whenever you are able to associate your persuasive object with another object that you know your listener views favorably or unfavorably, you may want to use the similarity relationship. In such cases the motivation factor is not a goal, value, or need. Rather, it is another attitude object. This kind of reasoning has frequently been referred to as *reasoning by analogy.* If you wish to convince your company to avoid a particular action, develop a step-by-step comparison of your company and a company that went bankrupt after adopting a similar policy. Granted, you may argue that such reasoning is cause-effect, and that the other company is merely evidence in the causal argument. However, let us stress that we are dealing with an example (a company) that must have vivid emotional effects on your listener—vivid enough that the example is inherently capable of accomplishing what strong needs, motives, and values normally accomplish in our linking process.

The warm welcome given to our fifty-two former American hostages was a sharp contrast to the reception afforded veterans returning from the Vietnam war. Some would-be persuaders utilized the similarity approach by asserting that prisoners of war and other Vietnam veterans had experienced similar situations to those experienced by the hostages in Iran; consequently, they should receive more recognition and assistance from the American people.

Approval Relationships.   The approval relationship involves the association of your persuasive object with a prestigious source. You argue that the prestigious source (whether it be another company, a person, or a group of people) approves or disapproves of your persuasive object. Politicians frequently rely on approval relationships during their election campaigns. Whether it be the mayor of Chicago, a popular movie or television personality, a nationally known professional football player, the AFL-CIO, National Organization of Women, or the NAACP that is endorsing a particular candidate, the identification of a relatively unknown politician with a well-known individual or organization can become a powerful persuasive appeal to a large portion of the electorate. In commercial advertising during the 1970s we were assured that the strong and tough Pittsburg Steeler football players had met their match with the strong and tough steel-belted radial tires. We were told that the young tennis star, Tracy Austin, would not think of going onto the court without a particular brand of tennis racket. As in the case of the similarity relationship, the motivational factor does not involve needs, values, and goals. Rather, the motivational factor *is* the approving agent (person, company, or group of people).

An interesting phenomenon occurs when an individual or group that we dislike is linked to concepts or people that are mildly favored. Research has indicated that mildly favorable concepts or people are negatively evaluated when evaluators are told that extremely disliked people approve of those concepts or individuals. This would explain why political candidates would not have desired an endorsement from Richard Nixon following his less-than-honorable departure from the Presidency in the early 1970s. We also have a tendency to be favorable toward individuals that we mildly dislike when an individual or group that we strongly dislike speaks negatively of those individuals. This would partially explain former President Jimmy Carter's dramatic rise in the public opinion polls shortly after he was denounced by Iran's Khomeni in the fall of 1979. One year later, when it appeared that Khomeni was *co-operating* with the White House to secure the release of the hostages on the eve of the November election, the President's credibility fell sharply.

Coincidental Relationship.   We include a discussion of one final relationship, not because we recommend its use, but rather because you, as a consumer of persuasive messages, should be aware of it. The coincidental relationship cannot be established by evidence and reasoning. Instead, this relationship is

Figure 7–5 Cause-effect arguments frequently are used to demonstrate relationships between audience motivation and a speaker's persuasive objective. In the picture above, the speaker is arguing that an end to the war will result in the return of prisoners held by North Vietnam. (Courtesy of Wide World Photos.)

implied by presentations of the persuasive object and motivational appeals in the same context. A series of Geritol commercials relied heavily on the coincidental relationship during the late 1970s. These commercials portrayed extremely healthy and attractive wives who asserted that they loved their husbands, that their husbands loved them, and that they took care of their bodies. Finally, the viewer was told that the women regularly took Geritol. There was a clearly *implied* relationship between health and happiness and the consumption of Geritol, but that relationship was *not* directly stated. Certainly, the manufacturers cannot assert a causal relationship. The F.T.C. would not allow such false advertising. However, the implied or coincidental relationship is permitted.

specific persuasive tactics

Having discussed the bases of attitudes and our recommended key to persuasion—the linking of the object of persuasion with motivational factors—we shall conclude this chapter with a brief treatment of several specific tactics that have proven successful for a large number of business executives. William S. Howell has listed ten "blockbuster formulas" for successful persuasion:

1. *The Yes-Response Technique.* Ask eight to ten questions in a carefully planned series. Make sure that each question will be one that demands a "yes" answer. At the end of the series ask for commitment to your object of persuasion. This little tactic has proven successful in selling everything from $100 vacuum cleaners to $100,000 homes.

2. *Putting It Up to You.* In order to ascertain that you are getting through to your listener, ask frequent questions such as "Is this clear?" "Am I making sense?" "Do you agree?" "Does this seem fair?" You will receive valuable feedback from the answers to such questions. In addition you will establish rapport with your listener by emphasizing your concern for clear understanding.

3. *Simulated Disinterest.* Resistance to persuasion frequently increases when the persuadee notices the speaker's anxiety over the outcome. Sometimes it is best to pretend to be disinterested in the outcome. It is difficult to explain, but some of us are unwilling to buy from salespeople who act as if they could not live without the commission from our purchase.

4. *Transfer.* The effect that the physical surroundings have on the outcome of our persuasive efforts is known as transfer. A positive attitude toward the surroundings will likely help create positive attitudes toward your object of persuasion. Don't forget: Negative surroundings transfer too!

5. *Bandwagon Technique.* Demonstrate that "everyone is adopting the idea" or buying the product. Our need to belong and to "keep up with the Joneses" is frequently too overbearing to resist the bandwagon appeals of persuaders.

6. *Say It with Flowers.* When you can honestly compliment your persuadee for some accomplishment, do so. Flattery can easily be overdone, but all of us appreciate recognition of our accomplishments.

7. *Don't Ask If, Ask Which.* Whenever possible, offer your listener the choice of *something* and *something else* rather than *something* or *nothing.* Walgreen drug stores managed to sell hundreds of thousands of eggs in their malted milks when their people started asking, "Do you want one egg or two in your malted milk?" rather than "Do you want egg in your malted milk?"

8. *The Swap Technique.* The swap technique involves the exchange of "favors." The Fuller Brush man is willing to *give* you a sample brush in exchange for your allowing a sales pitch. Beginning a sales interview with a sharing of a new idea that may be of value to the client is also an example of the swap technique. After receiving the new idea, the client feels obligated to buy something from you.

9. *Reassurance.* After you have persuaded people to buy a product or to work for you, send them a note which will give them reassurance that they have made the right decision. This technique has been particularly useful in effecting repeat sales.

10. *Technique of Irritation.* Although the technique can easily backfire, when carefully controlled it is often used to induce people to buy products and make decisions. The trick is to be clever enough that your prospects fail to recognize your *intent* to annoy them. If you can accomplish that bit of ingenuity, you may be successful in your desired response, if for no other reason than to "get you out of the hair" of your clients.[9]

ethics in persuasion

We dare not conclude this chapter on persuasion without at least raising the question of how one determines whether or not a particular persuasive appeal is ethical or unethical. The classical philosopher, Plato, distrusted oral argument primarily due to unethical behaviors of the practitioners of his day. His student, Aristotle, began his landmark work on rhetoric with an elaborate treatment of ethos, or the credibility of the speaker. Down through the centuries advocates have drawn rather fuzzy lines of demarcation to separate ethical from unethical argumentative strategies. Indeed, nations as well as individuals have frequently fallen into the trap of assuming that their arguments are "truth," while the other individual or nation's arguments are "propaganda." What does distinguish a "false advertisement" from a "slight exaggeration?" What separates "dirty tricks" from "aggressive campaign practices?" Since the most gifted philosophers, theologians, and politicians have failed to provide us with a definitive answer during the several thousand years that they have struggled with the issue, we cannot hope to offer you a magic formula for measuring the ethics of a particular persuasive effort. However, we do want you to be aware of the several different perspectives from which the ethics of persuasion can be measured. You will need to develop your own standard of ethics, borrowing from one or more of these perspectives.

[9]Ernest G. Bormann, William S. Howell, Ralph G. Nichols, and George L. Shapiro, *Interpersonal Communication in the Modern Organization.* Englewood Cliffs, N.J.: Prentice-Hall, 1969, pp. 233–241.

Richard Johannesen has identified seven different perspectives from which to measure the ethics of persuasion.[10] These perspectives include religious, philosophical, political, utilitarian, situational, legal, and dialogic vantage points.

The *religious* perspective is based upon what is prescribed by the literature of a particular religion. For example, the Moslem might base behavior on the Koran, while the Christian or Jew would refer to the specific teachings of the Bible. Such sacred literature would be used as the basis of avoiding lies, stealing, slandering, and so on.

The *philosophical* perspective is based upon the premise that there are "unique characteristics of man's nature that should be nurtured."[11] A specific persuasive technique is ethical if the unique characteristics of man's nature—that is, the capacity to reason or the capacity to make choices—are enhanced. A persuasive technique is judged unethical if man's unique nature is undermined.

The *political* perspective measures the ethics of persuasion on the basis of whether it enhances or undermines the basic value system of the political system. In the United States where there is a representative democracy and people are allowed to have a hand in the decision-making process, a particular persuasive technique would be judged unethical if it undermined the *rational* decision-making process.

The *utilitarian* perspective measures the means of persuasion in terms of the ends accomplished. The persuader is expected to advocate the "greatest good for the greatest number for the greatest length of time." The argument that the suppression of certain individual rights is in the interest of "national security" is an example of measuring persuasion or behavior from a utilitarian perspective.

The *situational* perspective avoids universal standards in favor of a specific situation or context. Consequently, a particular argument might be judged ethical for adults, but unethical when directed toward children. A method of reporting financial status might be acceptable for a business, but unacceptable for a political candidate.

The *legal* perspective is based upon the assumption that, if there isn't a law against it, it's ethical. Most commercial advertisements now carefully avoid the specific prohibitions of the Federal Trade Commission, and by doing so, would argue that their advertisements are ethical persuasive attempts. The discussion of the coincidental relationship in the previous section of this chapter illustrates how a technically "legal" commercial might be evaluated as misleading and unethical by some individuals who apply a more universal standard.

The final perspective is the *dialogic* viewpoint. This perspective views

---

[10]Richard L. Johannesen, "Perspectives on Ethics in Persuasion," in Charles U. Larson, (ed.), *Persuasion: Reception and Responsibility.* Belmont, Calif.: Wadsworth, 1973, pp. 214–219.
[11]Ibid., p. 215.

monologue (self-interest) persuasion as unethical and dialogue (two or more party interest) persuasion as ethical. It is based upon the age-old distinction between a self-orientation and an others-orientation. It asks the question of whether a particular politician is simply trying to get elected or does that politician really feel that he/she can help the country?

Regardless of which of the above viewpoints you embrace, it will be to your advantage to carefully consider the matter of ethics in each of your persuasive attempts. Certainly, you must be prepared for the allegation that certain of your arguments are unethical, and you must be able to explain from your own perspective your actions.

Summary

In this chapter we have discussed the relationships between opinions, attitudes, beliefs, attitude objects, and motivation factors. Attitudes are predispositions to react favorably, unfavorably, or neutrally toward an object or a group of objects. An opinion is a verbalized attitude. Attitude objects may be people, places, things, or concepts. Attitudes are based on beliefs. Beliefs are hypotheses regarding the nature and existence of an object and the object's relationships with other objects. Consequently, we have beliefs in objects and beliefs about objects. Our beliefs are developed from observations and experiences (facts, inferences, and judgments) in such a way that they are consistent with our motivational factors (goals, needs, and values).

Successful persuasion results from establishing relationships between the object of your persuasion and motivational factors. Five means of connecting the object of persuasion with motivational factors are: contingency relationships (cause-effect arguments), categorization relationships (parts-of-the-whole arguments), similarity (arguments by analogy), approval relationships (arguments based on testimony), and coincidental relationships (perceived relationship derived from a common context).

Ten specific persuasive techniques were discussed. They included the yes-response technique, "putting it up to you," simulated disinterest, transfer, the bandwagon technique, "say it with flowers," "don't ask if, ask which," the swap technique, reassurance, and the technique of irritation.

Religious, philosophical, political, utilitarian, situational, legal, and dialogic perspectives were offered as potential means of measuring the ethics of a particular persuasive appeal. One's own ethical position must be developed on the basis of one or more of the perspectives offered in this chapter.

Discussion Questions

1. In what ways do the definitions included in this chapter of opinion, attitude, belief, and motivation differ from your prior concepts of these phenomena? Do you know other people who use the terms in still different ways? How?

2. List ten to fifteen goals which you have adopted. Which are long-term? Which are short-term?
3. We have suggested that changes in beliefs usually cause attitude changes. Try to think of situations in which radical changes in attitude necessitated changes in beliefs.
4. In our model of a belief-attitude structure in Figure 7–3, you will notice dotted lines from the "observation experience" box to "motivational factors" and from "motivational factors" to the "observation experience" box. Explain the purpose of these lines.
5. Which of the five relationships (contingency, categorization, similarity, approval, coincidental) do you use most frequently in your attempts to persuade others? Which do you think is used most frequently on you?
6. Write two paragraphs concerning the ethics of the "specific tactics" of persuasion contained in the last section of this chapter. In one paragraph defend the tactics as ethical. In the next paragraph attack the tactics as unethical.
7. Which of the seven ethical perspectives do you feel is most applicable in today's business world? Why?

===== Study Probes

1. Ask a friend to join you in a brief study of television and radio commercials. Find a time when the two of you can watch the same commercials on television and listen to the same commercials on the radio. At the conclusion of each commercial, write down the type of motivational factor that the commercial played on. Compare notes to see if your friend perceived the commercial the same way that you did. Make a list of the motivational factors which the two of you discovered. Be prepared to discuss them with others who completed a similar task.
2. Carry a pocket notebook for one day. Every time that you hear someone attempting to influence another person's beliefs or attitudes, jot down the kind of motive appeal that was employed. Also, try to determine the kinds of relationships used to connect the persuasive message with the motivational factors.
3. Attend a political speech, a religious meeting, and a session of a courtroom trial. What kinds of persuasive appeals were common in all three settings? Which ones were predominant in each setting? Were there differences in the quality and quantity of evidence used to establish relationships?

===== Additional Reading

Beisecker, Thomas D. and Don W. Parson (eds.), *The Process of Social Influence: Readings in Persuasion.* Englewood Cliffs, N.J.: Prentice-Hall, 1972.

Bettinghaus, Erwin P., *Persuasive Communication*, 2nd ed. New York: Holt, Rinehart and Winston, 1973.

Cronkhite, Gary, *Persuasion: Speech and Behavioral Change.* Indianapolis: Bobbs-Merrill, 1969.

Kiesler, Charles A., Barry E. Collins, and Norman Miller, *Attitude Change*. New York: John Wiley, 1969.

Larson, Charles U., *Persuasion: Reception and Responsibility*. Belmont, Calif.: Wadsworth, 1973.

Miller, Gerald R., and Michael Burgoon, *New Techniques of Persuasion*. New York: Harper & Row, Pub., 1973.

Schein, Edgar, Inge Schneider, and Curtis Baker, *Coercive Persuasion*. New York: W.W. Norton, 1961.

Simons, Herbert W., *Persuasion: Understanding, Practice, and Analysis*. Reading, Mass.: Addison-Wesley, 1976.

Nonverbal communication

8

key points to learn

The relationship between culture and communication.

How nonverbal communication supports verbal communication.

Decoding body language.

Applications of nonverbal communication to international business.

Nonverbal communication and feedback.

Everything is communication—even silence.

Everything you do is a form of communication! (You'll see these words elsewhere in this book.) You are always telling somebody something whether you mean to or not. While sitting in class, you are sending messages to your teacher even though you may not be saying a word.

Nonverbal communication is an interesting and fascinating area that has received a great deal of attention in recent years. People have always been communicating nonverbally, but this form of communication has come into its own as an area of special concentration.

Nonverbal communication (as the term implies) is anything other than words themselves that communicates or affects (positively or negatively) the message "contained" in the words.

Metacommunication is a word used to describe the nonverbal process. *Meta* is from the Greek and means "beyond" or "in addition to"; hence, *metacommunication* is something "in addition to the communication." Thayer writes, "Anything which can be taken into account as relevant to our interpretation of what another is saying or doing beyond the manifest 'content' of what he is saying or doing—can be referred to as *metacommunication*."[1]

---

[1] Lee Thayer, *Communication and Communication Systems.* Homewood, Ill.: Richard D. Irwin, 1968, p. 118.

There are two types of nonverbal communication which we will discuss briefly before we look at the more common types. For lack of a better term, we will call these "special forms." You may not have thought of them as forms of nonverbal communication. They are paralanguage and silence.

You may have heard someone say, "It's not what he said, it's the *way* he said it." Inflection can have an effect on the impact of a message; and while inflection is applied to words, it is a nonverbal treatment which can completely change the meaning a person would be expected to attach to the words. Inflections or emphasis applied vocally to a message are known as *paralanguage.* Paralanguage many times sounds just the opposite from the words themselves. Someone may have greeted you with a "good morning," but the tone of the words revealed that it was anything but a good morning.

There are, of course, some messages which are transmitted entirely in a nonverbal manner through gestures and facial expressions. Pictures of Winston Churchill taken during World War II show him communicating encouragement to the people by raising two fingers in the familiar V-for-Victory sign. Probably each of us has had the experience of making a statement that was greeted either by a raised eyebrow (indicating surprise) or by a wrinkled brow (indicating confusion or doubt). And when the school bully took a step toward us with a raised, clenched fist, we got that message in a hurry, too.

Figure 8–1 (Courtesy of Wide World Photos.)

Silence is an important communication tool. Most of us find an extended period of silence rather oppressive and threatening, and we rush to fill the void with words—usually saying more than we mean to say. By using silence at strategic times, you can sometimes get your decoder to reveal certain feelings and attitudes that may be hindering effective communication. It is important that we find out how we are doing in our effort to communicate; we do this through feedback. Silence can be an effective technique to encourage feedback. By silence we mean nonverbal elements held to a minimum.

In this chapter we will discuss nonverbal communication under the major headings of culture, body language, space, touch, and dress and physical appearance, so that you will know what is involved but mainly so that you can make your nonverbal communication work *for* you and not against you. Become *aware* of nonverbal messages!

culture and communication

Webster defines culture as "the characteristic features of a particular stage or state of advancement in civilization." Or, another definition: Culture is the way a people think, act, live, and communicate. Since this is a book about communication, it seems helpful or desirable to get the word "communication" into the definition.

On the other hand, culture *is* communication; the two are very much bound together.[2] A culture develops as the result of interpersonal communication—the communication between people that we are concerned with in this book. At the same time, the form, the nature, the makeup of the culture results from the interaction of the people and the place and time in which they live. The "interaction of people" is just another way of saying "communication." Living together, working together, relating to one another is communication. We are always communicating—or attempting to communicate.

An awareness of the relationship between culture and communication as well as an understanding of the differences between cultures is helpful—and at times essential—in communicating successfully. We can see this on the rather simple and small scale which many of us have experienced right here in the United States. There are many "trademarks" of our culture which a large number of United States citizens probably share—mother, God, country, apple pie, and baseball, to name a few. These trademarks will be found to some degree in all parts of the country.

In addition to these common marks of our culture, various sections of the country have their own traditions and ways of doing things. Most United States residents from the North, East, and West, for example, think of the South as a place where the pace is slower and where living is relaxed and perhaps a little

---

[2]Edward T. Hall, *The Silent Language*. Greenwich, Conn.: Fawcett, 1959, p. 37.

more "elegant" than in the other parts of the United States. When people from other sections of the United States visit the South, they are immediately aware of a different style of speech as well as some words which may not be in their everyday vocabulary. And they also discover some different types of food on the restaurant menu. If they want to be friends with the local folk and enjoy their visit, the visitors adapt to these differences and are careful how they refer to them in their communications.

Perhaps the simplest way to explain culture and its relationship to communication is to say that people are different—we live, work, and play in different societies, environments, and climates, and we adapt to these in different ways. We are talking here not just about regional differences in the United States, but about even greater differences which are found in the numerous cultures of the world. As a result of living in different societies, environments, and climates, people develop special needs, acquire habits and customs peculiar to themselves, and have experiences (and since words are the names we give to our experiences, we have language differences, too) which, in general, result in particular patterns and methods and forms of expression and relating (communicating) with one another. Many examples of this could be given.

People in a warm, tropical climate, for example, live quite differently from people in a northern urban area of the United States. They live in a much more relaxed style from what we are accustomed to—life is much simpler. Communication is probably less complicated. Life in colonial United States was vastly different from our present-day pattern. The colonists were very independent and looked mainly to their own strengths and resources to provide food and shelter. They were religious folk who read the Bible and lived by its teachings. The simple pleasures of life were all they needed. American Indians and the elements were their main enemies. All these forces plus the old world background of the people are reflected in their culture and in their communication.

We need to know about people and their background if we are to understand their communications. This has important implications for those of you who may find yourselves doing business in a foreign country. It is important that you become acquainted with the local culture and be prepared to follow its rules while you are doing business there. For example, in some Latin American countries, men stand quite close together when talking—much closer than we stand in the United States. If you, as a United States business executive, were to find yourself in this situation, find the closeness uncomfortable, and back away, you would very likely offend your Latin American business friend. Your action would probably create a communication barrier because you would appear "cold and stand-offish" to your Latin American counterpart.

It is important for you to remember that people in different cultures and countries do not do things as we do them in the United States. Before you travel and/or do business in a foreign country, you should check carefully on local customs, cultures, and communications. In reality, your approach should not be very different from that of the President of the United States before he visits a foreign land. State Department officials who are experts on the culture of the country to be visited give the President elaborate and detailed briefings on all facets of the country's local scene so that the President will be able to do his best possible job of communicating. Any business person who must do business with a foreign company should prepare in the same way.

Remember that people do things differently. Remember, too, that people communicate in terms of their own experiences. Do not be offended (and communicate offensively) when something out of the ordinary happens. The situation may appear unusual to your frame of reference because it is not within the range of your experience; the situation may be perfectly "normal" to everyone else. It is small wonder that we seem always to be surrounded by wars and rumors of wars. In addition to the barriers of human behavior and language, our communication attempts also are complicated by cultural barriers (which actually are linked with language).

Many cultural differences take the form of nonverbal communications. The nonverbal area is relatively new and still is being studied and developed; however, most of us have had enough experience to be aware of its existence and importance. One must be careful to keep this area in perspective and to consider nonverbal elements as only a part of the total communication effort—while the nonverbal may be important, it is not always the whole story. If a person frowns while listening to you speak, it may indicate doubt or disagreement; on the other hand, the person may have a headache or the light may be bothersome. It is important for you to remain alert to nonverbal signals, but it is also essential that you decode them accurately.

body language

Probably the best-known type of nonverbal communication, at least to the layperson, is body language. Body language is also known as *kinesics*. A pioneer in the field, Ray Birdwhistell, writes, "The isolation of gestures and the attempt to understand them led to the most important findings of kinesic research. This original study of gestures gave the first indication that kinesic structure is parallel to language structure. By the study of gestures in context, it became clear that the kinesic system has forms which are astonishingly like words in language."[3]

Researchers have observed people involved in the communication process. They have studied body language and other nonverbal behavior, and they have

---

[3]Ray L. Birdwhistell, *Kinesics and Context*. Philadelphia: University of Pennsylvania Press, 1970, p. 80.

then related or identified these actions with actual content of the message being transmitted. The result is a dictionary of body language meanings. Inasmuch as body language is treated in detail in several books, our purpose here is to acquaint you with the subject, discuss possible applications, and direct you to some complete sources.

Both encoder and decoder send nonverbal messages as part of the total communication process."[4] The nonverbal messages of the encoder tend to reveal the degree of presence or absence of sincerity, honesty, conviction, ability, and qualifications; body language reveals a lot about the encoder and this person's attitude and feelings about the message being transmitted. Body language of the decoders also reveals a lot about them and their feelings; but most important, it frequently tells the encoder the extent to which the decoders are accepting or not accepting the message. In other words, body language provides instant feedback to the encoder and answers the question, "How am I doing?" It is this instant feedback which makes face-to-face communication such an effective form of communication.

Whether we are aware of it or not, each of us spends a lot of time decoding body language. We observe a wrinkled forehead, a raised eyebrow, a tug on the ear, fingers tapping on the table top, legs crossed and uncrossed, arms crossed over the chest. These movements should be considered in relation to the message itself; however, many times the nonverbal communications come through louder than the words that are actually being spoken. Have you ever found yourself in a difficult situation and realized that you were shifting your weight in the chair? Or running a finger around the inside of your collar? Or clearing your throat nervously? Nonverbal communication frequently reveals the emotional side of our communications.

A favorite sport of many individuals is "people watching." While waiting in an airport terminal, have you ever observed the crowd and tried to imagine the occupation, the problems, and the thoughts of various people? Have you observed an individual's dress and tried to conclude something about the person? Have you observed gestures, facial expressions, and manner of walk and tried to guess the nature of the topic under discussion?

To be a good reader of body language requires that you sharpen your powers of observation and perception. Observation is a form of decoding, and your ability in this area can be increased by three factors—education, awareness, and need. Education and awareness are interrelated. Through education, a person becomes aware of more things. In other words, a person knows what to look for; therefore, a person is more likely to observe it, to decode it. Likewise, realizing a need for something makes a person ready and eager to acquire it. If you have ever tried to find a certain house number in a strange neighborhood, you know that you were probably more alert and aware than usual; you saw

---

[4]Julius Fast, *Body Language*. New York: Pocket Books, 1970, p. 5.

things you had not seen before because you had a *need* to observe and to find the house number.

Perception has to do with your ability to observe, to remain alert, and to extract from a given communication incident the "realities" of the situation (recognizing, of course, that reality is different for each of us). You must try to take from the communication verbal and nonverbal messages which are similar for both encoder and decoder. While encoding your message, you must be decoding the body language of the decoder. (Communication is indeed a continuous process!)

Thayer says that while mastery of communication techniques is important, it is essential that the encoder be sensitive to the human relations aspects in the communication process[5]—and these human elements are often revealed vividly in body language and other nonverbal communication. The sooner you, as encoder, receive feedback in the form of a body language message, the sooner you can switch to a more effective encoding technique if necessary.

Probably everyone has had some experience with eyes as nonverbal communicators. Most of us have been stared at and have wondered why. Was it curiosity or ill manners? Or perhaps the starer had poor vision and was merely trying to get us in focus. But then there is the possibility the observer found us attractive and interesting and was issuing an invitation to get better acquainted. Most of us have decoded "eye language" even if we did not know about body language or nonverbal communication.

Fast points out that there are numerous messages that can be sent with the eyes, but the stare is the most important technique a person has. His reasoning is that in our culture, one does not stare at another person—one stares at *things*. Therefore, he points out that a stare can have a devastating effect because it reduces a person to nonhuman status.[6]

There is an endless number of messages which can be sent when one thinks of eyes combined with different positions and movements of the eyelids and eyebrows. As with all forms of nonverbal communication, messages sent by the eyes should be decoded in terms of the words accompanying them.

How can anyone hope to communicate without using hands and arms? And even legs are for something besides walking. No doubt each of us knows someone who "talks with his or her hands." Some people punctuate communications with such extravagant gestures that it is extremely dangerous to get too close to their nonverbal exclamations. Do you know people who during a conversation or a card game drum or tap incessantly with their finger tips? Are there people in one of your classes who constantly click the on-off switch of their ballpoint pens? Do you know people who frequently "pop" their knuckles? Do you notice individuals who tap their feet, who cross and uncross their legs, or who cross their legs and then swing their crossed legs back and forth?

---

[5]Thayer, p. 267.
[6]Fast, p. 130.

What do these nonverbal messages tell you? Is the person nervous? Insecure? Bored? Thinking? Happy? Craving attention? A nuisance? Perhaps the messages mean nothing. On the other hand, if nonverbal signs reveal the emotional side of a communication, it is often important for you to try to determine what message is being transmitted along with the verbal one. Sometimes they are the same; other times they are drastically different.

Most of you have observed a scene similar to the one in Figure 8–2. The total effect of the arms, body stance, and facial expressions indicates the feeling of the individuals. In a scene like this one, it is relatively easy to observe the nonverbal (and verbal) communication, to detect emotional elements, and to see the connection between actions and words. Body language is not always this easily read. Many people are devoting their entire life to the study of body language, and you can learn more about the subject in the suggested sources for additional reading. Body language is an interesting, fascinating area of nonverbal communication; much remains to be learned about it. By becoming a better observer, by sharpening your powers of perception, and by knowing as much as possible about your audience (decoders), you should be able to translate more accurately the nonverbal and verbal messages.

space

In an interesting book entitled *The Hidden Dimension,* anthropologist Edward T. Hall discusses space, how people structure it, and how space influences communication. "Proxemics" is the term Hall has coined

Figure 8–2 (From Albert E. Scheflen, *Body Language and Social Order,* Prentice-Hall, 1972, p. 24.)

"for the interrelated observations and theories of man's use of space as a specialized elaboration of culture."[7]

One use of space with which most of you are familiar is "someone's favorite chair." Frequently it is Dad who has a chair which is his, and it is extremely dangerous for anyone else to sit in it. The person who sits in "Dad's chair" without asking permission seems to be invading personal territory. When such an occurrence takes place, we frequently think of the intruder as ill-mannered. You will even find some people who become quite upset at this invasion of their private space.

Another place where most of you have observed special treatment of space is in business offices. Office space is usually allotted on the basis of a person's position in the structure and on the organization chart. This is such a common occurrence that it receives special attention in office management textbooks. Keeling, Kallaus, and Neuner write, "Private offices vary from 600 square feet for senior executives to 200 feet for senior assistants, and 75 to 100 square feet for cubicles in an open office space."[8]

Some companies have a "space manual" that lists the amount of room to which a particular level manager is entitled. One company has such a manual that lists not only size of office but also desk top size so that position in the organization structure also indicates and dictates desk top space. The manual also prescribes how many chairs "with arms" and "without arms" are permitted in an office which has a desk top of certain size.

In addition to the concept of physical space, Hall also discusses personal space. Each of us is surrounded by a "space bubble" varying in size according to the activity or type of communication taking place. Hall classifies these "space bubbles" or distances in four types (each with a close phase and a far phase):

Intimate Distance (Distance: Touching to 1½ feet)—"This is the distance of love-making, wrestling, comforting, and protecting."

Personal Distance (Distance: 1½ feet to 4 feet)—This distance is reserved for more than just a casual friend or fleeting encounter; however, it is a no-contact distance. Hall points out that "Where people stand in relation to each other signals their relationship, or how they feel toward each other, or both. A wife can stay inside the circle of her husband's close personal zone with impunity. For another woman to do so is an entirely different story."

Social Distance (Distance: 4 to 12 feet)—Impersonal business or casual conversations can be carried on in this space. People are very much aware of the presence of one another, but they neither interfere with each other nor are they oppressively near.

Public Distance (Distance: 12 to 25 feet, or farther)—A person at this distance is outside the circle of involvement. This is the distance reserved for public speakers and/or public officials or for anyone on public occasions.[9]

---

[7]Edward T. Hall, *The Hidden Dimension*. Garden City, N.Y.: Anchor Books, 1969, p. 1.

[8]B. Lewis Keeling, Norman F. Kallaus, and John J.W. Neuner, *Administrative Office Management*, Cincinnati: South-Western Publishing Co., 1978, p. 88.

[9]Hall, pp. 116–125.

Space and its use also make a contribution to your total communication effort. As you learned earlier in this chapter, the message sent by the use of space may vary from one culture to another. Be sure you know how to encode and decode "space messages"; as with other forms of nonverbal communication, they should be considered in relation to the words which accompany them.

touch

Among the earliest forms of communication for any human being is touch; it continues to be very important throughout our early years. Once past this period, however, we are relatively cautious about the use of touch in our culture. Except for the "intimate distance" noted in the previous section on space, touch is a rather carefully used means of communication in our society.

And yet a touch can often say as much as a lot of words. This is probably most obvious when someone you know is in trouble or in sorrow, taking hold of his or her hand or putting an arm around the shoulder often is much more effective than words. The nearness, the closeness, the touch says that you are ready to help if needed.

Earlier in this chapter you read about the relationship between culture and communication. Not only does verbal communication vary from one culture to another, but also so does nonverbal communication. Touching is no exception; and if you are interested in knowing more about the subject, you should read the book *Touching* by Ashley Montagu. As he points out, touch is not a widely used form of communication in the United States—we are not a tactile society. Touch is usually reserved for our most intimate relationships and for communication between close friends. Although it is acceptable for women to touch in public, it is not proper for men to do so. Even in the privacy of the home, a son may be embarrassed when he is embraced by his father. And so, we in the United States are a little surprised when we see pictures of men in other countries embracing or walking arm in arm.[10]

It is important for you to remember when communicating with people from other countries and other cultures that their nonverbal communications differ from ours just as their language may be unlike ours. Touching may be a very acceptable and a very common form of nonverbal communication in the country where you are transacting business; you should understand this and be prepared for it.

---

[10]Ashley Montagu, *Touching: The Human Significance of the Skin.* New York: Perennial Library, 1972, p. 303.

Always remember that people communicate in terms of their own experiences. You should keep this in mind as you encode and as you decode.

dress and physical appearance

Each of us has a self-concept or a self-image. This image has a great deal to do with the way we communicate. It is also reflected in our appearance and our dress. Knapp writes, "In addition to the importance of general physical attractiveness in influencing the responses of others, we have some information on stereotyped responses to specific features—e.g., general body build, skin color, hair, and clothes. These specific features may have a profound influence on your self-image and, hence, on your patterns of communication with others."[11]

You will probably find that when you are appropriately dressed for an occasion you will be more relaxed and will relate more effectively to other people. It is important that your clothes be pressed, clean, and properly fitted; while you do not want your attire to be too out of date, this factor is of secondary importance to the way your clothes look and fit. It is natural that a person just graduated from college would dress in a fashion appropriate for his or her age; however, it is important that the style not be too different from accepted styles currently being worn in the business world. If you do not trust your own judgment, secure the advice of a "clothes conscious" friend or a reputable clothing salesperson.

Proper attire is so important that you may want to hire the services of a specialist to assist you. Such a person is John Molloy, and he says, "Wardrobe engineering is just putting together elements of psychology, fashion, sociology, and art."[12] Everything you do is a communication!

It goes without saying that you should give close attention to your personal grooming. Cleanliness, neatly combed hair, and clean fingernails are extremely important; among other things, they tell other people what you think of yourself.

Reference is made to dress and appearance in the Appendix discussion of the employment interview. Once you become a part of the business world, your perception and observation should tell you what the accepted standards of appearance and dress are in your particular company and locale. While it is true that "clothes do not make the man" (or woman), your clothes and your personal

---

[11]Mark L. Knapp, *Nonverbal Communication in Human Interaction.* New York: Holt, Rinehart and Winston, 1972, p. 86.

[12]William Marling, "The Clothes Make the Man, If the Man Knows John Molloy," *Pastimes*, Aug. 1975, p. 15.

appearance are very important nonverbal communicators that tell other people a lot about you.

time

The way a person treats time reveals something about that person. A person who is consistently late may not be well organized; the person who is kept waiting may feel that he or she is not highly regarded by the other person. In the business world of the United States, a subordinate does not keep his or her superior waiting (at least more than two or three minutes); a "boss" may keep a subordinate waiting a few minutes, but a boss who is human-relations oriented will not take advantage of his or her superior position.

In some cultures, time is of less importance, but United States business people tend to move by the clock—a two o'clock appointment usually means two o'clock or something within five or ten minutes of it. In some cultures, a two o'clock appointment may mean three o'clock; and if you arrive to transact business at the "appointed" two o'clock hour, you may actually offend the other person. [13]

Summary

Everything you do is a communication. And actions often speak louder than words. Nonverbal communication—such as body language, cultural differences, space, touch, dress and physical appearance, and time—is a very valuable supplement to the intended communication expressed in words.

Nonverbal communication frequently expresses the emotional side of a communication; however, you should always decode nonverbal communication in relation to the words accompanying it. Nonverbal communication provides valuable feedback for both the encoder and the decoder.

Discussion Questions

1. What is the relationship between culture and nonverbal communication?
2. Why does silence frequently serve as an effective method for encouraging communication?
3. What nonverbal behavior do you observe most often in your communications classroom? Does this nonverbal communication serve any useful purpose for students and/or teacher?

---

[13]Hall, p. 15.

4. What nonverbal communications incidents have you experienced with people from other countries? With people from a section of the United States different from your own?

5. What "reserved" space or territorial zones can you identify in your own home? How does the "owner" of this space react when someone enters this space uninvited?

6. Why do you think ours is not a tactile society? Do you see any advantages to more use of touch as a means of communication?

7. What nonverbal communication do you find most effective as feedback when you are encoding a message?

8. What special or unusual uses of space have you noticed in companies where you have been employed or where you have transacted business?

9. Although most nonverbal communication is decoded in relation to the words accompanying it, what are some nonverbal communications that do not require any "accompanying text?"

10. What is your favorite nonverbal technique for terminating a conversation? What other methods do you know?

Problems

1. Involve a fellow student in conversation about a current, major issue at your school or in national and world news. After the person has expressed an opinion about the matter, use silence as a communication technique—that is, remain silent a few seconds after the person has stopped talking, and see what results you get. What was the person's next remark? What did you learn that was of interest or that you did not expect to learn? What was the person's reaction (verbal and nonverbal) to your silence?

2. What nonverbal communication does the teacher of your communication course (or the teacher of some other course) use most often? How do you decode these nonverbal messages—that is, what do they mean to you? What do these messages mean to the teacher?

3. At the next athletic event you attend, observe the coach of your college team. What nonverbal messages do you notice? How do you decode them?

4. Watch an interview, either live or on television. What nonverbal communications do you observe which we have discussed in this chapter? What other nonverbal messages are present? Does the nonverbal correlate with the verbal?

5. Perhaps you had not given nonverbal communication much thought until you read this chapter. With the background you now have, what nonverbal feedback do you look for most often in a serious conversation? Are you aware of nonverbal messages when you communicate socially, casually or informally? If so, what are these messages?

Additional Reading

Birdwhistell, Ray L., *Kinesics and Context*, Philadelphia: University of Pennsylvania Press, 1970.

Davis, Flora, *Inside Intuition: What We Know about Nonverbal Communication.* New York: McGraw-Hill, 1973.

Fast, Julius, *Body Language.* New York: Pocket Books, 1970.

Hall, Edward T., *The Silent Language.* Greenwich, Conn.: Fawcett, 1959.

Hall, Edward T., *The Hidden Dimension.* Garden City, N.Y.: Anchor Books, 1966.

Knapp, Mark L., *Nonverbal Communication in Human Interaction,* New York: Holt, Rinehart and Winston, 1972.

Mehrabian, Albert, *Nonverbal Communication.* Chicago: Aldine-Atherton, 1972.

Montagu, Ashley, *Touching: The Human Significance of the Skin.* New York: Perennial Library, 1971.

Sommer, Robert, *Personal Space.* Englewood Cliffs, N.J.: Prentice-Hall, 1969.

Visual communication in business

9

key points to learn

The importance of visual communication in business.

Why we use graphic and visual aids.

Various types of graphs and charts.

What are signs, symbols, and images.

The reasons for a corporate design program.

Means and methods of visual identification.

The meaning of color.

How design is used as an environmental communication element.

Jerome S. Bruner suggested that there are three major modes of learning: the enactive (direct experience), the iconic (pictorial experience), and the symbolic (highly abstract experience).[1]

> What a picture means to the viewer is strongly dependent on his past experience and knowledge. In this respect the visual image is not a mere representation of "reality" but a symbolic system.[2]

In this chapter we will examine some of the pictorial and symbolic techniques used in business to induce and reinforce learning; to aid and abet in communicating messages to a business firm's many publics.

"Ours is a visual world," says Gombrich.[3] We are almost continuously exposed to visual impressions from the moment we arise in the morning until we finally shut our eyes at night. A good many of these signs, signals, and symbols are commercially oriented. They represent an effort on the part of business to communicate with us nonverbally. The newspaper we read at the breakfast table, the package design on the box of cereal, the location signs,

---

[1]Edgar Dale, *Audiovisual Methods in Teaching.* 3rd ed. New York: Dryden, 1969, p. 14.

[2]Ernst H. Gombrich, "The Visual Image," *Communication.* San Francisco: W. H. Freeman, 1972, pp. 46–60.

[3]*Ibid.*, pp. 46–60.

the posters, the identified office buildings, factories, and vehicles we pass on the way to our jobs, our schools, and our recreation, etc., are examples of these. Regardless of our activities during the day, we will all most likely have to deal with pictorial representations of some kind. Illustrations, charts, maps, graphs, blueprints, photographs, trademarks, and instructions are just a few of the many we may deal with daily.

As a result of today's visual bombardment, some communication theorists are asserting that we are entering an era in which the image will take over for the written word. The question confronting us in this book and in this chapter is then, "When should one use words and when should one use pictorial or other nonverbal representations?" Communication experts are working to answer this difficult question. At best, this chapter will help you to inderstand the problem and how you may use visual images more advantageously.

is a picture worth a thousand words
===========or is a word worth a thousand pictures?

Confucius is reputed to have actually said, "A picture is worth 10,000 words," but somewhere along the line of history, somebody thought that this was an exaggeration and limited the number to 1,000 so that the statement might be more believable. In some cases, this might be true, but we must consider what words and what pictures we are using. Could you draw, or visualize (mentally picture), a representation that would immediately convey the meaning of this simple five-word sentence from a first-grade reading book:

"The dog is not here."

What dog? My dog . . . your dog . . . a dog? Where is here? And, besides, how do you convey "not"—by mere absence? The sentence is deceptively simple. Perhaps even more difficult would be the universal communication of an emotion and its meaning, say, love, through a single picture as opposed to a number of words.

To hammer home the point, Lincoln's Gettysburg Address contained 266 words; the preamble to the Constitution of the United States has but 53 words; and Psalm 23, the Psalm of David, contains only 118 words. Could pictures, regardless of number, ever be able to convey the impact and full meaning of those 437 words?

On the other hand, the use of a pictorial device such as a chart (broadly defined to encompass all types of diagrammatic illustrations, including graphs) may simplify and speed the communication of information or instruction. While a picture may not be worth a thousand words, when you are presenting the data in a report, graphic aids, *plus* words, can make a very useful combination to help you communicate.

using graphic or visual aids

Graphic aids is the name we give to such charts and other illustrations used for presenting data. These are excellent supplements to the written word or the spoken word. Your reader or listener may have trouble comprehending relationships when reading or hearing that "production costs rose an average of 5 percent from 1970 to 1974, 10 percent from 1975 to 1979, and are expected to increase 12.5 percent annually from 1980 to 1984." However, if the data can be seen in a graph a stronger mental image is received than from the words alone.

Almost everyone can benefit from having words reinforced with some graphic presentation; additionally, some people who are not particularly word-oriented will find the graphic aids of great value. Remember that meanings are in people and not in words. By quantifying data and presenting them in graphic form, you help to reinforce the "meaning" of the words in your report. Charts, graphs, and tables are tools that help you make this presentation of quantitative data more efficiently by enabling your reader to compare and contrast data.

If a good job is done in the preliminary planning, it is possible to determine in advance what types of graphic aids and how many of them will be needed to present the data effectively.

Purposes of Charts and Graphs

Charts and graphs can: (1) save user time as attention is focused on the matter at hand since superfluous material has been removed; (2) gain attention if well-done and pleasing to the eye; (3) show relationships over time; (4) speed comprehension if not unduly complex; and (5) aid in the interpretation of the data presented.

Care must be taken that the aids are free of error and of excessive detail that confuses rather than simplifies. When verbal information can be expressed graphically, its impact is likely to be enhanced.[4]

Principles of Graphic Presentation

There are a few principles of graphic presentation that you should observe regardless of the type of aid you are using. Attention to these principles will result in a much more credible report or presentation.

---

[4]Cecil H. Meyers, *Handbook of Basic Graphics: A Modern Approach.* Belmont, Calif.: Dickenson, 1970, p. 8.

Need.   A graphic or visual aid should be incorporated only when there is a purpose for it; there must be a need.[5] Aids should be included only when they enable you to present your data more clearly and/or when they allow you to present a lot of data in a relatively small space.

Graphic aids should not be used just to impress your viewer or make your presentation look more "professional." If report writers have done their jobs properly, the graphic aids were included because they were needed to help tell the story—not because they were pretty or "made the work look like a report."

Prepare the Reader.   You should always prepare your reader or listener for a graphic aid in the text of your report or speech—that is, tell your audience they are about to encounter a graph, a table, or a chart. When the reader comes to a graphic aid which has not been previously mentioned in the text, he or she is forced to pause and determine the purpose of the chart or table. This delay reduces the readability rating of your report. The speaker uses the visual aid as a reinforcement to what is being said. The listener can see and have reinforced the meaning of the words if alerted.

Do not make a major production out of introducing the graphic aid. The introduction can be made subordinately as you call attention to an important bit of data in the graphic aid.[6] For example, "In Table 3 on p. 5, you will see that a sales increase of 15 percent was realized, while advertising expense increased only 5 percent." Using a slide, a transparency, or just a graph on a blackboard would allow the audience to immediately see the relationship.

By calling attention to graphic aids before they appear in the report or on a screen, you enable your reader or listener to increase comprehension.

Explain the Graphic Aid.   It is not enough to say that "Table 3 is on p. 5," or "Look at the graph on the screen." You must never assume that your readers will read and study it. And if they do, you dare not assume that the message they received from it is the one you intended. After all, we communicate in terms of our own experiences, and you (as the writer of the report) are presumed to be the specialist who has studied the matter and who therefore is qualified to draw correct conclusions from the data. An explanation of graphic aids and other illustrations is important if they are to be of maximum use in the communication process.

After you have decided which graphic aid is best and most appropriate to convey a particular part of your message, you must make sure the data are presented honestly in the graphic aid. Assuming that the data themselves are accurate, dishonesty is most likely to occur because of improper handling of the mechanics of graphic presentation.

---

[5]Raymond V. Lesikar, *Business Communication*, 4th ed. Homewood, Ill.: Richard D. Irwin, 1980, p. 393.

[6]J. H. Menning and C. W. Wilkinson, *Communicating through Letters and Reports*. Homewood, Ill.: Richard D. Irwin, 1972, p. 525.

mechanics of graphic aids
for written reports

The mechanics of presentation concern the physical presentation of the chart, graph, table, or whatever aid you have chosen. When we talk about this subject, we are concerned with selecting and constructing an aid that will communicate effectively and accurately the data contained in the aid. The meaning of the data is important only to the extent that it is necessary to help select the appropriate graphic aid vehicle.

In addition to their importance in telling the report story, graphic aids can be a real help to improved readability and attention. Graphic aids provide spots of interest and color and break up what might otherwise be a sea of dark, dull type or drab words. Many people tend to think that reports must be dull and uninteresting; but since reports are a necessity in business, we must do everything we can to aid communication and understanding. The metacommunication and readability aspects of graphic aids can be important factors in gaining reader interest, acceptance, and attention for your reports; the same will be true of your oral presentations.

Location

You were cautioned earlier in this chapter always to prepare your reader for the appearance of a graphic aid and to interpret the data; therefore, the graphic presentation is usually preceded and followed by text. In typewritten reports such as are usually found in a business situation, graphic aids less than one page in size are usually centered horizontally on the page. If an aid occupies a full page, the rule still applies that it should be introduced before the reader encounters it.

Size

A graphic aid should be large enough to accommodate all the data that must be presented in it without looking crowded. Care must be taken to exercise consistency and honesty in the size of graphic aids. A large graph may tend to appear more important than a small one. If a one-inch space represents one year on one graph and ten years on the next graph, your reader may become confused and misinterpret your data. When such differences in size are unavoidable, it is your job to make sure your reader is not misled.

Titles

All graphic aids in a report should have a title and a number assigned to them. For example: Table 4—Average Production of Apples for the

Ten-Year Period 1940–1950 in the States of Washington, Oregon, Idaho. The title usually appears at the top of a graphic aid.

Although "tables" are usually discussed in connection with graphic aids, technically they are not graphic aids, as we will explain a little later in this chapter. In fact, we usually refer to "List of Tables and Other Illustrations." Graphic aids are titled and numbered for easy reference and identification in the body of the report as well as in the beginning section of the report.

When a report is of sufficient formality or length to require a table of contents, a list of tables and illustrations usually follows it.

_____ Color

Color can improve the readibility of a report. Color enables us to compare two or more things in a graph or a chart. In a graph, a red line can stand for corn, a blue line can stand for wheat, and a green line can represent oats. Your reader can easily compare statistics for all three products on the same graphic aid.

If color is not available for any reason (increased cost may be the main one), the same results can be achieved by the use of dots, dotted lines, broken lines, crossed lines, and other mechanical methods of comparing and contrasting.

types of graphic aids

Graphic aids enable the communicator to make a type of pictorial presentation of the research data. The graphic aids supplement the report, text, or speech, and should enable the reader or listener to visualize and comprehend the situation much better.

The most common types of graphic aids are discussed in the following paragraphs. Numerous variations and combinations of these basic types are possible.

_____ Tables

Tables are usually discussed in connection with graphic aids although they are somewhat different as you will realize when you compare Figure 9–1 with others that follow. A table is merely an orderly arrangement into columns of data so that comparisons and contrasts can be more easily made by the reader. More properly, a table may be thought of as a mechanical device for presenting data rather than as a pictorial presentation of the data.

Notice the necessity for descriptive captions on the columns (vertical) and on the stubs (horizontal). Accurate and concise headings are important if your reader is to understand the data contained in the table.

ECONOMIC ASSUMPTIONS

[Calendar years; dollar amounts in billions]

Item	Actual 1973	Actual 1974	Assumed for purposes of budget estimates					
			1975	1976	1977	1978	1979	1980
Gross national product:								
Current dollars:								
Amount_____	$1,295	$1,397	$1,498	$1,686	$1,896	$2,123	$2,353	$2,606
Percent change_____	11.8	7.9	7.2	12.6	12.4	12.0	10.8	10.8
Constant (1958) dollars:								
Amount_____	$839	$821	$794	$832	$879	$936	$997	$1,061
Percent change_____	5.9	−2.2	−3.3	4.8	5.6	6.5	6.5	6.5
Incomes (current dollars):								
Personal income_____	$1,055	$1,150	$1,232	$1,365	$1,536	$1,717	$1,900	$2,102
Wages and salaries_____	$692	$751	$792	$884	$999	$1,117	$1,236	$1,367
Corporate profits_____	$123	$141	$115	$145	$163	$185	$208	$233
Prices (percent change):								
GNP deflator_____	5.6	10.2	10.8	7.5	6.5	5.1	4.1	4.0
Consumer Price Index____	6.2	11.0	11.3	7.8	6.6	5.2	4.1	4.0
Unemployment rates (percent):								
Total_____	4.9	5.6	8.1	7.9	7.5	6.9	6.2	5.5
Insured [1]_____	2.8	3.8	7.5	6.9	6.4	5.1	4.4	3.6
Federal pay raise, October (percent)_____	4.77	5.52	5.00	8.75	7.25	6.50	5.75	5.25
Interest rate, 91-day Treasury bills (percent) [2]_____	7.0	7.9	6.4	6.4	6.4	6.0	5.0	5.0

[1] Insured unemployment as a percentage of covered employment; includes unemployed workers receiving extended benefits.

[2] Average rate on new issues within period; the rate shown for 1975 was the current market rate at the time the estimates were made.

Figure 9–1 Example of a table.

Tables are extremely convenient devices for displaying large amounts of data in a relatively small space. It would take many lengthy, involved (and perhaps boring) sentences to present all the data included in a large table, and to discuss the significant points. Remember that tables and other illustrations are always discussed, even though the discussion sometimes is brief.

_____ Graphs

A graph is an aid in which points on a scale are connected with a line in order to show increases or decreases. The degree of slope to the line gives the reader a better impression of the intensity of activity as well as a picture of the trend over a given period of time as shown in Figure 9–2.

If the purpose of a business report or presentation is to help someone make a decision, and alternatives are often considered in choosing the best solution,

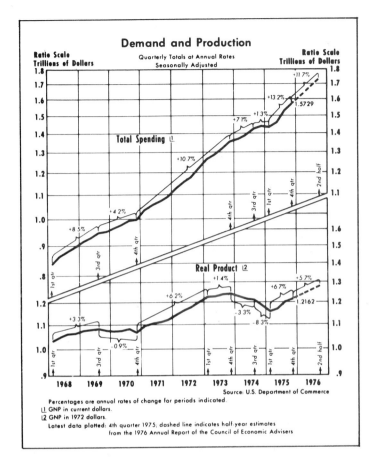

Figure 9–2 Example of a comparative graph. (*Survey of Current Business,* March 1976)

the decision maker sometimes needs to compare and contrast certain data. This is possible, as you can see in Figure 9–2, by the use of solid, dotted, and broken lines and by superimpositions.

_____ Charts

There are several types of charts—bar charts, multiple bar charts, and pie charts, to mention some of the most common ones. All of them permit the reporter to depict degrees of differences between and among data through variations in the size (length) of bars or wedges. Figure 9–3 illustrates a bar chart.

In using the multiple bar chart, you can see how comparisons between different classes of data are possible. Notice the mechanical techniques used to

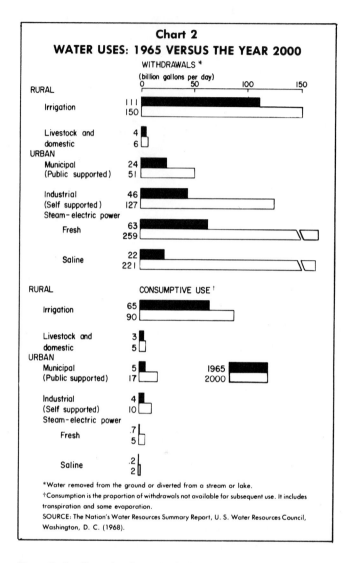

Figure 9–3 Example of a multiple bar graph.

distinguish the different classes and the legend on the chart describing the technique.

The pie or circle chart is so named because of its shape. Each wedge is a percentage of the total class of data being presented and described. Wedges usually begin at the top (twelve o'clock) and are sliced clockwise as shown in Figure 9–4.

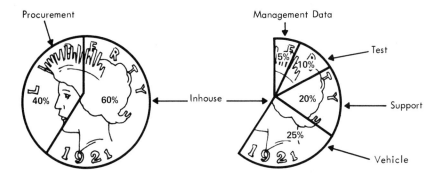

Figure 9–4   Example of a circular or pie chart. (*Defense Management Journal*)

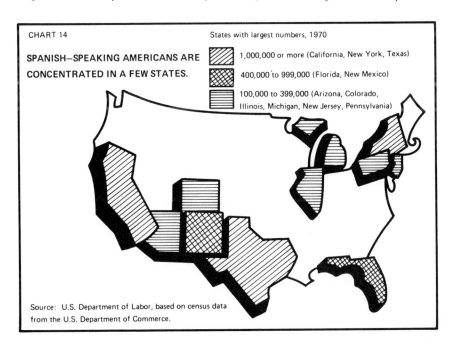

Figure 9–5   Example of an information-providing map.

_____Miscellaneous Charts

There are numerous variations and combinations of the different graphic aids. They are too numerous to mention here, but you should recognize them as a result of knowing about the basic types we have discussed in this chapter. The map in Figure 9–5 is very commonly used.

Information may also be conveyed using various other illustrative techniques. Pictures and photographs may convey explanatory data as can drawings of many types.

visual aids for oral presentation

The same mechanical details pertain to the presentation of visual aids to be projected or shown as to those to be printed in a report or book. Often the graphic aid is used as the base or art for the visual aid. Some of the more common visual aid forms are (1) slides; (2) overhead transparencies; (3) opaque projections; (4) signs and cards; and (5) miscellaneous forms.

Slides can easily be produced by photographing maps, charts, graphs, or other items. Care should be taken that the original material to be copied is in rectangular form and preferably horizontal rather than vertical. Simple to highly complex slide projectors are available for single screen to multimedia presentations.

Overhead transparencies can be quickly and inexpensively produced in a Thermofax copying machine and in others designed for this purpose. You may also make your own transparencies by drawing on special sheets of acetate with water-soluble felt-tipped pens. Transparency masters may be clear or colored; colors may be added in a number of ways to enhance the subject matter. Ease of production, low cost, and flexibility in use have made transparencies very popular.

Opaque projectors are capable of enlarging already printed or prepared material onto a screen without additional processing. Since the machine is somewhat cumbersome and material must be of size to fit, at times this method is awkward to handle.

Photographs, film strips, movies, video tape or cassettes, artwork, the blackboard, models, and signs are some of the many visual aids useful in communicating information and instructions, and in aiding persuasive attempts during an oral presentation.

signs, symbols, and images

Oddly enough, once a symbol has been designated by a language community, it tends to sound right. A table is called a table because a table is a table. Of course, if a table had been called a *glomph* by early speakers of our language, the argument would run that a *glomph* is called a *glomph* because a *glomph* is a *glomph*. [7]

---

[7] Jon Eisenson, J. Jeffrey Auer, and John V. Irwin, *The Psychology of Communication*. New York: Appleton, Century, Crofts, 1963, p. 113.

There is nothing in the nature of things that gives them meaning. Meaning is something we give symbols by agreement or convention so that they acquire a certain arbitrary character. There is a great deal of mysticism and symbolism related to the human eye. The sun, for example, was thought to be the eye of god. The ancient Egyptian god Ra, driven from the earth by evil, took refuge as the sun, and hence peered down on mankind's habits and misadventures.[8] Modley simplifies the definition of a symbol to mean "anything that stands for something else," and graphic symbols, "to be graphic devices that stand for something else."[9]

Cataldo considers symbols as the direct expression of subjective feelings and emotions. In the organization of information, the graphic designer uses these powerful communication devices that appeal more or less to universal modes of human behavior. Through the use of symbols, the artist can transform an abstract idea into graphic forms which are a common language of feeling between the graphic designer and the reader.[10]

Symbols have played a vital role in the communication of ideas throughout the history of human beings. To a botanist, a circle with a dot in the center is still a symbol for an annual plant while two dots in the center means a biennial plant. When a ring or circle is used with a seal it becomes a symbol for the International Olympics. Three gold balls signify a pawnbroker; supposedly they represent the three bags of gold St. Nicholas tossed into the window of the home of three poor sisters who needed dowries to obtain husbands.

A sign is different from a symbol although their functions are often combined in graphic design. Whatmough says, "A sign has a direct relation to its object, like water dripping from the trees is a sign of rain; but the word rain (which obviously is not rain or a sign of rain) is a symbol of rain or raining."[11]

A symbol and sign often go hand-in-hand. The familiar R_x is a symbol for a prescription and when used on a wooden, metal, or plastic form hanging outside of a shop, it indicates the services available within. The red and white stripes of the barber's pole signifying "bloodletting" or surgery are almost a symbol and sign of the past. The Ballingers note that "As part of a sign, the symbol is often strong and direct." They refer to coffee cups above a coffee shop obviously suggesting a coffee break; a pipe above a tobacco shop; seashells, gloves, etc., communicating a message about the services or products available within.[12]

Symbols, signs, and other ingredients of visual communication work together to help form and express what has popularly been called the corporate

[8]Faber Birren, *Color and Human Response*. New York: Van Nostrand Reinhold, 1978, p. 27.

[9]Rudolph Modley, "The Challenge of Symbology," in *Symbology*, Edward Whitney (ed.). New York: Hastings House, 1960, p. 20.

[10]John W. Cataldo, *Graphic Design and Visual Communication*. New York: Dun-Donnelley, Intext Educational Publishers, 1966, p. 64.

[11]J. Whatmough, *Language*. New York: New Amsterdam Library, 1956, p. 19.

[12]Louise Bowen Ballinger and Raymond A. Ballinger, *Sign, Symbol and Form*. New York: Van Nostrand Reinhold, 1972, pp. 13–16.

image. An *image* is the concept of someone or something that is held by the public. It is the character projected by this someone or something. The idea of image is important to the business firm since this is the way the firm is perceived by its customers, distributors, employees, suppliers, stockholders, and so on.

Eskell writes:

> Every company has an image shaped by its products, name, trademark, color, architecture, decoration, service, price range, advertising, etc., and its way of expressing itself in picture, word, and action. The image can be sharp or diffuse. The company's design policy can be logically and rationally executed by expert designers under a firm and uncompromising management, or it can be the opposite. A messy porridge of indistinct shapes without style or direction. The corporate image may connote good quality products, something pleasant, something desirable to taste, see, listen to, buy, own, and so on. The image may also have a negative impact: shoddy goods, vulgar taste, dreariness and *ennui* in general, a total lack of imagination.[13]

Visual communication does not create a company or corporate image but may play a large part in helping to establish and maintain it. The finest designers cannot correct or overcome poorly conceived and manufactured products, bad service, or overpricing. By the same token, poor design and visual communication usually will not erase the intrinsic good of a company or product but may retard its acceptance and popularity.

Chairman of the Board of Directors of the IBM Company, Thomas J. Watson, had this to say, "In the IBM Company we don't think design can make a poor product good, whether the product be a machine, a building or a promotional brochure. But we are convinced that good design can materially help a good product realize its full potential. In short, we think good design is good business."[14]

the corporate image
and visual communication

Some 83 percent of all the information a human acquires is acquired visually. The initial contact most people have with companies they purchase goods and services from are visual: through advertising and sales promotion. When we shop in a retail store, we do not transact business with an individual but rather with a representative of the firm. Without having experi-

---

[13]Ollie Eksell, *Corporate Design Programs*. London/New York: Studio Vista/Reinhold, 1967, p. 50.

[14]Ben Rosen, *The Corporate Search for Visual Identity*. © 1970 Litton Educational Publishing. Reprinted by permission of Van Nostrand Reinhold.

ence dealing with a company or using its products, we may still have formed an impression, based in part, by some visual communication form.

An interesting example of corporate image, symbolism, and visual communication came into play a few years ago when United Airlines changed its corporate design. Because of similarity of name (United Airlines and United States), similarity in the use of colors (red, white and blue), and use of the star as a symbolic design element, many people thought that United Airlines was a government owned or operated concern. The illusion of bureaucracy and the aftermath of Watergate contributed to a negative attitude. As a result, United changed its logotype and trademark as seen in Figure 9–6.

A company that is visually effective has a competitive edge over the firm whose visual communications are relatively ineffective. The poorer designs recede into the background rather than move into the forefront. The development of visual communications to enhance the desired corporate image does not happen by chance. The effort is usually a very carefully thought-out and planned endeavor with implicit, if not explicit, corporate design plans and policies.

_____The Corporate Design Program

While some business people have been concerned with corporate design for many years,[15] the importance of design and identification has become far more apparent since the late 1950s. Where design decisions were once made by middle managers, they are now made in the corporate board rooms and the offices of the presidents. Once decided at top levels, these design decisions are supported and observed throughout the firm via policies and guides such as manuals and style books.

The change in attitude and the upgrading of design in business came about for several reasons:

A New Look for United Airlines

Figure 9–6   United Airlines symbol before and after change. (Courtesy of United Airlines, Inc.)

_____

[15]Note: The Olivetti Company of Italy is considered a pioneer in corporate image and design. The principle of integrated design was laid down by their management in 1930 and has been implemented in many ways.

1. Recognition that the image of the business and the part played by graphic design and visual communication is an important factor in the profitability of the firm. Good design is good business.
2. Acknowledgement that a "total" identification program would have a greater impact (synergism) than the use of many different designs or variations.
3. Growth and dispersion of plants and facilities necessitated uniformity of identification.
4. Mergers, acquisitions, and diversification of products and services made necessary a means of identifying the corporate family.
5. Changes of long-standing corporate names to reflect new interests and diversification offered the opportunity to redo the entire design program. Some examples are: Pittsburgh Plate Glass Company to PPG Industries, the General Shoe Company to Genesco, Olin-Mathison Company to Olin, the Swift Meat Packing Company to Esmark, and so on.

A Top Management Decision

Instituting a corporate design program requires commitment from the top. The chairperson, the members of the board of directors, the president and his or her executives must fully support the idea as the program will usually take several years to implement, and will be costly from both an out-of-pocket and opportunity cost standpoint.

C. Peter McColough, President and Chief Executive Officer of the Xerox Corporation, said, "At Xerox we place special emphasis on total communications—anything written, said or seen which pertains to the company. This helps to accurately reflect who we are, what we are and our stated goals for the future, especially for those who cannot be a part of the day-to-day activities of Xerox on a first hand basis."

Once committed, the goals and objectives must be crystalized and provided to the designer or design team assigned the task. The designers will then familiarize themselves with the firm and its operations in attempting to embody its goals and perceived image into visible elements that represent the firm.

What Is Included

The items included in a corporate design program will vary from company-to-company based on the products and services offered for sale. Imagine the diversity of items to be included in a design program for an airline, a railroad, or a hotel chain. Ben Rosen lists the following as generally included in a corporate design program:

1. Corporate mark
   a. Logo or logotype
   b. Symbol
   c. Color

2. Corporate alphabet or type style
   a. Display style
   b. Text style or styles
3. Environmental design and structures
   a. Office architecture
   b. Plant architecture
   c. Reception areas, interiors, and entrance design
4. Product design
   a. Consumer items
   b. Service image
   c. Visual presentation
5. Package design
6. Advertising—all visual media
7. Sales promotion—all visual media
8. Company paper
   a. Stationery
   b. All business forms
   c. Transmittal envelopes
   d. Mailing labels and containers
9. Signage
10. Vehicle identification and uniforms
11. Exhibitions and displays
12. Design control manual.[16]

The above is only a partial list. Many subdivisions and other items could be included depending upon the type of business.

_____ **Design Program Components**

The balance of this chapter will be strongly visual and deal principally with four major design areas and their relationship to corporate visual communication. The four areas are identification, color, pictorial content, and environment.

_____ **Visual Identification**

Look at Figure 9–7. How many of the trademarks and trade characters can you correctly identify?

These symbols and signs cause you to recognize and identify many well-known companies. Other visual devices such as color, form, style, and typography further reinforce the recognition and identification of trademarks, logotypes or logos (design signatures). Without identification the competitive system could not be justified as there would be no means of advertising or sales promotion.

---

[16]Rosen, p. 233.

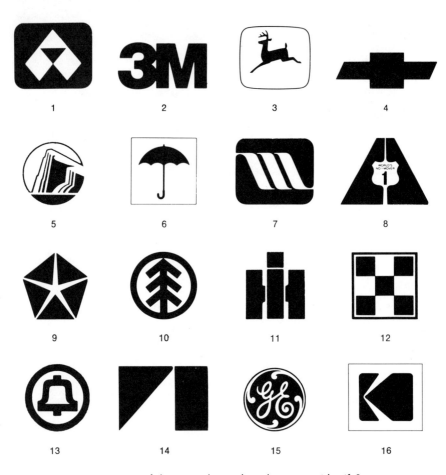

Figure 9–7   How many of these popular trademarks can you identify?

To create a total identification system, a graphic element must be used in a uniform manner. A partial list would include:

Stationery—letterheads, envelopes, forms, business cards, checks, postal indicia, labels, binders, folders, report covers, etc.

Products and packaging—product nameplates, labels, stencils, instruction manuals, guarantees, wrapping paper, boxes, cartons, crates, tape, decals, and more.

Advertising and public relations—all forms of advertising, premium and give-away items, publicity releases, bulletins, plant publications, etc.

Vehicles—autos, trucks, planes, boats, construction equipment, railroad cars, fork-lift trucks, and more.

As seen in Figure 9–7, some designs are directly related to the firm, its products, or its services, while others are simply designs that become associated over time. Along with a symbol or sign, we may find the firm name or the firm name may stand by itself as the identification. When the name alone is used, it is often written or printed in a distinctive lettering or typographic style. Type styles have a visual connotation and these may influence the viewers' image of the firm.

Once a trademark or character has been established, the design should be periodically reevaluated and changed or updated as need be. In an evolutionary manner, such trade characters as the Morton Salt girl and General Mills' Betty Crocker have been restyled and modernized to be in tune with the times. Subtle changes have been made to many familiar trademarks. Figure 9–8 illustrates these.

Form is another design element employed for identification purposes. Although the Coca-Cola bottle is slowly being phased out, it will be remembered as a classic case in product identification. Other packaging forms also serve to identify: Mrs. Butterworth's Maple Syrup bottle was in the form of a woman, Janitor in a Drum employed a unique package, and L'eggs hosiery items are immediately recognized. Although the prices and copy on the packages or labels may change, the basic form has been maintained. Some examples are shown in Figure 9–9.

Layout design and typography are used by advertisers seeking to gain instant identification as a reader or viewer turns the newspaper or magazine page. These styles also contribute to the image of the advertiser. Your newspaper will serve to illustrate the above points. Advertisers develop layout styles that promote identification even when the signature or logo has been omitted. Look through your newspaper and see how many advertisers you can identify without looking at the retailer's name. See if the ad styles reflect the nature or the image of the store. Airy designs with lots of white-space, graceful type, and art style to match lend to a quality image, whereas crowded layouts with heavy type connotate a low-priced or budget business. Penney's has developed a very easily identifiable style as seen in Figure 9–10.

_____ Color

Color is employed to: (1) identify, (2) communicate instructions, (3) capture attention, and (4) arouse symbolic and psychologically based images. If distinctive enough, color can serve as an identification device. You are all probably familiar with the brown and silver used by Hershey Chocolates and the shade of green on the Salem cigarette package.

Color is used in advertising and promotion to attract attention to the message, stimulate desire, arouse emotions, and set a scene or provide a mood. Internally, color is used for safety, direction, motivation, identification, and

1889

1900

1921

1939

1964

CURRENT

Figure 9–8 How American Telephone & Telegraph Co. has changed its corporate symbol in order to keep up with the times. (Courtesy of American Telephone & Telegraph Co.)

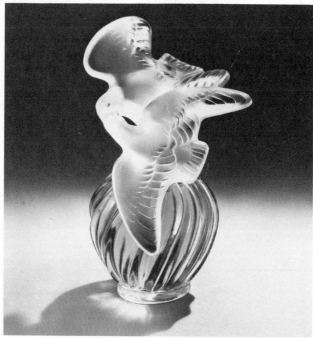

Figure 9–9 In addition to identification, packaging may also enhance the product and contribute to the image. The copy and colors may change over time, but the basic forms remain relatively the same. (Courtesy of Parfums Nina Ricci, Paris, and L'eggs, Hanes Hosiery, Inc.)

Figure 9–10   Example of distinctive advertising format and style. (Courtesy of J. C. Penney Co., Inc.)

other purposes. Pipes, cables, valves, and switches are color coded for immediate identification and safety. Color schemes are selected for their ability to provide an environment conducive to productivity, sales, or other desired goals.

Symbolic Value of Color

Like design, color has symbolic value and this quality along with psychological image serves the graphic designer. The Romans dressed in black for mourning, used red as a signal of danger, and signified quarantine (caution) with yellow. White has been the signal of light, and hence, signifies purity, joy, and glory. Red symbolizes fire and blood, indicating charity (the Red Cross) and sacrifice. Green is the symbol of nature and signifies eternal life, while purple symbolizes illness and melancholia.

Nine symbolic colors were and still are a part of the English culture carried over from heraldic days. Yellow or gold stood for honor and loyalty, while silver or white symbolized faith and purity. Red was a token for courage and zeal, and blue was used for piety and sincerity. Black signified grief and penitence while green stood for youth and hope. Purple was the mark of royalty and rank, with orange indicating strength and endurance. Sanguine, a reddish-purple color, had the meaning of sacrifice.

We still use a blue ribbon for first place, red for second, and white for third. Purple was and still is used to indicate the best of the classes. Color symbolism carries over into language in so many instances. We "color" our speech or writing when we want to influence opinions. We use such expressions as "green with envy," "feeling blue," "yellow journalism," and "red-hot news." Psychologically, different colors affect most people in the following way:[17]

R)			R)	
)	Exciting		)	Warm colors appeals to extroverted,
O)			O)	vigorous personalities
			Y)	
Y)				
)			G)	
G)	Tranquil		B)	
)			)	
B)			I)	
			)	Cool colors appeal to
)			)	introverted personalities
I)	Sedation		V)	
)			)	
V)				

(Note: An easy way to remember the spectrum of colors is to remember Roy G. Biv: red, orange, yellow, green, blue, indigo, and violet.)

---

[17]Faber Biren, *Selling Color to People.* Secaucus, N.J.: Lyle Stuart, University Books, 1956, pp. 159–160.

Howard Ketcham, a color engineer, suggests some good and poor color combinations for package design:

some good combinations:	**some poor combinations:**
Scarlet and turquoise	Scarlet and green
Scarlet and royal blue	Scarlet and yellow
Vermillion and purple	Orange and purple
Orange and dark blue	Olive and blue
Lemon yellow and dark brown	Beige and light gray
Chartreuse and violet	Charcoal and brown
Lime yellow and medium blue	Green and purple
Turquoise and violet	Turquoise and yellow green
Chartreuse and coral pink	Pink and orange[18]

The physical laws of color tell us that yellow is the brightest and most luminous of colors when all are viewed in the same light. As a result, the most legible of all combinations is black on yellow, followed by green on white, red on white, blue on white, and black on white. White, as you see, makes a good background but it lacks attention value.

Red and yellow are the best attention-getters with red being aggressive and yellow being visible. Brilliant red-orange is probably the most commanding color followed by yellow-orange, orange, yellow-geen, and pink. Attention value depends on the ability to startle the eye as well as to be seen clearly.

Knowledge of color can help the visual communicator overcome problems. Red, orange, and yellow can be seen clearly even through haze and distance, while blue and violet appeared blurred under the same circumstances. Yellow is seen as the largest and most advancing followed by white, red, green, blue, and black as the smallest of all. Bright colors appear large and warm colors appear close. Application of these rules has value in package and poster design. Prominent elements should be red, orange, or yellow set off against low-value green, blue, or purple backgrounds. For size, yellow and white will appear largest receding from warm to cool colors with black appearing smallest.

_____ Illustrative Material

Illustrations, art, or photography are used principally in advertising and promotion. Pictorial matter is employed to (1) attract attention, (2) speed communication, and (3) set a mood or atmosphere.

As important as it is to attract attention to an advertisement, the following table shows that the higher the index of attention the greater the percentage

_____
[18]Howard Ketchum, *Color Planning.* New York: Harper & Row Pub., 1958, p. 78.

TABLE 9–1 relationship of illustrative content to attention and to readership of copy

Type of Picture	Index of Attention	Percentage of Observers Who Read Some of the Copy
Result of use	96.9	80.0
Product	101.7	77.7
Irrelevant	102.8	88.9
Product in use	106.4	78.7
Testimonial	110.5	88.1
Result of nonuse	122.7	88.6

From ADVERTISING: ITS ROLE IN MODERN MARKETING, Third Edition by S. Watson Dunn and Arnold M. Barban. Copyright © 1974, The Dryden Press, a division of Holt, Rinehart and Winston, Inc. Reprinted by permission of Holt, Rinehart and Winston.

reading some of the copy. The table also shows that certain types of pictures stimulate a greater level of attention.

The high rate of readership for the irrelevant illustration would suggest that people read the copy to discover the relationship between the illustration and the product or company sponsoring the advertisement. The low rate for the "product in use" could possibly be explained if the illustration tells a very complete story.

_____ Pictures, Images, and Arousal

Fairfax Cone of Foote, Cone and Belding advertising agency had this to say:

> In projecting symbols, the projection counts as much as the symbol itself. And this makes it possible for the basic symbol that may appear tired and unappealing, to become fresh and convincing through the use of real imagination. It's seldom sufficient that a symbol be recognized. It also must be seen in context and be appealing.[19]

To illustrate his point, Cone cites a photograph of a ship, taken in the daytime showing its full profile against the background of a bridge. This is contrasted to the picture of the midship section of a ship taken at night and glowing with lights at every porthole. Cone's point was that people do not travel by ship to go somewhere but take a ship today for the cruise aspect. A picture of a ship can now be considered the symbol for a cruise. The daytime shot appeared static and would be a poor communicator of fun and activity

---

[19]Fairfax M. Cone, "Symbology in Advertising," *Symbology*, Edward Whitney (ed.), New York: Hastings House, 1960, p. 20.

whereas the night photo could stimulate images of dancing and dining in the romantic atmosphere associated with cruises.

Advertising, Illustration, and Product Image

Two of the most successfully contrived product images created through advertising and illustrative matter were the Hathaway shirt and the Marlboro cigarette images. David Ogilvy, co-founder of Ogilvy and Mather Advertising, always attempted to tell a story with illustrations. He conceived the idea of placing an eye-patch on the Hathaway shirt model. The image created by this symbol was one of mystery, excitement, and intrigue. Besides attracting attention, the ads sold a lot of Hathaway shirts.

The story of Marlboro cigarette advertising is replete with symbols and imagery. When first introduced with a filter and crushproof package, research showed the product to have a strong feminine connotation. Sales were not large. The Leo Burnett advertising agency set about to create another image and, hence, a turnaround in sales. At the risk of losing women smokers, Burnett used nonprofessional, rugged-looking men for their television commercials. On the back of the models' hands were tattoos! The brand was accepted as the smoke for the man who took pride in his masculinity (subconsciously), and sales climbed. Interestingly enough, women purchased more cigarettes as well. Today the Marlboro man is a cowboy. The symbol is again of a rugged individualist battling the elements of nature and proving his masculinity.

Environmental Design and Institutional Rhetoric

According to Irving J. Rein, *institutional rhetoric* is a communication program that an institution employs to impart its philosophy and values on its workers, products, and customers. Architectural design is one of the tangible marks of institutional rhetoric as an overall communication environment affecting our daily lives. Rein illustrates his point with this example common to us all: "The supermarket, in its strange way, fairly bristles with communication. Its communication however, usually is one way—enticing, not reflective. Perhaps it is too much to expect a supermarket to reflect the more subtle nature of a sensitive communication environment. The sole object is to move food items through the store at as furious a pace as is legally allowable, without regard to whether Brand A is better than Brand B." [20]

A corporate design program considers such factors as office, plant, store, warehouse, etc., architecture and interior design. It also includes the use of

[20]Irving J. Rein, *The Great American Communication Catalogue.* Englewood Cliffs, N.J.: Prentice-Hall, 1976, pp. 3, 60.

uniforms if and when considered a part of the identification program. The buildings, the entrances, the reception rooms, the uniforms, and the offices of a business should carry through the same identification designs and colors as all other visual communications. These identifying characteristics must also reflect the image planned and desired by the visual communication program.

Retail establishments, stores, restaurants, and other service businesses must not only maintain the image created in promotional activities but are largely responsible for initial creation of the image. Robert McClure lists several of the physical components—or rhetorical elements—of environmental design and their effects. These include space or spatial relationships, form, sound, temperature, light, color, windows/views, and height. Elaborating on height, he suggests that a tall building is prominent, emphasizing place and is a visual landmark. It is a physical symbol of size, power, and bulk that inspires awe. A tall building is a builder's response to man's "mountain-mystique": people who view it respond to the same "mountain-mystique." A building taller than neighboring buildings overwhelms them with its height. The famous Empire State Building and the twin towers of the World Trade Center in New York City and the Sears Tower and the Hancock Building in Chicago are examples of the rhetoric or symbolism of height.[21]

Years ago, banks were designed to convey the image of solid and trustworthy institutions. The high ceilings and use of marble were similar to government buildings. The symbolism of governmental authority and reliability was used by the banking and financial industry. The concept of banking has changed and along with this has been a change in image and design. Banks today are designed to appear warm, friendly, and helpful. Environmentally, this has been done through the use of carpeting throughout, warm wood paneling, and upholstered and living room-like furniture. Framed pictures are on the walls and the atmosphere is casual. Partitions and high barriers have been removed to convey accessibility.

The banking industry is only one example. The trend to incorporate environmental design in the corporate design program is in evidence in most firms today. Not only is this true about the interior but extends to the exterior design. The Howard Johnson restaurants are easily identified by their orange roofs and cupolas, as are the golden arches of McDonald's and a host of others. The Hyatt Regency hotels all have individualized designs but the panoramic lobbies and elevators maintain a thread of continuity. Environmental and architectural design are also valuable publicity tools. The Transamerica Building in San Francisco serves for immediate identification of the parent company and its subsidiaries, and is used in many ways other than by the Transamerica Company. The Sears Tower in Chicago is now the world's largest building and a constant reminder of the world's largest retailing firm.

---

[21]Robert McClure, unpublished research, Northwestern University, 1980.

Graphic or visual aids are valuable supplements to the written and spoken word in affecting communication with your audience. There must be a need for a particular table, graph, chart, or illustration for it to be included in your report or presentation. Graphic aids should not be included because they are "pretty" or "impressive looking."

A graphic aid should be announced before it actually appears. Important points in the graphic aid should always be discussed. You should never assume that your reader or audience will pay attention to the aid or see the significant data in it. Honesty of presentation is very important and is achieved through careful attention and proper handling.

Graphic and visual aids enable you to communicate more effectively not only from the standpoint of improved content (the message itself), but also with the result of improved understanding.

The visual communicator uses symbols and signals in the creation of an image. A symbol is something that stands for something else, while a sign has a direct relationship to an object. The so-called corporate image is the concept of the business form held by its publics. It is a collective view one has about a company; its products, service, personnel, sense of responsibility, reputation and more, rolled into one. While visual communication does not create a corporate image, it can help mold or reinforce thoughts in the desired direction.

Whereas corporate design and visual identification were relatively unimportant some years ago, dramatic changes now have elevated design decisions to the presidents and members of the boards of directors of major corporations. Corporate design programs spell out just how design should be used throughout the entire company to provide a singular view of identification.

Trademarks and trade characters are often the backbone of an identification program. Color, form, style, and other ingredients are used to provide a bridge between all units, product areas, and communication in general for the business.

Color functions as a visual language conveying mood, attracting attention, arousing the senses, and adding height to description. Like design elements, color also has symbolic values that are felt and understood universally. A designer should know the properties of color as this knowledge will enable more effective use.

Art and photography can communicate. Photographs are particularly valuable in creating a sense of immediacy, believability, and reality in advertising. A picture is often helpful to complete a statement where words alone may not be able to convey a complete meaning.

Visual communication is a very useful business tool along with verbal and written forms. All have their place in business communication, working together and creating a total effect in attaining goals that may be greater or beyond the ability of just one medium alone.

1. What is a graphic aid?
2. What is the main criterion you should use when deciding whether to include a particular graphic or visual aid in a presentation?
3. How do visual or graphic aids help to improve understanding?
4. Why is it important to prepare your reader for a graphic aid before it is reached in the body of a report?
5. Why is it necessary to discuss important points presented in a graphic aid? (Discuss in terms of overall communication principles.)
6. What value do you see in a firm having a corporate design program?
7. Discuss some of the factors leading to high-level concern over corporate design.
8. Explain, with examples, the difference between a symbol and a sign.
9. Do you agree or disagree with the psychological values placed on the colors discussed in this chapter?
10. How important do you consider environmental design as a part of the corporate design program?
11. Discuss this quote: "A supermarket fairly bristles with communication."
12. What do you think the future holds for visual communication in business?

============ Projects

1. Select some graphic aids from a current news and/or business periodical. Have the principles discussed in this chapter been observed in the construction of the aids as well as in the text surrounding them?
2. Take the data from the above graphic aids and devise several other chart or graph forms to present them.
3. Examine current periodicals for unusual modifications or combinations of basic types of graphic aids disucssed in this chapter. Does the modified graphic aid result in more effective presentation of data? Explain.
4. Look through several magazines and locate those trademarks you can identify on sight. Cut them out; paste them on a sheet of paper and see how well others do in identifying the companies using the marks.
5. Examine some of the trademarks or trade characters you have found and analyze them by symbolic meaning.
6. Seek out advertisements by competitive companies and compare the overall effort at creating an image. Also compare the illustrative techniques used in their communications.

============Additional Reading

Ashley/Myer/Smith, *City Signs and Lights*. Boston: Boston Redevelopment Authority, 1971.

Ballinger, Louise Bowen and Raymond A. Ballinger, *Sign, Symbol and Form*. New York: Van Nostrand Reinhold, 1972.

Dawe, Jessamon and **William Jackson Lord, Jr.**, *Functional Business Communication.* Englewood Cliffs, N.J.: Prentice-Hall, 1968.

Hereg, Walter (ed.), *Graphis Annual, 73/74.* Zurich, Switzerland: The Graphis Press, 1973.

Huff, Darrell, *How to Lie with Statistics.* New York: W.W. Norton, 1954.

Kepes, Gyorgy, *Language of Vision.* Chicago: Paul Theobald, 1951.

Lesikar, Raymond V., *Business Communication*, 4th ed. Homewood, Ill.: Richard D. Irwin, 1980.

Menning, J.H., and **C.W. Wilkinson,** *Communicating through Letters and Reports.* Homewood, Ill.: Richard D. Irwin, 1972.

Meyers, Cecil H., *Handbook of Basic Graphics: A Modern Approach.* Belmont, Calif.: Dickenson, 1970.

Rein, Irving J., *The Great American Communication Catalogue.* Englewood Cliffs, N.J.: Prentice-Hall, 1976.

Rosen, Ben, *The Corporate Search for Visual Identity.* New York: Van Nostrand Reinhold, 1970.

Turabian, Kate L., *Manual for Writers of Term Papers, Theses and Dissertations*, 4th ed. Chicago: University of Chicago Press, 1973.

Whitney, Elwood (ed.), *Symbology.* New York: Hastings House, 1960.

Some Periodicals to Read:
> *Advertising Techniques*
> *Art Direction*
> *Communication Arts*
> *Graphics*
> *Interiors*

Business Communication: Applications

III

Communication with one: interviewing

10

key points to learn

The distinction between interviewing and casual conversation.

The types of interviews frequently encountered in business.

Ways of opening interviews.

Types and uses of interview questions.

Advantages and disadvantages of various interview structures.

Specific guidelines for participation in interviews.

Employment interview questions that are illegal.

In the minds of millions of people *interviewing* is equated with *job hunting*. Indeed, employment is the issue in more than fifteen million interviews every year.[1] However, employment is only one of many reasons for participating in an interview. Every business day millions of interviews occur for purposes of appraising performance, selling ideas or products, giving instructions, receiving instructions, handling grievances, or solving problems. Add to that list the number of purposeful one-to-one communication transactions between lawyers and their clients, doctors and their patients, teachers and their students, police and their publics, and journalists and their sources and you will *begin* to comprehend the many uses of interviewing in our contemporary society.

the interview defined

Consider the following definitions of interviewing:

Interviewing is a conversation directed to a definite purpose other than satisfaction in the conversation itself.[2]

---

[1]Vernon R. Taylor, "A Hard Look at the Selection Interview," *Public Personnel Review*, July, 1969, p. 149; Lynn Ulrich and Don Trumbo, "The Selection Interview Since 1949," *Psychological Bulletin*, 43 (1965), p. 100.

Interviewing is a form of oral communication involving two parties, at least one of whom has a predetermined and serious purpose and both of whom speak and listen from time to time.[3]

Interviewing is a specialized pattern of verbal interaction initiated for a specific purpose, and focused on some specific content area, with a subsequent elimination of extraneous material.[4]

Collectively, the three definitions yield the following identifying aspects of the interview:

1. Effective interviewing presumes *purpose*.
2. Effective interviewing requires *planning*.
3. Effective interviewing involves *interaction*.

_____ **Effective Interviewing Presumes Purpose**

Chance meetings in elevators, hallways, or parking lots may result in conversations, but they should not be considered interviews. You will note that each of the three definitions cited earlier includes some statement pertaining to *purpose*. The phrases "definite purpose," "predetermined and serious purpose," and "specific purpose" are key elements in those definitions. Broadly speaking, the purposes of interviews may be classified into three categories: (1) giving and getting information; (2) seeking belief or behavioral change; and (3) solving problems. We shall discuss each of the specific types of interviews in the next section of this chapter (job application, performance assessment, grievance, reprimand, exit, sales, counseling, consulting, and stress). Each serves one or more of the three general purposes.

Giving and Getting Information.   Perhaps the archetype of an information interview is the journalistic interview. We can readily understand the reporter's need to determine who, what, why, when, and where. The journalistic interview, however, is only one of many interviews that are informative in purpose. Although the job application interview may be predominantly persuasive from the applicant's viewpoint, it is usually information-seeking from the recruiter's point of view. In addition, business people frequently engage in fact-finding interviews as a necessary investigatory activity prior to successful reprimand, performance assessment, sales, or problem-solution interviews.

Information sought and obtained through interviews is both objective and subjective in nature. There are times when interviewers are *more* interested in

---

[2]Walter Van Dyke Bingham, Bruce V. Moore, and John W. Gustad, *How to Interview.* New York: Harper & Row, Pub., 1959, p. 3.

[3]Robert S. Goyer, W. Charles Redding, and John T. Rickey, *Interviewing Principles and Techniques: A Project Text.* Dubuque, Iowa: Kendall/Hunt, 1968. Copyright © 1968 by the authors. Used by permission.

[4]Robert L. Kahn and Charles F. Cannell, *The Dynamics of Interviewing.* New York: John Wiley, 1964, p. 16.

discovering attitudes, personality, communication ability, ambition, and motivation than they are in gaining factual or biographical data. As a matter of record, the interview has survived as a data-gathering tool in spite of money and time requirements *primarily* because it's the only known means of gaining certain subjective kinds of information.

Seeking Belief or Behavioral Change.   Whenever information is exchanged with a conscious attempt to modify the beliefs or actions of either or both of the participants, we say that the ultimate purpose is persuasion. Persuasion is the motivating force behind a variety of interviews—ranging from the high-pressure salesperson pushing a product to a guidance counselor providing career advice. Obviously, reprimand and grievance interviews are purposeful attempts at belief or behavior modification. There are times when the surface purpose of an interview is information giving or getting, but the real motive is persuasion. For example, upon reading a report a junior executive discovers several innovative proposals. Concerned that his or her own standing is too low to warrant his suggesting the proposals to the company president on his or her own, the junior executive asks for an appointment for the purpose of *sharing* the information in the report. It is hoped, of course, that the information will have a persuasive effect on the boss.

In a later section we shall distinguish between directive and nondirective counseling. For the moment it will suffice to point out that psychologists and other counselors (and some skilled employees) are able to seemingly be discussing ideas on a purely informative basis, when, in reality, they are providing just enough suggestions to allow the client, counselee, or employer to arrive at a desired attitude or behavior "independently."

Solving Problems.   The examples discussed earlier as persuasive interviews could be considered as problem solving, providing one requirement was met. That requirement is that one or both parties approach the interview with the hope of *discovering* rather than *advocating* a solution. In other words, if a guidance counselor has already reviewed a worker's files and determined *in advance* the advice that she hopes the worker will accept, we are dealing with a persuasive purpose. If, however, the guidance counselor and the worker approach the interview as an opportunity to *discover* the best course of action, we are dealing with a problem-solving purpose. At least in theory reprimand and grievance interviews are conducted for problem-solving purposes, as well as for persuasive purposes. When a worker has a grievance and really doesn't know a solution for the problem, the motive for consulting the supervisor involves problem solving. If the worker is trying to convince the supervisor of a solution that will eliminate the grievance, the motive is persuasion.

Interviews for the purpose of solving problems might well be approached from a reflective thinking or creative thinking perspective. The reflective thinking approach (defining problem, analyzing causes of problem, suggestion of possible solutions, comparison of solutions, careful analysis of the apparently best solution) and the creative thinking approach (preparation, incubation, illumination, and verification) are discussed in Chapter 4.

_____ Effective Interviewing Requires Planning

Contrary to popular opinion, successful interviews do not "just happen." Successful interviews are the result of careful planning and preparation on the part of one or both of the participants. "The lack of adequate planning for an interview," notes Samuel Trull in the *Harvard Business Review,* "is the greatest single fault found in my studies of the interviewing process."[5] Obviously, certain types of interviews allow for considerable preparation by the interviewer and only minimal preparation by the interviewee. A worker may surprise a supervisor by using the occasion of a regularly scheduled appraisal session for a carefully planned airing of grievances. On the other hand, workers seldom have adequate advance warning to carefully prepare for reprimand interviews.

The conversational nature of interviewing precludes the kind of detailed planning allowed by a public speech. However, at least one of the participants should carefully consider the following aspects of planning *prior* to the interview.

Determine Exactly What You Hope to Accomplish.   Are you seeking information? If so, how much? What kind of information do you need? Are you seeking belief or behavior change? What specific beliefs or behaviors need to be changed? If you fail in your primary persuasive effort, are there compromise secondary responses that should be sought? What kind of problem are you trying to solve? Will time limitations permit a careful weighing of potential solutions? You should never enter an interview that *you* have initiated without thinking through what you hope to accomplish.

Analyze the Other Person.   Try to learn all you can about the other person prior to the interview. Is it usually difficult or easy to get this person to talk? What are the probable objections which will be raised? Does this person have the power to make the decision you are soliciting? A review of the receiver and source variables discussed in Chapter 5 will suggest additional questions that you will want to ask in your analysis.

Analyze the Context.   Will the interview take place in your office? In a coffee shop? During a drive to the airport? Is it likely to be interrupted? What time of day will the interview occur? What routine activities usually precede and follow that time of day? Will those activities affect your partner in the interview? Again, a general review of the section on communication context in Chapter 5 should prove helpful in your analysis.

_____

[5]Trull, p. 89.

Determine Structure and Questions.   How will you accomplish your goal of gaining or giving information, persuading, or problem solving? Will it be best to begin with general questions, followed by more specific questions? Should you gain detailed information first, and then progress to the philosophical questions? How should you arrange the points in your sales pitch?

In problem-solving interviews, which would be more appropriate, the reflective or the creative approach? The message variables discussed in Chap-

Figure 10–1. The interview context is extremely important in determining the degree of openness exhibited by the interviewee. In general, the more formal the context, the more inhibited the communication between individuals. (Photo on top by Ann Chwatsky, de Wys, Inc.; photo to the left by P. Vannucci, de Wys, Inc.)

ter 5 should be reviewed especially in the preparation of sales talks. Separate sections of this chapter are devoted to detailed discussions of interview structure and use of questions.

<hr>

Effective Interviewing Involves Interaction

Interviewing involves dyadic interaction—interaction between two parties. Even when team or group interviewing methods are used, we are still dealing with *two* points of view. Such dyadic or two-party interaction distinguishes the interview from small group discussion where as many as five separate points of view may exist among five members of a committee.

Interviewing involves both verbal and nonverbal interaction. Nonverbal cues, significant in all forms of human communication, are especially salient in face-to-face interviews. Meaning is frequently attached to the slightest changes in facial expression or tone of voice. The interaction achieved in the interview results from massive, sustained, immediate, and direct feedback—both verbal and nonverbal. The feedback cues demand moment-to-moment adaptations on the part of each participant.

The give-and-take conversational nature of the interview is essential for success. Many interviews owe their failure to accomplish the predetermined purpose to an over-talkative interviewer. Whether in sales, performance assessment, counseling, or job application interviews, interviewers must allow interviewees to participate frequently on the verbal and nonverbal levels. Goyer, Redding, and Rickey have observed: "Indeed, it is probably safe to suggest that if an expository interviewer finds himself talking uninterruptedly for as long as *two minutes*, he very likely is failing to 'get through' to his interviewee." [6]

<hr>

A Composite Definition of Interviewing

Based on our discussion of the distinguishing aspects of interviewing suggested in the definitions of earlier writers, we define interviewing as *purposeful, planned conversation, characterized by massive verbal and nonverbal interaction.*

types of interviews

We have already discussed information giving and getting, belief or behavior modification, and problem solving as the three general purposes for conducting interviews. There are many specific types of interviews to accomplish one or more of those general purposes.

<hr>

[6]Goyer, p. 14.

The role of interviewing in the hiring of employees is suggested in a recent American Management Association publication:

> Without exception, interviewing is the one technique universally used to help make decisions about job applicants and promotees. Even when interviewing is practiced in conjunction with other screening methods, it emerges as the most critical, pivotal, and potentially powerful technique.[7]

Estimates of the number of employment interviews conducted annually range from a low of 10 million to a high of 150 million. Regardless of whether we accept the higher or lower estimate, the number is staggering and the total cost is beyond calculation. Despite time and monetary requirements, we continue to use the interview in the hiring of personnel. Why? What does the employment interview accomplish that offsets the time and money loss involved? First, employers hope to discover information about the applicant— information not available by any other method. A well-prepared resume can convey biographical data, and letters of recommendation can suggest other people's estimates of the applicant. To gain insights into the applicant's general attitude, overall personality, ambition, motivation, and ability to communicate, however, a face-to-face meeting is often necessary. Second, employment interviews should provide the applicant with an opportunity to gain insights into specific job requirements and other matters of concern that are not discussed in available company brochures. The cost of training new employees makes the problem of turnover a special concern for most employers. We can only assume that employees who have an *accurate* picture of job requirements *prior* to accepting a position will be more likely to continue their employment than will employees who take their jobs without fully understanding their negative as well as positive aspects. Finally, the employment interview should build positive public relations for the company. Several recent studies have indicated that from thirty to fifty applicants are interviewed for each one hired by large, prestigious companies.[8] With such extensive interviewing prior to filling one position, the potential for public relations is tremendous.

_____ Performance Assessment Interviews

The selection process in hiring employees is far from infallible. Consequently, we do not always get the right person for the right job. In addition, there is no way of anticipating all the problems a new employee will

---

[7]Dean B. Peskin, *Human Behavior and Employment Interviewing.* New York: American Management Association, 1971, p. 10.

[8]Calvin W. Downs, "Perceptions of the Selection Interview," *Personnel Administration,* May-June 1969, p. 8; *Wall Street Journal,* Apr. 10, 1972, p. 1.

face once work is begun. These problems, coupled with the ever-changing environment in most organizations, have led to increased use of performance assessment or appraisal interviews. Such interviews usually involve communication between an employee and the immediate supervisor and range in frequency of occurrence from once a week to once a year. Norman Maier suggests several functions of performance assessment interviews:

> At the present time management supervisors conduct appraisal interviews with subordinates to (a) let them know where they stand; (b) recognize their good work; (c) communicate to them the directions in which they should improve; (d) develop them on their present jobs; (e) develop and train them for higher jobs; (f) let them know the direction in which they may make progress in the company; (g) serve as a record for assessment of the department or unit as a whole and show where each person fits into the larger picture; and (h) warn certain employees that they must improve.[9]

Although we are accustomed to thinking of the appraisal interview serving information-giving and information-getting purposes, supervisors also may use the appraisal session for persuasive and problem-solving purposes. Maier has noted the characteristics of appraisal interviews planned to accomplish each of the three general interview purposes.

TELL AND LISTEN APPRAISALS

Objectives: To communicate evaluation; to release defensive feelings.

Psychological Assumptions: People will change if defensive feelings are removed.

Role of Interviewer: Judge

Attitude of Interviewer: One can respect the feelings of others if one understands them.

Skills of Interviewer: Listening and reflecting feelings; summarizing.

Reactions of Employee: Expresses defensive behavior; feels accepted.

Employee's Motivation for Change: Resistance to change reduced; positive incentive; extrinsic and some intrinsic motivation.

Possible Gains: Employee develops favorable attitude toward superior, which increases probability of success.

Risks of Interviewer: Need for change may not be developed.

Probable Results: Permits interviewer to change his views in light of employee's responses; some upward communication.

TELL AND SELL APPRAISALS

Objectives: To communicate evaluation; to persuade employee to improve.

Psychological Assumptions: Employee desires to correct weaknesses if he knows them; any person can improve if she so chooses; a superior is qualified to evaluate a subordinate.

Role of Interviewer: Judge

Attitude of Interviewer: People profit from criticism and appreciate help.

---

[9]Norman R. F. Maier, *The Appraisal Interview: Objectives, Methods, and Skills.* New York: John Wiley, 1958, p. 3.

Skills of Interviewer: Salesmanship; patience.

Reactions of Employee: Suppresses defensive behavior; attempts to cover hostility.

Employee's Motivation for Change: Use of positive or negative incentives or both; extrinsic motivation is added to the job itself.

Possible Gains: Success most probable when employee respects interviewer.

Risks of Interviewer: Loss of loyalty; inhibition of independent judgment; face-saving problems created.

Probable Results: Perpetuates existing practices and values.

PROBLEM-SOLVING APPRAISALS

Objectives: To stimulate growth and development in employee.

Psychological Assumptions: Growth can occur without correcting faults; discussing job problems leads to improved performance.

Role of Interviewer: Helper

Attitude of Interviewer: Discussion develops new ideas and mutual interests.

Skills of Interviewer: Listening and reflecting feelings; reflecting ideas; using exploratory questions; summarizing.

Reactions of Employee: Problem-solving behavior.

Employee's Motivation for Change: Increased freedom; increased responsibility; intrinsic motivation—interest is inherent in the task.

Possible Gains: Almost assured of improvement in some respect.

Risks of Interviewer: Employee may lack ideas; change may be other than what superior had in mind.

Probable Results: Both learn, because experience and views are pooled; change is facilitated.[10]

_____ Counseling Interviews

A realtor friend of one of the authors of this text recently asked the question: "Have you ever had any experience in preventing suicides?" When we inquired as to why he was asking the question, he told us of an employee who was threatening suicide. The employee's marriage was breaking up; a son was on heavy drugs; one of the employee's parents had recently died; the other parent was sick; and finally, the employee had undergone two cancer operations within a period of sixty days. It is hoped that occasions of counseling involving employees with that many drastic problems are rare. However, alcoholism, inability to cope with stress and strain prompted by new responsibilities, drug abuse, and marital problems *do become company problems* when they prevent employees from doing their jobs. Managers need not always have the ability to *solve* the personal problems of employees, but they must be willing to lend a sympathetic ear and know the procedures for referral in cases requiring professional counseling. James Lahiff offers advice to managers

_____

[10]Norman R. F. Maier, *The Appraisal Interview: Three Basic Approaches*. La Jolla, Calif.: University Associates, 1976, p. 20. Used with permission.

regarding the creation of a climate suitable for counseling interviews. A proper climate will be created if the interviewer:

1. Secures the trust of the interviewee, possibly through the assurance that the information the interviewee provides will remain confidential.
2. Maintains a permissive atmosphere, one in which the interviewee will feel free to introduce any subject into the discussion without fear of offending, alienating, or embarrassing the interviewer.
3. Is nondirective in approach so that the interviewee, rather than the interviewer, will determine the subjects to be considered.
4. Is nonevaluative in words and demeanor. The interviewer should accept what the interviewee says, without any indication of approval or disapproval.
5. Empathizes with the interviewee. An empathic interviewer is able to sense the feelings and personal meaning of the interviewee as though he or she personally were experiencing them.[11]

Counseling interviews in business and industry are generally conducted for the purpose of solving a particular problem encountered by the employee. However, the purpose becomes persuasive if the interviewer is seeking to impose a predetermined solution on the interviewee.

_____ Reprimand Interviews

Being a supervisor would be considerably more enjoyable if employees always followed instructions and never needed to be disciplined. Without doubt, the least appealing part of a supervisor's work comes when employees must be confronted in a reprimand interview session.

Properly handled, however, the reprimand interview need not leave a bitter taste in the mouth of either the supervisor or the employee. The interview should be scheduled at a time when an "unhurried" atmosphere can prevail. The employee should be told that a problem apparently exists, and that the purpose of the interview is to determine the exact nature of the problem, and enable the employee to understand the policies and behaviors that are expected. Following a brief statement of the problem, the supervisor should invite the employee to tell his or her side of the story. In most cases the supervisor will gain information that will alter perceptions somewhat. A rational discussion will be easier to conduct if the supervisor refrains from temptation to "preach" to the employee before hearing the employee's story. It will be easier for supervisors to avoid accusatory beginnings if they wait until they have "cooled down" before arranging the reprimand interview. Too many supervisors discover a mistake and initiate a spur-of-the-moment encounter while they are "mad as hell."

---

[11]James M. Lahiff, "Interviewing for Results," in _Readings in Interpersonal and Organizational Communication._ Boston: Holbrook Press, 1973, pp. 341–342.

A reprimand interview should not conclude without the employee knowing exactly where he or she stands. Will additional disciplinary actions be taken? If so, what kind, and when? Can the employee appeal the disciplinary actions which the supervisor is imposing? If so, how? Above all else, the interview should conclude with a reminder that the discipline, whether in the form of a verbal warning or monetary penalty, will be confined to the issue at hand, and need not disrupt the working relationship between the supervisor and the employee in the future.

The most extreme form of reprimand is the firing of an employee. When this action becomes necessary, the employee should be told at the beginning of the interview that employment is being terminated. Rather than dwelling on what good things the employee has done for the company, the supervisor should explain the reasons for the termination and proceed immediately into an explanation of the termination process, with special attention given to such matters as severance pay, insurance benefits, and retirement funds. Although the interview will be unpleasant for both parties, and neither will want to unnecessarily prolong it, time should be allowed for questions from the employee. One question likely to be asked involves the kind of reference which the supervisor will forward to potential future employers. An honest answer is a must in this situation. You have nothing to gain, and the employee has everything to lose if you as a supervisor dodge this question.

Grievance Interviews

Grievance interviews are in many respects reprimand interviews in reverse. The need for these interviews may be lessened through effective management techniques. However, when a subordinate feels that a particular problem should be brought to the attention of a superior and arranges for a formal appointment to air the complaint, a grievance interview is appropriate. Grievance interviews present some unique problems that are not encountered in reprimand interviews. The status and power differences between the employee and the supervisor serve as considerable obstacles to free and open discussion of grievances. Many supervisors are unable to discuss grievances without experiencing extreme ego threats. The overreactions of some superiors to subordinate complaints are all too similar to that of ancient kings who were said to have cut off the heads of bearers of bad news. In corporations subject to union contracts, grievance procedures are usually specified in considerable detail. However, a more satisfactory solution to the problem will likely emerge if the principles of good interviewing are followed. For example, the employee should allow the supervisor to explain his or her side of the story immediately following the statement of the grievance. This will produce a foundation on which to build a rational discussion that will be more productive than ten minutes of "blowing off steam."

The fact that hundreds and sometimes thousands of dollars are invested in hiring and training an employee necessitates retention of valuable workers. Every year job turnovers require the expenditure of millions of dollars in the form of recruitment, training, and lost man hours as new employees are fitted into their jobs. Obviously, it is in the best interest of a company to keep turnovers at an absolute minimum. Consequently, whenever an employee voluntarily terminates employment, an exit interview should be conducted in an effort to determine the reasons for resigning. Lahiff points out, however, that obtaining the employee's *real* reasons for quitting may not be an easy task. He suggests several obstacles to successful exit interviewing:

> In the exit interview the interviewer is confronted with a number of unique obstacles to frank disclosure of reasons for leaving the job. A feeling of suspicion on the part of the interviewee is one of them. It is natural for him to wonder why, all of a sudden, has the company gotten interested in his thoughts and feelings. Another obstacle is presented by the interviewee's desire, often unspoken, to get a favorable recommendation from his employer. Another possible explanation for the interviewee's hesitancy to give reasons is his wish to keep a "foot in the door" by departing on a pleasant note and hence making it possible to return to this employer should his plans for the new job go awry.[12]

The interviewer may be able to overcome some of these obstacles by assuring the employee that information obtained in the exit interview will in no way affect future employment references. In addition, the interviewer must appeal to the interviewee's highest motives in seeking reasons for resignation. Basic areas that should be probed include strengths and weaknesses in supervisory methods, general working conditions, and pros and cons of company hiring policies.

The interviewer who prepares in advance of conducting an exit interview will know when to suspect "hidden" reasons for an employee's leaving the company. For example, the employee's prior employment record should be examined. You may simply be dealing with a job-hopper. Note the employee's physical condition. Does the employee lack the physical ability to continue in the assigned job? What is the employee's level of education? Educated people are more likely to become bored very quickly with menial jobs. What is the age of the employee? Younger employees change jobs more frequently than older employees. When you are confronted with an older employee's resignation, it is important to dig for the reasons for leaving.

The timing of the exit interview is of extreme importance. The interview should come somewhere near the end of the employment period, but should

---

[12]Ibid., p. 345.

not take place on the employee's last day with the company, when the employee's mind is likely to be filled with the details of severance procedures.

As a general rule, employees who are fired are not interviewed in a formal exit interview session. In cases where the firing results from unavoidable circumstances (loss of contracts from major clients, general economic cutbacks), however, the company may find the employee willing to submit to exit evaluation proceedings.

Other Specialized Interview Types

There is no general agreement as to how many different types of interviews actually exist. Consequently, we make no pretense of having discussed every conceivable type of interview in which one day you may participate. Before moving on to the next section, however, we shall briefly mention several additional types of interviews.

Induction Interviews.   Induction interviews are primarily informational in nature. After workers have been hired, they frequently are interviewed by their immediate supervisors for purposes of explaining specific operating procedures and expectations.

Consulting Interviews.   In today's complex company departmental structures, it is often necessary for members of one department to consult with members of another department prior to final adoption of policies or promotional campaigns. In addition, the bringing in of outside experts on a consultancy basis is still a frequent practice. Such interviews serve informational and problem-solving purposes.

Sales Interviews.   Sales interviews involve the selling of everything from schemes to skyscrapers. The basic principles of persuasion discussed in Chapter 7 will be useful in your planning for sales interviews. You will find William Howell's suggestions on pp. 139 particularly relevant. Remember, this is a sales *interview* rather than a sales talk! You should include your client in the communication process whenever possible.

Data-Gathering Interviews.   Usually, we think of data-gathering interviews as the stock in trade of newspaper and television reporters or the method used by the Gallup or Harris pollsters. However, such interviews are used increasingly outside the company in marketing research, and inside the company as materials are gathered from various department supervisors in preparation for policy determination and program planning.

Order-Giving Interviews.   Subordinates are frequently called into the boss's office for instructional reasons. Here the emphasis is on clear and accurate understanding of the instructions.

interview structure and content

At the same time that interviews resemble conversations in their informality and spontaneous interaction between the participants, the element of "purposeful planning" necessitates some form of structure. Although the structure will vary from a rigid, predetermined format to a loose collection of general topics or questions to be covered, most interviews share three common phases of development: an opening, a body, and a closing.

The Opening

A business card given to one of the authors of this text by a hair stylist contains the warning: "Remember, you only get one chance to make a first impression." Such advice might well be offered to interviewers. Regardless of whether you are seeking information, selling products or ideas, or attempting to solve a problem, the atmosphere established during the first few minutes will directly affect the interview outcome. Because of the process of receiver-self feedback, interviewees will be more likely to respond favorably to the second phase of your interview if they responded favorably to the first phase. Without consuming an unnecessary amount of time, you will need to develop an opening that *establishes rapport* and effectively *introduces the major content* of the interview.

Space would not permit even attempting to list all the possible techniques for opening an interview. However, the following list does suggest a few of the more popular openings.

1. Begin with a brief statement or rapid summary of a problem facing the interviewee and/or the interviewer. This technique is particularly effective when the interviewee is vaguely aware that the problem exists, but is not well informed about the details.
2. Begin with a brief explanation of how you (the interviewer) learned about the problem's existence, followed by a suggestion that the interviewee will probably want to discuss the problem with you. This technique encourages a spirit of cooperative, objective discussion of a mutual problem.
3. Begin by stating an interviewee goal that may be realized if your proposal is adopted. This technique can be either powerful or "corny" depending on the degree of honesty and sincerity you are able to convey to the interviewee.
4. Begin by requesting advice or help from the interviewee regarding a specific problem. This technique demands sincerity. If the interviewee views such an opening as a slick gimmick, you will begin with a serious disadvantage.
5. Begin by stating or striking fact. This technique is especially appropriate when a real emergency exists, and when the interviewee is apathetic and in need of arousal.
6. Begin by referring to the interviewee's known position on the particular problem. This technique is excellent in situations when the interviewee has taken a

public position, has asked the interviewer to bring in proposals, or when strong opposition from the interviewee is expected.

7. Begin by referring to the background (causes, origin, etc.) leading up to a problem, without actually stating the problem itself. This technique is useful when the interviewee is familiar with aspects of the background, but is likely to react in a hostile manner upon discovering what your proposal really is.

8. Begin by stating the name of the person who sent you to the interviewee. This technique is especially appropriate when the interviewee is a stranger, and an "entree" is needed. Two restrictions apply, however. The allegation must be true, and the third party must be respected by the interviewee.

9. Begin by stating the company, organization, or group that you represent. This technique results in added prestige for the interviewer and provides the interviewee with an explanation of why you are calling.

10. Begin by requesting a specified, brief period of time. You will need to avoid sounding overly apologetic when using this opening. The request for a brief period of time is most appropriate when you are dealing with an interviewee who is impatient, irritable, or very busy.

11. Begin with a question. The question may be either leading, yes-response, or direct interrogation. This technique compels the interviewee to respond in some manner, thus immediately becoming involved in the interaction process.[13]

_____ The Body of the Interview

Regardless of the type of opening that you use, you will want to exercise caution in preventing the use of too much of your allotted time in accomplishing introductory tasks. The major portion of your interview needs to be reserved for the asking and answering of questions, the seeking of solutions for problems, or the attempting to persuade the interviewee to buy your product or your idea. It would be safe to suggest that 95 percent of a 30-minute interview should be devoted to this phase.

Structuring the Body of the Interview. The degree of structure imposed on the interview by the interviewer will vary according to the purpose of the interview, type of interview, and time limitations. Interview structure is frequently described as *nonscheduled, moderately-scheduled, highly-scheduled,* and *highly-scheduled-standardized.*[14]

Nonscheduled interviews involve no advance scheduling or arranging of questions by the interviewer. The interviewer simply thinks through the purpose and determines a few possible topics or subtopics that will need to be explored.

Moderately scheduled interviews involve an advance scheduling or arranging of the *major* questions to be asked. In addition, optional probing questions

---

[13]Adapted from Goyer, pp. 10–11.

[14]Charles J. Stewart and William B. Cash, *Interviewing: Principles and Practices.* Dubuque, Iowa: William C. Brown, 1974, pp. 81–85.

are prepared as potential follow-ups to each major question. The optional probes are used only if the interviewee fails to provide the information which the probe is designed to gain.

Highly scheduled interviews involve an advance scheduling or arranging of *all* questions that will be asked, and those questions are asked in exactly the same way to each interviewee. Although some of the questions may be open-ended, most interviews of this type heavily rely on close-ended questions.

Highly scheduled-standardized interviews involve an advance scheduling or arranging of *all* questions and each answer option. Consequently, all questions are close-ended. For example, an interviewer might ask: "Do you antici-pate the automobile industry will be better, _____ worse, _____, or about the same _____ five years from now?"

Each type of scheduling has its advantages and disadvantages. You will want to consider carefully the purpose of the interview and the kinds of responses you will be seeking before deciding on a particular interview schedule. To assist you in considering the advantages and disadvantages of each schedule type, consider the following diagram in Figure 10–2.

Types of Questions.   The major portion of the body of an interview normally consists of questions and responses. Most likely, the role of questioner and respondent will alternate between the interviewer and the interviewee as the interview progresses. With questions and responses such a major part of the interview, it follows that the quality of questions and the kind of questions asked will directly influence the outcome of the interview. Consequently, you will want to become familiar with the basic types of questions and their uses.

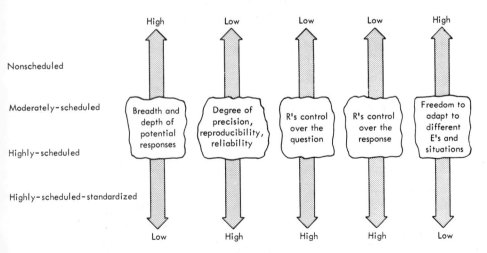

Figure 10–2   Advantages and disadvantages of four interview structure options. From Charles J. Stewart and William B. Cash, *Interviewing: Principles and Practices.* Dubuque, Iowa: Wm. C. Brown, 1974, p. 85. Adapted from B. Berelson and G. Steiner, *Human Behavior: An Inventory of Scientific Findings.* New York: Harcourt Brace Jovanovich, 1964, p. 30. Used by permission of Harcourt Brace Jovanovich, Inc. and Wm. C. Brown Company.

1. *The Direct Question.* When specific replies are sought on a definite topic, direct questioning is most often used. This kind of questioning is called *close-ended,* in that it permits the respondent little or no freedom of selection in response. *Examples:* "What was your major in college?" "How long did you work for Consolidated Industries?" In each of these examples the questioner is seeking and generally will receive specific, factual data.

2. *Bipolar Questions.* If for any reason the questioner wishes to limit the potential responses beyond the limitations imposed by direct questions, bipolar questions may be asked. While it may be argued legitimately that questions limiting potential responses to one of two possible answers are simply a subtype of direct questions, such questions are used with a great deal of frequency and probably deserve separate treatment. *Examples:* "Do you live here in the city?" "Can you come to work by the first of June?"

3. *The Open-Ended Question.* This kind of question allows the respondent maximum freedom in responding. *Examples:* "Tell me about yourself." "Describe the college level courses that you think might help people become better interviewers." "What are your reactions to the new contract with the union?" Although open questions may provide the questioner with an index of the respondent's ability to think, and may result in fruitful areas of discussion not previously anticipated by the questioner, considerable thought should go into their selection and use. Otherwise, a lot of time may be wasted in gaining answers to a few very general questions.

4. *The Laundry-List Question.* In *The Evaluation Interview: Predicting Job Performance in Business and Industry,* Richard Fear discusses a specific type of open question which he labels the *laundry-list* question. Fear is referring to the kind of question that may be asked to assist a respondent who is "blocking" mentally, and is unable to provide any appropriate response. *Example:* Assume that the respondent experienced a mental block when asked the question, "What do you look for in a job?" The questioner could come to the aid of the respondent by providing a laundry-list to stimulate the respondent's thinking: "You know what I mean. Some people are only interested in the money; others are concerned about working conditions; others are looking for long-term security, and others are concerned with the fringe benefits."

5. *The Yes-Response Question.* In Chapter 7 you were introduced to the value of the yes-response question. A series of questions resulting in affirmative answers will increase the potential of "yes" answers to questions that follow the series. Some authorities prefer to classify these kinds of questions as *leading* questions, and they suggest that the lead may be in a negative as well as a positive direction. *Examples:* "Don't you think the weather has been awful lately?" "You do agree that this is a good policy, don't you?" "There's no reason why a person with your income couldn't afford a monthly payment of $40, is there?" (This last example illustrates the desire of the salesperson to elicit a "no" response. In reality, however, a "no" by the respondent is an affirmative answer for the salesperson.)

6. *The Loaded Question.* The emotional loading of the words in some

questions indicates the desired response of the questioner. Such questions are sometimes used when the questioner is seeking to determine the respondent's reactions under stress, and when the questioner hopes to "crack" the respondent—that is, cause the respondent to become so angry or so emotional that true feelings or honest answers will emerge. An obvious example of such a stimulus followed by the sudden response that would not otherwise have been volunteered is as follows:

"Johnson, I have been informed by a reliable source that you weren't really sick yesterday. You were just too lazy to crawl out of the sack!"
"That's a lie, and I've got the fish to prove it!"

Other examples of loaded questions include: "What do you think about the stupid mistake the president made?" "How should we react to this ridiculous contract?"

7. *The Mirror Question.* You will recall from Chapter 4 that one authority has called the *tendency to evaluate* the major barrier to effective communication. In public speech situations we are unable to stop the speaker long enough to make sure that we fully comprehend what was meant by a statement. However, in the interview it is possible to *reflect* what you think you heard the respondent say by asking a brief summary question. *Example:* "Oh, then you're saying that you *favor* the new contract?"

8. *The Probing Question.* Frequently, the initial response given to a question may be lacking in detail or may indicate the need for a follow-up question. Consequently, the questioner may need to ask for additional information. *Examples:* "Could you give me an example of what you mean by poor management techniques?" "I don't think I understand what you mean by that." "Which of those reasons would you judge most important?" "Why?"

9. *The Hypothetical Question.* When the questioner wishes to determine how the respondent might handle some potential job-related situation, imaginary instances may be used to elicit such information. These questions are also useful in discovering prejudices, stereotypes, and other indices of respondent attitudes. *Example:* "Let's assume that you discover one of your employees using drugs during the lunch hour. What would you do?"

Sequencing of Questions.   You should give considerable thought to the sequencing of the questions that you have selected to use in a particular interview. The major sequencing patterns include the *funnel* sequence, the *inverted funnel* sequence, and the *tunnel* sequence.

The funnel sequence is characterized by broad, open-ended questions, followed by increasingly more specific, close-ended questions. The following list of questions follows a funnel sequence:

Tell me about yourself.
Tell me about your hobbies.
Which of those hobbies do you most enjoy?

How long have you been playing golf?
Have you ever played in golf tournaments?
What is your golf handicap?

The inverted funnel sequence begins with close-ended, specific questions and proceeds to the more general, open-ended questions. The questions below were taken from an employment interview in a placement center at a major university. They clearly follow the inverted funnel pattern.

So, you're a management major and advertising minor. Is that right?
I see your grade point average in your major was 3.2. Approximately what kind of overall GPA do you have?
When would you be able to begin work? About a week after graduation?
Why did you decide to interview for this job?
Where do you hope to be ten years from now?
Describe the characteristics that you think the ideal manager should possess.

The tunnel sequence is a series of similar questions. The questions may be all open-ended or all close-ended. You will want to use this type of sequence when your desire is to obtain initial answers to each separate question without asking follow-up probes. The following list is an example of the tunnel sequence.

Briefly describe your attitude toward automation.
Briefly describe your attitude toward labor unions.
Briefly describe your attitude toward profit sharing.
Briefly describe your attitude toward management by objectives.

Closing the Interview.   When the specified time limitations for the interview have been exhausted; when the information sought has been obtained; when persuasive goals have been realized; when the problem has been solved; or when it becomes apparent that further communication will be unproductive, the interviewer should close the interview. Generally, we suggest that interviews may be terminated by (1) briefly summarizing the accomplishments of the interview or the points of view expressed, (2) expressing gratitude to the interviewee for participating in the interview, or (3) agreeing on the next meeting or the actions that should follow the interview. Below are examples of each of these types of closing statements:

Brief Summary

"O.K. now, Charlotte, let me see if I have all of this right. You would consider our offer under the following circumstances. We would need to come up with another

$3,000. As I told you, I don't see any problem there. You would have to be assigned here in the New York office. That will be a little tougher. I'll get you an answer on that within a couple of days. Finally, you feel that you couldn't start work until September. On that, we will just have to see what the board wants to do. At our last meeting, we were of the opinion that we needed to fill this position by the first of July. Have I missed anything? . . . Very good! It's been my pleasure interviewing you. You'll hear from me in about a week."

Expression of Gratitude

"Well, that's all my questions for today. I certainly appreciate your taking the time to give me this information. If I can ever be of any assistance to you, just call."

Specifying Future Actions

"Well, if you have no further questions, Gerry, I'll let you take those forms home with you. Be sure to fill out both sides of the blue form. Now, you will get those back to us by next Tuesday, right? O.K! We will have our meeting on Wednesday afternoon and will be able to let you know our decision by noon on Thursday. Where will I be able to contact you Thursday morning? . . . All right, you will hear from us one way or the other next Thursday morning."

As the illustration of the brief summary indicates, the close may indeed be a combination of all three modes of concluding the interview. You may want to thank the individual, summarize your accomplishments, and specify what happens next in your concluding remarks.

At the risk of stating the obvious, we will close our discussion of concluding interviews with the reminder that your conclusion will include nonverbal as well as verbal behaviors. Very frequently, the close is indicated by the interviewer rising and extending a hand to the interviewee, or moving slowly toward the door. Sometimes the close will be initiated by the simple act of placing a cap on the end of a fountain pen and placing that fountain pen in your pocket, or by shuffling together all of the forms in front of you and stacking them neatly over to one side. All of these behaviors nonverbally indicate that you have concluded note taking, and, consequently, the substantive part of the interview is over.

suggestions for participants

In this final section, we shall simply list suggestions for effective participation in interviews. Our suggestions are divided into two categories: (1) interviews in general, and (2) employment interviews.

Anderson, Nichols, and Booth have listed several suggestions for participation in interviews. They provide their advice in three sections: (1) advice for both participants, (2) advice for the interviewer, and (3) advice for the respondent:

for both participants

1. Provide comfortable and cheerful physical surroundings.
2. Try to equalize status relationships.
3. Keep distractions to a minimum.
4. Concentrate both physically and mentally on the matter at hand.
5. Look pleasant and appear interested in the other person; smile.
6. Show by your facial expression that you are reacting to what has been said; avoid nonverbal manifestations of disapproval.
7. Speak directly to the other person.
8. Try to control nervous mannerisms.
9. Avoid too much warm-up (opening).
10. Avoid too lengthy a closing.
11. Avoid premature evaluation and judgment.
12. Identify your own prejudices, and attempt to keep them out of the interview situation.
13. Avoid arguing.
14. Analyze the situation in advance, and plan ahead.
15. Keep the purpose of the interview constantly in mind.
16. Avoid excessive note taking and excessive use of prepared notes.
17. Listen carefully and objectively.

for the interviewer

1. Show by actions that the respondent is welcome if he or she has come to your office for the interview.
2. Have a tentative structure for the interview planned.
3. Do not keep looking at your watch.
4. Avoid any actions that suggest boredom, lack of interest, disbelief, or opposition.
5. Have any needed equipment, supplies, or literature readily available.
6. Ask types of questions that will best achieve the objectives.
7. Be willing to understand the respondent's attitude and behavior, even though you may not approve.
8. Delay evaluation or judgment until you have all the information.
9. Wait patiently for answers; do not interrupt.
10. In the words of Balinski and Burger, your responsibility is to:

> Probe, not cross-examine
> Inquire, not challenge

Suggest, not demand
Uncover, not trap
Draw out, not pump
Guide, not dominate.

for the respondent

1. Take cues from the interviewer on degree of formality.
2. Sit down only when asked to do so.
3. Be prepared to take notes, if it is necessary to record information.
4. Don't smoke unless invited to do so.
5. Leave promptly when the interview is over.
6. Be neat and conservative in your appearance.
7. Prepare ahead of time by anticipating questions that might be asked.
8. Answer questions honestly and completely.
9. Don't attempt to bluff; be willing to say, "I don't know."
10. Generally attempt to expand your responses beyond a simple "yes" or "no."
11. Be polite, but friendly.
12. Keep your emotions in check.
13. Be sincere—be yourself.[15]

_____ Participating In Employment Interviews

All interviews discussed in this chapter can at one point or another become extremely important to each of us. The employment interview is, however, the interview situation that affords the most immediate reward to the interviewee. Consequently, we shall supplement the general advice about interview participation with some specific suggestions for the applicant and the employer in the employment interview.

Goyer, Redding, and Ricky provide several suggestions for the applicant and the employer involved in a job application interview:

specific suggestions for the applicant

1. Clarify the job requirements.
2. State why you are applying for this job with the company.
3. Present your qualifications in terms of having something of value to offer the company. Deal as much as possible in specific details and examples—job experiences, avocations, travel, activities, offices held, organizations, and school work.
4. Do not hesitate to admit potential weaknesses. Under no circumstances should you attempt to bluff or fake on these but wherever possible, make a transition from a weakness to a strength; or at least, when the facts justify it, show some

_____

[15]Martin P. Anderson, E. Ray Nichols, Jr., and Herbert W. Booth, *The Speaker and His Audience: Dynamic Interpersonal Communication.* New York: Harper & Row, Pub., 1974, pp. 495–497.

good extenuating circumstances for the weakness. (This does not mean supplying alibis or excuses!)

5. Do not depend merely on a "smooth front" (appearance and smile) to "sell yourself." Provide full information to the prospective employer.

6. Get as much information as possible on such "sensitive" matters as salary (usually in terms of a range, or of the going average).

7. Let the employer set the tone or atmosphere of the interview. Be a little more formal than usual—but not a stuffed shirt!! Be cautious about jokes, wisecracks, sarcastic asides, etc.!

8. Watch the opening moments of the interview. Avoid making remarks that create a "negative set" for the rest of the interview. Be positive. Avoid starting the interview with a remark such as: "I'm really not sure that my background will be appropriate for your company, or for this job." Or: "I'm sorry to say I haven't had any experience along these lines."

9. Be informed about the company: its history, geographical locations, general methods of doing business, reputation, etc.

10. Try never to have an interview concluded without some sort of understanding about where you stand, what is to happen next, who is to contact whom, etc. This does not mean you are to push the employer against the wall and force a definite commitment!

specific suggestions for the employer

1. Take the initiative in getting the interview under way; don't just sit back and stare at the applicant. Offer your hand first. Ask the applicant to be seated. Establish "rapport" before probing for pertinent information!

2. Make an easy, casual, smooth transition from opening greetings to the first serious topic of the interview.

3. Start off with "easy" materials and aspects on the applicant's background that are not sensitive areas. Encourage the applicant to talk freely about something which, according to the application blank, should be easy for him or her to discuss with specific details and examples.

4. Don't give a "sales pitch."

5. Do more listening than talking. Encourage the applicant to "open up." Listen carefully—including "between the lines." Insert brief "prompters" to encourage more talk; use "mirror" (turn-back) techniques.

6. Don't exaggerate the benefits of the company or the job! Create confidence and trust by being honest about potential or actual drawbacks.

7. Avoid evaluative comments on the applicant's answers such as "that's too bad," or "I'm certainly glad you said that!"

8. Without being mechanical about it, try to cover topics in a systematic order. Your objective is not only to avoid hit-and-miss jumping around, but also to avoid giving the impression you're engaging in an oral examination!

9. Be alert to "cues" in the applicant's answers and behavior. Adapt immediately to

---

[16]William D. Brooks, *Speech Communication*, 2nd ed. Dubuque, Iowa: Wm. C. Brown, 1974, pp. 203–204. Adapted from Robert S. Goyer, W.C. Redding, and J.T. Rickey, *Interviewing Principles and Techniques.* Copyright © 1968 by Goyer, Redding, and Rickey and used with their permission.

what is said so that you can "follow up a promising lead." Probe suspected weaknesses.

10. Ask questions that will reveal the applicant's attitudes and personality in terms of the job's total requirements.[16]

<hr />

Employment Interviews and the EEOC

To insure compliance with the Equal Employment Opportunity Commission's guidelines and to avoid charges predicated on Title VII of the Civil Rights Act, certain questions should be avoided during employment interviews. While there is no law that prohibits the *asking* of these questions, federal statutes do forbid discrimination on the basis of information that an employer might obtain in answers to these questions given by applicants. Consequently, by gaining such information, the employer becomes more susceptible to allegations of discrimination levied by rejected applicants. A recent publication lists "15 Questions You Dare Not Ask Job Applicants" (see *Administrative Management*, June 1974). The taboo questions include the following categories:

Figure 10–3 Equal Employment Opportunity Commission guidelines forbid discrimination based upon information gained during employment interviews. Care must be taken to avoid probing into an applicant's personal life in areas not specifically related to job requirements. (Photo by Sybil Shelton, Monkmeyer Press Photo Service)

1. Questions that reveal national origin.
2. Questions regarding membership in organizations possessing strong racial, religious, or ethnic identities.
3. Asking the applicant to submit a photograph with the job application.
4. Questions requiring the identification of "nearest relative."
5. Questions pertaining to the applicant's "general" military service (i.e., "Your discharge was honorable?")
6. Questions pertaining to educational levels not directly related to job performance requirements.
7. Questions pertaining to applicant's height, weight, or marital status.
8. Questions regarding home or automobile ownership.

For the most part, courts and review panels have ruled against *any* potentially discriminating question which is not a B.F.O.Q. (bona fide occupational qualification). In other words, you may ask the question, "Do you speak Spanish" *if* the job for which the applicant is applying requires the use of that language, but you cannot ask such a question if it is not related to basic job qualifications.

We will conclude our discussion of the employment interview with an attempt to answer a very practical question. What do you as an applicant do if an interviewer asks you an obviously illegal question? Do you answer that question? Do you confront the interviewer with the illegality of the question? The answer lies within your own estimation of the intent of the interviewer and just how much you want the job. If you go ahead and answer the question, be sure to make a note of the interviewer's name and write down the specific question that you were asked. Later on, if you are denied the job and feel that the information gained from the forbidden question was part of the reason for the negative decision, you may contact your regional EEOC office and file a complaint. However, you must be realistic in your expectations for redress of your grievances. There are currently a large number of cases backlogged in the courts and review panels, and it takes months and even years for action to be taken under the Equal Employment Opportunity Act.

Summary

In this chapter we have focused on interviewing as purposeful, planned conversation, characterized by massive verbal and nonverbal interaction. Specific characteristics of employment, performance assessment, counseling, reprimand, grievance, exit, induction, consulting, sales, data-gathering, and order-giving interviews have been discussed. The three phases common to most interviews—an opening, a body, and a closing—were discussed, with special attention given to structure, types of questions, and sequences of questions.

You have been provided with a number of specific suggestions for participating in interviews both as the interviewer and as the interviewee. Since the employment interview is generally of vital importance to most of us from time to time, special suggestions regarding participation in employment interviews were included.

Discussion Questions

1. Compare and contrast interviews and chance conversations.
2. Discuss several ways in which the environment influences employment interviews; counseling interviews; and reprimand interviews.
3. Write out your own definition of interviewing. In what ways does your definition differ from ours?
4. Which of the interview types do you feel you could participate in with the greatest degree of competence as an interviewer? An interviewee? In which of the types do you feel you would be least effective as an interviewer? An interviewee? Explain why in each case.
5. List and discuss three ways of opening an interview that were not discussed in the section on interview structure and content.
6. Explain the advantages and disadvantages of nonscheduled, moderately-scheduled, highly-scheduled, and highly-scheduled-standardized interviews.
7. List and discuss three methods of concluding an interview not mentioned in this chapter. The methods may be either verbal or nonverbal.
8. Construct two sample questions to demonstrate your familiarity with each of the types of questions discussed in this chapter.
9. Examine the suggestions regarding participation in interviews. Do you question any of the suggestions? Which ones? Why?

Study Probes

1. Select three people of varying status and power. Prepare three separate interviews complete with an indication of the opening, the kinds of questions that will be asked, the sequence of questions, and the closing. Clearly indicate the specific adaptions you have found necessary for each of the three interviewees.
2. Secure permission to witness an interview conducted by an experienced interviewer. Carefully observe his or her methods, and write a critique of them.
3. Select an interview from *Newsweek*, *Time*, the *New York Times*, or another current source. Try to identify the kinds of questions asked, the sequence of questions, the opening, and the type of closing.
4. Observe an interview on the *Today* show, the *Tonight* show, or the *Tomorrow* show. Does the interview you observed fit our definition of interviewing? In what ways? How does the television interview differ?

Additional Reading

Benjamin, Alfred, *The Helping Interview*. Boston: Houghton Mifflin, 1974.

Gorden, Raymond L., *Interviewing: Strategy, Techniques, and Tactics*. Homewood, Illinois: The Dorsey Press, 1969.

Goyer, Robert S., W. Charles Redding, and John T. Rickey, *Interviewing Principles and Techniques: A Project Text*. Dubuque, Iowa: William C. Brown, 1964.

Huseman, Richard C., Cal M. Logue, and Dwight L. Freshley, *Readings in Interpersonal and Organizational Communication*. Boston: Holbrook Press, 1973.

Kahn, Robert L., and Charles F. Cannell, *The Dynamics of Interviewing*, New York: John Wiley, 1957.

Stewart, Charles J., and William B. Cash, *Interviewing: Principles and Practices*. Dubuque, Iowa: William C. Brown, 1974.

Communicating within groups: discussion and conference

11

key points to learn

Trends that account for increased reliance on conference and group meetings in business and industry.

Advantages and disadvantages of the small group decision-making process.

Key variables affecting the small group communication process.

Suggestions for effective participation in small group meetings.

Suggestions for leading discussions.

Guidelines for developing a discussion agenda.

"A camel is a horse designed by a committee." "A meeting brings together a group of the unfit, appointed by the unwilling, to do the unnecessary." "A conference is a meeting to decide when the next meeting will be held." "A conference is a meeting of a group of people who singly can do nothing, but who collectively agree that nothing can be done." The preceding statements reflect the frustrations and cynicism of people who have tried the "group method" of decision making and found that it left something to be desired. Indeed, a large number of people view the appointment of a committee to study a problem as a waste of time and energy and as a delay tactic on the part of those who are willing to give an idea "lip-service," but are unwilling to *act!* Perhaps *you* have experienced wasted hours in group meetings and find yourself agreeing with those who question the value of conferences and committees. Maybe you number among the thousands who impatiently insist on quick actions, without wasted hours of talk. *The problem is not so much committees in management as it is the management of committees!* Meetings need not be a waste of time. When meetings fail, human beings have failed as participants and leaders. It is our hope that an understanding of the group communication process will enable you to see why you or others have experienced nonproductive conferences and committee meetings, and that you will use this understanding to become a more effective leader or participant and to assist others in doing the same.

small group communication defined

Increasingly, the demands of contemporary business and industry require face-to-face communication with small groups of people. Whether in the form of regularly scheduled staff meetings, committee meetings, workshops, or conferences, you are likely to find small group communication activities occupying a significant segment of your total work time. One leading executive recently reported spending half of his time, or more than 1,000 hours per year, in conference and committee work.

Why has small group communication become so vital in modern business and industry? Zelko and Dance outline five trends that partially account for increased reliance on conference and group meetings:

1. The trend toward a more social interacting work climate and environment. (We have become so specialized in our vocations that we are interdependent upon one another. Consultations and conferences are an essential part of just doing our jobs.)

2. The trend toward giving more participative opportunities to employees to express themselves and be heard and to have a "voice" in matters that concern them puts the conference in a dominant position as a major forum for such opportunities.

3. The practice of more consultation with subordinates, now characterized as "consultative management," relies heavily on the conference setting for drawing out opinions and judgments of members of a work group.

4. The degree of reliance on group decision making by anyone who supervises the work of others has a direct effect on the amount of use of the conference method.

5. The total objectives of democratic management put the group-leader relationship in focus very strongly.[1]

When we consider the amount of time we spend in some form of small group communication activity, and when we realize that this amount of time is likely to *increase* as society becomes more complex, it begins to make good sense to seek a better understanding of group interaction phenomena. In the remainder of this section, you will be introduced to the process of small group communication. After defining small group communication, we shall briefly discuss some of the advantages and disadvantages often encountered when the group method of decision making is used.

Definition

You may feel that there is little need to define small group communication. After all, the phrase obviously refers to *communication within small groups:* conferences, committees, etc. However, in order to understand

---

[1]Harold P. Zelko and Frank E.X. Dance, *Business and Professional Speech Communication.* New York: Holt, Rinehart and Winston, 1965, p. 161.

the implications of small group communication, we do need to agree upon a definition of *small group*. For our purposes here, we shall consider a small group "a number of persons who communicate with one another often over a span of time, and who are few enough so that each person is able to communicate with all others, not at secondhand, through other people, but face-to-face. . . . A chance meeting of casual acquaintances does not count as a group for us."[2]

According to our definition, the crowd at a football game, several business people conversing during their ride to work on a train, or five people who happen to be in an elevator at a given moment *are not small groups*. The crowd at a football game is too large to allow face-to-face communication with *each* person present, while the other two examples constitute *chance* meetings.

_____ Advantages and Disadvantages of Small Group Decision-Making

The widespread use of small group communication in organizations is ample testimony that committees and conferences in some ways are advantageous. However, the small group method of decision making has a number of disadvantages that must be reckoned with. When considering whether it would be best to make a decision autocratically, or whether to involve a group of people in the decision-making process, consider the following advantages and disadvantages.

Advantages.   Considerable research has focused on the effects of active and passive participation in the making of a decision, and levels of commitment to that decision once it has been reached. The results of these studies suggest that people are more committed to a decision (e.g., have better attitudes toward the decision and are more faithful in executing the decision) when they are included in the decision-making process.[3] Such results may be explained by two factors. First, involving a group of people in the determination of a policy ensures that members of the group are made familiar with the nature, background, and need for the policy. Consequently, the group understands why the policy is necessary. Second, attitudes are more favorable because of a sense of personal involvement in the decision.

A group of people is capable of making a decision that is superior to that of an individual working alone.[4] The very basis of the American jury system rests upon the premise that the collective wisdom of twelve ordinary people will prove superior to that of a learned judge. There are, of course, exceptions to the

_____

[2]George C. Homans, *The Human Group.* New York: Harcourt Brace Jovanovich, 1950, p. 1.

[3]Howard H. Martin, "Communication Setting," in *Speech Communication: Analysis and Readings,* Howard Martin and Kenneth Anderson (eds.). Boston: Allyn & Bacon, 1968, pp. 70–71.

[4]Wayne N. Thompson, *Quantitative Research in Public Address and Communication.* New York: Random House, 1967, pp. 97–105.

rule. Juries do not always reach the *right* verdict, and committees do not always make the right decisions. At times, the creative and innovative suggestions of an individual are stifled by a conservative majority. However, groups should be able to make better decisions for two reasons: (1) by dividing responsibilities for research among a number of people, more information can be brought into the discussion; (2) the fact that each member of the group represents a unique frame of reference should improve the quality of the final decision. Taken together, these two advantages may indicate the reasoning behind the statement "two heads are better than one." It's easy to comprehend how five or more people can conduct more interviews, read more reports, or conduct more surveys than one member acting alone.

However, the second advantage which pertains to individualized frames of reference bears further explanation. Problems of selective perception and selective retention, coupled with very different backgrounds and experiences of individual group members, will likely result in one member "seeing" aspects of the discussion problem that were not perceived by other members. By the time that the collective perceptions have been brought to bear upon the problem, a higher quality solution should be the result.

Disadvantages.   Group decisions require the expenditure of a considerable amount of time. It is not uncommon for Congress to spend several months on a particular piece of legislation before bringing it to a vote, whereas the President has the power to issue "executive orders" on the spur of the moment. Although we considered the different frames of reference as an advantage earlier, we must view them as disadvantages if we consider the time required to satisfy each member's desires to comment and react to the comments of other members. There are times when the necessity of prompt action precludes the use of committees and conferences.

The length of time required to reach a group decision wouldn't be so bad if it weren't for the fact that much of that time is *wasted*. Groups waste time in a number of ways: (1) too much time is spent pursuing a single train of thought, with the result that the agenda cannot be completed; (2) members insist on discussing irrelevant points; (3) members spend so much time maintaining group morale and other human relations matters that time does not permit solving the problem assigned to the committee.

Groups sometimes assume irrational risks. In the days of the wild, wild West, "necktie parties" were occasionally celebrated by normally rational and conservative men caught up in a frenzied group identity. To some extent the mob psychology is evidenced in some group decisions. Indeed, there is a tendency for groups to take actions for which the individual members would be unwilling to assume responsibility. Such a tendency has been called the *risky shift phenomenon*.[5]

---

[5]Stewart L. Tubbs and Sylvia Moss, *Human Communication: An Interpersonal Perspective.* New York: Random House, 1974, pp. 207–208.

Groups sometimes substitute *talk* for *action*. Here we are not concerned with such intentional filibusters as sometimes occur in the United States Senate. Rather, we are dealing with the tendency of some committees to exhibit a willingness to discuss just about any problem, but solve none. Certainly, there is an element of catharsis (emotional cleansing) involved in simply discussing an important social or business issue. Some groups are so satisfied with their talk that they never get around to acting to implement a realistic solution.

variables affecting small group communication

Space will not permit a discussion of all the variables that affect the small group communication process. However, eight of the more significant variables have been selected for consideration here: (1) purpose of meeting, (2) size of group, (3) leadership styles, (4) interaction patterns, (5) orientation, (6) degrees of conflict and cooperation, (7) conformity, and (8) cohesiveness.

Purpose of Meeting

The type and purpose of the conference or committee meeting will exert a significant influence on the small group communication process. Classified according to purpose, meetings are described by business executives as *information-sharing* (exchange of views and information), *persuasive* (recommending action), *creative* (generating ideas), and *policy-determinative* (making major decisions). Of these four purposes, information-sharing and persuasion are the most common. One survey of committee and conference purposes led the investigator to conclude that most executives use "meetings" as sources of information to assist them in their decision making and as occasions to "sell" their ideas and recommendations to subordinates.[6] This same study reports that 60 percent of the executives who hold regular staff meetings make their decisions either before or after their meetings, rather than during their meetings. This is not to imply, however, that decision-making groups are insignificant in today's business community. On the contrary, one survey of 1,200 respondents revealed that 30.3 percent of the firms responding used policy-determination committees. On the average, these policy-making committees consist of 8.6 members and meet 27 times per year.[7]

---

[6]Martin Kriesberg, "Executives Evaluate Administrative Conferences," *Advanced Management*, 15 (March 1950), pp. 15–17.

[7]Tillman, p. 12.

Small group discussions in business and industry may also be classified according to type. By far the most frequent meeting is the *staff conference*. Such conferences bring together a supervisor and the immediate subordinates, usually on a weekly basis, for purposes of solving problems, determining policies, and sharing information. Committees are in reality small-scale conferences. They either may be standing committees or ad hoc committees. *Production conferences* are special variations of staff conferences. The aim of the production conference is the solution of production-line problems —quotas, schedules, etc. *Training conferences* are special internal or external meetings that almost always involve the development of desirable attitudes and understanding, rather than straight presentation of information.

_____ **Group Size**

Earlier in this section we reported a survey that indicated an average of 8.6 members on policy-making committees. Is this the optimal size? Would it be better to have more or fewer members? Most recommendations are for committees of no fewer than three and no more than nine members. One recent *Harvard Business Review* survey of 1,658 committees revealed an average committee of eight members. However, respondents to the survey indicated that their preference as to committee size was around five members. The wisdom of these respondents' preference for five-member groups was vindicated in a study by P. E. Slater of groups ranging in size from two to seven members. Slater's conclusions were:

> Size five emerged clearly . . . as the size group which from the subjects' viewpoint was most effective in dealing with an intellectual task involving the collection and exchange of information about a situation, the coordination, analysis, and evaluation of this information, and a group decision regarding the appropriate administrative action to be taken in the situation. . . .
>
> These findings suggest that maximal group satisfaction is achieved when the group is large enough so that the members feel able to express positive and negative feelings freely, and to make aggressive efforts toward problem solving even at the risk of antagonizing each other, yet small enough so that some regard will be shown for the feelings and needs of others; large enough so that the loss of a member could be tolerated, but small enough so that such a loss could not be altogether ignored.[8]

You will need to realize that as group size increases, the amount of available time for each participant to communicate decreases. In addition, the distribution of participation is influenced as group size increases. More powerful or forceful individuals begin to dominate the available communication time. Because of the complexity of potential interactions, participants in larger groups fail to perceive feedback cues and fail to respond with feedback cues as

_____

[8]P.E. Slater, "Contrasting Correlates of Group Size," *Sociometry*, **21** (1958), pp. 137–138.

Figure 11–1 Group size plays a significant role in small group communication. As group size increases, the degree of involvement of each individual committee member decreases. (Photos by Al Kaplan, D.P.I.)

group size increases. One study by Bostrom indicates the complexity created by the addition of even one member to a group. In interviews there are only two possible interactions—either A talks to B, or B talks to A. With the addition of one member (C), the number of potential interactions increases from two to nine:

1. A to B	*6.* C to A
2. A to C	*7.* A to B and C
3. B to A	*8.* B to A and C
4. B to C	*9.* C to A and B
5. C to B	

Bostrom, fascinated with the impact of including one additional person in a discussion, calculated the potential interactions for groups ranging in size from two to eight members:[9]

NUMBER IN GROUP	INTERACTIONS POSSIBLE
2	2
3	9
4	28
5	75
6	186
7	441
8	1,056

There is some indication that larger groups at times are able to solve a greater variety of problems because of the increase in potential skills accompanying increased group size. However, this is only true involving tasks with clearly defined criteria of correct performance. In our opinion, the gains achieved by pushing group size past seven members are far outweighed by the disadvantages that will result.

_____ Leadership Styles

The style of leadership is a significant variable that will influence small group communication. Andersen, Nichols, and Booth have summarized the comments of a number of theorists regarding the three principal leadership styles—*democratic, autocratic,* and *laissez-faire:*[10]

In a *democratic-leadership climate* we may expect to find the following:

---

[9]R. Bostrom, "Patterns of Communicative Interaction in Small Groups," *Communication Monographs,* **37** (1970), pp. 257–258.

[10]Martin P. Andersen, E. Ray Nichols, Jr., and Herbert W. Booth, *The Speaker and His Audience: Dynamic Interpersonal Communication.* New York: Harper & Row, Pub., 1974, pp. 534–536.

1. Policy decisions are made by the group, encouraged and assisted by the leader.
2. Activity plans are made by the group, technical advice being provided by the leader when needed.
3. Member satisfactions are gained in making own decisions.
4. Members grow in self-confidence and self-acceptance.
5. Leaders and members function as peers.
6. Emphasis on status decreases and emphasis on respect for others increases.
7. Listening improves, with the result of greater acceptance of the ideas of others.
8. Little stress is placed on discipline, unless imposed by the group. The leader's relation to the members is friendly, helping, and tolerant.
9. There is a fundamental belief on the part of the leader that the members can attain their own ends by using their own resources.
10. Subgroup assignment and task decisions are left up to the group.
11. Responsibilities are placed on all members.
12. Status in the group is earned by the contribution made to the achievement of the group's goals; praise from the leader is objective and factually based.

In an *autocratic-leadership climate* we may expect to find the following:

1. Activity plans are made by the leader, with some uncertainty on the part of members about what the next steps may be.
2. All policy decisions are made by the leader.
3. Unless productivity is high, member frustrations may increase, resulting from high standards set by the leader.
4. Member discontent may develop when leaders seek dominance for its own sake.
5. Considerable status differences exist between leaders and members.
6. Aggressive status-seeking activities develop among members who have need of status.
7. Members listen carefully to leader's instructions; they may pay little attention to what others say, unless productivity is at stake.
8. Considerable stress is placed on discipline and on getting the job done.
9. There is a fundamental belief on the part of the leader that constant direction is necessary for goal achievement.
10. Subgroup assignment and task decisions are made by the leader.
11. Limited responsibility is placed on all members; members are chosen for specific tasks.
12. Status comes from praise from the leader, which is usually personal and subjective.

In a *laissez-faire-leadership climate* we may expect to find the following:

1. Members of the group are given help in activity plans by the leader only when it is requested.
2. The group has complete freedom to make policy decisions without any help or guidance from the leader.
3. Members do not know what is expected of them and develop disunity and dissatisfactions.

4. Members have little sense of accomplishment.

5. Few contacts exist between leader and members. Little friendship for the leader develops.

6. Status-mindedness develops, resulting in competitive hostility.

7. Members focus primarily on their own concerns. Listening to others' comments is infrequent.

8. There is no concern for discipline. Members develop self-assertiveness without regard for others.

9. There is little concern for goal achievement.

10. Comments by leader on member activities are infrequent. No attempt is made by the leader to interfere with group's activities.

11. Leader places no responsibilities on members, who are left to develop activities if they wish.

12. Lack of development of feelings of unity, self-confidence, or friendliness.

Despite the modern trends toward democratic management, we do not recommend democratic leadership in all situations. There are times when the executive must make the final decision *after* consultation with workers; times when the executive must make a decision *prior* to consultation with workers; times when the executive should allow workers to assist in determining the decision; and times when the executive may allow the workers to make the decision. In Figure 11–2, Zelko and Dance graphically depict the various leadership options and their effects on group decision making:[11]

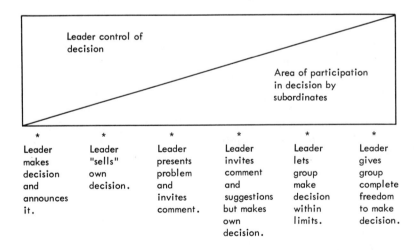

Figure 11–2   Control over decisions.

[11]From *Business and Professional Speech Communication*. Harold P. Zelko and Frank E.X. Dance, Copyright © 1965 by Holt, Rinehart and Winston, Inc. Reprinted by permission.

The willingness of group members to interact verbally and nonverbally has a significant effect on the type of meeting you will have. Earlier in this chapter in our discussion of group size we mentioned the potential number of interactions for groups ranging in size from two to eight members. Unfortunately, many small groups appear to be unaware of any interaction other than that which occurs between members and the leader. If ideas are to be discussed in depth, and if the collective wisdom of the group is to become a factor, maximum interaction among all participants is a must. Figure 11–3 is a diagram of two types of small group interactions. The diagram labeled "wrong way" depicts interaction between the leader and the members, without member-to-member interaction. The diagram labeled "right way" illustrates maximum interaction among all participants. Members' comments are directed in any one of many directions, rather than exclusively to the leader.

_____ Orientation

A few years ago a popular definition of discussion included the requirement that a group with *group orientation* purposefully interact orally. By group orientation that writer meant that individual goals had been subjugated to group goals. Participants were seeking the greatest good for the greatest number, rather than a solution that would benefit any individual participant. Such is indeed a lofty goal. City councils, boards of regents, boards of directors, and almost any committee you could name would become more effective policy-making groups if members were less selfish in their deliberations. Unfortunately, groups are frequently composed of members who are either *self-oriented* or *task-oriented* to the extent that the group process is short-circuited. Members who are self-oriented may be so busy "making points" in an effort to gain recognition and peer approval that significant contributions to the content of the discussion will be lacking. Members who are overly task-oriented may be so determined to "get the job done" that they are willing to run roughshod over the social and emotional needs of other group

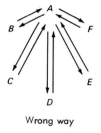

Wrong way

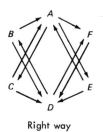

Right way

Figure 11–3   Patterns of interaction.

members. Simply getting the committee assignment accomplished may prove of little value if, in the process, worker morale has diminished as a result of "railroading" techniques. Groups probably will be most productive when members exhibit a combination of group orientation and task orientation. Remember, it is possible to become so concerned about maintaining the social and emotional needs of the group that too much time is wasted, and the task is not completed. On the other hand, it is possible to be so task-oriented in pushing a committee through its agenda that interpersonal losses outweigh group productivity.

_____ Conflict and Cooperation

Studies that have concentrated on the variables of conflict and cooperation in small group activity have shown rather consistently that "group members who have been motivated to cooperate show more positive responses to each other, are more favorable in their perceptions, are more involved in the task, and have greater satisfaction with the task."[12] It is essential to note that the kind of conflict that we are describing here is somewhat related to our previous discussion of self-oriented group members. We are not dealing with lively competition of ideas. As we shall see in the next paragraph, competition on the idea level is essential for effective group decision making.

_____ Conformity

Whenever group members assume that cooperative delibera-tion prohibits constructive conflict, many of the advantages of the small group method of decision making are lost. Indeed, one of the recurring problems faced by committee leaders is that of getting members to express views when those views in all probability will be minority opinions. You will recall that one of the advantages of the group method lies in the different perspectives that potentially can be brought to bear upon a particular problem. When individual members feel pressured to conform to the will or viewpoint of the majority _prior to expressing their views_, everyone loses. A recent cartoon focuses on the tendency of members of small groups to conform without expressing minority viewpoints. The cartoon pictures eight of the nine Supreme Court justices looking at the ninth in anticipation of his decision. With a sheepish grin, the ninth justice responds: "Well, heck! If all you smart cookies agree, who am I to dissent?"

---

[12]A. Paul Hare, _Handbook of Small Group Research_. New York: The Free Press of Glencoe, 1962, p. 254.

The attractiveness that a group has for its members is defined as cohesiveness. Obviously, the level of cohesiveness will exert a direct influence on individual members' determination to abide by group decisions. Groups that are high in cohesiveness will generally tend to enjoy one another's company, are interested in the well-being of other group members, and tend to help each other with problems. Although highly cohesive groups tend to exhibit conformity behaviors such as the establishment of rigid norms for their members, their members are more likely to disagree *openly* than are members of less cohesive groups.

leading and participation in discussions

We have already discussed the three major styles of leadership. In this section we will comment briefly on the functions of group leaders and list the requirements for effective member participation in small group discussions.

———————— Responsibilities of Group Leaders

Effective leadership in conferences and committees has been the theme of literally thousands of workshops and seminars in business and industry. There is a growing belief that the *management* of meetings is to blame for many of the failures of conferences and committees. What should an effective chairperson or leader do during a meeting? What should the leader do preceding or following a meeting?

Although leaders need not attend to the physical labor themselves, they have the overall responsibility of preparing the meeting room before the meeting. The leader must see that ashtrays are provided, water glasses and pitchers of water are available, adequate seating arrangements are made, and that members are notified about the time, purpose, and, if possible, the agenda of the meeting.

At the beginning of the meeting, the leader should serve an introductory function. If the participants are not acquainted with one another, the leader should either introduce them, or allow them to introduce themselves to the group. Following the introduction of the participants, the leader should briefly introduce the agenda for the meeting. Such introductions will vary from one or two sentences to several paragraphs. If there are special time limitations, the leader should state these during the introduction. In some instances several committees will be working simultaneously, and your committee will be charged with one limited aspect of a total problem. When this is the case, you will want to explain this to the group during your introduction, urging members to avoid discussing the facets of the problem that are the concern of other groups.

After the introduction and from time to time during the discussion, the leader must stimulate members by asking appropriate questions. The types of questions discussed on pages 208–209 may be used in group discussions as well as in interviews. The function of stimulating members goes hand in hand with the regulatory function of leadership. The leader is responsible for regulating the amount of time spent on any given portion of the agenda, as well as for regulating the amount of time the various members talk. For the group method to realize the advantages discussed earlier in this chapter, each member must have input. First, the leader should not dominate the total talk time. After that, the leader should try to get every participant involved in the discussion. This may require interrupting a too-talkative participant and calling on the reluctant participants for their thoughts. This may be accomplished by commenting as you interrupt the too-talkative participant, "Now there's an interesting point. What do you think about that, Miss Walters?" In a recent issue of *Supervision*, Lawrence Loban suggests that effective use of questions can aid the chairperson in both regulatory and stimulation functions. After asserting that members get bored, discussions get off the track, the same few people doing all the talking, there is too much griping, some people do not talk at all, some items drag on and on, and leaders do all the talking are the responses participants most frequently give to the question, "What's wrong with meetings?," Loban offers five suggestions regarding effective use of questions:

1. Phrase questions to avoid "yes" or "no" answers.
2. Keep questions brief.
3. Use only the most simple words.
4. Use questions with a direct relation to the topic.
5. Use questions that cover a single point.[13]

In stimulating and regulating the discussion, the leader should also be aware of the four possible directions of questions. Questions may be *overhead*, i.e., asked by the leader to the group as a whole, with any member free to answer. Questions may be *direct*, i.e., asked by the leader and directed to a specific group member. Questions may be *reverse*, i.e., a question asked by a member is referred by the leader straight back to the one who asked it. Questions may be *relay*, i.e., a question asked by a group member is relayed by the leader to the group as a whole.

The leader must also serve a guidance function. Whenever a group member begins discussing matters that are irrelevant to the issues before the group, the

---

[13]Lawrence N. Loban, "Questions: The Answer to Meeting Participation," *Supervision*, Jan. 1972, pp. 11–13.

leader must attempt to get the discussion back on track. Again, the effective use of questions is necessary in fulfilling guidance functions.

In an effort to keep issues clearly in focus for the benefit of the entire group, the leader should summarize from time to time. A few brief summaries interspersed throughout an hour-long meeting will assist the leader in accomplishing other functions—i.e., stimulation, regulatory, and guidance.

The leader also should attempt to keep the discussion on an idea level, rather than allowing it to slip to a conflict of personalities among members. Hidden agendas, competitions between members, and emotion-laden statements made by group members must be dealt with properly or else social and emotional concerns rather than task considerations will become the major focus of your group. You will probably need some help in accomplishing this task. Research has indicated that the social-emotional leader of a group is frequently someone other than the designated leader.

Finally, once the conference or committee work is completed, the leader must see that the committee report is properly prepared and placed into the hands of the appropriate person or persons. A letter should be sent to committee members notifying them that the report has been submitted. If possible, a copy of the report should be made available to each committee member. Such simple acts of follow-through will ensure that the meeting's objectives are accomplished and will enable members to feel that their time was well spent.

Responsibilities of Participants

One of the first and fundamental requirements of a good participant is to become thoroughly familiar with the leadership functions discussed in the previous segment and assist the leader in accomplishing those tasks. Leadership is a dynamic phenomenon. During an hour-long meeting various leaders may emerge from time to time, even though the same person remains as the official committee leader.

Participants must be informed on the topic. This may require considerable time and effort, but the quality of a meeting can rise no higher than the quality of information possessed by the group members.

The specific traits of effective discussion participants are summarized in a study by Major Herman Farwell. Farwell's study, based on a comprehensive review of more than 25 leading small group scholars, revealed eight consensus traits:

1. An attitude of respect and open-mindedness toward others in the group.
2. A favorable attitude toward flexible, permissive interaction.
3. An awareness of communication barriers and a desire to overcome them.
4. An awareness of the need for understanding of group process.
5. An ability and desire to speak clearly and to the point.
6. An understanding of the need for attentive listening.

7. An ability to think logically and analytically.
8. A desire to cooperate and conciliate in order to reach group goals.[14]

When should you participate during the meeting? The answer should be "when you have something to say!" You should never talk just to be talking. However, be ready to get involved on the spur of the moment. Contribute your ideas at the moment that group interest in your contribution will be strong. Do not sit back waiting patiently until everyone else has had a say. There is some indication that members who contribute early in a discussion gain the initial respect of the entire group and are perceived as credible sources as the meeting progresses.

the discussion agenda

Much of the time you will find the agenda for a particular meeting consisting of five or six "items of business" that individually must be dispensed with during the one to two hours of meeting time. In these cases some care should be taken to ensure consideration of items in the most appropriate order. As a general rule, whenever several brief items of discussion are on the agenda, tend to those first, allowing the rest of the meeting to be concentrated on the more time-consuming matters of business.

In arranging the subpoints of an informative conference, you will profit from an examination of the methods of arranging issues on pages 245–247. For useful formats of problem-solving or policy-determination discussions, you will want to review the reflective thinking and the creative thinking approaches on pages 60–61.

In preparing the agenda for a meeting, you will want to remember that questions stimulate a greater variety of responses than do affirmative statements. This is particularly true if care is taken to structure questions in an open and unbiased manner. The agenda, then, should consist of a carefully thought out series of questions.

Summary

A number of trends in contemporary business and industry have resulted in an ever-increasing reliance on small group communication. In this chapter we defined a small group as "a number of persons who communicate with one another over a span of time, and who are few enough so that each person is able

---

[14]Major Herman Farwell, "An Evaluation of a Televised Method of Teaching Group Process," (M.A. unpublished thesis). University Park: The Pennsylvania State University, 1964.

to communicate with all the others, not at secondhand, through other people, but face-to-face."

The use of the group decision-making method will result in increased motivation of employees, more information being available as the basis of solving a problem, and better decisions as a result of varying perspectives being brought to bear upon the problem. The group method has several disadvantages. Among them are the time required to reach a decision, the waste of time, the risky shift phenomenon, and the substitution of talk for action.

Several variables were discussed as they pertain to small group communication. The eight variables treated in this chapter include meeting purpose, group size, leadership style, interaction pattern, orientation, conflict and cooperation, conformity, and cohesiveness.

Leadership responsibilities include planning, introductory, regulatory, guidance, stimulation, socioemotional, summary, and follow-through functions. Participation involves a willingness to assume some leadership functions and a willingness to contribute your comments spontaneously. Several specific traits of effective participation were discussed.

The specific agenda will vary from meeting to meeting. However, more variety in responses will result from an agenda that consists of a series of questions, rather than declarative statements.

Discussion Questions

1. What is meant by emerging leadership? How does an emerged leader differ in influence from an officially designated leader?
2. Examine carefully the cynical statements about conferences and committees listed at the beginning of this chapter. Discuss the breakdown or problem that probably prompted each of those statements.
3. List all of the groups to which you belong. Which of those groups conform to the definition of "small group" provided in this chapter? Which ones do not?
4. List and explain two additional advantages and two additional disadvantages of small group decision making.
5. Define risky shift phenomenon. Can you think of examples from your own experiences of this phenomenon?
6. Several purposes of small group communication were discussed in this chapter. Can you list additional purposes?
7. According to Bostrom, there are seventy-five potential interactions for a group consisting of five members. Using A, B, C, D, and E to represent the five members, list each of the possible seventy-five interactions.
8. Provide a one-sentence definition of the three styles of leadership: democratic, autocratic, and laissez-faire.

9. What is a group *norm?* Give several examples of norms. How do norms affect group cohesiveness?
10. What is an agenda? Of what value is an agenda in a conference or committee meeting?

=============== **Study Probes**

1. Attend a city council meeting, board meeting, or other small group decision-making session. Which one of the members dominates the discussion? Is that member the official leader? Keep a list of leadership functions assumed by members of the group. Does there seem to be a willingness to share leadership functions? Characterize each member of the group as predominantly self-oriented, group-oriented, or task-oriented. What were the major successes of the discussion? Failures?
2. Interview five managers regarding their involvement in small group communication. Try to determine the approximate amount of time spent by each manager in committee and conference meetings. What is each manager's philosophy of conducting meetings? Ask each manager what the advantages and disadvantages of the small group method are in his or her particular business.
3. Prepare an agenda for a problem-solving discussion using the reflective thinking format. Be sure that each item on your agenda is phrased in the form of a question. You may select any problem that you please.

=============== **Additional Reading**

Cartwright, Dorwin, and Alvin Zander, *Group Dynamics: Research and Theory.* 2nd ed. New York: Harper & Row, Pub., 1960.

Davis, James H., *Group Performance.* Reading, Mass.: Addison-Wesley, 1969.

Gulley, Halbert E., *Discussion, Conference, and Group Process.* 2nd ed. New York: Holt, Rinehart and Winston, 1968.

Haiman, Franklyn S., *Group Leadership and Democratic Action.* Boston: Houghton Mifflin, 1951.

Hare, A. Paul, *Handbook of Small Group Research.* New York: The Free Press of Glencoe, 1962.

Phillips, Gerald M., *Communication and the Small Group.* Indianapolis: Bobbs-Merrill, 1966.

Communicating with groups: presentational speaking

12

key points to learn

The concept of "expanded conversation."

The types of analyses that should precede speechmaking.

Useful patterns of arrangement for developing key points in a speech.

The distinction between presentation and preparation outlines.

Types of support materials used to clarify and prove statements.

Ways of beginning a speech.

Effective use of transitions.

Ways of concluding speeches.

Philosophical assumptions behind effective delivery of speeches.

Opportunities to communicate with organized groups abound within business organizations, between business organizations, and between businesses and their publics. "Get your crew together and explain the new guidelines." "I want you to present this program to the entire board at our next meeting." "If anyone can convince our employees of the value of this new insurance package, Jones, you can do it. Meet with the group tomorrow and sell them on the idea." "This contract is vital to us, Smith! We'll be pulling for you next week when you present it to the people at General Motors." "You take this invitation to speak to the Lions Club, and remember, stress the new ecology-minded programs that we instituted at the beginning of the year." "One of us should attend the ABCA convention in New York this year and explain our new approaches in facilitating upward communication."

Similar statements are made thousands of times during the course of a typical business day throughout our country. Whether addressing audiences within his or her own organization, one of the 75,000 annual convention gatherings, or one of the 4,500 Rotary clubs, the modern business executive must learn to favorably and effectively present both self and ideas to organized groups.

presentational speaking
is expanded conversation

During the past few decades it has become increasingly popular to think of "public speaking" as *presentational speaking*. Perhaps the trend results at least in part from the tendency of a great many people to attach very restrictive connotations to the word public. In the minds of many, "public" evokes visions of the politician standing before a political rally, of the lawyer addressing the court, and of the minister speaking to the congregation. There is a tendency to assume that only politicians, lawyers, and preachers need to concern themselves with public speaking. No matter what line of work you are in, however, you will probably face many situations requiring an ability to communicate with a number of receivers by means of a formal presentation.

Whenever you find it necessary to communicate a particular message to a number of receivers, you will discover that you have essentially two choices. You can communicate with each member *individually*, or you can call the group together and present the message to the entire group. Whenever you select the latter means of communicating your message, you have expanded your conversation from one receiver to several or many receivers. If you will keep these choices in mind, you may be able to overcome many of the negative stereotypes of speechmaking. You do not need to use sweeping gestures, develop pedantic pronunciation, or any other artificial vocal or physical behavior while presenting speeches to audiences. You simply need to *converse* with the entire group simultaneously. Accordingly, we have followed the lead of a number of earlier writers in defining *presentational speaking* as *expanded conversation*.

preparing for presentations: analysis

Regardless of the communication setting, whether internal or external, the preliminary analysis on the part of the speaker should consist of such basic questions as: (1) Do specific audience or occasion variables require specialized adaption? (2) What kind of response do I hope to obtain from this presentation? (3) Exactly what is it that I hope to communicate to this group?

Audience and Occasion Variables

Information concerning the audience and the communication occasion will provide you with valuable clues pertinent to the function and scope of your presentations. Such information should be used *throughout* the entire preparation process in determining the most appropriate introduction, the optimum organization scheme, most potent support materials, and the best

Figure 12–1 Presentational speaking should be viewed as expanded conversation. Whether before small audiences or large audiences, speakers are frequently asked to deliver presentations to groups of people. (Top photo by Al Kaplan, D.P.I., bottom photo by E. Johnson, de Wys, Inc.)

method of concluding the presentation. While you may have "first-hand" knowledge about receivers and occasions within your own organization, you will probably need to engage in considerable research to obtain information about external audiences. If you neglect to do your advance analysis, you will probably encounter problems similar to those faced by the oil company executive who was invited to speak to a local civic club on the subject of the energy crisis. Without asking any questions, he assumed that the audience would have little or no knowledge about his subject, beyond that obtained through general news media coverage. Accordingly, he prepared a 20-minute speech covering the energy crisis "waterfront" in very general terms. He lost his smugness when the leader introduced him as the fifth speaker in their "energy crisis series." We cannot forgive the leader for failing to provide such critical information along with the speaking engagement invitation. However, a few simple questions from the speaker at the time of the invitation would undoubtedly have averted considerable embarrassment. In your efforts to achieve effective presentational speaking, you will need to actively solicit input concerning your audience, the communication occasion, and the physical environment of the room where the speech will be given.

Although there are many different approaches to analyzing an audience, it is convenient for our purposes to suggest two inventories that you should conduct: (1) an analysis of membership groups with which the audience identifies, and (2) an analysis of probable audience attitudes toward you and your message.

Audience membership groups are of two types: (1) demographic and (2) voluntary. *Demographic* groups are those associations over which audience members have little or no control, i.e., sex, ethnic origin, age, or socioeconomic status. Religious affiliation, political affiliation, civic club affiliations, and professional affiliations are all samples of *voluntary* membership groups.

Probable audience attitudes toward you and your message may range from hostile to extremely favorable. You probably will encounter all of the following types of audiences at one time or another: (1) hostile (obvious disagreement with your ideas and/or with you as a person), (2) apathetic (totally unconcerned with your ideas and/or with you as a person), (3) neutral (mixed feelings about your ideas and/or about you as a person), and (4) favorable (support for your ideas and/or for you as a person).

In analyzing the occasion you should determine the exact purpose of the gathering. In addition, you should attempt to discover as much as you can about the background and history of the occasion. You should also seek input regarding the ramifications of the occasion.

Any speaker who has ever experienced the embarrassment of preparing a slide presentation for delivery in a room without adequate electrical outlets knows the significance of surveying the physical environment of the communication setting. Will there be a need for a public address amplification system? Can enough light be blocked out of the room to permit a daytime filmstrip presentation? Will there be a blackboard equipped with chalk and erasers? What is the seating capacity of the room? You will need to secure answers to these and similar questions in your analysis of the communication environment.

Although occasionally you may be asked to deliver a presentation aimed at entertaining your audience, most of your speeches will focus on one of four general purposes: (1) to inform, (2) to stimulate, (3) to convince, and (4) to actuate. A side-by-side comparison of these four general purposes is included in Figure 12–2.

Once you have selected your general purpose from among the four possibilities, you are ready to specify your *specific purpose*. Using the occupational safety act as the general topic, observe how the four different general purposes and four specific purposes can be derived:

1. (Inform) "I want my audience to understand the major features of the occupational safety act."
2. (Stimulate) "I want my audience to become vividly aware of the importance of the occupational safety act."
3. (Convince) "I want my audience to believe that the occupational safety act has too many loopholes."
4. (Actuate) "I want my audience to sign a petition calling for amendments to the occupational safety act."

Note: In each of the above examples, the specific purpose is an explicit behavioral statement of the desired audience response.

PURPOSE	DISTINGUISHING CHARACTERISTIC	EXAMPLES
Inform	Seeks to secure understanding	1. Technical reports 2. Operating reports 3. Research reports
Stimulate	Seeks to intensify old beliefs	1. Sales manager's appeal 2. "Kick-off speech" 3. Tribute speeches
Convince	Seeks mental commitment	1. Feasibility of zero defects? 2. Should prices be increased?
Actuate	Seeks specific behavior	1. Give blood 2. Support United Fund Appeal 3. Accept this contract

Figure 12–2 General purposes of speeches.

Far too many speakers talk "around" their topic for 20 or 30 minutes without knowing themselves what it is that they are attempting to communicate. One thing is certain—if a speaker doesn't know what he or she is trying to say, members of the audience are not likely to discover the message accidentally. One vice-president asked another as they filed out of a general staff meeting: "I missed the president's speech yesterday. What did he talk about?" The other replied, "About 20 minutes!" Unfortunately, many speakers do talk about several subjects for 20 or 30 minutes without having a central idea in mind. You can avoid this problem through careful preparation and analysis. Ask yourself the following question: If I had to deliver my presentation in one sentence, what would I say? Once you have determined an answer to that question, you are ready to move on to the next phase of speech preparation. In his autobiography, Grove Patterson wrote: "As to the preparation of a speech, write down exactly what you want to say in one sentence. Make up your mind: This is it. This is the idea I want to sell."[1] Patterson's advice is well worth heeding.

preparing for presentations: the middle phase

Let's assume that you have completed your analysis phase of preparation. After careful consideration of the audience and occasion, and after determining your general and specific communication purposes, you have developed the central idea that you hope to convey to your listeners. How do you develop that central idea into a 20- to 30-minute presentation? The answer to that question lies in the middle phase of speech preparation. Immediately after determining the central theme of your presentation, you are ready to (1) select the main points that you will need to develop, (2) arrange those points into some meaningful order and prepare an outline, (3) support each point, and (4) develop your introduction, conclusion, and transitions.

_____ Select Your Main Points

Main points, or *issues*, are the individual points that are critical to an understanding or acceptance of the central idea that you are communicating. Although we can provide you with a few examples of the derivation of main points, each individual topic must be broken down into meaningful issues consistent with your general and specific purposes. Assume

_____

[1]Grove Patterson, *I Like People: The Autobiography of Grove Patterson*. New York: *Random House*, 1945, p. 241.

that you are attempting to convince an audience that city taxes are too high. In order to determine your main points, you need to ask several questions: "What taxes do we pay in our city?" "Which ones are too high?" "Will I need to discuss each of the taxes that I feel are too high, or will I be able to concentrate on one or two of the most significant taxes?" Let's suppose that the answer to the first question indicates three taxes: sales, property, and income. If you feel that all three are too high, you will need to develop three issues or main points—one for each tax. The derivation of several other issues will be indicated in our examples of patterns of arrangement. Before we move on to that section, however, consider the relationships between general purpose, specific purpose, central idea, main points, and support materials as diagrammed in Figure 12–3.

According to Figure 12–3, the three main points (I, II, and III) must stand before the central idea can be accepted. You might say that the main points become the *key* to acceptance or rejection of the central idea, while the various support materials (A, B, and C) become the basis for acceptance or rejection of each individual main point. It is hoped that this diagram will impress on your mind the necessity of adequately supporting your assertions. Indeed, the support materials form the foundation of a good speech, just as they form the foundation of the pyramid in Figure 12–3.

_____ Patterns of Arrangement

An understanding of potential patterns of development should assist you in selecting the exact points to develop. The most popular patterns of development are (1) chronological, (2) spatial, (3) problem-solution, (4) cause-effect, (5) topical, and (6) motivated sequence.

The *chronological* pattern of development requires a division of issues according to a logical time progression. You may move from the most remote to the most recent time frame, or from the most recent back to the most remote. A speaker wishing to inform an audience of recent changes in the corporate tax laws might use the following points:

I. Changes from 1955–1965.
II. Changes from 1965–1975.
III. Changes since 1975.

The *spatial* pattern of development requires adherence to systematic progression through geographical space. A persuasive presentation emphasizing the ecological activities of Gulf Oil Corporation might be arranged spatially as follows:

I. Gulf Oil is concerned with worldwide ecology.
II. Gulf Oil is concerned with ecology in the United States.
III. Gulf Oil is concerned with ecology in Pennsylvania.

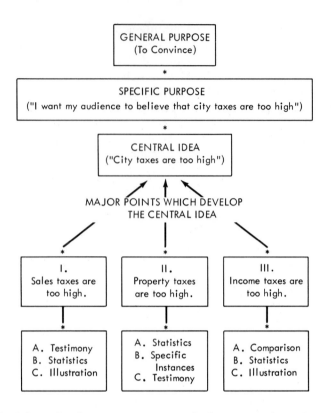

Figure 12–3 Relationships between main points and other aspects of speech preparation.

An informative presentation emphasizing the taxes paid by a corporation might be arranged spatially as follows:

I.   Federal taxes paid by IBM.
II. State taxes paid by IBM.
III. Local taxes paid by IBM.

If you are advocating a particular solution to a problem, you will probably want to use the *problem-solution* pattern of development. In the problem-solution pattern, you must first explore the nature, causes, and extent of a particular problem, and then provide a detailed treatment of your recommended solution. A speaker advocating an energy allocation program might develop the following two-point speech:

I.   Problem: A serious shortage of fuel oil will exist in the midwest this winter.
II. Solution: A federally-initiated, state-administered allocation system must be implemented.

The *cause-effect* pattern of development involves a discussion of factors that cause certain effects. For public relations purposes, a banker might arrange a two-point speech for presentation to local civic clubs:

I. Cause: The development and growth of City National Bank.
II. Effects: The impact of City National Bank on the economy of the area.

The cause-effect pattern may be reversed by discussing effects that people are somewhat familiar with, and moving into a discussion of the causes of those effects.

I. Effects: Indications of a recession economy.
II. Causes: Factors which created the recession.

The *topical* development pattern frequently involves a discussion of the individual components of a given phenomenon or of the steps involved in a process. In our earlier example of the city-taxes speech, the development is topical. The individual taxes paid by residents of the city become the issues in such a speech.

I. Sales taxes are too high.
II. Property taxes are too high.
III. Income taxes are too high.

Remember, when you are using a topical sequence, you have the option of saving your strongest point until the end of your speech (climax order) or placing it at the beginning of the speech (anticlimax order). You will recall from our discussion of message variables in Chapter 5 that placing your strongest point in the middle (pyramid order) is not advisable in most instances.

The *motivated sequence* is a five-step pattern of arrangement that is particularly suitable for developing persuasive messages. The five steps are as follows:

1. Attention: Secure the audience's attention and focus that attention on the message.
2. Need: Explain the nature, scope, and implications of the need or problem.
3. Satisfaction: Provide a solution that will eliminate a significant portion of the problem which you discussed in the preceding section.
4. Visualization: Mentally picture the future as it will be if your solution is adopted and/or if your solution is not adopted.
5. Action: Call for specific adoption of your solution. Let the audience know specifically what they need to believe or do in order to realize the benefits or avoid the perils that you have just visualized for them.[2]

---

[2]Alan H. Monroe and Douglas Ehninger, *Principles and Types of Speech Communication.* Glenview, Illinois: Scott, Foresman, 1974, p. 355.

Once you have determined the pattern of development of your speech, you are ready to prepare a rough outline. Preparing the outline will allow you to develop an overview of the entire speech and will enable you to see points in need of additional development. In addition, a well-prepared outline will indicate the degree of support for each of the major points. A sample outline is presented in Figure 12–4.

The outline that you prepare at this stage should be as detailed as you can make it (even to the extent of writing out full sentences). Please note, however, that this kind of outline, the *preparation outline,* differs significantly from the *presentation outline,* the outline that you take with you to the lectern when you

General Purpose:_____

Specific Purpose:_____

Central Idea Sentence: _____

INTRODUCTION: Get attention? Establish rapport?

TRANSITION TO BODY:

BODY:

I. First Main Point

    A. Support
    B. Support
    C. Support

II. Second Main Point
    A. Support
    B. Support
    C. Support

CONCLUSION: Summary? Wrap-up statements?

Figure 12–4 Sample outline.

deliver your speech. As a general rule, presentation outlines should contain only a few key words and phrases to jog your memory from time to time. Speakers who use full-sentence outlines have a tendency to "get lost in their notes" and lose valuable contact with their audiences.

_____Supporting Your Main Points

Your major points must be well supported if they are to be understood and accepted. Some of the supporting materials discussed in this section serve a clarifying function, while others serve a substantiation function. We shall briefly explain each of the major methods of supporting assertions and follow our explanation with an example drawn from a contemporary speech by a business representative.

Testimony.   Quoting from some outside source is generally used to lend credence to a point, although some use of testimony is of a clarifying nature (especially quotes from dictionaries, etc.). In support of his argument that risk-taking is essential to success in the modern business world, Walter B. Wriston, Chairman of Citicorp, quoted a statement made by George Gilder:

> The odds against success of any kind in our society are formidable. Some 300,000 businesses are started each year in America and only about a third of them survive as long as five years. Proponents of a safe, stagnant, boring tomorrow view this as a wasteful process, to say nothing of its being irrational. On the contrary, George Gilder has argued that:
> ". . . such waste and irrationality is the secret of economic growth. Because no one knows which venture will succeed . . . a society ruled by faith and risk rather than by rational calculus, a society open to the future rather than planning it, will call for the an endless stream of innovation, enterprise, and art."[3]

Statistics.   Statistics are numbers demonstrating some relationship. In speeches, statistics are used both for clarification and for persuasion. A recent speech by David Rockefeller, Chairman of the Board of the Chase Manhattan Bank, includes the use of statistics as support for his assertion that Americans are better off financially today than they were in the past:

> I would add that the miseries of trying to live on an inadequate income have been substantially reduced in the past 30 years or so. In 1949, 15 percent of American households had incomes of less than $3,000 in today's dollars. During the 1970s, this figure has been less than 4 percent. At the same time, more and more people are becoming more and more affluent. Right after the second World War, fewer than 15 percent of American households had incomes of more than $15,000 in today's dollars. In 1977, more than one-half enjoyed such incomes.[4]

_____

[3]Walter B. Wriston, "Risk and Other Four-Letter Words," *Vital Speeches*, 46 (Dec. 15, 1979), p. 159.
[4]David Rockefeller, "The Values By Which We Live," *Vital Speeches*, 46 (Dec. 1, 1979), p. 108.

Richard L. Lesher, President of the Chamber of Commerce of the United States, wanted to illustrate statistically the impact of 10 percent inflation over a 20-year period. He offered his audience the following statistical support:

> Well, let me try to bring the evil of inflation home to you more vividly. Our rate of inflation is going to run this year around 10 percent. If that continues for 20 years, the results will be mind-boggling.
>
> Today, it costs $71 per week to feed a family of four. Twenty years of 10 percent inflation will bring that to $478 per week.
>
> Today, the average new car cost is $5,000. Twenty years from now, adjusting only for 10 percent per annum inflation, the cost will be $33,000.
>
> Today, the average new house costs $59,000; 20 years from now, that same house will cost $397,000. (If that doesn't shock you, the 30-year figure is $1,030,000.)[5]

Specific Instances.   Specific instances involve the bare mentioning of several examples in support of a point. Although none of the examples is discussed in detail, the cumulative effect of listing a number of instances is very significant. Addressing the annual meeting of the Northeastern Poultry Producers Council, Dr. L.M. Skamser of the American Cyanamid Company suggested that *radicals* are the people who make things happen. In support of that claim, he briefly mentioned a number of instances:

> Radicalism: movement away from the usual or traditional.
>
> Norman Thomas made his first race for the presidency of the United States, on the Socialist ticket, in 1928. He made his last effort in 1948. Early in 1952, he announced he was through running. His traditional, radical platform, he said, had either been enacted into law by others or was contained in the platforms of the major parties.
>
> Henry Ford, radical, brought the automobile within reach of the average man.
>
> Wilbur and Orville Wright, radicals, put man into the air.
>
> Stokstad and Jukes, radicals, put Aurcomycin into poultry and livestock feeds.[6]

Analogies.   An anology is a comparison between objects of the same class (literal analogy) or objects of different classes (figurative analogy). Comparing a United States company to a company in the Soviet Union is a literal analogy. Comparing a company to a machine is a figurative analogy. In her speech, "Why Corporate America Fears Women," Jean Way Schoonover, a public relations executive, compared contemporary business with a hunting expedition:

> The future will be spent in a brand-new, unprecedented way: men and women will be hunting together. Not hunting each other, mind you, but hunting together.

---

[5]Richard L. Lesher, "Business Leadership: The Next Era in American History," *Vital Speeches*, 45 (July 1, 1979), p. 553.

[6]L. M. Skamser, "Radicalism: An Approach for the Poultry Industry," *Vital Speeches*, 40 (Jan. 1, 1974), p. 189.

All of business is a mighty hunt. Until recently men hunted alone: the game was the customer: The sale. Men, in order to be effective, did what they did millenia ago; they formed hunting tribes. This time they called the tribe the business or the corporation. The women did as they had always done—stayed behind, at home, in the caves of Scarsdale and Westport, raising the children, unable to run with the men, bound by apron strings. A few were closer to the hunt—closer to the cliffs and canyons, hills and valleys of business—and they were called secretaries. Clerks. Typists. And they brought some of the comforts of the cave to the office—steaming cups of coffee, for example.

Men were the chosen people. THE CHOSEN SEX. The hunters.

But now—Uncle Sam—traitor to his sex, has ordered that the hunt be opened to women, that there be equal opportunity, that the Man's World hang out *both* "his" and "her" signs.[7]

Explanation.   One of the best ways to get listeners to grasp your meaning is to provide explanations when you use unusual, technical, ambiguous, or foreign words. Harry R. Hall, who at the time of his speech was president of the Michigan state chamber of commerce, described his view of education as "Bewitched, Bothered, Bewildered." He then explained what he meant:

—*Bewitched* by the demonstrated values of education.

—*Bothered* by the immensity and intensity of the festering problems.

—*Bewildered* by the benign involvement of a sclerosed bureaucracy, characterized by a labyrinthine lacework of divided authority between a variety of agencies at the federal, state and local government levels, ill-structured, ill-equipped and ill-willed to take decisive action leading to solutions of problems, leaving willing and able administrators shackled with traditional rigidities that prevent maximum use of manpower and money.[8]

Illustration.   An illustration is a detailed example. To qualify as an illustration, the narrative must include a setting, a few characters, and vividly told action. In his speech on "Urban Crime: Its Causes and Control," Dr. William A. Stanmeyer used a number of vivid illustrations to point up the "ridiculous" implications of several Supreme Court rulings on search and seizure.

A woman who lived alone was awakened in her bedroom by the defendant, who threatened her with a knife, robbed her, and raped her while she was forced to lie on her stomach with a pillow over her head. With the aid of a night light she saw the knife and also noticed that the defendant was wearing leather boots. As soon as he left, she called the police. They searched the area and found boot tracks outside her house. They traced the tracks to the vicinity of the defendant's house. After knocking and entering, the officers observed defendant standing with his boots on. He was questioned and told to go outside and place his boots in the tracks. Later, the boots were confiscated and defendant taken before a magistrate. One of the officers

---

[7]Jean Way Schoonover, "Why Corporate America Fears Women," *Vital Speeches*, 40 (Jan. 1, 1974), p. 189.

[8]Harry R. Hall, "Business Views Education," *Vital Speeches*, 39 (Jan. 15, 1973), p. 210.

returned to his house, conducted a warrantless search and found the knife used in the rape. But defendant's rape conviction was reversed with the court holding that the arrest and search, without a warrant, were illegal.[9]

Example. An example is an illustration in abbreviated form. All but the essential detail has been omitted. On a detail-nondetailed continuum, we would place illustrations on the detail end, specific instances on the non-detailed end, and examples somewhere toward the center.

Visual Aids and Displays. Visual aids may range in complexity from a few lines drawn by the speaker on a blackboard during a presentation to expensive and elaborate models and diagrams prepared by professionals. Holm suggests several guidelines to remember when using visual supporting material (graphs, diagrams, charts, models, etc.):

> Keep the display simple, do not allow its significance to be obscured by nonessential details.
>
> Be certain that it can be seen easily by everyone. Do not stand in front of it. Make certain that it is large enough for the expected viewing distance and for the number of people in the audience.
>
> While using the display, talk to the audience and not to the visual aid.
>
> Keep displays out of sight until you are ready to use them; get them out of sight again when you are through. Do not allow a visual aid to compete with you for the attention of your auditors.
>
> If a visual is too small to be seen, do not use it. Never pass one through the audience where it will distract your listeners from what you are saying.
>
> If you use pass-outs to your listeners, do not try to talk until they have been distributed.
>
> Remember visual aids should be used to explain or prove a point; they are not a substitute for an idea or for skill in speaking.[10]

_____ Introductions, Conclusions, and Transitions

Many experienced speakers make the mistake of trying to write an introduction as the first step in preparing a speech. We have saved our discussion of introductions and conclusions until now, because they should not be written until you have thoroughly planned the body of the speech.

Introductions. A good introduction will accomplish three things: (1) attract and focus audience attention on your speech; (2) assist you in establishing rapport with the audience; and (3) orient your audience to your message. A review of Chapter 4 should be sufficient to make you realize the vital importance of attracting the audience's attention at the very beginning of your

---

[9]William A. Stanmeyer, "Urban Crime," *Vital Speeches*, 39 (Jan. 1, 1973), pp. 183–184.

[10]James N. Holm, *Productive Speaking for Business and the Professions.* Boston: Allyn & Bacon, 1967, p. 406.

presentation. You will be faced with enough barriers to communication with cooperative listeners. However, if you fail to gain a willingness and desire to receive your message from the audience, you are doomed to become a miserable failure. Because it is so important to *start out on the right foot,* we will suggest a number of potential ways of beginning your speeches. In light of your analysis of the audience and the occasion, you should be able to determine the most appropriate opening for each presentation experience that you encounter.

1. You may begin your speech with a startling or shocking statement. The statement may be either fact or opinion; a reality of the moment or a projection for the future. C. Howard Hardesty, Jr., shocked the members of a leadership conference on energy and the environment with two fictitious announcements:

> Ladies and gentlemen, I have been asked to make two announcements: "Because of fuel shortages, the local utility is unable to continue generating electricity at full capacity. At noon the lights will go out, elevator service and telephone service will be discontinued. To avoid any hazard, the management requests that we vacate the hotel by 11:30 A.M."
>
> Regrettably we have also just received the following news bulletin: "An oil well platform off the Delaware Coast has blown out and is on fire. Unless containment efforts are successful, oil will wash ashore along the Delaware and New Jersey Coasts."
>
> Let me quickly add that I hope you've surmised that these notes are pure fiction and were used to bring two important problems into clear focus.[11]

2. You may begin your speech with a hypothetical illustration. Hypothetical illustrations either project us into the future for a glimpse of what might be or take us back into the past for a view of what might have been. V.A. Langille used a hypothetical illustration to open his speech on "The Misinformation Crisis":

> It is the year 2002. The great American social contract glossed over in the history books of the 1970s has been supplanted by what is popularly known as the "Break-Even" society. Free market enterprise, that famous old bulwark of capitalistic democracy, is dead.
>
> Profits are not just a dirty word; they are prohibited.
>
> Personal and corporate taxes are at the 100-percent level.
>
> The government takes care of everybody with living stamps for food, clothing, medical care, recreation, everything.
>
> All housing is public and free. . . .
>
> Now there is still quite a difference between the USA as we know it today and this facetious society of 2002 . . . but the gap is narrowing.[12]

---

[11]C. Howard Hardesty, Jr., "Energy vs. Ecology," *Vital Speeches,* **39** (Mar. 1, 1973), p. 314.

[12]V.A. Langille, "The Misinformation Crisis," *Vital Speeches,* **39** (Mar. 15, 1973), p. 470.

3. You may begin your speech with a reference to the occasion. Jacqueline D. St. John, Associate Professor of History at the University of Nebraska at Omaha, opened her speech at the Conference on Women and Work with: "I am happy to be here this morning and to participate in this Conference on Women and Work sponsored by the Coalition of Labor Union Women and the Nebraska Committee for the Humanities."[13]

4. You may begin your speech with humor. This type of opening is especially effective when the punch line of a humorous anecdote conveys the theme of the speech. George Dixon, President of First Bank System, wanted to explode a number of myths about trade with mainland China. He effectively began his speech with the following anecdote:

> It is a genuine pleasure to be here in Duluth again today to share with you some thoughts on trade with the People's Republic of China. This being a speech, we might as well begin with a brief anecdote about another speech which can give us an early insight into the nature of the Chinese people. It is the story of a well known American professor who once spoke at a Chinese university where an interpreter translated his talk into Chinese symbols on a blackboard. The professor noted that the interpreter stopped writing during most of the speech and at its conclusion he asked why. "We only write when the speaker *says* something," was the blithe reply.
>
> Then there is the story about a young American who at a banquet found himself seated next to the eminent Wellington Koo, a Chinese diplomat. Completely at a loss as to what to say to a Chinese, this young man ventured, "Likee soupee?" Mr. Koo smiled and nodded. Later when called upon to speak, Wellington Koo delivered an eloquent talk in exquisite English, sat down while the applause was still resounding, turned to the young man and said, "Likee speechee?"[14]

5. You may begin your speech with a reference to a historical event. Jay Van Andel, Chairman of the United States Chamber of Commerce, began a presentation to the Atlanta Downtown Kiwanis Club in the following manner:

> Two hundred years ago the American Colonies were far down the road to becoming a government regulated totalitarian society. Big government headquartered in London was taking over. Free enterprise was being destroyed. Personal freedom had become more and more limited. Taxes were going higher and higher. Government bureaucrats—not elected and not responsive to the people—were forcing people to do that which the bureaucrat wanted—never mind what the people wanted. Local government was weak, the power was in London, and London wasn't listening.
>
> Now this was nothing new. Most of the world lived that way 200 years ago and had from the beginning of time. Freedom—free enterprise—Liberty—these were only a lovely but unrealizable dream to most of the world's people then—and so it had always been. A distant Camelot—a tale told around the campfire at night but disappearing into the harsh realities of life each morning.
>
> But then something happened. . . .[15]

---

[13]Jacqueline D. St. John, "Women and Work," *Vital Speeches*, **45** (Sept. 1, 1979), p. 691.
[14]George H. Dixon, "Trade With China: Opportunity or Illusion," *Vital Speeches*, **46** (Nov. 15, 1979), p. 83.
[15]Jay Van Andel, "Business Leadership Against Inflation," *Vital Speeches*, **45** (July 1, 1979), p. 555.

6. You may begin your speech with a question or a series of questions. Such questions are usually called *rhetorical*, since they are asked to stimulate thought rather than to get answers. Charles J. Dibona, President of the American Petroleum Institute, began his speech with two important questions: "I suspect that the first two questions you'll ask me today are: 'Will we have enough heating oil this winter?' And, then, 'Will we have enough gasoline next spring?' "[16] The remainder of his speech on U.S. energy policies sought to answer those two questions.

7. You may begin your speech with a personal reference. Such an opening is more effective when you know that your listeners will be interested in hearing your personal experiences. The president of the Plaza Hotel began his address to the American Medical Association with a personal reference:

> I came from the balcony to the hotel business. For ten years as a corporate director of Sonesta Hotels with no line responsibility, I had my office in a little building next door to the Plaza. I went to the hotel every day for lunch and often stayed overnight. I was a professional guest. . . .
>
> In my ten years of kibitzing, all I had really learned about the hotel business was how to use a guest toilet without removing the strip of paper that's printed "Sanitized for your protection." . . . Paul Sonnabend, President of Sonesta, didn't help much when he introduced me to my executive staff with the following kind words: "The Plaza has been losing money the last several years and we've had the best management in the business. Now we're going to try the worst."[17]

8. You may begin your speech with a reference to some current event. The executive vice-president of the Continental Oil Company began a speech on "Fuels, Feedstocks and the Future" with a reference to the latest statement from Arab oil czars:

> You should have invited the Shah of Iran to be your speaker. He has more money, more oil, and more credibility. The other day, he observed that the industrial nations should ban the burning of petroleum and reserve it entirely for petrochemical manufacturing. The high importance he recently attached to petrochemicals is one of the most sensible statements to come out of the Middle East. America's "burn-it-up" philosophy is coming to an end, but the present stringency will force us to continue burning—wasting if you will—oil and gas.[18]

9. You may begin your speech with a quotation. Speaking on the topic "It's Your Freedom They're After!", Herbert E. Markley, Chairman of the Board, National Association of Manufacturers, began by reading from a letter sent to Kentucky Senators and Congressmen by one of their constituents:

---

[16]Charles J. Dibona, "U.S. Energy: Moving Off the Razor's Edge," *Vital Speeches*, **46** (Dec. 1, 1979), p. 104.

[17]James Lavenson, "Think Strawberries," *Vital Speeches*, **40** (Mar. 15, 1974), p. 346.

[18]C. Howard Hardesty, Jr., "Fuels, Feedstocks and the Future," *Vital Speeches*, **40** (Feb. 15, 1974), p. 274.

Thank you. In seeking a suitable way to open this talk, "It's Your Freedom They're After!", I could not identify a more appropriate vehicle than a letter sent to Kentucky Senators and Congressmen by one of their constituents. The letter from Mr. Henry Heuser, President of Vogt Machine Company, I shall not quote in full, but I will extract for you two or three of its key paragraphs, for they set the stage for what we will be talking about in the next several minutes. Asking his readers to "give us less," less control of people's lives, less government encroachment into our everyday affairs, and a less horrendous level of taxation that is gradually but surely wrecking our country, he went on to say:

"Who do you think you are? Are you really smart enough to design our automobiles, tell the farmer how to raise his crops, establish minimum wages, and tell us when to retire? Do you really know enough to tell us where and how to build our plants, price our gas and oil, regulate each package in the grocery, and tell us how and where to educate our children? . . . You run the most inefficient operation in the history of the world. . . . You employ more people to generate more paper to make more rules to harass us working people more than ever before in history. You dole out money to more undeserving recipients who make absolutely no contribution to our standard of living than ever previously conceived by man."[19]

10. You may begin with a reference to the audience. When the executive director of the National Urban League addressed the 33rd annual Convention of the National Newspaper Publishers Association, his opening words were "I have never before addressed an audience that included so many of my bosses—over sixty of you are publishers of newspapers that carry my weekly To Be Equal column."[20]

11. You may begin your speech with a reference to your subject. A Charles F. Kettering Foundation official began his talk with: "In preparation for this address, I utilized the extensive resources of the Charles F. Kettering Foundation to investigate how much we have learned about education during the past decade."[21]

Conclusions.   Your conclusion should include (1) a summary of your most important points and (2) a wrap-up statement. Summary should be self-explanatory, but you may wonder what we mean by a wrap-up statement. Your last words need to be more powerful than what you normally communicate in a simple summary. Consequently, it is recommended that you prepare some kind of closing in addition to your summary. The wrap-up statement can be a statement of personal intent, a challenge to the audience, or any one of the methods used to open your speech.

1. *Concluding with a Quotation.* Frequently, the speaker will elect to close a speech with the words of another individual, lines of poetry, or lyrics from a song. The late Dr. Martin Luther King was inclined to conclude his messages with lyrics from hymns, such as the old slave hymn that ended with the lines "Free at last! Free at last! Thank God Almighty! I'm free at last!" Jay Van Andel,

[19]Herbert E. Markley, "It's Your Freedom They're After!", *Vital Speeches*, **45** (September 15, 1979), p. 731.

[20]Vernon E. Jordan, Jr., "A Black Press," *Vital Speeches*, **39** (July 15, 1973), p. 586.

[21]Samuel G. Sava, "To Russia, With Love," *Vital Speeches*, **39** (May 1, 1974), p. 444.

Chairman of the United States Chamber of Commerce, concluded his address to the Atlanta Downtown Kiwanis Club with a quote from Winston Churchill:

> We must continue to work as leaders of American business, to preserve our free enterprise system and its Siamese twin—personal liberty. There is no greater inspiration to do so than that contained in the words of Winston Churchill as he spoke of another compelling challenge at the onset of World War II:
>
> "Still if you will not fight when you can easily win without bloodshed, if you will not fight when your victory can be sure and not too costly, you may come to the moment when you will HAVE to fight with all the odds against you and you have only a precarious chance of survival. There may even be a worse case; you may have to fight when there is no hope of victory because it is better to perish than to live as slaves."[22]

2. *Concluding with a Challenge.* Sometimes speakers choose to close their speeches with direct challenges to the audience members. John Tupper, President of the California Medical Association, concluded his remarks before the California Medical Association, with these words:

> Upon each of us in the medical profession, in education, in government and in the community rests an important responsibility to do all that we can to help guide and direct these changes and to increase the efficiency of the energy expenditure toward the production of more light and less heat.
>
> We must participate! We must communicate! We must educate! We must legislate! And we must litigate! For private medicine is a major bastion in the protection of freedom and of private enterprise in the United States of America.
>
> Thank you.[23]

3. *Concluding with an Illustration.* Just as illustrations are effective devices for opening speeches, they are of proven value in closing your message. Armand Hammer, Chairman of the Board of Occidental Petroleum Corporation, spoke to the City Club of Cleveland about the need to reduce our dependence on foreign imports. He concluded his remarks with a brief historical illustration:

> Having spent a great deal of my life in France, I have always particularly liked the philosophy of that great Marshal of the Army, General Lyautey, who was greeted one day in the advanced years of his life by his gardener. The gardener showed him a fruit tree, a gift sent to the Marshal from some friends in Africa.
>
> "But General," said the gardener. "It will take many years for this tree to bear fruit."
>
> "Then we have no time to waste," said the Marshal, "plant the tree immediately."
>
> My friends, there is no longer any time which can be wasted on endless debate. The most critical moment is now at hand and we must for our very salvation undertake real, possible actions which can begin to turn the tide which has begun to wash away our resources and our confidence.[24]

---

[22]Jay Van Andel, "Business Leadership Against Inflation," p. 558.

[23]C. John Tupper, "A New American Revolution," *Vital Speeches*, 45 (May 15, 1979), p. 465.

[24]Armand Hammer, "Our Dependence on Foreign Imports," *Vital Speeches*, 46 (Nov. 1, 1979), p. 47.

Transitions.   Transitions may be either verbal or nonverbal. Verbal transitions include such phrases as "in addition to," "besides this," "however," "consequently," "later," "looking ahead," "provided," "in spite of this," etc. Nonverbal transitions may take the form of body movement or even silence. A few seconds pause between your introduction and the body of your speech can be an extremely effective transition. Regardless of whether you choose to use all verbal or all nonverbal transitions, or even a combination of the two, you will want to give special attention and planning to the task of developing clear transitions.

rehearsal for presentations

When you have completed the polishing phases of preparation, you are ready to prepare a presentation outline (key words and phrases) from your preparation outline and begin practicing your speech aloud. Thinking through the speech will be beneficial, but there is no substitute for standing in front of a mirror and actually talking through your presentation. Remember, since you will be receiving self-feedback during your actual presentation (hearing your own voice through the bony structure of your head and through the channel), it makes good sense to get somewhat accustomed to the sound of your own voice in presentational situations.

As you rehearse your speech, however, remember that it is wise to avoid memorizing the content of your message. A multitude of delivery problems can be traced to the simple act of attempting to "recite" your speech, rather than conversationally *sharing* well-thought-out ideas with other human beings. Only the most skilled speaker is able to make a memorized speech "sound" natural and conversational. For most of us, a memorized speech results in an unnatural phrase pattern and a predictable rising and falling inflection pattern. Your best approach will be to speak extemporaneously. This approach will allow your exact wording to be spontaneous and reflective of audience feedback.

delivering your presentations

Many people have trouble maintaining control over their voices and their bodies during presentational speaking situations. You should, however, be able to talk with twenty to thirty people with the same degree of confidence that you have when you are conversing with one or two people.

If you want to be as effective in the control of your body and your voice in presentational speaking situations as you are in small group communication situations, you will need to remember that presentational speaking is expanded conversation. Therefore, you should think of the audience as *a collection of individuals.* Try to communicate directly with three or four individuals scattered throughout the room. Chances are that if you are getting through to the three or four people that you have singled out, you are getting through to the rest. Don't forget this principle. The more that you feel a need to avoid direct contact with individual members of the audience, the more you need to force yourself to establish and maintain contact. Several years ago students with stage-fright problems were told that it was all right to look over the heads of audience members. What these well-meaning counselors didn't realize, however, is that they were actually making the stage-fright problems worse in allowing the students to break direct mental contact and eye contact with members of the audience.

Effective delivery presupposes the following:

1. That you have something to say that *you* think is important.
2. That you really care whether or not you are being understood by members of the group.
3. That you are willing to say what you have to say as simply and as directly as you are able.

Finally, remember that mother nature gives you an extra supply of energy when you face a speaking situation. That excess energy can work for you or it can work against you. If you are afraid to move (either by taking a few steps to the side of the lectern or by using your body in emphatic and demonstrative gestures) you will likely exhibit meaningless, distracting body movements as your body attempts to work off the excess adrenalin. You will want to review Chapter 5 regarding the use of gestures, eye contact, and vocal variety to increase your communicative effectiveness.

Summary

In this chapter we have defined presentational speaking as expanded conversation. In addition, we have discussed the phases of preparation of a presentational speech. The first phase is the *analysis phase.* Here your concern is with determining audience and occasion variables requiring specific adaptation, selecting your general and specific communication purposes, and developing your central thought into a one-sentence statement.

The middle phase of preparation for speechmaking involves: (1) selection of the main points that you will need to develop; (2) arrangement of those points into some meaningful pattern of development; (3) supporting each main point, and (4) developing of introduction, conclusion, and transitions.

The final phases of speechmaking involve careful rehearsal (preferably by speaking aloud in front of a mirror) and delivery of the message. Effective delivery presupposes proper attitudes toward yourself, your message, and your listeners.

Discussion Questions

1. Give your own definitions for each of the support devices in this chapter. Provide an example of each type of support.
2. Construct an example and provide definitions for at least two methods of beginning a speech that were not discussed in this chapter.
3. Distinguish between central idea sentence and specific purpose.
4. List five uses of presentational speaking in the type of work you are in or plan to enter.
5. Distinguish between each of the speech purposes discussed. Which one will you probably rely most heavily on in life? Which one least?
6. Distinguish between demographic and voluntary membership groups.
7. What are some of the ways that an individual may gather materials concerning audiences?
8. Construct a sample outline to demonstrate your familiarity with each of the patterns of arrangement.

Study Probes

1. Attend a college lecture, a courtroom trial, and a church service. Keep accurate notes regarding the presentations in each context. How do the three contexts affect the type of communication and interaction?
2. Write a speech in two forms. Adapt one form to a favorable audience and the other form to an unfavorable audience. In each case be sure to note the type and frequency of support materials, pattern of arrangement, and type of conclusion.
3. Ask a friend to help you conduct a survey of the make-up of a civic club in your town. Once you have discussed the results with each other, try to outline the characteristics and specify the kind of adaptation required on the bases of those characteristics.

Additional Reading

Holm, James, *Productive Speaking for Business and the Professions.* Boston: Allyn & Bacon, 1967.

Howell, William, and **Ernest Bormann,** *Presentational Speaking for Business and the Professions.* New York: Harper & Row, Pub., 1971.

Redding, W.C., "The Empirical Study of Human Communication in Business and Industry," in *The Frontiers of Speech-Communication Research,* Paul Ried (ed.). Syracuse, N.Y.: Syracuse University Press, 1965.

Zelko, Harold, and **Frank Dance,** *Business and Professional Speech Communication.* New York: Holt, Rinehart and Winston, 1965.

Preparing
for effective
writing

13

key points to learn

The importance of words in the communication process.

How background and experience affect vocabulary and word choice.

The importance of tone in written communications.

The part readability plays in letters and reports.

Some grammar trouble spots.

Develop a writing style that is comfortable for you.

It is difficult to think about written business communications without thinking about words. Words are the "tools of the trade" for writers of business communications.

But it is probably a safe bet that many readers of these pages have not given much thought to words or vocabulary. Oh, you may find yourself thinking, "What is that word I want?"; but most of the time we get along without too much thought given to words. After all, we've been communicating with words ever since we learned to talk, haven't we? Studies have shown that most of us think we communicate pretty well.

Someone has said that "words are the names we give to experiences." We have an experience, something happens to us, or we are involved in a particular incident, and we must have some means of telling other people about the happening, or we must have some means of filing it in our own minds. We do this by means of words; therefore, you can see that words are just symbols that stand for "the real thing." The four-wheeled, metal vehicle in which I drive to work is out in the parking lot; however, I can let you know that I have one of these contraptions by using the symbol "a-u-t-o-m-o-b-i-l-e." And it probably won't take very long for us to discover that "automobile" means one thing to me and another thing to you. Words are an important area of study in the communication process.

semantics

A layman's definition of "semantics" might be "the study of the meaning of words." But words in themselves have no meaning. Meanings are in people.

The ancient Greeks held two views about the meaning of words. One was that the gods gave words their meanings; the other view held that people gave meanings to words. We, of course, adopted the latter view. Words mean whatever you and I say they mean. Since you and I have had different experiences and different backgrounds, the same symbol (word) will mean something slightly different to each of us. If I say the word "desk," I may picture the one in my office at the University (metal, formica top, four drawers). You, on the other hand, may visualize the desk in your father's executive office (solid wood, six drawers). We have agreed on the general type or category of object, but we are definitely not "seeing" the same desk.

To carry this one step further, if you and I were to agree that the four-wheeled, metal vehicle we drive to work each day is a "d-e-s-k," then we can communicate effectively when we tell each other we are going to get in our "desks" and drive home. Meanings are in people!

Menning, Wilkinson, and Clarke say that "fundamental to communication is this general [semantic] principle: *The symbols used must stand for essentially the same thing in the minds of the sender and the receiver.*"[1] Notice the word "essentially." When communicating with a serious purpose in mind, we usually strive for "perfect" communication; but we rarely achieve perfection. Knowing this in advance, we should attempt to come as close to the ideal as possible. Inasmuch as we know that words mean different things to different people, we select a word which we think our reader will understand (decode) in "essentially" the same way we understand (encode) it. This is one reason it is very important to keep our reader in mind as we write. If you do not know your reader personally and if you have no clues about the person's vocabulary level (e.g., the word choice used in the letter he or she sent to you), then you must write at a level you think most people would understand. You must be careful, however, when writing at this lower level that you do not select words which sound condescending—that is, do not seem to be "talking down" to your reader. Condescension is an element of "tone" which we will discuss later in this chapter.

Another semantics problem is that we tend to take words "at face value." Words are only "the tip of the iceberg," as it were; there is much more to the story or to the statement than that which is expressed by the words. Be very

---

[1]J. H. Menning, C. W. Wilkinson, and Peter B. Clarke, *Communicating through Letters and Reports.* Homewood, Ill.: Richard D. Irwin, 1976, p. 590.

careful about making broad, sweeping statements. When you hear an absolute statement, check it carefully. "All politicians are crooked." Who says so? What level politician? What does "crooked" mean? As we have said, words are only symbols; do not confuse the word (symbol) with the real thing; some people tend to react as violently to the word "snake" as they might to the real slithering reptile.

If there is one thing of which we can be certain, it is that things are going to change. "Time marches on." You must remember that word meanings change, too. Just as words mean different things to different people, words mean different things to the same person at different times in his or her life. As a result of our changing experiences (and our perceptions), the meanings we attach to words will change, too. It is one thing to read about Paris; a visit to the city will add new meaning to the word "Paris." It is one thing to watch a professional football game on television; attendance at a Super Bowl game will guarantee an entirely different definition of "professional football" for the viewer from that point on. And a final example, "going to pot" probably conjures up a completely different mental image now from what it did 30 years ago.

We can sum up this portion of our discussion about words by urging you to remain *aware*, to stay tuned in as you communicate. Communication requires effort and planning. You must work at it! When communicating, try to place yourself in the position of your receiver. Try to think of the frame of reference of the other person and encode or decode words accordingly.

_____ **Words about Words**

Words have certain qualities or characteristics called "denotation" and "connotation." Denotation refers to the "meaning" of the word as given in the dictionary; it is the definition of the word usually accepted or understood by most people. "Connotation," on the other hand, refers to the emotional response to the word; it is the mental, and sometimes overt, response a given person will have to the word. A man may have no particular reaction to the word "football" other than it is a pleasant experience he has on Sunday afternoon in front of the TV. His wife, on the other hand, may become quite upset at the mention of "football" because she is tired of having the games interrupt social activities in which she wants to participate.

If you have not already had the experience, you will sooner or later witness the spectacle of someone reacting "connotatively" to your words. It can be a very interesting—even frightening—experience.

Two more words about words you should have in your vocabulary are "euphemism" and "dysphemism." A euphemism is a pleasant-sounding word that is substituted for an unpleasant-sounding one. Probably the best example of a euphemism is the extent to which we go to avoid saying someone is dead—the person "passed away," "went to the happy hunting ground," or "expired"; but we have great difficulty in using the word "dead."

A dysphemism is the opposite of a euphemism; it is an attempt to give a bad or unpleasant flavor to a situation. A person who is very much opposed to the consumption of alcoholic beverages might refer to a cocktail lounge as a "booze joint." After experiencing several days of almost constant rainfall, a person who is extremely tired of the wet weather might be inclined to refer to the next gentle shower as a "monsoon."

Word choice might be thought of as a "nonverbal element of verbal communication." You need to be sensitive to words and their "meanings." And you need to be aware of how you use words, and to the greatest extent possible, how other people use words. If you can develop this awareness of and sensitivity to words in general as well as to the concepts of connotation, denotation, euphemisms, and dysphemisms, you will on many occasions get a more accurate communication than you will just by taking the message at surface value.

you and written communication

It is important that you know something about your intrapersonal communication and the "state of the art" concerning *your* use of words. That is, you need to do some self-analysis to discover your strengths and weaknesses with regard to word usage and language. While a lot of your communication patterns may be established, there are still some things you can do to compose more effective written communications.

A frequently heard comment explaining miscommunication goes something like this, "I don't understand what happened, I told him. . . ." All too often we say words and assume we have communicated. A teacher can fall into this trap very easily because the teacher may have taught certain material for several semesters and may forget that it is new ground to the students. You need to be aware of some of the intrapersonal (*intra* = within) elements which affect the communication process. As a result, when you are involved in a very important business deal, for example, you can plan your communication encounter more effectively.

We said earlier in this chapter that words are the names we give to our experiences. If you know some of the things that make up this experience, you may be able to make some predictions about the person's vocabulary. Some of the factors which go to make up this experience are: age, education, travel, organizations where employed, organizational memberships, family background, section of the country where the person has lived. This is just a partial list, but it is sufficient to point out how these factors result in your experience and in your vocabulary.

It should be quite obvious that you know more words now than you did when you started school—age and education have accounted for this. Travel introduces us to new places and new customs—hence, new words. We pick up the jargon of the business world in which we are employed. The varied backgrounds and interests of other members expose us to many new and different words when we join an organization. Your family background or your home life has had a great effect on your vocabulary. Was there emphasis on a variety of activities? Were there family discussions on current events and other subjects? Was attendance at cultural events encouraged? Finally, the section of the country where we live has some effect at least on the types of words we know. For example, people who live near the ocean are going to use a set of words dealing with life in and around the water which people in the desert Southwest are going to have little use for in their daily life. On the other hand, people in the Southwest are going to have a set of words peculiar to their section of the country which would be of little use in the daily conversation of people living near the ocean.

We can achieve a lot of our experiences vicariously through reading books, through talking with other people, by watching television. One need not break a leg in order to have some idea of what is involved; after all, each of us has had some bout with pain and we have observed people with broken legs and perhaps we have even talked with someone using crutches. However, it is quite certain the term "broken leg" will take on new meaning for us if we should ever have the misfortune to have this experience.

One factor we have not mentioned in connection with words and experience is "money." Money or the attainment of a certain fairly high level of financial income is definitely not a necessity in the attainment of experience and vocabulary. However, one can assume that a person with adequate financial reserves can "buy more experience." The person with money can go to college, can travel, can join more organizations, and can engage in many different activities. Notice we are saying only that money makes the experiences potentially available. Obviously, people spend their money in different ways.

Another factor we should discuss in passing is "individual differences." The mental ability or the mental capacity of an individual will certainly affect the extent to which an individual can become involved. Along the same line, some people have more acute senses than other people; thus, some people will experience a happening which other people will miss entirely or they will experience the same event more intensely than other people.

A common thread which runs throughout most of our discussion is *people*. People are the focal point in many of our experiences. It is interesting to note that development of our intrapersonal communication depends to a great extent on the depth and extent of our interpersonal communications. It is through your contacts, interactions, and relationships with other people that you identify, define, and determine who you are. In other words, our communications with other people help us to determine our self-image.

How you view yourself or how you think of yourself helps to determine how you act—how you communicate. If you are told often enough that you have a pleasing personality and if you accept this evaluation, then you are probably going to spend time cultivating this personality and selecting words that tend to make you sound likeable, that give you a positive appearance, and that make people want to be with you. And when you do something that makes you appear "nasty" or which violates this self-image of a pleasant person, you develop guilt feelings that are very annoying to you. In short, a great deal of our communication effort is spent in developing, maintaining, and increasing the images we have of ourselves and which we think other people have of us.

Basically, what we are talking about in this section of the chapter is *perception.* Perception is synonymous with or similar to your self-image, the filter of your mind, your frame of reference, and various other concepts which are used in discussing intrapersonal communication. The experiences you have with people and things will determine your values, your opinions, your beliefs, your attitudes, and how you use words. They will determine how you perceive events. Peter Drucker says, "Communication is perception."[2]

Although this is only a surface treatment of some very involved and complicated concepts, perhaps by now you realize that the way you view yourself and the various experiences which have resulted in this person called "you" determine how you use words—how you communicate.

Grouping the Words (Tone)

While it is important that you have enough words in your vocabulary to enable you to communicate effectively by selecting just the proper shade of meaning, it is important that you pick the word or combinations of words that impress the reader as polite, pleasing, and proper. This quality of your writing is known as *tone.*

Poor tone can creep into your writing very quickly if you do not stay alert to what you are writing and/or if you are not aware of your own true feelings about what you are writing. The end result in either case will probably be the same: you will offend or annoy your reader. Let's consider a few examples.

"We are looking forward to having several prominent business people in attendance at our meeting, and you may come, too." While this sentence would probably be annoying only to someone who was looking for trouble, there is still no need for it to be written this way. If you cannot eliminate errors in tone as you compose your written communications, then you will have to catch them as you rewrite or as you proofread. When you proofread, proofread for meaning as well as for mechanical errors. The error in "I have you letter" would probably pass inspection, if you are not proofreading for meaning as well as for mechanics.

---

[2]Peter F. Drucker, *Management: Tasks, Responsibilities, Practices.* New York: Harper & Row, Pub., 1974, p. 483.

Watch the use of superlatives; keep "est" words to a minimum. In other words, don't brag. You need a good self-image, but let the facts speak for you. If you use strong evidence, the reader will realize how "great" the subject under discussion is.

Closely related to bragging is the "big I, little you" approach. It is not difficult for some employees of large, successful, multimillion dollar companies to be impressed with themselves and to write from their lofty perch. When you are employed by a business organization, you will have to deal with other business organizations, and this should enable you to realize that all business organizations have problems. You and your company will make mistakes, too, so very few of us can afford to take a superior position or attitude towards other people and other organizations. Perhaps the Golden Rule applies here.

Another danger of the "big I, little you" attitude is that you may condescend to your reader—that is, you may "talk down" to your reader. You must not use words which make your reader seem to be beneath your level organizationally and/or mentally. "With just a little more effort and persistence, you can make certain that your growing little organization gets on the right track." Not a statement designed to build good will for you or your organization.

With just a little additional effort, the person who condescends to his readers can become a preacher. There is rather a fine line between "telling people something" and "preaching to them." Many of the letters we write, especially persuasive types, involve a job of educating the reader. But in educating, you may be preaching, if you are not careful.

Once you recognize that you are writing with a rather superior, conceited tone, be very careful that in your efforts to reform you do not go overboard and suffer a serious attack of humility. Inferiority feelings in print do not have a good tone either; they make you seem negative, weak, and indecisive. Such tone will not inspire confidence in your reader. Consider the weak tone of this statement: "We have our problems like all other companies, and we make mistakes, too; however, in our own small way we try to do our best."

Many of these problems of tone come about because the writer fails to maintain a balance with the reader. Indeed the writer may not even be thinking of the reader as a human being. The writer may not even be thinking of the reader period! When you are writing to a customer or a client, you should always try to think of him or her as a real, live, flesh-and-blood human being. Your reader is more than just an account number. Your reader is a person much like yourself, and you should treat this person as you would want to be treated. If you will try to maintain this balance between yourself and your reader, you will go a long way towards choosing words which will result in acceptable tone in your written business communications.

Many authorities suggest that the business writer should try to be conversational—write the way you talk. This approach may be all right provided you do not become folksy, chatty, and long-winded. However, one aspect of the conversational approach which does have merit is that as you write you picture yourself actually using face-to-face communication (still the best form of communication), and this may force you to be more careful of your tone. Immediate feedback is an advantage. And one final suggestion about tone: Don't forget to use an occasional euphemism.

The end result of all your attention to tone is that your writing will sound much more courteous and sincere.

Making Your Writing Inviting (Readability)

Readability is the ease with which a person can read your words, sentences, and paragraphs and comprehend their meaning. As we have tried to point out, you must do everything you can to make your writing inviting. You must attempt to get all factors in the communication process working *for* your message. The way you group words together in sentences and paragraphs and the appearance all this mass of type has on the page can have an influence on reader acceptance of your message.

Because you have your reader in mind as you write and because you are thinking of your reader as a person and not as an account number, you should automatically adapt your writing to the reader. Because communication takes place in the mind of the reader, you will want to use words, sentences, and paragraphs that will invite the reader to read and which will make it easy for him or her to understand and remember what you have written. It is not necessary to limit yourself to one-syllable words if you know your reader is capable of understanding six-syllable words; however, if you do not know your reader, you will want to use words that the "average" person can understand.

You will want to use sentences of many different lengths. A good average sentence length is fifteen to twenty words, but this does not mean that all your sentences should fall within this range. Having all sentences approximately the same length would result in very dull reading. Variety is the spice of life in sentence structure, too. A very short sentence tends to break your reader's stride and to receive special attention. Be sure the content of the sentence deserves all that attention. There is nothing wrong with an occasional sentence containing thirty or forty words, provided you can handle the construction of such a sentence; be aware, however, that a long sentence presents many opportunities for faulty construction. Write carefully!

In addition to watching the length of your sentences, you can also do a lot to make your reader's job easier by paying special attention to topic and transitional sentences. A topic sentence is one that introduces the subject to be discussed in a paragraph. It is much like the headline in a newspaper. The topic sentence is usually the first sentence in a paragraph, although it may on occasion be the last sentence. A transitional sentence is usually the last sentence in a paragraph, which prepares the reader's thoughts and attention for the subject to be introduced by the topic sentence in the following paragraph. Effective topic and transitional sentences enable your reader to progress easily and logically through your letter or report.

Just as a variety of sentence lengths makes a written message more readable, so does a variety of paragraph lengths appear more inviting. Each paragraph is supposed to contain one basic idea. A long paragraph of thirty or forty lines of black type appears rather dull and forbidding to the reader who must begin at the first line of the paragraph and wade through all those lines just to obtain one idea. An occasional paragraph of this length is acceptable, but too many of them are very discouraging to the reader. Too many short paragraphs may overwhelm the reader with an excessive number of ideas to be absorbed from one page of writing. This is *overparagraphing;* too many long paragraphs result in *underparagraphing.* A mixture of paragraph lengths, like a variety of sentence lengths, is desirable.

Readability, then, is another element of written communications which when handled effectively should enable the writer to achieve attention, understanding, and acceptance of his or her message by the reader.

some grammar hints

Millions of people have argued, "What if my grammar is incorrect; you got the message, didn't you?" A college professor might respond, "Well, if you want to write like a grade-school dropout, why spend your time and money here at Higher Education U?" The discussion of "correct" versus "understandable" grammar has actually been going on for centuries; and while it is not our purpose either to join the battle or to attempt to settle the fight here, we do want to make a few points in favor of correct grammar.

Importance of Correct Grammar

Correct grammar makes communication easier. Obviously, people who have a good background in the fundamentals of grammar are going to get your message more easily than they would a poorly written communication. Subconsciously, they will appreciate your command of the language. People who do not have a strong background in grammar will also read your message more easily than they would one that is poorly written. While they may not realize why you have communicated with them so easily, the net result is still the same. In addition to making communication easier, correct grammar is flattering and pleasing to the reader. You are telling your reader that he or she is important and that you think he or she is discriminating and will know and appreciate a job well done.

Another reason correct grammar pays dividends is that it makes your company look good. It suggests attention to quality and detail. In a way, incorrect use of language is not unlike incorrect use of numbers; it says to your reader, "I'm careless, and other parts of this message may not be accurate either." You must make all segments of your communications work for you.

We want to mention here just a few of the grammar trouble spots we encounter most often in students' papers:

Agreement of Subject and Verb.   The subject and the verb of a sentence must agree in number. If the subject is a singular noun, it must have a singular verb. If the subject is a plural noun, it requires a plural verb.

(No)   *Profits* of the partnership *was* not up to budget.
(Yes)   *Profits* of the partnership *were* not up to budget.

Incomplete Sentence.   This is a group of words which does not make complete sense. Something is missing. Frequently, the writer has created the incomplete sentence by using a period instead of a comma.

(No)   Knowing that you are interested in buying additional computer equipment. I have asked our sales representative to call on you.
(Yes)   Knowing that you are interested in buying additional computer equipment, I have asked our sales representative to call on you.

Tense.   The time of an event is expressed or revealed by the tense of the verb. Use the tense which is sensible and which fits the situation.

(No)   We *were* glad to get your order.
(Yes)   We *are* glad to get your order.
(No)   What *was* the name of that building we just passed?
(Yes)   What *is* the name of that building we just passed?

Agreement of Pronoun and Antecedent.   The number of a pronoun (singular or plural) should agree with the number of the word to which it refers (the antecedent).

(No)   *Everyone* had *their* own idea about what should be done.
(Yes)   *Everyone* had *his or her* own idea about what should be done.

"Ing" Words.   Whenever you see a sentence beginning with a word ending in "ing," watch for potential trouble! You are dealing with a dangling participle, which means there is some doubt about what the "ing" word modifies.

(No)   Going to school this morning the United Nations Building was shrouded in fog.
(Yes)   Going to school this morning, I noticed that the United Nations Building was shrouded in fog.

Adjective or Adverb Misuse.   Adjectives modify nouns or pronouns; adverbs modify verbs, adjectives, and adverbs. ("Real" is an adjective; "very" is an adverb.")

(No)   They are *real* efficient workers.
(Yes)   They are *very* efficient workers.

Although these are just a few examples, they are very common grammar trouble spots. If you recognize your own mistakes in some of these problem areas, a little time spent in grammar review could prove worthwhile. You will find books on the subject at your college bookstore, or your instructor can give you some help. A few book titles are listed at the end of this chapter. Your grammar review time will be time well spent.

the end result

The sorts of things we have discussed in this chapter are the ingredients of your writing style. Your background and experiences are revealed in the way you express yourself on paper. Check your intrapersonal communication to make sure that your personal feelings and attitudes enable you to express yourself in writing with good tone and genuine you attitude.

Be friendly but not folksy. Be businesslike, but remember that your reader is a human being as well as an account number. If you handle mechanics well, and if your writing sounds sincere and includes a certain amount of reader involvement, your written business communications should get the results you want.

Summary

Words are the tools of the trade for the business writer. Therefore, it is important for you to learn about them and how to use them effectively. These words about words should be in your vocabulary: euphemisms, dysphemisms, denotation, and connotation.

Your background and experience—those things that make you "uniquely you" in intrapersonal communication—determine how you perceive events and use words. Some patterns may be set, but there are things you can do to change if you want to.

Tone, the way your words sound to the reader, is achieved by the words you choose as well as by the way you group them. Make your writing sound sincere. You will also want to choose and group words carefully in order to achieve good readability. Readability means that someone can peruse your written communications more easily because you have paid attention to word, sentence, and paragraph length or difficulty.

It is important to use correct grammar because it makes communication easier, it makes your company look good, and it makes the reader feel important. Grammar trouble spots can be eliminated with a little review of a basic grammar book.

Discussion Questions

1. Words are the "tools of the trade" for the writer of business letters. Explain.
2. "A word is a symbol." Explain.
3. Why is it doubtful or unlikely that a person will ever achieve perfect communication?
4. How can *awareness* help a person solve some miscommunications resulting from language or word misuse?
5. Select several words and consider and discuss their denotative and connotative meanings.
6. Of what value is a knowledge of euphemisms and dysphemisms to the writer of business letters?
7. What is the relationship between perception and intrapersonal communication?
8. What is readability? What are the factors involved in readability?
9. "Why should I worry about my grammar as long as people understand what I'm saying?" Discuss.
10. What is meant by "writing style?" What factors go to make up your writing style?

Word Exercises

Select the Correct Word:

1. It is a personal matter between (him, he) and (I, me).
2. She writes (very, real) (good, well).
3. The envelope (lay, laid) on the table unopened.
4. Your class participation will have little (affect, effect) on your grade in the course.
5. I will be glad to speak to your management team (providing, provided) I do not have a conflicting engagement.
6. Give the package to (whomever, whoever) answers the doorbell.
7. I understand (you, your) wanting to finish your college program.
8. Standard letterhead (stationery, stationary) measures 8½ × 11 inches.
9. What (is, was) the name of that building we just passed?
10. His book about birds (was, were) on the best-seller list last week.

11. She (don't, doesn't) own a typewriter.
12. (Lie, Lay) down.
13. The old lady was (sitting, setting) in a chair on the front porch.
14. I would like to bring my friend with me to your party if I (can, may).
15. Neither of us (are, is) going.
16. It seems unlikely that our team will (loose, lose) the game.
17. (Who's, Whose) pencil is this?
18. They (should have, should of) tried harder.
19. (Between, Among) the five of us there are 73 years of experience.
20. He took the loss in stride (like, as) a good sport should.

(If your score on these sentences is not what you would like it to be, you may be able to improve it by studying one of the books in the additional reading section.)

════════ Additional Reading

Branchaw, Bernadine P., *English Made Easy*. New York: Gregg/McGraw-Hill, 1979.

Brusaw, Charles T., Gerald J. Alred, and Walter E. Oliu, *The Business Writer's Handbook*. New York: St. Martin's Press, 1976.

Burtness, Paul S. and Robert R. Aurner, *Effective English for Colleges*. Cincinnati: South-Western, 1975.

Glazier, Teresa Ferster, *The Least You Should Know about English Basic Writing Skills*. New York: Holt, Rinehart and Winston, 1977.

Hodges, John C. and Mary E. Whitten, *Harbrace College Handbook*. New York: Harcourt Brace Jovanovich, 1977.

Keithley, Erwin M. and Margaret H. Thompson, *English for Modern Business*. Homewood, Ill.: Richard D. Irwin, 1977.

Whalen, Doris H., *Handbook for Business Writers*. New York: Harcourt Brace Jovanovich, 1978.

Writing effective business letters

14

key points to learn

The place of letters in the business communication process.

How to plan a business letter.

Types of business letters.

Techniques for beginning and ending a business letter.

The importance of writing in terms of the reader.

Nonverbal elements in business letters.

════════introduction

Except for using the products and services of a business organization and for reading advertisements, the only direct and individual communication contact many people have with a company is a business letter. You, as the writer of a business letter, have the tremendous opportunity to help your company meet its objectives and to help a customer while at the same time building good will.

Letters are only a small part of the total business communication scene, as you can tell by reading this book; however, they are an important part, and when letters are decided upon as the appropriate communication medium, they require the same careful attention and effort as do other forms of communication.

_____ Cost

A business organization can continue to serve the public only so long as it makes a profit. Communications costs are part of the total expense of doing business. Perhaps you have thought of the cost of a business letter as only the price of a piece of stationery, an envelope, and a postage stamp.

A business letter is not an inexpensive method of communication. In addition to stationery and postage, there are such costs as handling through the company mailroom, filing time, filing equipment and space, and the biggest item—salaries for the composer and the secretary. It follows, then, that the higher these salaries, the higher will be the cost of their letters.

According to the Dartnell Institute of Business Research, *average* costs for a face-to-face dictated letter climbed from 30 cents in 1930 to $2.54 in 1968 to $4.77 in 1978. . . . Some cost consultants have asserted—after considering stopwatch timings and misuse of expensive machines—that too many business and government letters cost as much as $15 to $20 each.[1]

Knowing this, you may discover that it is less expensive to make a telephone call. (In some extremely delicate and/or important matters requiring face-to-face communication, it may be "less expensive" to fly across the country and handle things personally.) How does a person decide whether a letter is the least expensive and/or most effective form of communication? You can make this decision if you know some of the advantages and disadvantages of the business letter.

_____ Advantages

Although not necessarily the most important, one advantage of a business letter is that it does provide a written record of a transaction or an event. Since it is frequently very important that a written record be kept, this need alone may help you to decide whether written communication is the answer to your problem.

Time and timing are important factors in communication, and you can write a letter when you have the time and when "you are in the mood." Therefore, it is hoped you will achieve a more effective, more carefully thought out communication than you would have had you used spoken communication. Inasmuch as the person to whom you are writing can read your letter at his or her convenience, it is possible you will get better results for this reason.

_____ Disadvantages

Probably the biggest disadvantage of a business letter is that instant feedback is not available. When you communicate with someone face-to-face, you have the opportunity to receive both verbal and nonverbal feedback as you talk. This should allow you to modify and change your communica-

---

[1]Herta A. Murphy and Charles E. Peck, *Effective Business Communications*. New York: McGraw Hill, 1980, p. 9.

tion so that you can achieve better results. With a business letter you probably get only one chance, so you must write carefully the first time. We can't remember ever receiving a business letter with a postscript stating, "If you don't like the way this letter is written, return it to me and I'll try to do a better job."

Many people either do not communicate well in writing or they think they do not communicate well in writing—which can add up to the same thing. Therefore, they find themselves at a disadvantage when it is necessary to write a letter. The suggestions in this chapter should enable you to build your confidence so that you will be able to handle any letter-writing situation.

As a beginning, you should become acquainted with some letter-writing principles which apply to all types of business letters. Study these principles and use them in your letters.

==================letter-writing principles

Many students (and business people) think that just because they have been writing for several years they know how to write a business letter. The shock of discovering this is not true is difficult for some people to accept.

There are a few principles of letter writing that you should keep in mind regardless of the purpose for which the letter is being written. Actually, these principles of written communication also have applications in the area of spoken communication. Although the concept of a conversational approach or of "talking one's letter onto the page" can result in some rather "folksy" and poorly organized letters, the psychology involved in face-to-face spoken communication can also be employed effectively in written communications.

The person to whom a business letter is written should be treated as a human being. This person is more than just an account number. He or she is a person who has a family, friends, a mortgage, hopes, indigestion, aspirations, dreams—and is, in fact, not much different from you, the writer. Apply a bit of the Golden Rule concept. Treat other people as though you expect to meet them personally the day after they read your letter. Constant attention to a few basic concepts or principles should enable you to write an effective letter.

_____Tone

"It's not what he said; it's the way he said it."
"Smile when you say that."
"You can call me anything you want to as long as you smile when you say it."

Although we discussed tone in Chapter 14, we need to say more about it in relation to letter-writing principles. Tone—good tone—is an essential element of a successful business letter. It is achieved in written communication by the careful selection and grouping of words. Use pleasant words whenever possible, "thank you," "agree," "glad," "pleased."

Although it is not possible always to avoid unpleasant words, you should try to keep such words to a minimum, subordinate them through sentence structure and physical placement in the body of the letter, and use euphemisms when appropriate. No one wants to be called "ignorant"; however, your reader probably will not object if you say "perhaps you did not understand" or "perhaps you have not heard."

When you are about to use an unpleasant word, check to see whether some alternative is available. To refresh your memory, here is a list of some pleasant words and some unpleasant words:

Pleasant words	Unpleasant words
yes	no
thank you	refuse
appreciate	ignorant
agree	not
cooperate	stupid
glad	careless
happy	delay
willing	cancel
good	unable
excellent	unacceptable

Tone is basically a reflection of your attitude toward yourself, your company, the reader, and the problem you are attempting to solve in the business letter. Good will is a major benefit that you and your company will realize from the effective handling of tone (as well as from the proper application of the other principles discussed in this section).

In this book we are concerned with the preservation of good will through effective communication. There are times when it becomes obvious that a customer is not going to pay an account or otherwise do what we expect (and what *should be done*), and it is necessary to tell the person that we no longer

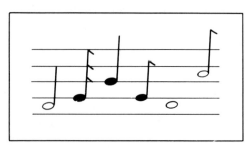

"At the sound of the tone . . . "

want him or her as a customer. Even this should be done in a firm but as friendly a manner as circumstances permit—that is, with good tone.

_____ "You Attitude"

"You attitude" is a well-known, frequently used concept in the field of letter writing. Anyone who professes to write effective business letters not only must know the term but also must make use of it. "You attitude" means that the writer thinks and writes in terms of the reader. The writer is motivated by what the reader wants and needs. The best way to achieve "you attitude" in a letter is to stress "what's in it" for the reader. Explain how this will be beneficial or profitable for the reader rather than how your company will gain.[2] It is not nearly so important to tell a customer, "our company has grown because we provide quality furniture and fast service," as it is to say "your new furniture should reach you within one week, and you'll be enjoying the most beautiful home in the neighborhood."

Instead of telling a customer, "Send in your order promptly so that we can begin to fill it," say "As soon as your order reaches us, your stereo will be on its way to you, and your life will be filled with beautiful music." People buy products because they expect to get certain benefits and/or pleasures from them, not necessarily because the objects themselves do anything for the buyers. Although a stereo system may be encased in beautifully grained wood and may be controlled with gleaming metal knobs, the real value to the buyer should be the sounds that come from the speakers. Whether you are selling a product, a service, or an idea, do it by involving the reader and by showing where the reader fits into the picture. You may want to describe a product physically, but you will want especially to tell your reader how ownership of the product will be beneficial.

It should be noted that "you attitude" is not necessarily achieved by frequent use of the pronouns "you" and "your." It is possible to talk about "you" and still be very "me" oriented. You must forget your own ego trip and write in terms of your reader's situation. A genuine interest in people, an empathetic approach, and an understanding of the reader's needs will help a writer to achieve the *real* "you attitude."

_____ Positive Approach

Business moves at a frantic pace, and many companies find themselves having to run in order to stand still. Under these conditions and with human beings involved, it is only natural that mistakes occur. It is easy to

---

[2]J. H. Menning, C. W. Wilkinson, and Peter B. Clarke, *Communicating through Letters and Reports.* Homewood, Ill.: Richard D. Irwin, 1976, pp. 40–42.

become negative and to decide that everything is falling apart, that nothing is done correctly. However, as a song writer put it several years ago, we need to "accentuate the positive and minimize the negative."

When talking or writing about a thing or an event, you should emphasize its plus rather than its minus factors. For example, do not write to a customer saying that you do not sell cashmere sweaters. Instead, explain, "we have orlon sweaters that are soft, warm, and inexpensive." Stress what your product has rather than what it does not have.[3]

Negative elements in a situation will not "go away" if they are ignored; however, they can be made to seem less important if they are subordinated through word choice, sentence structure, or placement in the letter. Instead of writing, "Your order will not be shipped today, but will be sent in one week when we receive more merchandise," write this way: "Your order will be on its way to you in one week when we receive a new supply of merchandise."

Positive approach (like "tone" and "you attitude") requires a change in attitude and thinking for many people. It requires a new psychological outlook. Listen to your friends in conversation sometime and notice how many of their comments are negative or derogatory. There are negative elements at work around us all the time, and they cannot be ignored; but everyone can do a better job of taking a positive approach in communications without becoming "nauseatingly nice" or "sickeningly sweet."

_____ Complete Coverage

A business letter usually is written to help solve a business problem of some sort. In order to meet this objective, all pertinent factors must be considered in the letter. If essential information is omitted from the letter, the reader will have to write (or telephone) and again request the information.

If a potential customer writes for information about a product, the sales correspondent must be careful to answer all questions. Failure to do so creates doubts in the mind of the reader which might result in the possible loss of a customer. If the correspondent is unable to answer a question, he or she should say so, rather than ignore the question; and, if the reason is not confidential, the writer should tell why the question is unanswerable. A complete, thorough answer inspires your reader's confidence.

As we will discuss in the chapter when we talk about planning, the competent, qualified secretary will annotate and underscore important points in incoming letters, thus calling to the manager's attention points to be considered in writing replies. The secretary should also provide a complete correspondence file before the manager begins to dictate a reply so that he or she will have a complete record of events on which to base an answer.

_____

[3]Ibid., p. 46.

A letter is a failure if it omits any information that makes it necessary for the reader to write and ask again. Careful planning of written communications will help you to achieve complete coverage of the topic.

Organization

Your letters must be well organized so that you lead your reader step by step through the various points you want to discuss. Once again, planning is essential.

A brief outline of such points will help you to achieve an organized approach as well as the complete coverage that we discussed previously. Once you know what you want to say, you will be able to approach the writing in a logical manner. Furthermore, you will be able to use location or placement in the letter for emphasis of important elements as well as for de-emphasis of unpleasant news.

Organization, planning, and the application of letter-writing principles are essential to the writing of a successful business letter. People who can apply these concepts successfully in the "body" of the business letter, the writing that occurs between "Dear Sir" and "Sincerely," can communicate their messages effectively.

beginning a letter

Beginning a letter is "sort of" like getting the first olive out of the bottle. After you get that one out, the rest is easy . . .

The most important thing for the writer to remember in beginning and ending a letter is that these places are the most important locations in the body of the letter for emphasis—that is, *the first sentence and the last sentence in a letter should be reserved for the news you really want to emphasize.* [4] Conversely, if you want to de-emphasize or minimize something, do not put it in the first or last sentence of a letter.

Too many letter writers waste the first sentence of a letter with an unimportant comment such as "I am writing to thank you for your order," or with an obvious statement such as "We have your order." Obviously the writer has the order or he or she would not be able to acknowledge it. A much better beginning would be "your order is being shipped today by motor freight and should be in your store for the weekend crowds." The reader gets the important news first, along with a bit of "you attitude" that enables the reader to see customers ringing the cash register.

Here are some techniques that will help you *begin* a letter.

Favorable Elements

"Yes" is a pleasant word to hear. Inasmuch as the first sentence of a letter is the most important place in the physical layout of the letter to emphasize a point, it is the place to write favorable messages—things the reader wants to hear. For example: "Here is your check." "Your order is on its way." "Yes, I'll speak at your business conference." Once you agree with your reader or say you will do what the reader wants, it is difficult to make him or her angry. So, check through your letter plan, determine a favorable element or elements, and begin your letter with this idea. See the sample letter in Figure 14–1. It opens with presentation of favorable news and closes with a subtle reminder of the pleasant news; the letter includes some other techniques that are discussed in this chapter.

If there is no favorable element in the letter plan, then you should begin the letter with "good will" or "resale" elements (see following discussion). You *should not* begin a letter (i.e., the first sentence and/or first paragraph) with an unfavorable or negative idea. If you refuse your reader's request or say "no" in the first sentence, the rest of your letter may not be read. By not refusing in the first sentence and by offering an explanation before you introduce negative elements, you should be able to keep your reader reading and then you may be able to win the reader to your side with your explanation and with the offering of possible alternatives. This letter beginning is similar to the principle of positive approach discussed earlier in the chapter.

There is no better way to begin a letter than to tell your reader the news he or she wants to hear.

---

[4]Jessamon Dawe and William Jackson Lord, Jr., *Functional Business Communication.* Englewood Cliffs, N.J.: Prentice-Hall, 1974, p. 38.

THE LETTER	THE EXPLANATION

Dear Customer:

Your Toastee Toaster is on its way to you today by U.S. Mail.

The opening sentence tells the reader what he really wants to know.

The Toastee is a fine toaster; and as a result, it's our best seller. You picked a good one! It toasts bread quickly to "any shade of done" you select.

Resale keeps the customer happy while he's waiting for his order to arrive.

Your check for $34.50 is exactly the correct amount to cover th cost of the toaster and the mailing charges.

Money should always be mentioned even though the order "obviously" was received.

When you're ready to add other fine electrical appliances to your kitchen, just let us know. We can supply you with electric skillets, grills, coffee pots, and blenders which will complement your Toastee.

While you have the reader's attention and he's in a good mood because his order is on its way, why not try to make an additional sale?

The enclosed order card will help us speed future orders to you. You'll like our other products just as much as you're going to enjoy your new Toastee Toaster.

The letter ends on a note of helpfulness with a bit of resale and a touch of you attitude.

Sincerely,

Figure 14–1 How to begin and end a letter.

_____Good Will

A "good will" beginning to a letter is one that uses words such as "thank you," "we appreciate," or "we are glad to hear." Although these pleasant words may not "excite" the reader, they do not cause annoyance either. (See the section on "tone" for a list of pleasant and unpleasant words.) Beginning a letter with pleasant words requires no creative ability. Indeed, the reader will tend to read quickly past them, but they are better than beginning a letter with unpleasant news.

Since one major objective in our business letters is to maintain and/or build good will, use of pleasant words is always a good idea. By beginning a letter with good will ideas and subordinating unpleasant news until you have had a chance to explain, you should be able to do a better job of selling your reader on your approach. Notice the letter in Figure 14–2. It opens with a good will approach and ends with "you attitude" (reader benefits). The actual refusal is subordinated by physical placement in the middle of the message.

_____ Resale

Resale means keeping a person sold, and it can be used in reference to a product or a company. In effect the writer says, "You are smart to have bought X brand," or "You could not have picked a better company than Acme with which to do business."[5]

THE LETTER	THE EXPLANATION
Dear Mrs. Smith:	
Thank you for writing to us about your dress. We are always glad to hear from our customers because this enables us to offer you better service.	This letter begins with good will words and contains a "touch" of you attitude. There is no direct reference to the unfavorable news.
By treating all our customers fairly, we are able to keep prices at a reasonable level which all of our customers appreciate. One way we do this is by making adjustments only when they are warranted. The tag in your dress specifies "dry clean only." Inasmuch as the dress has been laundered, we are not able to replace it.	An explanation prepares the reader for the actual refusal which appears at the end of the paragraph. Notice that a direct refusal is used—i.e., "we are not able to replace it." An attempt to minimize the refusal is made by placing it at the end of the paragraph (subordination by physical placement).
Having bought the dress, you must like the brand. We are having a sale of dresses by this manufacturer beginning October 1. Why don't you come in and get another one at a bargain price?	An attempt is made to reason with the reader by suggesting that since she bought one previously, she might enjoy another one. Although we are not going to replace her mishandled dress, we do tell her that she can get another one on sale at a good price.
You'll continue to be one of the best dressed women in town.	The letter ends with a suggestion of reader benefits.
Sincerely,	

Figure 14–2   Using good will to begin and end a letter.

_____

[5]Menning and Wilkinson, p. 63.

Many people have doubts about the wisdom of their decisions. When these doubts occur, the person involved needs to be resold, or reassured. The customer needs to be told, "You certainly were smart to buy the purple thingamajig; the pink ones were it last year, but the purple ones are 'in' now." Resale is especially valuable in written business communications because there usually is a lapse of at least several days between the time an order is sent by the buyer and the time she receives shipment from the seller. This gives the buyer time in which to wonder whether the purchase is the correct one; resale helps to overcome these doubts.

The idea of resale is a good beginning for letters of a sales nature—whether the sale involves a product or an idea. "Your order for Spiffy sweaters shows how attuned you are to today's fashions." This beginning is equally appropriate when unpleasant news, such as a delay in shipping, follows:

> Your order for Spiffy sweaters shows how attuned you are to today's fashions.
>
> These superior sweaters have been our top seller for many years; public acceptance is tremendous. And because of this great acceptance, we are always having to order more sweaters from our supplier. We expect a shipment in one week and we'll have your order in your store two days later.

Resale is an excellent way to begin a letter because it reinforces the reader's good self-concept and decisions. It is an especially effective way to begin a letter in which unpleasant news regarding a product or service must be transmitted. Resale preserves the concept of the excellent judgment of the reader while giving the writer a chance to tell "what happened."

Exclamation or Question

Exclamations or questions are very acceptable beginnings for letters of a sales or persuasive nature. They may be used to start any letter in which the objective of the writer is to gain the reader's attention quickly. See Figure 14–3 for a sample of a letter that begins with a question and ends with a question. Each one contains some "you attitude." A question involves the reader quickly and, as in this example, provides a bit of mystery and suspense to keep the person reading until you can explain where he or she fits into the picture.

The question is an especially appropriate beginning because the reader is flattered to be asked for an opinion; also, the question involves the reader immediately and gets the letter off to a fast start. Be sure to word the question in such a way that it brings an answer in the desired form. Thought-provoking questions are usually better than questions that can be answered simply "yes" or "no." However, there is nothing wrong with a "yes" or "no" answer if that amount of information is sufficient.

THE LETTER	THE EXPLANATION
Dear Mr. Speaker:	
Would you like the opportunity to win some votes while helping educate young voters about the operation of their state government?	A question involves the reader quickly; and even though this is a "yes" "no" question, it's not likely to get a "no" answer.
As a part of its continuing program to broaden the experiences of students, State University is holding a conference with the theme, "Educating the Voter." It is important that our country have well informed citizens, and you can help us to achieve this goal (while meeting several hundred potential voters) by being one of our speakers.	This paragraph builds interest and explains the situation so that the reader knows what it is all about and where he fits into the picture. He's prepared for the request when it arrives.
We would like for you to speak on October 5 at 2 p.m. in the Student Center Ballroom. We have allotted thirty minutes for your talk on the subject, "What You Can Do to Help Your State Senator."	The actual request makes sense now that the explanation has been given. Complete details of time and place must be included here.
So that we will have plenty of time to publicize your visit, won't you telephone me at 123-4567 before August 31 and tell me you'll speak to our students on October 5?	The possibility of publicity motivates the reader to reply quickly. The action required and a deadline are given. And it is all included in a question.
Sincerely,	

Figure 14–3 Using a question to begin and end a letter.

ending a letter

Having got your letter off to a good start and having applied all of the relevant principles of good letter writing to the body of the letter, you are now ready to bring your letter to a proper close.

Many letter writers have trouble "going home in their letters." In other words, they do not know how to exit gracefully. As a result, an otherwise good letter can be ruined by being dragged out. Perhaps you have had occasion to observe a guest at a party who wanted to leave but could not figure out how to say goodnight and depart; the guest reached the front door, but a half hour later was still standing there, on one foot and then the other, making small talk and trying to depart. Some people have a similar problem in their letters.

After you have covered all the essential topics in your letter, it is time to quit. And it can be easy to quit. Here are a few techniques you should find helpful. Notice that most of them are similar to the ones we suggested for beginning a letter, but with a slightly different twist.

Favorable Elements

We all want to end a letter with a favorable element, with a positive tone. It is desirable to leave the reader in a good frame of mind. In a letter that contains favorable news throughout, it is a simple matter to stop on a positive note by reminding the reader that he or she got what was wanted—that is, that you answered "yes" to the request. You must watch your tone, however, to make sure that you do not sound overbearing or obnoxious. Having told your reader, for instance, that the order is on the way, and having completely covered all important points, you can end the letter by saying, "You soon will realize what a wise purchase you have made when your customers demand more and more of X products."

Good Will

Although it *is* possible to overdo a good thing, you do not need to worry about too many good will elements in your letters. Pleasant sounding words always are easy to take. Although they may be a little trite, good will endings such as "thank you" and "we appreciate your order" always are acceptable.

Many business letters primarily contain disappointing news. Since the end is the second most emphatic place in the letter, you should not close your communication by reminding the reader of the disappointment. Sometimes the simplest, farthest-removed ending is the term "good luck."

You should make efforts to use synonyms in the ending as well as elsewhere in your letter. There is no need to close with "thank you again." Exercise your vocabulary and find something other than "thank you" so you will not have to use it "again."

Resale

Sometimes it is appropriate to end a letter by reassuring the reader that the purchased product is right for the customer or that the company the customer is dealing with is the one that can do the best job for him or her.

Ajax Company sells only quality sporting goods. The fishing rods we are sending you are the finest in our line and they'll certainly help your customers land the big ones while you land big profits.

If reassurance seems needed or if confidence appears to need strengthening, resale is the way to end the letter.

Action

In every letter that involves a request, the action the reader is expected to take must be specified—usually near the end of the letter. This technique will leave the subject uppermost in the reader's mind.

Requests for action should not be vague statements. Do not ask your reader to "notify" you or to "let you know." Tell the reader to "telephone collect" or to "reply on the enclosed postal card." A letter containing a request for an individual to speak at a meeting is useless if it does not specify that the reader should communicate acceptance or refusal—as well as how, where, when, and to whom.

A sales letter that whets the reader's appetite for a particular product and then fails to specify the action to be taken to obtain that product is a failure. In addition to telling the reader how to reply, you also may find it advisable to establish a deadline for action. Avoid vague statements such as "at your convenience" or "as soon as possible." A better ending would be:

> Simply indicate your acceptance of our offer on the enclosed postcard and mail it by June 1. Ten days after we receive your acceptance, you will be setting records with your new golf balls.

"Action required" is a convenient, and essential, way of ending some types of letters.

Question

In certain situations, a question is an exciting, interesting, and intriguing way of bringing a letter to a conclusion. A question adds a touch of "suspense" to the letter. It seems to shift the burden of proof to the reader by saying, in effect, "now it's your turn." For example, in a letter attempting to collect an overdue account, the writer, after presenting the facts in the case, may end the letter quite effectively by asking, "May we hear from you?"

With your knowledge of some basic letter-writing principles as well as some techniques for beginning and ending letters, you are now ready to apply what you have learned to specific letter-writing situations. If you studied Figures 14–1, 14–2, and 14–3, you have had a preview of the sorts of things we will be discussing in the next section of this chapter.

plan your letters

Have you ever listened to a speaker whose presentation seemed to ramble? Have you ever read a letter that seemed very disorganized and which seemed neither to "start anywhere" nor "to end anywhere?" It is probably safe to say that neither the speech nor the letter had been planned. Letters that get results do not just "happen."

If you are to write effective business letters, you must give them the necessary thought, planning, and effort. To plan well for your message, you should review, if necessary, all previous correspondence you have had on the subject. Your secretary can be a big help by underlining key points in incoming correspondence as well as by making annotations in the margins. Or, if you prefer, you can perform the underlining and annotation steps as you read incoming mail; they help you to see key points, to organize, and to give complete coverage as you answer the letters. Also, you may find it helpful to make a short outline of your proposed message before you begin to dictate.

As you review the correspondence you are to answer, the nature of the business problem you have to solve should become apparent. When you have isolated and identified the problem, you then can determine the type letter you must write in order to solve the problem. For example, if the problem to be solved by your letter is to refuse to make an adjustment requested by a customer, a certain type of letter with a certain organization will be indicated. If your purpose in another letter is to send a refund check, another type of letter will be suggested. All it takes is a little planning!

You will probably find that most of the letters you write will fall into one of four categories or a combination of two or more of these categories. The categories are: favorable, neutral, unfavorable, and persuasive. A special type of letter we call "human relations letters" will be discussed after we study these four basic categories. The employment application letter, also a rather specialized type, is presented in the appendix.

Some authorities say that "every letter is a sales letter"—that is, "you are always selling something." You also should remember that "most" of the time you are trying to build good will and keep a customer. It does not take a lot of training to tell people you no longer want them as customers or clients of your organization—except that you will want to word your letter carefully in order to avoid legal action. In large companies, cases of this nature are turned over to specialists in this type letter. Therefore, a big element in most of the letters you write is going to be the preservation of good will.

Having determined the purpose of your letter and having planned your letter, you are ready to begin writing. We will now look at basic patterns of organization for the various letter categories.

A favorable letter is one in which you agree to do something for the reader. You will speak at the meeting; you are sending a check; you shipped the order yesterday. It is an easy letter to write because you are saying what the reader wants to hear. Favorable letters have basically a three-step formula:

1. A fast, direct, good news first sentence
2. Complete coverage
3. A pleasant ending.

Dear Customer:

Your order for one case of Flavormints Chocolate Candies left here this morning by Fleet Truck Lines and should reach you in ample time for Christmas shoppers.

The candies have been charged to your account.

You will be glad you ordered Flavormints when you see how fast they sell. And you'll probably want to buy at least one box to satisfy your own "sweet tooth." The delicious light chocolate and the refreshing minty flavor are an unbeatable combination. These candies are our number one seller, and they will be favorites of your customers, too.

Happy Holidays!

Sincerely,

Figure 14—4 The letter begins with the most important news; this is followed by "you attitude," details about money, and resale (keeping the customer sold, see page 335).

Inasmuch as a letter of this type must contain no negative elements if it is to be classified properly as a favorable letter, there really is nothing about the message which should give you any problems. Remember to discuss the most positive item in the first sentence; be sure you cover every topic that needs to be treated in the letter; and, finally, stop on a pleasant note. Since the entire letter is positive in nature, you should have no trouble stopping the message with a good tone—perhaps you could remind the reader in the last sentence that she got what she wanted in the first sentence.

Two very common types of favorable letters are letters granting a request and letters acknowledging and sending an order. This is a very simple letter granting a request:

> Yes, I'll be glad to speak at your public relations conference on May 6.
>
> Public relations concerns all of us, and it is an activity in which each of us is engaged to some extent. The topic you have asked me to discuss, "Sales Letters," is an important one and one of my areas of specialization. I will prepare about a half-hour presentation.
>
> I will appreciate your making hotel reservations for me, and I will let you know early next week about my travel arrangements.
>
> The enclosed resume and photograph will enable you to proceed with publicity and program plans. I look forward to being a part of your conference.

A letter acknowledging and sending an order is very common in the business world. An example of this type of letter is shown in Figure 14–4. You will notice that the letter has a pleasant tone throughout. Many writers feel that they must be what they consider "helpful" and suggest "If the merchandise is not satisfactory when it arrives, just let us know." There is no need to suggest trouble and introduce this negative element. You can be quite sure your reader will let you know if he or she is not satisfied.

Neutral Letters

Neutral messages are just what the name suggests: they are neither favorable nor unfavorable. Many letters in this category are what we might call "mutual back-scratching" in the business world. You may have to write a letter of recommendation for a former employee who is seeking employment with another organization. As far as you and your company are concerned, such a letter is neither favorable nor unfavorable; it is just one of those helpful letters you will have to write in the everyday practice of business. Another letter in this category is a credit reference. In this type letter you will supply another company with information about the payment habits of one of your customers—that is, how fast or how slow did the customer pay bills.

In some of these letters there may be negative elements you will want to include. You should follow our usual practice of discussing good points of the person first and placing unfavorable news in the middle of the letter. You will also have occasions when the news concerning an individual is mostly negative. You may still use the neutral, direct approach—that is, negative news in the first sentence—because the reader of your letter is not the person about whom you are writing. Here is an example of a letter of recommendation which contains only a small bit of unfavorable information:

> Julie Ainsworth, about whom you inquired, compiled a very good record during her five years as an employee of Elkins Electronics. She was assistant manager of our supplies department when she left us.
>
> Ms. Ainsworth was an extremely efficient worker, and she kept her department operating on schedule. She was open to suggestions and quick to make any change which would result in a better operation. Because of her energy and drive, she tended at times to lose patience with her subordinates who did not measure up to her standards of performance.
>
> I was sorry to have Julie Ainsworth leave our organization, and I would be glad to rehire her. I feel sure she would do a fine job for your company.

The main things to remember about neutral letters are a direct opening and complete coverage. If there is only a limited amount of negative news, it is always a good idea to minimize the negative by relegating it to the middle of the letter.

Unfavorable Letters

An unfavorable letter is one in which you must refuse to do something for the reader. It is a difficult letter to write because when you say "no" to a person, there is a chance you may lose that person as a customer and/or friend of your organization. It should be obvious, then, that this type letter requires "liberal doses" of good will.

Because you want to de-emphasize the refusal or the negative part of your message, you will not want to put it in the first sentence of your letter. As you learned earlier in this chapter, "good will" and "resale" are acceptable ways to begin a letter of this type. If neither of these approaches is applicable, you may begin with some general statement dealing with the subject of the letter on which you and your reader can agree. This is the technique we have used in the unfavorable letter in Figure 14–5.

Whichever technique you use for beginning your unfavorable letter, your objective is the same: to keep the reader reading and give yourself time to win him or her over to your viewpoint. After you get the letter underway, you will want to offer explanations and/or reasons which will justify the refusal which you offer about midway in the letter. If you have an alternative to offer your reader, you should do so following the refusal.

You are now ready to end your letter. Inasmuch as this is the second most important place for emphasis, you will not want to remind the reader of the

Dear Program Chairman:

The Public Relations Forum you are sponsoring this fall is
certainly a worthwhile activity and one which should prove
helpful to everyone who attends the sessions.

Fall is an extremely busy time of the year for me because I
make my annual visit to each of our regional offices to consult with management and to discuss objectives for the new
year. Having scheduled these trips so far in advance, I must
carry through with my plans. On the date you have asked me
to speak, I must be in Tucson.

Let me suggest the editor of our employee publications, George
Simpson, as an ideal person to speak in my place. George is
much in demand as a speaker because he does such a fine job.
"Communicating with Internal Publics" would be an excellent
topic for him. You may contact him here at our offices.

Best wishes for a successful Forum!

                              Sincerely,

Figure 14–5 Because the letter contains unfavorable elements, it opens on a pleasant note
related to the Forum. This is followed by an explanation ending with the refusal stated indirectly.
The writer offers an alternative and then ends the letter with a good will idea.

unfavorable news at this point. Be careful not to apologize or become negative.
Use a pleasant ending, perhaps some sort of good will words like "thank you" or
"good luck."

Unfavorable letters contain these steps:

1. Positive beginning with no reference to refusal
2. Reasons or explanation
3. Refusal or unfavorable news
4. Alternative if available
5. Pleasant ending with no reference to unfavorable news.

These steps are shown in the example of an unfavorable letter in Figure 14–5. This is a letter refusing a request, and it is a type of letter you will probably have to write at some time. Your attention is called to the indirect refusal in the letter. Several times we have stressed the importance of being positive, of minimizing negative or unfavorable elements in your messages. You can minimize negative elements by physical placement in the letter (keep them out of the first and last sentences), by sentence structure (make negatives subordinate, dependent, and, if possible, place them at the end of the sentence), and by word choice (use pleasant, positive words). Many times you need tell your reader only what you can do or will do; this will frequently eliminate the need to tell what you cannot do or will not do.

Notice the writer of our refused-request letter has said that he will be in Tucson on the date he was asked to speak. If the reader of the letter is in Philadelphia, it will be quite obvious to that person that the request has been turned down; but the tone is so much softer than, "No, I will not give a talk at your meeting." You need not eliminate all negative words; in fact, there will be times when you will need to use unpleasant words. Our purpose here is to make you aware of the unpleasant effect of negative words and to urge you to avoid as many of these words as possible.

Let's look now at two other types of unfavorable-letter situations. It is sometimes necessary to write a customer to report that a product is not available or that it will not be available for some time (back order). If the product is not available at all, this could be very bad news for the reader; and you will want to rely heavily on good will ("thank you" and "we appreciate") and resale of your company (stress customer service, quality merchandise, dependability, upcoming sales). Many times when a product is unavailable, you will have in stock a product which you believe will meet the needs of the customer just as effectively as the product that was ordered. In this case, your problem is one of selling an alternative or a substitute. These steps should get the results you want:

1. Open with an agreeable statement on the *type* products under discussion (not brand names).
2. Discuss an alternative or substitute.
3. Make it clear that the ordered product is unavailable.
4. Push for positive action on the substitute.

Now, let's look at these steps in letter form:

A good flashlight is certainly a necessity today; in fact, it's sensible to have at least two—one in the house and one in the car.

In our constant efforts to supply our customers with new and improved merchandise, we talk with every supplier we can find. That is how we ran across a new flashlight which is very lightweight but strong and durable. This flashlight, called "Beacon," is only six inches long and about as big around as a silver dollar. Beacon uses a new type battery which lasts twice as long and costs half as much as most flashlight batteries. For these many good reasons, we now stock Beacon instead of the flashlight you ordered. Oh yes, the best news is that Beacon sells for only $2.95.

We are sending a Beacon flashlight for your inspection. We think you will like it; but if we are wrong, return it at our expense. We will be glad to charge the Beacon to your account.

The safe and secure feeling which your Beacon flashlight provides will make you glad you own one. May we send you a second one?

Notice that we have not referred to Beacon as a "substitute." Many people consider a substitute as not so good as the real thing. Also, notice that we sent the flashlight but gave the customer the option of returning it at our expense. In some cases you might wish to ask the customer's permission before sending the product. In selling an alternative or a substitute, spend your time talking about the substitute product. Don't spend time talking about what you want the reader to forget—that is, the product he or she ordered.

An unfavorable letter dealing with a back order is no great problem, provided the delay is not too long. About all there is to this letter is a bit of resale on the product (to keep the customer wanting it) and a realistic estimate of when the customer can expect to receive the product.

The Green Grass lawn mower you ordered is a very popular piece of equipment. Inexpensive operation and easy maintenance appeal to a lot of people.

The Green Grass mower is so popular that we have had to submit several reorders. We are expecting our latest order to be filled soon, and your mower will be on its way to you at once. Your Green Grass mower should reach you no later than ten days from today.

Your lawn will look beautiful when you take care of it with a Green Grass mower.

Whether you want to put someone "on hold" for a back order will, of course, depend on the nature of the product and the time factor, among other things. If someone were to order five sets of Christmas tree lights, and you would be unable to deliver them until January 15, you might want to check with the customer to see whether to go ahead and fill the order.

One other type of unfavorable letter we need to consider is the incomplete order or any situation where there is a problem of incomplete information. We listed "complete coverage" as one of our letter-writing principles; therefore, whenever a writer fails to fulfill this principle, it becomes necessary to write a letter requesting that this gap be filled in.

This creates a potentially unfavorable climate because you must request the missing information in such a way as not to make the reader feel stupid for having omitted essential data. Words like "careless" or "you forgot" will not build the kind of tone you want here. Tell your reader what you need to know, not what he or she forgot to tell you. Here is an example:

Many people tell us Champion tennis shoes are an essential part of their tennis equipment. We can understand why you are so eager to receive yours.

If you will tell us your shoe size right away, we will have your shoes in the mail to you the day we receive the information.

Good luck with your tennis game!

Even though unfavorable letters are probably the most difficult kinds of letters to write, they need cause you no trouble if you use the suggestions we have given here. Remember the importance of setting the stage before you actually refuse. And make use of your knowledge of euphemisms and "you attitude": reader benefits are important even in refusal letters.

Persuasive Letters

Probably all who are reading this book will, sooner or later, have to write a persuasive letter asking someone to do something for them. Such a letter could range anywhere from asking someone to donate $5 to a charity to requesting a $500 refund on a refrigerator. The $5 charity donation letter we would call a "persuasive favor or request" and the $500 refrigerator refund is known as a "persuasive claim." Your approach in writing the letter is basically the same for each situation.

A persuasive approach is important in these situations because you are not sure whether the reader will say "yes" to your request—but you feel sure that once the reader knows the facts and/or your reasoning, agreement with your position will be forthcoming. The situation is similar to subordinating refusals in unfavorable letters: you want to keep the reader reading until you get to the real purpose for the letter. Use this time to reason, to stress reader benefits, and to show why the request makes sense. A persuasive letter asking a favor is shown in Figure 14–6.

What you have observed in this letter example is the application of a well-known persuasion formula: attention, interest, desire, action. A persuasive letter is one in which you must *sell* someone on an idea or a product. To do this you must be sure the reader is paying attention to what you have to say. Then you create interest and desire in your proposition or product through explanation and reader benefits, and you conclude with a request for a specific type of action.

If you think about it, the persuasive letter is no different from the approach you use in a face-to-face persuasive encounter:

"Wouldn't it be great to get away from the books and the classroom grind?"
"We'd feel better; we'd have a better mental outlook; our grades would improve because of improved concentration; we'd meet some fun people."
"Let's go skiing this weekend. It will cost only $50 and it will be worth it."
"Call me this afternoon and say you'll go!"

Whether you are selling an idea or a product, the approach is the same. Let's

```
Dear Mr. Businessman:

Don't you agree that it's important for people in business
to know what is going on in the field of education?

We think it is.  People in business and educators can learn
much from each other.  As a result, each of us should do a better,
more efficient job.  You can help us with course content, and
we can reduce some of your training time.  You can help reach
these objectives.

The Management Club at City University would like for you to
talk to our members on November 1 at 8 p.m. in the Student
Center.  You may select your own topic of you wish; or, if you
would like a suggestion, we would enjoy knowing more about how
things really operate in the business world.

Your pay for participation in this event will be the knowledge
that you have helped some young people, and that you have built
good will for your company.  It also will be a fine opportunity
for you to meet future customers and potential employees.

We'd like to begin publicizing your visit at once.  Please
telephone me at 456-7890 and tell me you will be with us on
November 1.

Sincerely,
```

Figure 14–6 Persuasive letter. Notice the letter begins with a question; hopefully, it is a question on which the writer and reader can agree. This is followed by explanation and then the request itself. The reader learns in the fourth paragraph that he will be paid, but not in money. The letter ends with a bit of "you attitude" and a request for action.

look very briefly at sales promotional letters—the sort of letter you receive occasionally in your mailbox at home. Sales promotional letters are a specialized type of letter that you will want to study in depth if you plan to write many of them. Special courses are offered on this one type letter. We will offer only a few comments on sales promotional letters so that you will have a little different perspective on them and a little better understanding of what the writer is trying to do.

Writers of these letters use questions, exclamations, startling statements, headlines as techniques for getting your attention. Having accomplished this, the writer goes on to create interest and desire through a description of the product and by telling how the product will help the reader (reader benefits). The interest/desire portion of the letter will go on at some length with the writer using various approaches to product description and then translating these into reader benefits. When the writer feels that the reader's appetite is sufficiently aroused, he or she moves into the action ending. He or she tells the reader what action is wanted and makes it easy for the reader to perform this action: telephone an 800 number, use the enclosed stamped envelope, take enclosed coupon to retailer.

An example of a persuasive letter is presented in Figure 14–7. This example relies mainly on message to make the sale rather than on a combination of message and mechanical gimmicks. Many sales promotional letters seem to consist mainly of gimmicks, such as capitalized words, words underscored, paragraphs indented, certain words typed in a different color ink, or paragraphs or words written in longhand. Study the next sales letter you receive and determine the number and types of gimmicks which have been used.

Sales promotional letters fill an important need in the business world. If they hold a special interest for you, you should investigate the possibility of further study.

Dear Homemaker:

Would you like to save money on your food bills?

If you're like most people these days, you have about all the bills you can handle; and you are looking for ways to economize. In addition to the fact that we have to eat, most of us like to eat. Imagine being able to serve delicious, tasty meals while saving money at the same time!

Beautiful, flavorful meats, fruits and vegetables can be yours at reduced prices. Colorful, eye-appealing meals will provide your family with the vitamins and body-building ingredients they need. All these advantages can be yours when you join the Thrifty Meals Food Club. This organization is made up of people like yourself who want to eat well and save money at the same time.

All we've tried to do here is "whet your appetite" by telling you what a membership in the Club can mean to you and your family-- good food in your stomachs and more money in your bank account.

To learn more about the Thrifty Meals Food Club, just fill out and mail the enclosed postcard. Within a week we'll send a representative to tell you how you can begin to enjoy better, more economical food.

Sincerely,

Figure 14–7 Persuasive letter. The letter opens with a question that involves the reader. Through the use of "you attitude," which stresses reader benefits, the reader is persuaded to take the desired action of requesting a representative to call and explain the Club in detail.

A final type of persuasive letter we need to mention is the *collection letter*. Perhaps we should say collection letters, because they usually are thought of as a series of letters ranging from mild reminder to a threat of legal action. Collection letters, too, are a specialized type that will probably require further study on your part if you are to spend much time writing them.

Actually, the monthly statement you receive from a department store or the gasoline company is the first message in a collection series. If payment is not received within a "reasonable" time, a mild reminder will probably be sent. Messages become increasingly stronger thereafter and may end in a threat of legal action. As good will becomes less of a factor, letters will become more direct in approach. The writer of collection letters appeals to the reader's sense of duty, obligation, and fair play. He or she also attempts to educate the reader about the importance of a good credit rating. Some letters are designed to find out whether anyone is really receiving our letters. Business organizations are frequently willing to make special arrangements with people who are having financial problems and can't pay.

Collection letters do present some unique challenges created when we begin to talk about a person's bill-paying habits. Fortunately, most of us pay our bills—some people pay more promptly than others; but the relatively small group of people you will deal with in writing collection letters is a group which will really test your letter-writing ability!

Human Relations Letters

The final letter type we will discuss is the human relations letter. A human relations letter really contains nothing but good will. Good will is an element in all the letters we have discussed, but in human relations letters, good will is everything. Here are some types of human relations letters:

1. Congratulations
2. Welcoming new customers
3. Opening a new office
4. Reaching a sales quota
5. Birthday
6. Christmas
7. Sympathy.

Everyone has several opportunities each day to write human relations letters. In fact, one could spend most of his or her time writing such letters if he or she is not careful. These letters can play an important part in your success because of the friendships you can build with them. In addition to the fact you *need* to write these letters, you should *want* to write them.

There is no formula, outline, or pattern for human relations letters. The important thing is that you remember to write them. People like to be remembered and to be made to feel important. If you need a little help, why not use a direct beginning? "Happy Birthday!" "We're glad to have you as a new customer!" Write another sentence or two and end the letter, if that's all you can think of. Your letter will have accomplished the results you want.

In addition to the important elements of message and content we have been discussing in this chapter, there are additional communication factors involved in your business letters. The remainder of the chapter is devoted to a discussion of mechanics and appearance.

metacommunication

Everything you do is a communication. This is true in letter writing, too. As the writer of a letter, you send your reader messages in addition to the one you intend to send. It is important that you make all your messages work for you.

Metacommunication is a word that encompasses the elements involved in a communication other than the message itself. "Meta" is from the Greek and means "beyond" or "in addition to"—thus, metacommunication means "beyond the communication" or "in addition to the communication." Our spoken communication is augmented by inflections, gestures, body language, nonverbal communication. Metacommunication also is present in a business letter. Let us consider some of these elements now.

Stationery

Letters written to customers and other people outside our corporate family should be typed on *bond paper*. Rags are used in the manufacture of bond paper, as opposed to the wood pulp used in the newsprint on which your daily newspaper appears. Thus, bond paper makes a person or a company look successful because the paper is durable, strong, "looks good," and "feels good." Subconsciously, perhaps, the reader forms additional impressions beyond the message in the letter while looking at and holding the stationery.

Standard letterhead stationery measures 8½ × 11 inches. The letterhead design occupies about two inches at the top of the page. Included in the letterhead design is the name of the company, the address of the company, and the type of business, if this is not apparent from the company name. Other data such as names of company executives, slogans, telephone numbers, and founding date of the organization are sometimes found in the letterhead; however, stationery and letterhead design should not become so busy that it detracts from the message (which is still the important thing). Just as "basic black and pearls" are correct attire for a woman at most formal social gatherings, so a simple letterhead design on plain, good quality stationery still is a good idea for most business letter writing situations. The effect of this combination is to complement the message and to inspire added confidence and acceptance in the mind of the decoder.

Another size of stationery often used for correspondence going outside the company is known as "monarch" or "executive." This paper measures approximately 7½ × 10 inches. Usually, it is used by executives who are middle management or above for what might be called a "personal-business" letter. This size of stationery tends to give a less formal and more personal flavor or tone to the letter. Frequently it is used when the letter deals with noncompany business in which the writer wishes to give the company some recognition.

_____ Typing

A business executive is responsible for the letters that are typed "over" the executive's signature—that is, the executive approves the content *and* the appearance of whatever he or she signs. Whether you type with one finger or not at all, you must know what a well-typed letter looks like on the page. (Notice the examples in this chapter.) The "how to" of setting up and typing a business letter is not within the scope of this book, but the appearance of the letter is relevant here.

A letter that is not centered, that is sloppy in appearance, or that contains strikeovers and/or messy erasures detracts greatly from the content of the message. The reader may well wonder whether the entire organization is run in such a slipshod manner. In addition, a messy letter actually is an insult to the reader, who may be justified in believing that he or she is not considered important enough to merit a properly typed letter.

_____ Letter Styles

Sometimes a company will prescribe a letter style and format that must be used throughout the organization. If this is not the case, the secretary typing the letter may determine the letter style. However, since the person who signs a letter is responsible for the communication and the metacommunication involved, it is important that you have at least a "nodding acquaintance" with basic letter styles.

Most of the letters written in business firms of the United States are set up in one of two letter styles. These are (1) block style, and (2) modified block or semiblock style. Be sure to read the sample letter in Figure 14–10.

The block style, shown in Figure 14–8, is just what the name suggests; all parts of the letter are blocked on the left margin.

The modified block style letter is different from the block style in that the heading and the closing of the letter are moved to the center or right of the page. The modified block style is shown in Figure 14–9.

Figure 14–8   Block style letter.

Figure 14–9   Modified block letter style.

```
                                         The Date


Mr. John Businessman
Large Corporation
Metropolis, U.S.A.

Dear Mr. Businessman:

     Appearance is important in a business letter!  An attractively
typed, well centered letter invites attention and puts the reader in
a frame of mind to accept your message.

     This letter is set up in modified block or semiblock style.
This is probably the letter style most frequently used in American
business organizations.  The first line in each paragraph of the letter
you are reading has been indented; if you prefer not to indent these
lines, they may begin at the left margin (blocked).  Most letters not
typed in modified block style are typed in what is known as block
style.  In this style, the date, the complimentary close (sincerely,)
and everything following it also begins at the left margin (in the
same relative position as "Mr. John Businessman: and "Dear Mr.
Businessman:").  Paragraphs should not be indented in a block style
letter.

     Notice, too, that this letter is placed on the page using visual
centering.  Visual center is one-half inch higher than actual center.
If a letter cannot be typed in the actual center of the page (and this
is neither easy nor necessary), it should be high on the page rather
than low because this treatment is more pleasing to the eye.

     Yes, the appearance of a letter is an important factor in its
success.

                              Sincerely,



                              A. Letterwriter

AL/me
```

Figure 14–10 **The appearance of a letter.**

It is important for you to recognize these two letter styles. Many of you will be typing your own employment application letters, and it is important that these letters be typed properly since "first impressions may be last impressions." Business people who deal extensively in written communication (and personnel managers fall into this category) know letter styles; and when they see letter styles that are "nonstandard," they immediately make a mental note about the writer. Even before your letter is read, you have communicated something—perhaps something you really do not want to tell.

Everything you do is a communication!

Mechanics

There are many items that might be listed under the heading of "mechanics." Some of these are grammar, spelling, punctuation, and syllabication. Although mechanics also fall into the secretary's province, the emphasis in this book is not on the secretarial aspects of written communication. The importance of the secretary's role in the successful handling of many communication elements should be obvious by now. Managers may delegate, but they may not abdicate. This applies to written communications as well.

To help solve some of these metacommunication problems, managers should make sure that their secretaries have (and use) a copy of a reference manual (such as *Complete Secretary's Handbook* by Doris and Miller, published by Prentice-Hall) that contains answers to most problems in the area of mechanics. Another source book that should be used frequently by both boss and secretary is the dictionary.

Everything you do is a communication. There are many metacommunication elements working for you (and against you?) in your written communications as well as in your spoken communications. With attractive stationery, consistent letter style, and correct mechanics, you can make metacommunication work *for* you.

Summary

Although letter writing is only one part of business communication, it is an important part. Before a business letter is written, it should be planned. You will find a business letter easier to write if you will study the situation and determine the nature of the problem you need to solve. The type problem will dictate whether the letter is favorable, neutral, unfavorable, persuasive, or a combination of these types. Human relations letters are also very important to your career.

The business letter writer must be well acquainted with some basic principles of letter writing: tone, "you attitude," positive approach, complete coverage, and organization.

Many people have trouble beginning and ending letters. Once these hurdles are overcome, the letter progresses smoothly. Some suggested ways to begin and end a letter are with (1) favorable elements, (2) good will, (3) resale, (4) action required, or (5) a question.

Everything a person does is a communication. A business letter contains many messages in addition to the one that the writer purposely expresses between "Dear Madam" and "Sincerely." The metacommunication, or "beyond the communication," elements in a business letter are revealed in the stationery, the typing, the letter style, and the mechanics of written communication (grammar, spelling, punctuation, and syllabication).

Discussion Questions

1. What are some metacommunication factors in written communication? In spoken communication? What do these factors have in common?
2. What are some of the techniques to be used in organizing a business letter? Why is good organization important in a letter? Do you see anything of a metacommunication nature that is revealed by the way a writer handles organization in the letter?
3. What is the difference between sympathy and empathy? Which of the two terms do you think is more important to the business letter writer—that is, should the business writer be sympathetic or empathetic? Apply your reasoning to the techniques for beginning a business letter.
4. Making liberal use of the principles of "tone" and "you attitude," explain how you would tell an instructor you are not particularly happy with the grade you received on the latest test.
5. Bring to class a sales promotional letter received by you or by someone of your acquaintance. What techniques for beginning and ending the letter have been used? What metacommunication elements are present in the letter? Does the letter motivate you to buy the product? Why or why not?
6. What is the psychological effect on the reader of a business letter when negative elements are introduced early in the letter? How does proper organization help the writer deal with this problem?
7. Why is it permissible to introduce negative elements in the opening sentence of a direct approach letter?
8. What negative reactions may be created in the reader of a business letter when mechanical factors are poorly handled by the writer of the letter?
9. Bring some samples of business stationery to class and study them. What impression does the paper itself have on you? What effect does the letterhead design have on you?
10. What are the advantages of using a question as a technique for beginning a letter? What are its advantages for ending a letter?

COMBINING THE STEPS

What we have suggested in this chapter is that you follow these steps when you write a business letter:

1. Plan your letter. What category is it?

    a. Favorable
    b. Neutral
    c. Unfavorable
    d. Persuasive
    e. A combination

2. Decide how to begin. What approach is best?

    a. Favorable elements
    b. Good will
    c. Resale
    d. Exclamation
    e. Question

3. Decide how to end. What approach is best?

    a. Favorable elements
    b. Good will
    c. Resale
    d. Action
    e. Question

4. Remember letter writing principles. What am I saying?

    a. Tone
    b. You attitude
    c. Positive Approach
    d. Complete coverage
    e. Organization

5. Apply metacommunication concepts. What else am I saying?

    a. Typing
    b. Letter styles
    c. Mechanics

Figure 14–11 Combining the steps.

11. What are the possible details or requests for information which should be included when you end a letter with a request for action?

12. Where does the business letter fit into the total business management/ business communication picture? The letter is only one form of encoding a business communication. What are some advantages and some disadvantages of the business letter as a form of communication? Relate the cost of a business letter to your discussion.

Letter Problems

Favorable Letters

1. As claims manager for the Gigantic Department Store, write to Mrs. Ralph Spencer, 6785 Ridgecliff Road, Des Moines, Iowa, and tell her that you are sending three champagne glasses to replace the ones broken in your shipment last week. Thanks to her comments, you have checked the packing department and have found some weaknesses in packing procedures. The glasses will arrive in time for the party she mentioned.

2. Herman Shiller, owner and manager of Shiller's Automotive Supply, has asked you to rush him six sets of floor mats for the two-door 1980 Sensational Foreign Car. This is really a very small order and a bit of a nuisance to you, but you decide to do it because Shiller is a good customer. Include some sales promotional material and a bit of resale on your company in the letter.

3. Write to Ralph Smith, 435 Brownfield Street, Green City, Nebraska and tell him that his order for an Ideal fishing rod and a Superior reel is on its way to him. Begin and end the letter properly and incorporate such important items as resale and "you attitude." Is there a related product you might attempt to sell Mr. Smith? Have you covered all the important points in your letter?

4. Jim Johnson, president of the Accounting Club at State University, has asked you to return to your alma mater and tell the students "how it really is" out there in the world. You've done very well since you received your degree in accounting from State U just four years ago. Write to Jim and tell him you will be glad to speak to the students. Ask him for any suggestions he may have about topics for your speech as well as for details about the meeting itself.

5. In your position as sales representative for Empire Publishing Co., write to Dr. Bruce Stoneham, Professor of Economics at Mid-America University, Chicago. He has requested a desk copy of *Current Economic Thought.* You are happy to send this book free of charge since there is a good possibility he will adopt it for use in his classes at Mid-America. Dr. Stoneham has sent you a check for $15 to pay for transparencies and other visual aids to accompany *Current Economic Thought.* You decide not to charge him for the visual aids either since he is a good friend and user of Empire books. Write the letter to Dr. Stoneham telling him he will receive the book and the visual aids free of charge. Be sure to return his check.

6. Select from a newspaper or a magazine an advertisement for a product in which you have some interest. Write a letter of inquiry requesting specific information about the product.

neutral letters

7. You receive a letter from the employment manager of a large manufacturing company saying that a friend of yours has given your name as a reference. Write the letter of recommendation which will help your friend get the job she is seeking as a management trainee.

8. Ruth Simpson did an outstanding job as your secretary and office manager during the ten years she was in your employ. Then she moved to Tucson when her husband was transferred there by his company. Today you receive a letter from Frank Abernathy, sales manager for Desert Real Estate Co., wanting your evaluation of Ruth as a person and as a potential salesperson for his company. You know Ruth has no sales experience, but you know she has many good personal qualities and outstanding business ability. Write a letter of recommendation which will help her get the job by showing how her background and experience in an office will serve her well and enable her to succeed in real estate sales.

9. As credit manager for Nu-Style Dress Shops, you must answer a request for credit information on Janice Lovington, a customer of your company. The credit manager of Fashion Clothes, Inc. wants to know how Ms. Lovington has handled her account with Nu-Style. You consider her a good customer, as she has always paid her bills. She is, however, rather slow to pay at times. Supply any additional details you think may be helpful.

unfavorable letters

10. Write to Jim Johnson, president of the Accounting Club at State University (problem 4) and refuse his request to speak at the next meeting of the organization. You are grateful to have been asked, and you appreciate the part State U played in your success. Suggest an alternate speaker and indicate your willingness to speak at another meeting yourself.

11. Hubert Yelverton, 980 Englewood Drive, Albany, New York, wants your company to replace his wrist watch which he thinks "should have lasted longer than it did." You examine the watch and find that it has had something other than normal wear and use. You will, however, repair it for $20 and guarantee it for one year. Write a letter that will keep Yelverton's good will.

12. Mary Hanson wants your company to replace her electric blanket which does not heat properly. Your inspectors agree that the blanket has apparently not been mistreated; then you discover that the one-year guarantee has expired. You can offer to replace the blanket with a new one at your cost of $20.

13. Sara Peterson, owner of Sara's Cosmetics, 810 Central Mall, Spokane, Washington, orders 12 dozen lipsticks in "cranberry pink." It's obvious this is the lipstick of the season because you can't keep it in stock. You have some on order which should reach you in two weeks. You'll have it on its way to her immediately. Write the letter which will keep the order—include sales promotion, resale, and "you attitude."

14. You'd be happy to fill Phillip Sander's order for a wool sweater if he had only told you what color and size he wants. Apparently he's eager to be off to the snow country because he forgot to give you this important information. As customer service representative for Acme Retail Co., write to Phillip and request the needed information. Why not suggest a pair of matching gloves to go along with the sweater?

15. Vivian Vardaman, 2056 Hawthorne Road, Centerville, California, ordered a set of dishes from your company, Mercantile China and Crystal, Inc., for a wedding gift. She said she wanted the ones you advertised in last Sunday's *Tribune.* Your ad said the dishes were available in service for six or eight people. Vivian forgot to tell you which she wanted, and since she wrote "charge them to my account" you can't tell from the price which she wants. Write the letter requesting the needed details. You'll want to hurry in order to get the gift on its way before the wedding.

16. Fred Finch is in charge of coffee making at his house, and he has always had great success with the Kofee-King appliance he bought from your company. He has enjoyed this coffee maker so much during the years he has had it that he decides to order another one just in case his present one should get tired and quit. You must answer his enthusiastic letter ordering another Kofee-King, but you must tell him you no longer handle that brand. Your firm is always looking for new and better products, and you now sell Coffee/Magic. This brand is the same price as Kofee-King, but it boasts sturdier construction and is much easier to keep clean. Coffee/Magic also makes coffee to the desired formula in less time. Inasmuch as you no longer sell Kofee-King and cannot tell Fred where to find it, write a letter which will switch his allegiance to Coffee/Magic.

persuasive letters

17. As leader of a committee of students charged with planning the program for the annual All-Business Day at your school, write to a local business person asking him or her to speak. Plan your letter carefully and be sure you have complete coverage.

18. A social organization to which you belong is planning a charity auction. Alpha Beta Gamma Delta is planning the event to benefit a local orphanage. Items to be auctioned are being solicited from local business firms. Contributors will receive great publicity in newspapers, on TV and radio, and in a program at the auction itself. As chairperson for the event, write a letter which will persuade local business persons to donate merchandise to the auction. Be sure to stress reader benefits. You will follow up the letter with a personal visit to the merchant.

19. In an effort to save money on his clothing bills, George Granfeld bought a half dozen dress shirts made of a new miracle fabric. The shirts were supposed to be long-wearing, color-fast, no-iron, and just the last word in everything. Now, after only a few months of use, the shirts are definitely beginning to show signs of wear. In addition, they have faded a bit, and they always did look better with just a bit of ironing. Write a letter persuading the company to give George the adjustment he desires.

good will letters

20. Write a letter of congratulation to a friend of yours who has just graduated and accepted a position in business. (It often is necessary for a person to write letters of congratulations, appreciation, or sympathy. Such letters are important to your personal and professional life. There is no certain formula for these letters; the important thing is to remember to write them.)

================ *Additional Reading*

Dawe, Jessamon, and **William Jackson Lord, Jr.,** *Functional Business Communication,* 2nd ed. Englewood Cliffs, N.J.: Prentice-Hall, 1974.

Himstreet, William C., and **Wayne Baty,** *Business Communications.* Belmont, Calif.: Wadsworth, 1977.

Lesikar, Raymond V., *Basic Business Communication.* Homewood, Ill.: Richard D. Irwin, 1979.

Level, Dale A., and **William P. Galle, Jr.,** *Business Communications: Theory and Practice.* Dallas: Business Publications, 1980.

Menning, J.H., C.W. Wilkinson, and **Peter B. Clarke,** *Communicating through Letters and Reports.* Homewood, Ill.: Richard D. Irwin, 1976.

Murphy, Herta A., and **Charles E. Peck,** *Effective Business Communications.* New York: McGraw-Hill, 1980.

Wolf, Morris P., Dale F. Keyser, and **Robert R. Aurner,** *Effective Communication in Business.* Cincinnati: South-Western, 1979.

Communicating through reports

15

key points to learn

The importance of reports to the attainment of organizational objectives.

The importance of problem definition and report assignment.

Types of business reports.

Construction of the memorandum report

Principles of report writing.

Preparation of minutes of meetings.

purpose of business reports

Business reports may be considered as business letters written and sent within the company, or to groups in the corporate family such as shareowners. A business report, like a business letter, is usually written with the idea of helping to solve a business problem.

A business organization has goals and objectives that it is constantly striving to attain. By providing its customers with a service and/or a product, the organization seeks to meet these objectives, not the least of which is profit. Reports are an essential communication tool of management in the attainment of these goals and objectives. Reports are used to communicate with both internal and external publics—employees and nonemployees—people with some interest in the company.

Reports, then, may be considered as business letters containing data and/or information needed to help solve a business problem that are written within the company. Reports for external publics are not too different from those for internal publics, and these differences will be pointed out later in the chapter. Business reports as discussed in this chapter are mainly those that are encoded and decoded within the company; emphasis is on the communication of ideas that will help solve problems and enable the company to meet its objectives.

Although business reports must be well written, literary style is not important nor is there any attempt to entertain.

business reports and problem solving

The purpose of this chapter is to give you an understanding of the written communications known as "business reports." To do this, however, it is important to relate them to the "big picture." Reports result because management must have data that can be converted to information and can be used to make decisions that will solve problems.

You will notice that management takes data and translates it into information or into a useable form for the solution of a problem. The report writer and the problem solver (manager) are frequently not the same person. The manager or problem solver is a person with the experience, the frame of reference, and the filter that enable him or her to perform the feat of changing data into information which will help the organization reach its objectives.

The person who assigns the writing of a report is usually rather well up the organizational ladder. The person to whom the writing of a report is assigned is usually not so far up the ladder. While each individual must have a considerable amount of skill to do the job effectively, it is essential that the manager be able to recognize, isolate, and define the problem clearly and precisely, because the researcher and/or the report writer will research and write about the problem that is assigned. It makes no difference how good the research effort is or how well the report is written if the wrong problem has been tackled.

This is not a chapter about problem solving; however, it is important that the relationship between problem definition and problem solving be pointed out. As the researcher and/or the report writer, you must be sure that you understand the assignment (problem definition). If you do not understand the assignment, ask questions of your superior until you *are sure*. An assignment of this sort should be made in writing to assist you in your work as well as for your protection.

origin of reports

Depending upon the type problem to be solved, reports may originate within the company or outside the company. Except for reports required by the government, even external reports originate within the company—that is, they are *authorized* by the company.

Internal

Internal reports (reports written and used within the company) usually fall into one of two categories: (1) routine, or (2) special.[1]

Routine reports originate because management anticipates problems to be solved. Management establishes quantitative markers to determine whether the company is on schedule in meeting major company goals or objectives. The budget is one of the best known markers; others are sales quotas and production units. Progress toward achieving these various markers or quotas is communicated routinely to management in the form of reports. Results, good and bad, are reported routinely to those responsible for company operations.

Special reports originate because of problems to be solved which management cannot anticipate. Special reports frequently result because of problems that become apparent in routine reports. A routine report may reveal that sales in District A are far below quota. Management investigates and determines that production is below quota because of morale problems. Based on this determination, a special report on sales personnel morale may be authorized. This is a special report that management did not expect but that management authorized because it is necessary to the attainment of company goals.

A few reports come about because of the independent action of individual company personnel. Although no attempt is made here to explain motivation, some individuals (probably a relatively small number) of their own volition will detect, research, and report on some problem they identify in company operations.

External

Reports to governmental agencies are probably the most frequently produced reports originating (authorized) outside the company. And even though they are authorized externally, they originate—that is, the research is performed—internally. Other examples of external reports would be those going to trade associations or to chambers of commerce.

Occasionally there will be problems to be solved which the personnel of a company may not be qualified to solve. Having isolated the problem(s), management calls upon an outside organization to research and report the findings. Once again, though, the problem is usually defined internally. Sometimes, even though company personnel have the necessary abilities and skills to research and write a report, an external source is hired to do the job in order to obtain the essential report element of objectivity.

---

[1]Raymond V. Lesikar, *Report Writing for Business*. Homewood, Ill.: Richard D. Irwin, 1973, p. 12.

types of reports

Countless numbers of people have spent countless numbers of hours trying to categorize the various types of reports. Some of the types they have identified are: informational, progress, administrative, independent, periodic. But many, if not most, reports overlap several categories and are difficult, if not impossible, to fit into one particular mold (category). Think for a minute about the monthly report—a report found in many business organizations. The report is a periodic report. It is prepared monthly. It is a progress report. It relays to top management how the unit is doing in efforts to meet company objectives. It is informational. It supplies facts and figures to top management. It is administrative. It is sent to management. So, even though the report carries the label "monthly," it is a mixture of this and several other types.

Actually, it is not terribly important which label is placed on a report so long as the report is constructed according to good report-writing principles and helps management to solve a business problem. When a report assignment is well made, the report writer knows not only the type report to write, but also the proper format and construction for such a report.

Reports may be classified effectively under the two major headings of *informal* and *formal*. The corporate annual report is a third category that we will consider separately.

Reports are sometimes referred to as "short" and "long," and people tend to assume that a "short" report is "informal" and a "long" report is "formal." This is not necessarily true. It is quite possible that a formal report might have fewer pages than an informal report. We will use the informal and formal designations in our discussion. It may help you to think of reports as ranging along a continuum from a very informal memorandum type (To, From, Subject, Date; Figure 15–1), perhaps written in longhand, to the formal report of many parts discussed in Chapter 16.

Within the informal and formal frameworks, however, it is helpful to think of the *purpose* of the report stated by the person who assigned the report—that is, were you (1) asked merely to supply data, (2) told to analyze and interpret the data, (3) requested to go a step further and specify some action. Dawe and Lord classify reports at these three levels as (1) informational reports, (2) interpretative reports, and (3) analytical reports.[2] Within the informal to formal continuum, you may write reports which content-wise range all the way from merely supplying data to the reader, through analysis and interpretation of the data, and on to a proposed recommendation of action.

A report concerning proposed nationwide expansion of a company will differ greatly from a report on the adoption of a new janitorial service for the

---

[2]Dawe and Lord, p. 188.

INTER-OFFICE MEMORANDUM

To: John Clinton, Office Manager   Date:

From: Frank Ingersoll, Procurement Manager

Subject: Recommended use of 16 lb bond paper

Introduction

Rising costs are a problem in the office area as well as in other
areas of the company. One of the major expenditures for office
supplies is bond paper. A telephone survey of leading office
suppliers in Metro City reveals that a saving of approximately
$2,500 annually is possible in our purchases of bond paper.

Analysis

Bond paper is used for all correspondence going outside the
company and it is used for certain important correspondence
within the company, too. It has been company policy to use 20
lb paper; and in some cases, 24 lb paper has been used. The cost
for this weight paper is about $3.00 per ream.

It is possible to buy 16 lb bond stationery for $2.50 a ream.
While this paper is not so heavy as that presently in use, it is
a good quality and would fill our needs nicely. (A sheet is
attached for your inspection.) By buying a lighter weight paper
and by stocking only the 16 lb paper, the company could realize
the $2,500 annual saving.

Recommendation

It is recommended that the company purchase and use only 16 lb
bond stationery for correspondence going outside the company and
for certain important communications within the company.

Figure 15-1   Inter-office memorandum.

company. Whether a report should be formal, informal, or somewhere in between is determined by one or more of several factors. Among these factors are: size and/or complexity of the research effort; company policy regarding reporting and report writing; cost of the research effort upon which the report is based; method of funding, especially if government or foundation funds are used; relationship of the superior to the subordinate. You will usually want a record of everything connected with the project from assignment and definition of the problem through the research to the final write-up of the results.

Within the limits specified by company policy, the superior-subordinate relationship and the need for written "evidence" will sometimes determine the degree of formality and informality that can be permitted. As with any form of communication, a report must be prepared in terms of the decoder. The audience to whom a report is directed and the relationship of that audience to the writer will help to determine the type report. The amount and the type of data that must be available to help management *make* a decision and the amount and type of documentation that must then be kept on file to *support* that decision will help determine the type of report, too.

Sometimes company policy specifies what type report should be written. Obviously, this solves one problem for the writer. It is impossible to predict what name a company will apply to a particular type of report, or what format (to be discussed in the next section) a company will require. All we can do here is acquaint you with some of the major alternatives and emphasize that good report-writing style does not change regardless of report type or format. As Lesikar points out, "With small exception, the basic writing principles, the rules of logical organization, techniques of writing style and tone and so on, remain the same in all reports."[3]

Differences between formal and informal reports should become more apparent when we discuss report writing format in the next section.

Corporate Annual Report

The corporate annual report is a type needing special attention here. The annual report is probably the type of report best known to the "average" American. Most companies prepare an annual report as a summary of their financial achievements as well as their activities in all major areas of operation during the year. Many make this annual report available to the general public. Many are required by the Securities and Exchange Commission to publish an annual report.

An annual report usually begins with a letter to the stockholders of the company signed by the chairman of the board of directors and/or the president

---

[3]Lesikar, p. 9.

of the company. The letter may give background information, report the major achievements in the year's operations, and indicate areas of concern to management that will receive special attention in the next year. A balance sheet, income statement, and various other financial analyses usually occupy several pages. In addition, many annual reports inform the reader about product acceptance, new product development, expansion plans, use of human resources, and company involvement in local, national, and world affairs.

The annual report serves not only as a financial report and a progress report but also as a public relations tool. While some people read an annual report to find out how their investment "did" during the year, other people read the annual report to learn about the company and to decide whether to invest in the company. This report, too, helps solve several business problems for the many publics of an organization.

Because the annual report at times does serve as a sales tool, it has undergone some major changes in format in recent years. Many companies go to great expense to turn out an interesting, eye-appealing report in order to attract investors. The people who write annual reports keep their audience in mind as they write, too. For example, in recent years increasing numbers of women have become shareowners in American business. To produce added appeal for this group of people, annual report writers have made increased use of color, pictures, and other eye-catching techniques of communication.

Annual reports are usually prepared by public relations specialists, and it is unlikely that you will be involved with the actual preparation of an annual report unless you enter this particular type of work. It is important, though, that you be aware of this important business communication tool.

report-writing format

Having assessed the situation and the nature and complexity of the data to be reported, the writer must determine which report format to use. Report format may be anything from the formal report having all, or most, of the parts discussed in Chapter 16, to the informal "To, From, Subject" memorandum report shown in Figure 15–1. Experience, company policy, and a well-defined assignment will help the writer make this choice of appropriate report format.

Regardless of format or style, all reports contain these three sections, although they may not be called by these titles:

1. Introduction
2. Data
3. Ending.

An informal report usually contains only these three sections. A formal report includes all these sections in the *body* of the report; in addition, the report body is preceded and followed by some additional material that makes it take on more the appearance and characteristics of a book. Even though an informal memorandum report contains introduction, data, and ending, the three sections may be compressed into five or six sentences.

Let us look in a little more detail at the formal and informal report formats.

Formal Format

We will make only a brief mention of the formal report format here because formal reports are discussed at some length in Chapter 16. Because formal reports are just that—formal—you will probably find that most companies using formal reports will have developed a formal report format and will have identified those occasions where formal reports are needed.

A research effort that produces a large amount of data, or extremely complex data, will probably require a formal report presentation because the formal report format makes it easier for the writer to departmentalize, compartmentalize, categorize, and organize the vast amount of material he or she has to work with. Both formal and informal reports must be well organized, and the same techniques for achieving organization will work for all types of reports.

Informal Format

The most informal type report format is the memorandum report shown in Figure 15–1. As we pointed out earlier, this report also contains the three major areas of introduction, data, and ending. Although these three sections are very definitely set forth in the example by means of marginal headings, it is not necessary to use the marginal headings. If the headings are not used, you will need to make effective use of topic and transitional sentences to lead your reader through the report.

Whether you use a personal writing style (first person) or an impersonal style (third person) in your informal reports will depend on such factors as company policy, organizational climate, and superior-subordinate relationship. Report content could also be a factor in your decision.

The informal format is relatively simple and plain. The content is a somewhat abbreviated version of the body of the formal report which we will discuss in Chapter 16. Another type report that may be listed under the "informal" heading is the letter report. The letter report can be organized and set up in the same way as the memorandum report, or set up in one of the accepted letter styles discussed in the chapter on business letters. Marginal heads are optional but helpful. The writing style is usually formal and businesslike. An example of a letter report is shown in Figure 15–2.

```
                                        September 15, 198-


Office Facilities Committee
Dependable Insurance Company
P.O. Box 5607
Atlanta, Georgia    30300

Gentlemen:

Here is the information about the Abington and Smithfield elec-
tric typewriters you requested in your letter of September 10.
In as much as we handle both these machines, we know what they
can do, as we can give you an impartial viewpoint.

Features

Both machines are powered by sturdy, dependable electric motors.
The Abington has the automatic erasing feature; the Smithfield
does not have it.  The Smithfield has more type styles available
than does the Abington.  The Abington typewriter comes with a
number of special keys for technical typing jobs.  Both machines
are available in several colors to match your office decor—red,
green, brown, yellow, and blue.

Costs

Because you plan to order more that 50 typewriters, we can give
you a special price of $850 each for the Abington and $800 each
for the Smithfield.  We will allow you a $150 trade in on each
of your old typewriters.

Both the Abington and the Smithfield typewriters give excellent
service with a minimum of problems.  Should you have problems, we
can have repair persons at your office within one hour of your
call.  The typewriters come with a one-year warranty on parts.

Action Requested

I know you are eager to ger your new typewriters as soon as pos-
sible, so I know you will follow up promptly.  It will take us
approximately two weeks to get the typewriters after we receive
your order.  Please telephone me at 123-4567 when you make your
decision.

                                        Sincerely,


                                        Frank Reynolds
                                        Sales Manager
```

Figure 15–2 **Example of letter report.**

Please remember that good report-writing style does not change. What is good and acceptable in a formal report is equally good and acceptable in an informal report.

Report Organization

As we have pointed out, most reports, whether informal or formal, contain three basic sections: introduction or opening, data or analysis, and ending. When a report is set up in this sequence, it is said to have *logical* organization.

Some executives prefer the ending or action section of the report to be placed at the beginning of the report format. This approach is known as *psychological* organization. This format saves time for certain members of management who need to know only what the *results* of your research are; these people are not concerned with all the details of your research. Also, some people like to know the conclusions or recommendations in your research so that they can relate your data to them as they read. The psychological organization means that you will begin your report with what would normally be the ending (summary, conclusions, recommendations) and follow this with introductory or background information and then data or analysis.

A third form of report organization is *chronological*. As the word "chronological" indicates, a report organized in this fashion is set up in a time sequence in which events occurred.

Readability

Readability was discussed at some length in Chapter 14. You will remember that we defined it as the ease with which a person can read your words, sentences, and paragraphs and comprehend their meaning. You will need to consider readability factors as you write your reports.

Inasmuch as reports are usually assigned and the assignment should tell you to whom to report, you will have some idea about the audience for whom you are writing. This will make word choice and sentence structure somewhat easier for you.

Your basic guide to an acceptable readability rating is to keep your reader in mind and write for him or her. Since you usually know something about the audience to whom a report is aimed, you should be able to do a good job with readability.

Marginal Heads

Marginal heads (an example of which you see just above this line) are very effective devices that aid readability in reports. They serve the same purpose as headlines in a newspaper. Marginal heads tell your readers what to expect in the paragraphs following and thus channel their thoughts into a certain area and prepare them for a certain vocabulary. In addition to this function, marginal heads help break up the monotony of paragraph after paragraph of dark type. They give the readers a chance to take a mental breath before plunging into the next topic.

In addition to marginal heads, there are centered heads, run-in heads, and variations on these. All of them help the writer to achieve a good readability rating by directing the reader gently but firmly through the report. You should refer to a style manual (such as Turabian) for help in setting up these heads.

_____ Spacing

We have touched on spacing in our discussion of paragraph length and marginal heads. Well-centered, typed material with a good balance and blend of dark type and white paper invites a person to read your report. Suggestions for proper and effective spacing may be found in a style manual.

The body of a report may be either single spaced or double spaced, depending upon the preference of the person assigning the report or the person writing the report. Some companies have an established report format and style which includes spacing.

report-writing style

Good report-writing style does not change from one type of report to another. Good grammar and good sentence structure are always to be hoped for; any deficiencies you may have in these areas must be remedied elsewhere than in this course. By now, you have a certain writing style or pattern that you use in term papers or in writing letters. You should check now to make sure this style includes the ability to handle some areas especially pertinent to report writing.

Our purpose in this section is to point out some very important report-writing principles. It is not that these principles have no place in letter writing, but rather that they have special importance in report writing; much of what you read here about report-writing style has applications in letter writing, too. We will consider these headings: objective, concrete, organized, impersonal.

_____ Objective

Reports must be written objectively. Care must be taken to avoid words that slant or color your writing. Let the facts speak for themselves and let the business decision be made on the basis of the facts.

Avoid such statements as, "It is obvious that the plan will not work," or "It is clear that action should be taken now." It may be "obvious" or "clear" to you, but not to your reader, and this tends to make the reader feel a little stupid. Notice how the facts speak for themselves:

> In a preliminary survey, we found that 87 percent of our 353 employees believed a suggestion system would yield no positive assistance with company operational problems. Of the 98 suggestions submitted during the last four months, only 6 relate to company operational problems.
>
> (Note: It could be argued that the word "only" colors the writing by reflecting the opinion of the writer. Some people might consider 6 to be a good response for that particular technical area. "Only" could be omitted. The credibility of the writer is an important factor in report acceptance, too.)

Be very careful of absolute words, "always" and "never" for example. Something which will "never happen again" is usually the first thing that happens. Don't forget the existence of gray areas.

Do not make a statement such as, "The following figures were carefully checked." You are paid to be careful and thorough; therefore, when you call attention to it at a specific point in your reporting, the reader may well wonder whether the figures on the other pages in your report were *not* "carefully" checked. Write so that the reader will have no reason to question or doubt the quality of the research or the accuracy of the report.

_____ Concrete

Concrete means that your report-writing style must be firm and solid; it must contain facts and figures. Management needs facts and figures (data) in order to make a business decision. Therefore, whenever possible, supply your reader with facts, figures, numbers, percentages, rankings, ratings which will prove of value to him or her. In other words, avoid vague statements such as, "many people," "several respondents," or "a few businessmen." How many are "many," "several," or "few"? Be *concrete* and specific":

Two out of three respondents favor the new insurance plan.
The four-day week is requested by 75 percent of our employees.

_____ Organized

A business report must be organized and orderly. Not only does this characteristic contribute to readability, as we have discussed already, but also it inspires the reader's confidence in the report writer, in the research and in the entire organization.

We pointed out earlier that reports (formal or informal and regardless of length) may be organized under the three heads of introduction, data, and ending. So, we organize our report by telling our readers why we conducted the research (and perhaps how we conducted it), then we tell them what we found in our research, and then we tell them what we suggest doing with what we found in our research (if we were requested to make such a suggestion). Even a short memo written in longhand by a busy executive follows these basic steps of organization:

> Because of the unkempt appearance of the lawn and shrubs around our plant, you requested at yesterday's staff meeting that I check with Property Maintenance to see what is being done about the situation. Yard Work, Inc. has been hired to take over this work for $300 a month. They will begin work Monday.

The entire report should be carefully organized and outlined before any writing is attempted so that the readers are lead firmly and logically from beginning to end.

Impersonal

Formal reports are usually written in the impersonal third-person style. However, there is nothing wrong with using the personal style, provided you know the proper degree of informality exists between researcher and audience. Some report writers prefer the impersonal approach even in informal reports, but the use of first person in informal reports is acceptable. Probably the main reason the use of the impersonal style in reports has been frowned on in the past is that when a person says "I" in a report, there is a tendency for the person to go ahead and say, "*I* think. . . ." While we hope that what the writer of the report thinks is important and worthwhile, we should not forget the importance of having the facts speak for themselves. Facts, numbers, figures are essential.

Management wants these facts and figures to help solve business problems. If the subordinate is qualified to furnish opinions and is asked to do so, the writer should give his or her opinions, but label them as such.

Informative and Instructive

Perhaps it will help you in developing your report-writing style always to remember that basically you are trying to inform and instruct your audience. Because your reader(s) will usually use your report to help solve a business problem, he or she needs to be informed and/or instructed. Your report is not supposed to be entertaining, but this does not mean it should not be interesting. And you must still use language effectively and properly.

All we are saying is that your basic objective in report writing is to *report*, to inform, and to instruct. Everything else we've said in this section just supports you and enables you to do a good job of informing and instructing.

Adherence to these few principles will help you to strengthen your report-writing style. Do not destroy good solid research efforts with poor reporting.

```
                    COMBINING THE STEPS


        What we have suggested in this chapter is that you follow
    these steps when you write a business report:

        1.  Obtain a clear assignment

            a.  Be sure the problem is properly stated
            b.  Be sure you understand the assignment
            c.  Be sure you know the purpose of the report

        2.  Determine report type

            a.  Formal (chapter 17)
            b.  Informal

        3.  Determine report format

            a.  Major sections
                1.  Introduction
                2.  Data (analysis)
                3.  Ending
            b.  Formal (chapter 17)
            c.  Informal
            d.  Readability
            e.  Margin heads
            f.  Spacing

        4. Apply report-writing style

            a.  Objective
            b.  Concrete
            c.  Organized
            d.  Impersonal
            e.  Informative and Instructive
```

Figure 15–3 Combining the steps.

miscellaneous report forms

In addition to the formal and informal business reports we have discussed in this chapter, there are a few miscellaneous report forms we should mention briefly.

Minutes of Meetings

Although you may not have thought of them in this category, minutes of meetings are reports. Minutes of a meeting may vary all the way from a statement of the motion and the action taken on it to a verbatim presentation of the entire meeting (in which case a tape recorder will probably be used). The amount of detail required in the minutes of a given meeting should be ascertained before the formal proceedings begin; this decision can be made by the chairman and/or the members of the group.

Subjects discussed in a meeting are usually recorded in the minutes under marginal heads as we have already discussed. After Subject *A* has been reported in the minutes, marginal head Subject *B* is introduced and that topic is discussed. Sometimes each subject entry is numbered for easier, quicker reference. With permanent groups that meet on a regular basis (daily, weekly, monthly), certain subjects will probably be discussed frequently; the reporter should make certain that the subject is reported under the same subject head wording in each set of minutes. For example, the sales staff probably discusses progress of the sales force at each meeting. The reporter should decide upon a proper heading for the minutes ("Sales Progress," "Sales to Budget," "Sales Income") and record like data using the same heading in each set of minutes.

The first page of minutes of a meeting is usually headed with the words "Minutes" or "Minutes of Meeting." Also included are date, time, and place of meeting. It is customary and desirable to include the names of the people present; and, in the case of a formally organized group with designated membership, the names of absentees should also be included. In some groups it is customary to record the time of arrival or departure should a member of the group come into the meeting late or leave early.

News and Publicity Releases

Large business organizations have public relations departments or hire outside public relations firms (or both) to handle news and publicity releases for them. If you should find yourself assigned to this type of work, you will receive or you will have received the additional training necessary to carry out this specialized type of reporting.

If you are employed by a company without a public relations department, you may find yourself involved in some of these activities. The broadcasting and newspaper media have specialists who will assist you with advertising. We are more concerned here with the communication of news about the company and its employees. Some events are so special (new company president, new office building, major expansion), that you will have no trouble getting reporters to come to the company offices. For events of a more routine nature, reports (news releases) may have to be prepared and sent to the media offices.

News releases are usually typed, double-spaced, on copy paper—an inexpensive paper. The newspaper staff will edit your writing, so you need not worry about perfection as you write; however, assuming that you have a worthwhile news item to report, media personnel are more likely to make immediate use of it when it is presented to them in an accepted form and format. With experience you will learn to put the story into more publishable form each time. Remember, too, that newspaper personnel are available to help you with the learning process.

Reference is made quite often to the five W's of journalism—who, why, what, where, when. Here is where you put them to use. Think about them and use them as guides when you are deciding what to include in your news release (report).

Miscellaneous

There are other forms of reports, less obvious and more simple, but reports nonetheless. For example, you are making a report when you fill out your income tax form for the Internal Revenue Service. The person filling out an expense account form is reporting. The authors are asked frequently to make recommendations for students who are graduating and seeking employment; the report consists mainly of checking boxes or circling words such as "average," "outstanding," "superior." It is still a report.

And even though the report seems so simple and consists only of filling in a blank or checking off a box, it is important that you remember to be objective, specific, factual, and impersonal. It is still a report.

Summary

Reports are business letters written within the company which contain data and/or information needed to help solve a business problem. It is important that the report writer and/or the researcher understand the assignment perfectly so that the correct problem will be researched, reported, and solved.

Reports originate either within the company or outside the company, and they come about through either routine needs or as the result of special problems which arise. It is not terribly important how a report is classified as to type—formal and informal or long and short will suffice. The situation necessitating a report will usually dictate quite clearly whether the report should be of one type or another.

All business reports regardless of length contain three sections—introduction, data, ending. Both formal and informal reports contain these sections, but the sections vary in complexity and length. In addition to these parts, a formal report contains opening and closing sections which give a more complete, detailed, and documented picture than the reader will find in an informal report.

Readability is an important factor in any type of writing. Word, sentence, and paragraph length or difficulty affect the ease with which a person is able to read and digest what you have written. Marginal heads and proper spacing are mechanical assists that help you achieve good readability ratings in your reports.

Report-writing style is actually not too much different from other forms of business writing, but you will achieve better results if you will remember four key words as you write your report—*objective, concrete, organized,* and *impersonal.*

=========== Discussion Questions

1. Why is the definition of the problem so important in the research/report-writing situation? What are some techniques that are helpful in securing accurate definition of the problem?
2. Why are the report writer and the person who defines the problem frequently not the same person?
3. What are the two basic ideas which should be incorporated in the introductory section of the report body (i.e., ideas which should guide your thinking when you are deciding what to include in the introductory section)?
4. What are some of the main differences between a formal report and an informal report?
5. "Good report-writing style does not change from one type of report to another." Explain.
6. "A good report 'ends,' it does not 'stop'." Explain. What is the function of each of the four sections which may be found in the ending section of the body of a formal report?
7. Distinguish between logical, psychological, and chronological forms of report organization.
8. Why is it usually safer to make assumptions about the reader of a report than it is about the reader of a business letter? What evidence is available to the report writer on which he may base his assumptions about the report reader?

Problems

1. Interview some business people and/or administrators at your college concerning their methods of accurately defining problems and then solving them.
2. Secure a copy of a corporate annual report and study it. Identify the various parts in the report. What mechanical techniques (metacommunication) have been used to aid in the communication?
3. Visit a local company and determine the types of reports they use and the way reports are categorized in that company. Does the company make use of formal reports? What format is used?
4. Some reports are initiated by the report writer. Identify a problem with which you are familiar and write a short, informal, memorandum report to the appropriate person. Be sure to include a brief analysis as well as the recommended action.
5. Assume that you have been asked by the president of your college to serve as chairperson of a student-faculty committee to study some current problem on campus. Prepare a statement of the problem (definition) as you understand it, and prepare a broad, general plan for researching the problem.
6. Collect data for the research project you have outlined in Problem 5 by means of questionnaires, interviews, or observation, or a combination of these methods. Tabulate the data. Prepare graphic aids for some of the data after you have studied the chapter on presenting data.
7. As office manager for your company, you are considering the use of some temporary help in the secretarial/clerical area. Management of your company has become very cost conscious, and it has been suggested that savings might be gained by using some temporary office help supplied by an employment agency specializing in this type personnel. You presently employ two full-time people who "float" from department to department filling in where needed; each of these individuals receives $150 a week. At certain times of the month they have more work than they can handle; at other times, they "have time on their hands." You think perhaps you might level off this situation by using outside help rather than your own employees. The employment agency will supply temporary help for $6 an hour.

   In making your decision you will want to consider factors such as the convenience of having people always on hand who are familiar with your company's operations. On the other hand, you have a rather high turnover rate in these positions because the people do not feel that they belong any particular place in the company—and it costs money to hire and train our own people. What other factors do you need to consider? Write your findings and recommendation in memorandum report form and send them to the president of the company.
8. You are an assembly-line supervisor at a manufacturing company. One of your employees, Frank Findley, has become something of a problem. The situation began about a year or so ago when Frank and his wife separated. You could understand this was a difficult experience, so you forgave him some of his increased errors and lack of attention to details. He seemed to straighten out for a while, and then he began to come to work late or many times would call in sick. You suspect he has developed a drinking problem.

   Frank's attitude and actions have become a problem and he is now adversely affecting morale and production in the department. The situation has reached a point where you must take action. Write a report of the situation and your recommended action to the personnel manager. (You may supply any needed facts and figures to support your position.)

9. Your instructor has asked you what makes a textbook good. He or she wants input from students to help in selecting a new textbook for use next year. Obviously you cannot compare the content of a chemistry book with the content of a grammar book, but you can decide how readable you think each is. How interestingly is the material presented? You can also look at such items as size of print, color of ink, quality of paper, and number and types of illustrations. Are there other factors you look for? Compare two of your textbooks and present your analysis to your instructor in memorandum report format.

10. Could you and a group of your fellow students be of help to a small businessman in your community? Contact some businessmen and find out whether they have problems which you might help solve. With the help of the businessman, identify the problem, research it, and write the report. This is a project which might involve not only your communication instructor but also instructors from other departments and disciplines. It might also be helpful to draw the members of your committee from the several business majors.

══════════ Additional Reading

Dawe, Jessamon, and William Jackson Lord, Jr., *Functional Business Communication*, 2nd ed. Englewood Cliffs, N.J.: Prentice-Hall, Inc., 1974.

Lesikar, Raymond V., *Report Writing for Business*. Homewood, Ill.: Richard D. Irwin, 1977.

Level, Dale A., and William P. Galle, Jr., *Business Communications: Theory and Practice*. Dallas: Business Publications, 1980.

Menning, J.H., C.W. Wilkinson, and Peter B. Clarke, *Communicating through Letters and Reports*. Homewood, Ill.: Richard D. Irwin, 1976.

Murphy, Herta A., and Charles E. Peck, *Effective Business Communications*. New York: McGraw-Hill, 1980.

Turabian, Kate L., *Manual for Writers of Term Papers, Theses, and Dissertations*, 4th ed. Chicago: University of Chicago Press, 1973.

Writing a formal report

16

key points to learn

The relationship between the formal report and the research effort.

How to determine the degree of formality required.

The way in which the structure of the report assists the researcher in dealing with all aspects of the research effort.

The parts of the formal report.

the formal report and research

The formal report is the end result of a rather lengthy and involved process. Problem definition is the beginning of a rather lengthy and involved process. Between these two focal points—problem definition and formal report—come many hours of research and writing. The process is shown in Figure 16–1.

The point is that the formal report is not something isolated and by itself. It is the product toward which the entire problem/research process is directed. By keeping the structure of the formal report in mind, the researcher is able to do a more effective job of organizing his or her efforts.

Our model calls attention to that important subject of problem definition, which we have already discussed in Chapter 15. Perhaps we should make a distinction between "problem identification" and "problem definition." We have tended to use the terms synonymously here, but there is a difference. A problem must be *identified* before it can be *defined*. As we use the term "problem definition" in these chapters, we have assumed that the correct problem has been identified before it is defined. It should be obvious that if we identify the wrong problem, we are going to solve the wrong problem. As we pointed out earlier, it is essential that the person or persons who identify and

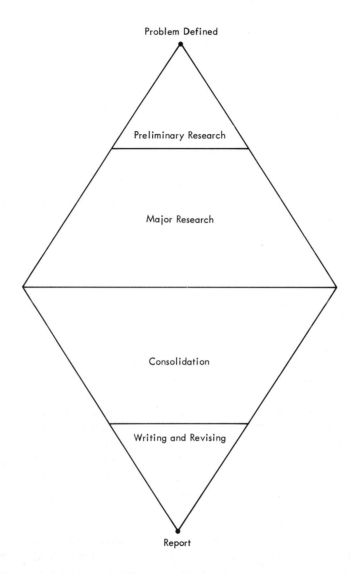

Figure 16–1 The process of writing a formal report. (James T. Watt and Wade S. Hobbs, "Research and Report Writing: A Model of Their Interrelationships," *ABCA Bulletin*, September 1979, pp. 22–24.)

define a problem be experienced and informed so that they do the job well. This group must then communicate their instructions to the researcher/ reporter.

At this point we can return to our model (Figure 16–1). The researcher begins preliminary research. He or she should read about the subject and talk with people to learn as much background information as possible. This background information should include arguments for and against a premise or thesis about the subject. The problem should be approached from as many angles as possible.

Once the researcher has determined the factors involved and developed a research strategy or design, the research effort can begin. Data are obtained through primary and secondary research. Primary research consists of data obtained from original sources and through the efforts of the researcher using such techniques as interviews, questionnaires, and observation. Secondary research involves data collected from the works of others and is frequently referred to as "library research." Completion of data collection brings us to the center, or widest portion, of our model. At this point, the researcher does something of an "about face" in his or her work.

So far, the researcher has been moving outward, as shown by the model. He or she has been reading, talking, experimenting, questioning—in short, gathering as much data as possible. Now, surrounded by a mass of facts and figures, the researcher must move in the opposite direction by consolidating the data into a manageable, meaningful, usable set of facts and figures that can be applied to the solution of the problem.

In preparing the data for use in the report, the researcher must do four things: tabulate, edit, classify, and analyze. *Tabulation* (counting the data) can be accomplished with pencil and paper or with a computer. Sometimes data do not fit into categories established by the researcher; when this happens, he or she must *edit* the material. If it cannot be determined which category the data belong in, they will still be accounted for (tabulated) by being placed in a category such as "no answer" or "not usable." It is also necessary to *classify* all data. The only way the researcher can make sense out of all the data is to group them in appropriate ways. Appropriate groups may be determined before the research is undertaken, or they may become obvious after the data are gathered. In order to compare like things, it is important that "all the oranges be in one pile" and "all the lemons be in another pile" before *analysis*, the last step. The facts and figures in the various classifications of data must be compared and contrasted so as to reveal similarities, dissimilarities, or relationships of whatever kind. In the process of analyzing the data the researcher makes use of the appropriate statistical treatment. When all data have been prepared, the writing process can begin.

Please remember that the things you learned about good report-writing style in Chapter 15 apply to the formal report, too. It might be helpful to you to read again the sections headed *objective, concrete, organized, impersonal,* and *informative and instructive.* Also, you will want to read elsewhere in this book about the use of graphic aids in the presentation of your data. A formal report will demand all the skills you possess.

factors determining need for formal reports

It was necessary for us to discuss informal reports and reports in general in Chapter 15 before talking about the more detailed formal report in this chapter. As you can see, all reports have many things in common. It is not likely that you will have trouble recognizing the need for a formal report (rather than an informal one). We will make a few more comments here about this list of factors that may suggest handling a subject within the structure of a formal report.

1. Company policy
2. Size of research project
3. Amount of money expended in research effort
4. Funding agency, if any
5. Need for documentation and analysis
6. Audience.

It is possible that company policy may specify that reports dealing with certain topics, or projects costing a specified amount of money must be presented in formal format. A project of major proportions can be handled more easily in a formal report, as you will see. ("Major proportions" could refer to scope, money, time, personnel, and amount of data.) We have mentioned money as a factor twice. You will definitely need a formal format if your research is being funded by a foundation or a government agency, and the foundation or agency may very well specify what that format will be.

A need for thorough documentation and detailed analysis could also dictate the formal format. Finally, as you've read several times in these pages, remember your audience. Is your report for internal or external consumption? If internal, to what level in the organization structure is the report directed?

parts of the formal report

As you read the remainder of this chapter, remember that the layout, organization, and appearance of the formal report will vary from one company to another. However, the types of material presented in the reports will not vary.

You have learned that a report has three sections: introduction, data presentation, and closing. In the formal report, these sections become the body of the report. In addition to these three sections, the formal report contains three *major* divisions: an opening division, the body (to which we just referred), and a closing division.

As you have probably concluded from the discussion of the factors determining the need for a formal report, we are talking about dealing with a large amount of material. Therefore, it is proper at this point to speak of a *long*, formal report. Because of the length of the report, additional divisions are needed to organize the material for ease of reading.

_____ Opening Division

The opening or preliminary division of the formal report is an overview of the report. It gives the reader an idea of what the entire report is about. A member of the organization not vitally concerned with the details of the report should be able to read only the opening division and have enough information to do his or her job.

Parts of the opening division of a formal report are:

1. Title page
2. Letter of authorization
3. Letter of transmittal
4. Table of contents
5. List of tables, charts, illustrations
6. Synopsis.

These are *available* parts; it is not necessary that each one be included in every formal report.

The *title page* contains the title of the report, for whom the report was prepared, by whom the report was prepared, and the date. This is the same information found in the To, From, Subject, Date heading of the informal memorandum report.

Because of the dimensions and complexity of a formal report, it is frequently authorized in writing. In order to complete the report package, a copy of the *letter of authorization* should be included. And, a *letter of transmittal* is included to pave the way for the report. A considerable amount of time has probably elapsed since the report was assigned, and the reader may need to be reminded what this is all about. If there is no letter of authorization, authorization facts may be included in the opening paragraph of the letter of transmittal. The letter usually begins with "Here is the report," and it concludes with an offer of further assistance or with an expression of appreciation for being allowed to help. Beyond this you may include any significant facts you wish concerning the research effort or the report. The letter may be set up in one of the letter styles we discussed in Chapter 14.

Inasmuch as a formal report is lengthy and may even have chapters like this book, a *table of contents* will help your reader to find needed sections. A *list of tables, charts, illustrations* is included for the same reason.

An important part of the opening section is a *synopsis*. (The word "synopsis" is used to avoid confusing this part with a similar part which appears at the end of the body of the report.) The synopsis is a brief presentation of the most important data in the body of the report. It should also include the major recommendation(s) or other appropriate ending material. The synopsis should be approximately one-eighth the length of the body of the report. A well-written synopsis can save valuable reading time for many executives.

Body or Report Proper

The body or report proper is what the concerned reader is interested in. This division of the formal report contains details of the total research effort. Parts of the report proper are:

1. Introduction
   A. Purpose
   B. Historical Background
   C. Sources of data
   D. Methods of collecting data
   E. Scope
   F. Limitations
   G. Definitions
2. Presentation of Data
3. Ending
   A. Summary
   B. Findings
   C. Conclusions
   D. Recommendations.

The *introduction* serves two very important purposes:

1. It brings the reader up to the level of understanding of the researcher and/or the writer, and
2. It gives details of how the research was conducted so that a follow-up study may be undertaken at a later date if it is needed.

Therefore, it is important that the introductory section be carefully prepared. We have repeatedly stressed the importance of problem definition. If our advice has been followed, it should be relatively easy to write the *purpose* of the report. A very simple way to begin this part is to say, "It is the purpose of this report to. . . ."

The *historical background* section is the place where you fill in any lack of understanding or experience in the reader so that he or she will be able to handle the material in the report. You must include enough historical background to enable your reader to see the data presentation in the proper context. Bring the reader up to your level of understanding.

The remainder of the introductory subheads fulfill the second major purpose of this section by giving details of the research effort. *Sources of data* refers to libraries and other depositories; it does not refer to specific books or periodicals (these are listed in the bibliography). *Methods of collecting data* should include specific details of the methods used to obtain primary and secondary data. Please notice that sources and methods do not include specific titles of books and articles or the names of people interviewed; you would, however, list the names of the libraries and companies where the interviews were held. Details of interview techniques used and related matters such as interview guide construction and pretesting methods would be given.

The *scope* of the report lists the parameters or boundaries within which the research was conducted. For example, "General Motors manufactures Chevrolets, Buicks, Pontiacs, Oldsmobiles, and Cadillacs, but this report deals only with Chevrolets and Buicks." This statement will save time for a person interested in knowing about Pontiacs. The *limitations* are such things as time, money, and library resources. Limitations should be discussed so that the reader will have a good idea of the extent to which they may have affected the research. None of these statements should be looked upon as "excuses." The writer/researcher is merely telling the reader, "I did this. I did not do this. I found this."

The previous sections are essential in your introduction. In addition, you may have a *definitions* section if needed. If the report is technical and contains many specialized words or if it has been necessary to coin words or to use words with other than their usual "meaning," the words should be defined somewhere in the report. If only a few words need to be defined, they should be defined in the introduction section. If the list of words is lengthy, it should be labelled "glossary" and placed in the appendix. If a word requiring definition is used only one time, it should be defined in a footnote at the point where it is introduced in the report.

Have I told everything necessary to enable another researcher to duplicate this study sometime in the future? Does the reader now have enough background to know how the research was conducted and to understand the data I'm about to present? If you can answer "yes" to these questions, you are ready to present the data gathered in the research project.

The *presentation of data* is the focal point of the report. It is the section toward which everything has been channeled since the title page. Using all your writing skills, with special attention to report-writing style and technique, you now present the data gathered through primary and secondary research. If your company does not have a prescribed style for presentation of data, you may obtain help from style manuals such as Turabian. Proper handling of these details is important because if any part of the report-writing effort is not well done, the reader may wonder about the quality of the research which preceded it. There must be nothing in the total effort to cause the reader to doubt the value of this document in helping him or her to make the decision that will solve the problem that started this whole process.

The *ending* section of the body of the report is where you wrap up the project and bring your statements to an appropriate close. A well-written report *ends;* it does not *stop.* Having presented all data, you are ready to end your report. The ending of a formal report frequently includes these four parts: summary, findings, conclusions, recommendations. These words are not synonyms; each is a different concept.

A *summary* is a "repeat report" of the high points of the body of the report. It is usually longer and more detailed than the synopsis we discussed earlier. An executive who requires more information than is contained in the synopsis, but who still does not need the entire report, can find what he or she wants by reading the summary. (A reading of the entire ending section, if it includes more than a summary, should give a very complete view of the report.)

Findings are the major or most important facts and figures uncovered in the research. In effect, it is a summary that includes only the most important facts, figures, numbers, revealed by the research. Based upon these important findings, the *conclusions* are written. Because conclusions are the opinions of the researcher/writer based upon the findings, it is permissible to use the first person pronoun in this section of the formal report. "Because 75 percent of the respondents said such-and-such, I conclude that we should do this-and-this."

Having concluded that a certain decision should be made because it will produce favorable results, the writer is ready to *recommend* specifically what should be done. A recommendation should be a recommendation and not a "hint." Do not hesitate to say, *"It is recommended* that the company borrow $100,000 immediately." "It seems like a good idea to borrow $100,000" lacks a certain ring of conviction. Do not be afraid to state your recommendation in clear terms. Your superior always has the right to make the final decision.

_____ Closing Division

The third major division of the long, formal report is the closing division. Although this division contains important information, it is often not needed for an understanding of the report proper (with the possible exception of a glossary, should there be one). There are three major parts which may be in the closing division of a formal report, although it is possible that a formal report may have none of them. The parts are:

1. Bibliography
2. Appendix
3. Index.

If library research has gone into the formal report, it must be documented. A complete listing of printed sources should appear in a *bibliography.* Quoted or paraphrased material in the body of the report must be footnoted.) Documentation is not an invention of the devil; it is used for two very important reasons:

1. To give credit where credit is due, and
2. To enable the interested reader to go to the original information source and learn more if he or she wishes.

The *appendix* contains information that is helpful or interesting to the reader but which is not absolutely essential to his or her understanding of the report. For example, if some data are secured by means of a questionnaire, it is helpful to the reader to see a copy of the questionnaire (which could be placed in the appendix): but it is not necessary for the reader to see the questionnaire in order to understand the presentation of the data gathered on the questionnaire.

An *index* is the third section of the closing division of a formal report. An index cross-references major topics and enables a reader to locate quickly references to a given topic wherever they appear in the report. The index is similar to the one at the end of the book.

These are the major parts of the formal report format. There are some additional areas we need to consider before we conclude our discussion of the report.

miscellaneous

Here are some additional suggestions that will prove helpful to you in your preparation of a formal report.

Spacing

Readability is an important factor in the formal report. The report may be double-spaced or single-spaced. Inasmuch as these reports are bound on the left like a book, you will want to leave a 1½-inch margin on the left; use a 1-inch margin top, bottom, and right. Notice this one exception: the first page of a major section (big roman numeral in your report outline) should begin at least 1½ inches from the top of the page. And, always double-space before and after headings.

There are many more rules and variations on rules for spacing, but these are important ones to begin with. For more help, see a style guide.

Pagination

Pagination is just another word for the process of numbering pages. Pages in the opening division are numbered with small roman numerals. All pages, beginning with the title page, are counted; but the first page that actually carries a numeral is the table of contents. Therefore, in a report with a title page, a letter of transmittal, and a table of contents, the table of contents would be numbered "iii." Pages in the body or the report proper are numbered in arabic numerals. The first page of a major division is numbered at the bottom; however, if you wish, you may not number the page. You *do* count the page even though you do not put a number on it. Pages in the body, other than the first page of a major division, are numbered at the top of the page, centered or in the right corner.

Mechanics

Although you should realize by now the importance of the effective handling of mechanics in written communications, we must mention it again in connection with the formal report. Poor typing, incorrect grammar, and misspelled words always have a negative effect on your reader. A report contains many facts and figures that are being used by someone to make a business decision. Don't force the reader to question the accuracy of any of your figures or statements because of poorly handled mechanics in your report!

Documentation

We have already made reference to documentation in our discussion of a bibliography. Do not overlook the ethical and moral responsibility you have to give credit to the original source of your material. Failure to do this is just one more way you can cast doubt upon the quality of your research. On the plus side, documentation makes it easy for your reader to do additional research if he or she so desires. And, having a voice of authority (or many voices of all sorts) on your side strengthens your research. Documentation is a very detailed process, and these details can best be understood by using a reference book.

Reference Books

A report writer needs several reference books on his or her desk: a dictionary, a thesaurus, perhaps a stenographer's reference manual, and a style guide are some examples. Your instructor will probably be the first person to admit that he or she does not have all the answers to the countless numbers of details involved in writing and setting up a formal report, but your instructor undoubtedly knows where to go to find the answers. When in doubt, investigate!

A final word of advice in this chapter: check your references, select the correct spelling, or style, or whatever, and then continue to use the chosen method throughout your report. In other words, *be consistent.* Lack of consistency is quickly apparent to the reader who is accustomed to well-structured, well-organized reports. Inconsistencies of any kind can cast serious doubts on the quality of your work.

Summary

A formal report is the end result of a research process that had its beginning with the definition of a problem. Data to be used in the solution of the problem are collected by means of primary and secondary research. To prepare the data for use in the report, the researcher must tabulate, edit, classify, and analyze.

Some of the factors that determine the need for a formal report are: company policy, size of research project, amount of money involved in the research effort, funding agency (if any), need for documentation and analysis, and audience. A formal report consists of three major divisions: opening, body, and closing. Each division has several subparts. The available parts of the formal report are listed in Figure 16–2 so that you can see them all together. And, samples of key elements in a formal report appear in Figures 16–3 through Figure 16–7 to show actual structural techniques.

Some additional topics that require your attention when writing a formal report are: spacing, pagination, mechanics, and documentation. You will need a variety of reference books. A style guide is one of the most important, and one by Turabian is well known and widely used.

Discussion Questions

1. Distinguish between "problem identification" and "problem definition."
2. What is the relationship between the research effort or the research project and the report itself?
3. What is the difference between "editing" and "classifying," as applied to data preparation?
4. What are some of the factors to be considered in determining the degree of formality of a report?
5. What are the three major divisions of a formal report? What, in general, is the main purpose for each section?
6. What are the three major sections of the body or report proper? What, in general, is contained in each section?
7. Discuss briefly the nature and importance of spacing, pagination, and mechanics in report preparation.
8. What are some of the most important reference books needed by a report writer? What is the value of each to the writer?

```
┌─────────────────────────────────────────────────────────────────┐
│                                                                   │
│                                                                   │
│                     FORMAL REPORT FORMAT                          │
│                                                                   │
│                                                                   │
│                                                                   │
│    Opening Division                                               │
│                                                                   │
│            Title Page                                             │
│            Letter of Authorization                                │
│            Letter of Transmittal                                  │
│            Table of Contents                                      │
│            List of Tables, Charts, Illustrations                  │
│            Synopsis                                               │
│                                                                   │
│    Body of Report                                                 │
│                                                                   │
│            Introduction                                           │
│              Purpose                                              │
│              Historical Background                                │
│              Sources of Data                                      │
│              Methods of Collecting Data                           │
│              Limitations                                          │
│              Definitions                                          │
│            Presentation of Data                                   │
│            Ending                                                 │
│              Summary                                              │
│              Findings                                             │
│              Conclusions                                          │
│              Recommendations                                      │
│                                                                   │
│    Closing Division                                               │
│                                                                   │
│            Bibliography                                           │
│            Appendix                                               │
│            Index                                                  │
│                                                                   │
│                                                                   │
│                                                                   │
│                                                                   │
└─────────────────────────────────────────────────────────────────┘
```

Figure 16–2 Outline of a typical formal report.

═══════════ Problems and Additional Readings

The problems and additional readings given at the end of Chapter 15 apply also to Chapter 16.

The possibilities for topics of long, formal reports are limitless. A teacher and student working together can easily come up with a topic that will be helpful and of interest to the student.

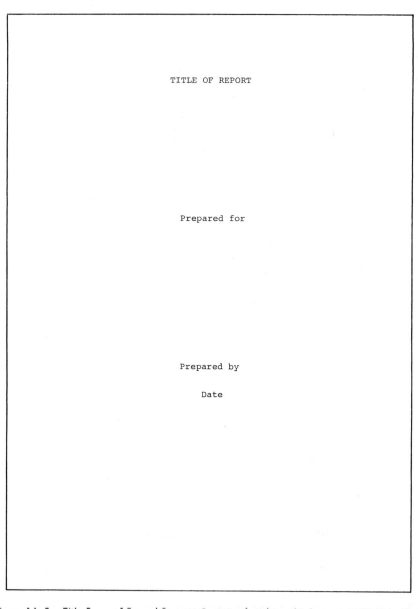

Figure 16–3   Title Page of Formal Report. Contains four bits of information: (1) Title (2) for whom the report was prepared (3) by whom the report was prepared (4) the date.

```
Heading


X
X
X
X

Dear

The letter of transmittal which accompanies a formal report
usually begins by saying "here is the report you asked me to
write."  Since many months may be required to research  and write
a formal report, your letter of transmittal may be needed to
explain what the report is all about.  If the report was not
authorized in writing, authorization facts may be included here.

The letter may include any details the writer wishes: any sig-
nificant or major findings, special thanks to important individ-
uals who assisted in the project, comments on specific points.

The letter of transmittal usually ends by expressing thanks for
the privilege of working on the project, and by offering to be
of further help in interpreting or researching the data.

                                        Sincerely,


                                        Name
```

Figure 16—4   Letter of Transmittal.

```
                       TABLE OF CONTENTS

Synopsis .................................................  iv

INTRODUCTION .............................................   1

     Subtopic ...........................................

     Subtopic ...........................................

MAJOR HEADING ............................................

     Subtopic ...........................................

     Subtopic ...........................................
```

Figure 16—5   Table of Contents. The outline of a formal report becomes the table of contents. Just add leader lines and page numbers.

```
                              SYNOPSIS


          A synopsis is a "brief summary" of the major points in the
     report proper.  The synopsis is sometimes called précis, epitome,
     or summary.

          The synopsis is generally about one-eighth the length of the
     body of the report.

          It is usually single spaced, and it need not be centered
     vertically on the page.

          Be sure that the synopsis is a summary and not an overview—
     i.e., do not tell the reader he or she will find the report "a
     description of word processing in the office."  Instead, give de-
     tails of equipment cost, speed of reproduction, training time for
     operators, etc.
```

Figure 16– 6   Synopsis. This section contains highlights of the report for people who do not need to read the entire report.

```
                            TITLE

                         INTRODUCTION

The "body" or "report proper" begins at this point.

Remember that the Introduction serves two very useful purposes:

1.   It brings the reader up to the level of understanding of
     the researcher and/or the writer, and

2.   It gives details of how the research was conducted so that
     a follow-up study may be undertaken at a later date if it
     is needed.

Subtopic

     Subtopics of major headings (such as "Purpose" or "Methods
of collecting data") are presented as marginal heads or as sub-
heads of some type.

     Consult a style guide (such as Turabian) for help in these
areas.

                            DATA

     After you have presented the introductory section of the
report proper, you are ready to begin the presentation of data.
This is the focal point of the entire research effort and the
report itself.  It is in this section that you present the re-
search findings; i.e., the reason for the entire project.

     In addition to quality research and accurate, clear report-
ing, you will want to add to the readability by use of headings,
subheadings, and by attention to details.
```

Figure 16–7   *Body or Report Proper.* This section is the culmination of the research effort and report preparation.

Mass communication for business application: advertising and public relations

17

key points to learn

How mass communication is used by the business firm.

Development of the mass communication model.

Differences between advertising and other forms of mass communication.

Classifications of advertising.

Characteristics of advertising media.

How an advertisement is developed.

The purposes of public relations.

Steps in the public relations process.

The future of public relations.

Can you imagine a world without mass communication? Can you envision *your* life without mass communication? How would you learn about world events or news in your community? Where would you shop for the best buys in town or hear or read about the winners of sporting events? You needn't worry about the evening's TV schedule or what movies were playing . . . there wouldn't be any TV or movies—nor would there be any newspapers, magazines, records, tapes, or books, for that matter.

We are great consumers of mass communications. Over 97 percent of all households in the United States have one or more TV sets and 80 percent of these are turned on daily. One or more persons per household watch an average of better than six hours each day. It is estimated that an American child watches 15,000 hours of television between the ages of 3 to 16. That is more time than is spent in school.

There are almost three radios in every household, on the average, and almost 77 percent of these households receive one or more newspapers. The average home receives six magazines on a regular basis ranging from very specialized publications with limited circulation to *TV Guide* with 20 million copies sold weekly. Over 5.5 billion individual copies of various magazines are sold each year, and the average reader spends almost an hour and a half (83 minutes) with each magazine.

Typically, we tend to think of newspapers, television, radio, and magazines when the subject of mass communication is discussed. This is due to the impact that these media, and the advertising carried, have had upon our lives. Mass communication, mass media, and advertising have come to mean the same thing to many. Taking a broader view, the book you are reading is a form of mass communication and librarians often consider themselves a part of the mass communication process. Film is certainly a mass communication vehicle as are impressive structures, works of art, musical and dramatic events. Mass communication can be either commercial or profit-making, or be noncommercial, generating returns other than profit.

Mass communication can be differentiated from other kinds of communication by these criteria: (1) messages that are addressed to a large section of the population, (2) some technical means are employed in transmission, and (3) the message is delivered simultaneously to the audience. Other criteria include limited and indirect feedback, monetary purpose, and greater efficiency due to low unit cost, among others.

═══════════business and mass communication

What is the relationship between business and mass communication? Between business and mass media? For one thing, *business in the United States pays for all radio and television through advertising! Newspapers and magazines would cost substantially more if they were not subsidized by advertising revenue!*[1] The business firm employs mass media to present and to promote its products, services, and ideas through the advertising message. Public relations, publicity, and employee relations use mass media to convey information or promote an image to employees, customers, creditors, community neighbors, suppliers, and others. In addition to using public or external mass media, the business firm has its own private and internal channels.

A business organization may also publish such internal items as magazines, TV programming, and newsletters to reach employees, stockholders, suppliers, and distributors. The annual report is a very important publication as it is addressed to those who are or may become stockholders of the corporation. On-premise signs, bulletin boards, and posters all serve to provide additional

---

[1]Advertising supports the media almost solely, with the exception of some relatively small government and private grants to educational TV and radio networks and stations. These are nonprofit and supported by these contributions. Only recently have newspaper and magazine publishers attempted to pass along increasing costs to the reader rather than impose them on the advertiser.

channels of mass communication to the business firm's many publics. Hundreds of films are produced annually by business. These cover a wide range of subjects, some dealing with the firm and its products while others are informative or entertaining. Many of these are distributed free of charge. Often there is no commercial message, just the mention of the business firm producing and making the film available in the film credits.

Another subtle way business communicates with its various publics is through visual communication, as discussed in Chapter 9. This nonverbal form is evident in almost every city and is seen in the design of the local bank building or a glistening skyscraper bearing the name of its major tenant. Impressive manufacturing plants and attractive store fronts are seen daily by thousands of motorists and pedestrians. Attractive interior designs, displays, and packaging are other forms of nonverbal and visual communication employed by a business in reaching a mass audience.

Mass communication is very important to the success of a business today. The theory and process should be understood by those who will work with it or be affected by it.

developing a mass communication ===============model[2]

In developing a mass communication model, let's start with a basic communication model as shown in Figure 17–2.

As the illustration shows, a *communicator* with an objective (stimulus) in mind originates the process of sending a message to the *receiver*. To do so, the *message* must be *encoded* or translated, using words and other symbols that have meaning to the intended receiver. A suitable *channel* is employed to deliver the message. The receiver engages in a process of *decoding* or a screening of content for message interest that takes place between becoming aware of the message and actually receiving it. The final step of *feedback* is an indication or result of how successful the communication effort has been. As indicated in Figure 17–2, if the sender's objective (O_1) meets the receiver's expectancy (O_2), then the process has been successful. If they don't match up, the process has failed to some degree.

The communication process does not take place in a controlled laboratory or in a vacuum, but in an environment subject to constant change with many sources of physical and psychological interference. A radio commercial will never reach its intended listener if there is a power failure (physical interference). If the commercial message was geared to status-seekers, but a listener

[2]Much of the material in this section was adapted from Karl-Erik Wärneryd and Kjell Nowak, *Mass Communication and Advertising*. Stockholm, Sweden: Economic Research Institute, Stockholm School of Economics, 1967.

Figure 17–1 An array of public relations and advertising communications produced by The Royal Bank of Canada in both English and French, to meet the required needs of their audience. (Courtesy, The Royal Bank of Canada, Montreal)

was concerned with security, the message will fail due to psychological interference.

In Figure 17–2, the O_1 (AIM) was addressed to a specific person. In the mass communication model, we have one message on one channel but many receivers who may have similar or dissimilar characteristics or needs. The basic premise of the mass communication model is the assumption that there are shared characteristics among a large number of the audience so that a single message, O_1 (AIM), would or could affect many.

The conceptual basis of this model is the "bullet" theory. Early in communication research, it was thought that the audience was relatively passive and defenseless, and that a communication could be fired at them like a bunch of sitting ducks.[3]

A realization that different people reacted differently to the same message resulted in the "category" approach. Demographic, reference group, personality (or psychographic), and saliency (utility or need) factors modify message perception. Advertisers found that young people reacted differently than older people to their message, and this held true for other demographic classifications as well. As more research was done in audience measurement, it was found that people with different clusters of attitudes and beliefs would behave differently from those with other belief and attitude clusters. Group membership was found to affect communication habits, and group belonging led members to choose and react to messages in such a way as to defend group norms and values. Intrapersonal communication was found to be involved along with the effect of the mass communication message. Many receivers are reached simultaneously but they are not independent of each other. They are

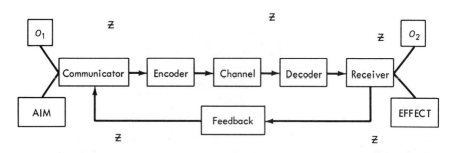

Figure 17– 2   Basic communication model illustrating the communicator's objective (O_1) and the receiver's objective (O_2). If the sender's aim is good and the message received as planned, the effect will reflect this. (Adapted from Wärneryd and Kjell, *Mass Communication and Advertising*, 1967, p. 13.)

---

[3]Wilbur Schramm, ed., *The Process and Effects of Mass Communication*. Urbana, Ill.: University of Illinois Press, 1965, pp. 8 and 9.

affected by one another and more generally influenced by the whole milieu of the society in which they live.

Figure 17–3 shows the more complicated mass communication model. We see many identical messages directed toward potential receivers. These receivers are members of groups and have interpersonal relationships as members of these groups. Most are members of more than one group and so we have intergroup transactions as well. The entire system operates in a changing environment introducing a continuous flow of stimuli and interferences.

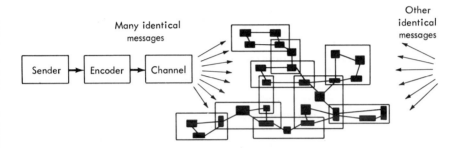

Figure 17– 3   Mass communication model showing group membership and interaction between receivers. The individuals and groups are exposed to more than one message in this illustration.

Using this model, let's examine some concepts and theories underlying the mass communication process.

Individual Difference or Selective Attention[4]

As the twentieth century progressed, psychologists discovered new concepts to replace the idea of universal instincts. The idea of "attitude" was elaborated upon and means of measurement were developed to explain individual differences in people.

Research showed that people varied greatly in their psychological organization. These differences were in part caused by biological factors but in greater part by differential learning. From different environments and experiences, different sets of attitudes, beliefs, and values develop. These differences result in the way we perceive stimuli. Two people viewing the same picture and hearing the same words will perceive these symbols according to their individual personality structures.

---

[4]Much of this material was adapted from Melvin L. De Fleur, *Theories of Mass Communication*, 2nd ed. New York: David McKay, 1970, and Norman Velsenthal, "Orientation to Mass Communication," *Modcom*, Module Series. Chicago: SRA, 1976.

Instead of thinking of an audience as a monolithic, homogeneous collection subject as one to a message, an audience is now seen as a large group of individuals with unique characteristics. The "bullet" theory evaporated into the realization that members of an audience exercised the "principle of selective attention and perception." The "individual differences" theory implies that a message and/or medium has particular stimulus attributes that have different interactions with differences in the personality characteristics of the audience. Attorney Lee Loevinger expanded this idea in his theoretical approach to mass communication published in the *Journal of Broadcasting,* Spring 1968. His "reflection-projection" theory sees society reflected by media as an organized group(s), but audience members watching as individuals. Each observer, through selective perception, projects his or her own view of themselves and of society into the media mirror. One sees or is what one wishes to see or be.

Social Categories Theory

Stemming from sociology, and sometimes overlapping the psychologically derived "individual differences" theory, is the social category approach. The approach assumes that broad groups exist in our urban, industrialized society and that group behavior is more or less uniform to a given set of stimuli. These groups can be identified by age, sex, income level, area of residence, religious preference, educational attainment, and other demographic variables.

Evidence of this theory can be seen in advertising media selection. Magazines sell the demographics of their readership by the categories mentioned above. Editorial content is so designed and planned to attract particular readerships: *Sports Illustrated* appeals to men, while *Redbook* appeals to women; *Fortune* readers will have higher income levels than the readers of *Popular Mechanics*, and married women would read *Parents' Magazine*, while unmarried women might read *Bride's Magazine*. The basis of this theory rests on evidence that in spite of the differences in a modern society, people having similar characteristics have similar folkways.

Social Relationships Theory

Also called the "opinion leadership" theory of mass communication, it is based on the leader-follower relationship that exists in groups. The concept was discovered accidentally and called the "two-step" theory of communication. In studying the 1940 presidential election, it was found that almost none of the voters seemed to have been influenced by mass media but that ideas seemed to flow from radio and print to opinion leaders and from them to less active group members or followers. Another way of stating the principle is that "individuals who are influential for others are more likely to be exposed to relevant mass media than are the people whom they influence."[5]

Opinion leaders tend to be very much like those they influence. They conform to the norms of their groups and are leaders in one or more areas, not necessarily in others. Opinion leadership is often horizontal rather than vertical, although this may vary depending upon the issues. Opinion leadership is often based upon status and may be seen in a hierarchy. Diagrammed, the principle would appear as in Figure 17–4.

The same message is received by the leader and members of the group, but the interpretation is based on that of the leader. R_1 indicates leaders in each of the groups; members tend to look up to the leader for direction in making up their own minds about a product, an issue, or whatever the question. Examples have been found in agriculture where farmers turn to the area leader for an expert opinion although they have been exposed to the same information or message. In fashion promotion, we still see a certain amount of filtering-down from fashion leaders to mass adoption of styles.

Recent research now questions the importance of the leader and the value of the two-step theory. Criticisms are based on such factors as verbal limitations, since only the most and least important news appears to be transmitted by word-of-mouth. And, there are difficulties in identifying the leaders, there are leader hierarchies, and so on. Although simplistic, the basic theory has led to further study and interpretation of message transmission.

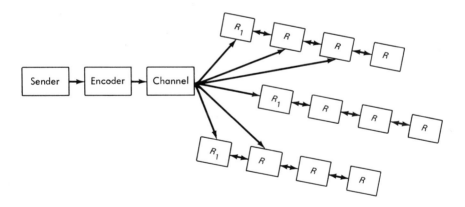

Figure 17– 4 The two-step or opinion-leader concept implies that the members of a group look up to the group or opinion leader for advice or opinion on an issue, a decision, a form of behavior. The message may be received by both the leader and the member, but interpretation is rendered by the leader. The leader is usually more message or communication conscious due to the role.

[5]Carl I. Hovland and Walter Weiss, "The Influence of Source Credibility on Communication Effectiveness," in Schramm, p. 275.

Although never stated explicitly, De Fleur sees mass communication media creating cultural norms (or what the writer, actor, director, etc., see these to be). These norms could then serve to influence behavior. Media could define a situation which provides guides for action appearing to be approved and supported by society. Conduct or behavior is then directly shaped by exposure to communication. The use of pills, drugs, or alcohol could then be shown as a normalized and condoned social institution and accepted that way by an audience.

There are three potential ways media can influence norms and define situations for individuals: (1) reinforce existing patterns, (2) create new shared convictions, and (3) change existing conditions.

Media has tended to be conservative and to reinforce existing patterns. For many years motion pictures perpetuated the accepted stereotypes of racial and ethnic groups. TV would avoid showing controversial issues or those challenging conventional norms. Today we see some changing of these patterns—but is media taking the lead, or only following society?

Media has sold just about everything from new clothing styles to new life styles. During the 1950s, the Davy Crockett television show influenced children to wear raccoon-tail hats as television had influenced older brothers and sisters to put on big, floppy ears like Mickey Mouse. The hula hoop attained national popularity almost overnight after being seen on a television show. Today, many charge that the drug culture found its roots in the pharmaceutical advertising and that the increasing crime rate and violence are a result of what is seen on TV and in the movies.

_____ "The Medium is the Message"

In 1964, Professor Marshall McLuhan published *Understanding Media*, which provoked great comment and controversy. His major thesis dealt with television's altering our patterns of perception, our thought processes, and our very environment. TV ended the dominance of print technology and its linear approach to building and returned us to a mosaic pattern of impressions, or multisensory perception.

McLuhan believed that the media alter not only the environment but the very messages they convey. He suggested that the medium or channel of transmission was more important than the content of the message, and that an audience would react differently to the same news presentation in a newspaper and on TV. Media, said McLuhan, was "hot" or "cold." A medium filled with data or detail leaving little to the receiver's experience or knowledge was "hot" and the opposite would be "cool." He considered TV to be the "coolest" medium requiring the highest level of receiver participation. Radio, photography, film, and print he considered hot while direct conversation, the telephone, and cartoons were cool. His analysis was not limited to media but extended also to people. Cool people were best presented on TV and hot people on radio.

He cited the John F. Kennedy and Richard Nixon debates to support his ideas. Those who viewed the debates on TV saw Kennedy, the "cooler" candidate, as victor over his "hot" opponent. Those listening on the radio perceived Nixon as having won.

The Play Theory

Psychologist William Stephenson theorizes that mass communication is utilized more for pleasure than for information or improvement. He cites proof in the type of stories people read first in newspapers: the comics and features gaining more attention than news events. Those stories or articles read first are those one identifies with or knows about.

The content of magazines, movies, and the broadcast media are even more entertainment-oriented than newspapers. Although some content is information- or reality-directed, the major portion of it is designed to entertain rather than inform.

mass communication theories and persuasion

Advertising and public relations operate to alter or direct behavior on the strength of a persuasive message directed to satisfy the needs of the receiver. Theories of motivation, perception, and learning suggest ways in which beliefs, attitudes, opinions, fears, and self-concepts are related to persuasion. Using psychological variables such as sexual urges, status drives, needs for social approval, and so forth, the persuasive communicator attempts to influence need-satisfying behavior. Viewing the process as follows:

PERSUASIVE	ALTERING OF	DESIRED
MESSAGE $\longrightarrow$	PSYCHOLOGICAL PROCESS $\longrightarrow$	ACTION

Those in an audience tend to relate and act upon suggestions or directions that solve their problems or fill their needs. The message suggests means for satisfying instrumental behavior.

A persuasive model can be based on the "cultural norm" concept discussed earlier. A message is received and defined by the individual in light of the existing social situation. Group-derived definitions of situations often provide ready-made answers to persuasive efforts. In some societies the culture has institutionalized behavior with respect to innovations, new ideas, and beliefs.

Other cultures provide the individual with no guidance. In the United States, society appears to lie somewhere between the two extremes.

Groups provide members with a shared orientation by which they can interpret realities. This has been called the *reality* principle and the interaction employed has been called the *consensual validation* process. New products are often introduced in a manner suggesting acceptance and proven product qualities. The communicator provides a message or demonstrates how acceptance is normal with that particular reference group thought to be the best prospects for the product. Testimonials are often used for this purpose.

This technique is widespread and used in many situations. Sometimes a negative approach is used. Many community efforts or social projects are organized in such a way as to identify those who refuse to participate or support the happening. Wearing a United Way pin or a red poppy on Veterans' Day separates those who gave from those who didn't. Some organizations and institutions make a fetish of awarding prizes to those having perfect attendance records. Have you ever been made to feel that if you didn't do a particular thing or go along with an idea, you were a deviant member of society, or at least of your peer group?

the variables of mass communicating

Earlier you were introduced to the Lasswell framework for examining an act of communication. The same structure will now be used for mass communication. Let us examine these questions:

Who
Says What
In Which Channels
To Whom
With What Effect?

The *Who*, or source of the message, is subject to such considerations as credibility, trustworthiness, expertise, attractiveness, and other considerations. Hovland and Weiss found that agreement is usually higher with an identical message if the statements are attributed to "high prestige" sources.[6] With all other variables held constant, the effect of the message may depend on the source.

The *Says What*, or message characteristics, play an important role in determining audience effect. Should the communicator present one side of the story or both sides? What appeal should be used? In what order should evidence be presented?

The *Channels*, or media, are the vehicles by which messages are transmit-

---

[6]Schramm, 1965, p. 89.

ted and also subject to choice. The communicator may ask: What use does the audience make of the channel? Newspapers for news? Television for entertainment? How reliable does the audience perceive the medium to be? What can one channel succeed in doing better than the others?

In choosing channels, Cantril and Allport found the following:[7]

1. Television ⎤
2. Radio ⎦   Best suited for exchanging and sharpening opinions

3. Form letters ⎤
4. Newspapers ⎥
5. Billboards ⎥   Swift and widespread communication of information.
6. Magazines ⎦

Many other factors would have to be considered. If time is of the essence, then television or radio should be used. Newspapers would come next, followed by magazines. Print media allows time for study and reflection. If permanence of the message is desired, then certainly radio or television could not be the choice, but rather magazines and newspapers. The more permanent media are, the most likely they will be used for organizing meaning, while the less permanent for reporting and persuasion.

The *Whom*, or the audience, is still another variable affecting the mass communicator. A mass communication audience is no longer viewed as a homogeneous glob but as a heterogeneous, viable group of interacting individuals. These receivers often test the message within their groups or rely upon the judgment of the group opinion leader.

Audiences for mass communication messages may be categorized according to the reach of the medium, or geographically. Demographic classifications can be used as well as psychological or psychographic characteristics. By using psychological measures instead of such items as sex, age, or marital status, a message could be designed to satisfy emotional needs. A psychographic appeal would cut across the more traditional demographic classifications. An advertising message often seeks to enhance the listener's or reader's perception of role and status. Berelson and Steiner stated, "People tend to see and hear communications that are favorable or congenial to their predispositions; they are more likely to see and hear congenial communications than neutral or hostile ones."[8]

With What Effect?—or, why engage in mass communication in the first place? Obviously a mass communicator produces specific messages with some intent in mind. The intended effects may be simple or extremely complex and may range from providing data or information to sophisticated efforts of persuasion and attitude change. More about effects will be found in the next section of this chapter in the discussion of advertising and then again in the public relations section.

---

[7]Schramm, 1971, p. 211.
[8]Bernard Berelson and George Steiner, in Schramm, 1971, p. 287.

advertising in the business system:
the voice

While advertising is a very small part of business it is the best-known and most widely discussed activity. As the voice of a business firm, it is self-publicizing and always subject to public scrutiny. In terms of dollars spent, the annual rate has been about 2½ percent of the Gross National Product (GNP), now over $50 billion annually. We may not know how large a business firm might be, or where it is located, or who its managers are, but we do know its products and have an image of the firm through advertising.

Advertising, Old and New

Many think of advertising as a relatively new business development. A 5,000-year-old clay tablet was found in Babylon promoting the services and wares of an ointment dealer, a shoemaker, and a scribe. An ad written on papyrus was found in the Egyptian ruins of Thebes dated approximately 1000 B.C. When the ruins of Pompeii, destroyed in 79 A.D., were excavated, advertising signs and messages were found inscribed on the walls of many buildings.

Advertising Defined

The definition committee of the American Marketing Association developed this four-part definition, "Advertising is any *paid form of nonpersonal presentation and promotion of goods, ideas or services by an identified sponsor.*" This definition distinguishes advertising from other forms of communication. Publicity is provided at no cost, while propaganda is not identified. Personal selling is face-to-face rather than nonpersonal, while the sign painted on a truck may or may not be advertising depending on whether the truck belongs to the publicized firm or whether the sign space is leased. By definition, word-of-mouth advertising, although very important in the successful promotion of a product, is not truly advertising as personal communication is involved.

Classifications of Advertising

There are many ways to classify advertising. Some of the more popular ones are:

1. Consumer advertising—messages directed to those who purchase goods and services for their own personal satisfactions.

Somewhere West of Laramie

SOMEWHERE west of Laramie there's a broncho-busting, steer-roping girl who knows what I'm talking about. She can tell what a sassy pony, that's a cross between greased lightning and the place where it hits, can do with eleven hundred pounds of steel and action when he's going high, wide and handsome.

The truth is—the Playboy was built for her.

Built for the lass whose face is brown with the sun when the day is done of revel and romp and race.

She loves the cross of the wild and the tame.

There's a savor of links about that car—of laughter and lilt and light—a hint of old loves—and saddle and quirt. It's a brawny thing—yet a graceful thing for the sweep o' the Avenue.

Step into the Playboy when the hour grows dull with things gone dead and stale.

Then start for the land of real living with the spirit of the lass who rides, lean and rangy, into the red horizon of a Wyoming twilight.

Figure 17–5 An example of a classic. This advertisement ran over fifty years ago yet the sparkling copy and idea concept are as timely as today.

2. Business/Professional advertising—advertising directed to people who use products and services in manufacturing or who resell goods for profit.

3. Product advertising—specific messages to sell products or services immediately or at some time in the future.

4. Institutional advertising—a mass communication effort to create a favorable image or impression of the firm and its products. Also called corporate advertising or public relations advertising.

5. Local advertising—advertising efforts by retailers and area services promoting in a relatively small geographical area. Selling the idea of where the product or service is available as well as the items themselves.

6. National—preselling a brand on a large regional or national basis.

Many other subclassifications exist but the advertising process will remain basically the same. Figure 17–6 serves as the basis for a good advertising/communication model.

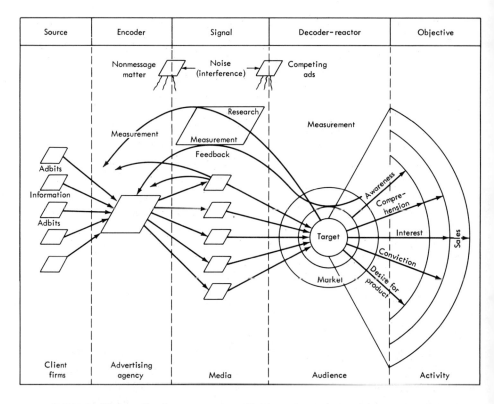

Figure 17– 6   The process of communication. (Charles E. Lee and Jarvis W. Mason, "Advertising Objectives, Control and the Measurement of Controversy," p. 39, MSU Business Topics, Autumn 1964. Reprinted by permission of the publisher, Division of Research, Graduate School of Business Administration, Michigan State University.)

the process of advertising

The advertising process deals with an open social system. Advertising must constantly be adjusted to the changing environmental conditions and to the whims and fancies of target market members. We are dealing with a dynamic process that is as sensitive and subject to change as you are.

As shown in Figure 17– 6, the source of the message is the business firm or advertising agency client wishing to reach a mass market. These advertisers range from the giants of industry making and selling billions of dollars of soap, cars, appliances, groceries, and so on, to the local advertiser in your city telling where these products are available locally.

Advertising is generally associated with profit-making enterprise but there has been a large increase in use by government agencies and other nonprofit organizations. Just a few years ago the federal government spent almost nothing on advertising, but with changes in the environment, an all-volunteer armed service, and an attempt at a self-sustaining postal service, the federal government is now among the top ten largest advertisers.

Nonprofit organizations utilize advertising to recruit members, to raise funds, to endorse politicians, and to seek action of one sort or another as the result of increased interest in consumerism, environmental, and socially-related problems. Indications point to the increased use of advertising in these nonprofit sectors of our society.

The advertising message is the responsibility of the encoder. The advertising encoder may be the advertising agency, an internal company advertising department, an individual within the firm charged with the task, or the medium by which the message will travel. To encode is to transform the message into terms meaningful to the potential receiver.

The purpose of the message is to bring about a desired goal: to sell a product, to increase awareness of a company or brand, to stimulate a favorable attitude toward the advertiser, or to have the reader or listener/viewer request more information. Creating or encoding a successful message requires an understanding of the prospective receiver's needs and desires. The cardinal rule therefore is: *KNOW THY AUDIENCE!*

The choice of media will depend on the audience to be reached and the behavior sought. An advertising medium or channel is a paid carrier of messages to given segments of the population or what has been determined as a market of potential purchasers.

Newspapers cover a limited geographical area very intensely. Almost everybody reads the local paper; rich or poor, old or young, man or woman, employer or employee. A newspaper is geographically selective (reaching a certain marketing area), making it an ideal medium for local and retail businesses. National advertisers use the newspaper to reinforce the message in that particular area.

Television and Radio signals cover defined geographical areas, but through the use of networks (systems joining individual stations together for programming and advertising purposes) national and regional audiences can be reached. Electronic media are not qualitatively selective by nature but take on some selectivity due to the nature of the programs offered and when they are offered. Radio stations appeal to different age and interest groups by the music featured. Television stations and networks base their programming on the interests of the audiences they wish to attract. Cable television stations have provided some selectivity where economically sound. Foreign language and ethnically-oriented programming is currently being provided as are special series that have appeal to select audiences. The future growth of cable is expected to be in the area of target or segmented programming.

Outdoor advertising is geographically selective with little qualitative selectivity other than motorists being the major audience. *Transportation* advertising with its cards inside the vehicles and posters on the outsides is also geographically limited with little or no qualitative appeal.

Magazines are used when an advertiser wishes to reach a very well-defined audience. Magazines are classified into two major groups, with subclassifications in each. The two major divisions are consumer magazines and business publications. Within the consumer group, we find such subdivisions as general, sports, hobbies, crafts, men's, women's, shelter, and others. The business magazines are subdivided into four categories: (1) trade publications that are read by retailers and wholesalers; (2) industrial publications read by manufacturers of products; (3) professional magazines that are read by those that may recommend goods but never purchase the products for their own use (doctors, architects, professors, etc.); and (4) agricultural publications read by farmers, ranchers, and others engaged in agri-business.

Direct advertising, and specifically direct mail, are the most selective of the mass communication channels. Through the use of the computer and sophisticated techniques of obtaining and qualifying lists of names, an advertiser may reach a large number of prospects who fit a particular description, and do this in a highly personalized manner.

Miscellaneous media offer other channels of communication between the advertiser and the prospect. *Specialty advertising*, often called goodwill or reminder advertising, includes such imprinted and free give-away items as calendars, matchbooks, pens, and other novelties. *Movie advertising* is projected on the screen before the main feature or during intermissions. It is far more popular abroad than in the United States. *Directory advertising* is used very extensively by both business and consumer advertisers. The most familiar directory is the telephone company's "Yellow Pages."

Related media generally serve to identify products and assist in the promotion of the goods for sale. Included are packaging with such identifying devices as the trade and brand names and marks, trade characters, and labels. Point-of-Purchase advertising (POP) includes all display and sign material used where the purchasing decision is actually made and the product is purchased. Related media have taken on added importance with the growth and development of self-service stores where the customer has no help in choosing products other than past experiences and immediately placed promotional devices.

In moving from media to audience in the process of advertising, bear in mind that few if any products are presented or promoted via a single channel or on only one level. In our society we are constantly being bombarded with advertising stimuli; an estimated 450 daily advertising exposures per average adult.

The audience to be reached is specified early in the advertising process by those responsible for marketing. The advertising personnel then create the message and select the media that will best reach the predetermined prospects or audience. In the final analysis, what we want to know is "How was the individual's behavior affected by the advertising?"

To measure the effect, or the effectiveness of advertising, Russell H. Colley established a framework for examining the "hierarchy of effects," which he called DAGMAR (Designing Advertising Goals for Measured Advertising Results).[9] He designated four levels: (1) awareness; (2) comprehension; (3) conviction; and (4) action, as the means by which to evaluate how successful an advertisement was. The first step in his method was to translate the purpose of the message into communication terms and then evaluate the communication qualities only. As, for example, if the purpose of a retail ad was to draw people into the store, then measure the effectiveness in terms of the number of people attracted and not on the volume of sales for that day.

To measure the effects of advertising, we can pre-test and post-test. Pre-testing involves the use of different techniques to measure a reader or viewer's attraction, interest, or attitude in the appeal or presentation of an ad idea. These tests usually take the form of comparisons, with the interviewee being asked for his or her opinion. Advertisements are also test-marketed under actual conditions. The ideas under test are tried in different areas to see which produce best. In the case of immediate or direct response advertising such as sale by mail or phone orders, the results can be compared by dollars of business when different approaches are tested.

Two methods are generally used for post-testing advertising, recognition techniques and recall testing. In conducting recognition tests, respondents are asked whether they remember seeing the ads in a magazine as the researcher turns the pages. Three questions are asked: (1) Do you remember seeing this ad—*awareness?* (2) Can you associate the ad with the product, the advertiser—*seen-associated?* and (3) Did you read half the copy or more—*read most?*

---

[9]Russell H. Colley, *Defining Advertising Goals for Measured Advertising Results.* New York: Association of National Advertisers, 1961.

The recall, impact, or playback method asks how much of the ad was remembered. The respondent is asked to playback what was recalled or remembered about the ad, its message or illustration. Research has shown that there is a high positive correlation between measures of awareness and product sales. As the awareness tends to increase, so do sales of the product.

planning advertising

The effective advertising campaign, the individual ads, are all part of a team effort calling upon the skills and expertise of many. Before work can start on the advertisements, a number of marketing decisions must be made. These include choosing the product to be advertised and the goals and objectives sought as a result of the promotion. The target market must be identified, a budget allocated, and the timing determined. Along with the preliminary marketing decisions are a number of advertising decisions that must be made before the first words of copy are written or the first design sketched. These include a media plan and strategy; determining what additional information will be required; and plans for testing the creative effort. While creativity is usually thought to be the property of the writers, the designers, and the artists, the seeking of unique solutions to the advertising problem is the responsibility of all concerned and is required at these primary steps.

A Universal Approach

Advertising is problem solving and the following framework is suggested for whatever the ad problem is. Modifications may be required for a particular situation but basically the steps are:

1. Define the problem from an advertising standpoint.
2. Gather required information needed for a solution.
3. Determine the appeal, the approach, the message, and then implement.
4. Pretest.
5. Modify as test results imply (pretest again if possible).
6. Run the ad, post-test, and evaluate the results.

Define the Problem: Given the problem by marketing and/or advertising management, it must be redefined or translated into advertising objectives. These should be stated in communication terms. In the process of redefinition, we can assess what is known and what additional information is required. This also helps establish criteria to evaluate the results.

Gather Information: The 3 *P's*—product, prospect, and purchasing—are useful as a guide in information gathering. The advertising person should have as complete a knowledge of the product as is possible. This includes knowing all about competing products. Next, one must know as much as possible about the most potential prospects for the product. Finally, knowing about the purchasing habits of the prospects sets the scene for the next step.

Determine the Appeal: An analysis of the information about product, prospects, and methods of purchasing should lead to the determination of appeal to be used in the message. This step is crucial as the advertisement is now ready for implementation.

Pretest: To be certain the target market will be most effectively reached, the formulated ideas may be tested in a variety of ways. A panel of potential prospects can be shown the proposed ad and asked for their reactions. The advertising ideas can be actually tested in a small way, in a test market, before they are used on a broad national basis. There are several experimental ways to test ideas and concepts: pairs of ads can be shown prospective purchasers of the product for an opinion; ads being tested can be placed in dummy magazines and tested for recognition and recall; television commercials are being tested in pairs over cable television lines and into select homes.

Modify: Incorporate into the message or overall presentation any ideas that will help the effectiveness of the ad.

Post-test and Evaluate: Test the advertisement after it has run to see whether the objectives were attained and to what degree. Analyze what happened and why as an aid to further advertising plans.

_____ **Anatomy of Advertising**

Although different in form depending upon medium, advertisements share similar structures and characteristics. Figure 17–7 identifies the various parts of a print ad whether it appears in a newspaper, magazine, or as a direct mail piece. Variations can be made to the basic structure: ads without body copy, without headlines or illustrations, or just an illustration with a logo. Placement or design adds to the infinite variety possible.

Outdoor advertising is seen by a passing vehicle for an average of six seconds; therefore, just a few words (maximum of ten), a bold illustration, and some form of product identification are all that can be employed.

Where a headline, an illustration, or both can be used to attract attention to a print ad, radio advertising depends on an attention-compelling opener. If attention is not gained early, the entire message may be missed. Music, sound effects, or dramatic words can gain attention for the advertiser. The body of the radio commercial is similar to that of body copy in a print ad. It is the development of the story. A musical theme or slogan can close the radio announcement as does the advertiser's logo.

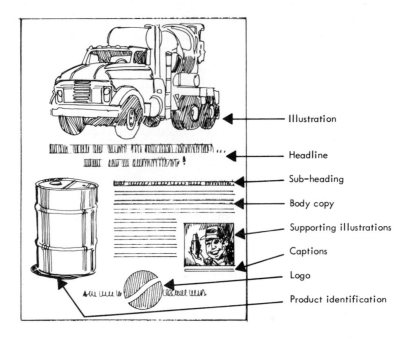

Illustration

Headline

Sub-heading

Body copy

Supporting illustrations

Captions

Logo

Product identification

Figure 17-7 Anatomy of a print ad.

Television must also attract immediate attention. Television of course has the advantage of a motion picture and sound. The time limitations on radio and television copy limit the message to one basic idea. As television is a visual medium, greater emphasis should be on the picture telling the story rather than words.

creative advertisements

Copy Thinking. Before a word is written, before a line is drawn, the creative team must seek out the approach or guidelines to be used. This is the most difficult step as success hinges upon it. The more time and care spent in thinking out the problem and the approach, the faster will be the implementation. Having analyzed the product, prospect, and purchasing information, ranking the possible approaches, a decision is made as to the best one.

Copy Structure. Once a theme is chosen, it must be translated into a message. The message must reflect logical and orderly thinking. The persuasive proposition must have some order. The AIDCA formula is frequently suggested as a basic starting point:

A for attracting attention
I for developing interest
D to stimulate desire
C to provide conviction
A call for action.

Following this formula should result in a logical copy path toward the desired advertising goal.

Copy Style.   Given an idea and a structure, there remains the style to be determined. By style, we mean the way the advertisement is presented, not the way an individual develops a writing or an art style. For example, an ad for flashlight batteries may be presented in a straightforward manner. It could also be presented in a story or a narrative style, or as a testimonial. In contrast to a serious approach, humor may be employed with cartoon or animated characters used. These are all different styles that add variety to advertising. Each style is capable of accomplishing its purpose if executed properly.

Attention Getting: Headlines or Openers.   The headline is considered the most important element in the ad. One writer suggests that half the time spent in doing an ad should be spent in developing the headline. Headlines can be classified in a number of ways. The two most important are: (1) those that promise a user benefit, and (2) those that convey news. Other categories include emotional, imperative, questions, selective, label, gimmick, and more. The copywriter seeks out that USP ("unique selling proposition" as named by Rosser Reeves) and then conveys to the reader or viewer what this means in terms of user benefits or satisfactions. Some examples of benefit headlines are:

Smith-Corona typewriters: " . . . announces a new form of scholastic aid."
Sanka: "the 100 percent real coffee that lets you be your best."
For newness:
"Introducing the first Chevrolet wagon with diesel power."
Phillip's Milk of Magnesia ad starts with, "Introducing New Chocolate Phillip's."
Many headlines are emotional such as these:
Naturalizer Shoes: "No, thanks, I'd rather walk."
Vitabath's: "Every woman should have an experience."
A curiosity headline from GE states: "The computer radio at 6:00 A.M.: it's smarter than you are."
The Investment Company Institute uses the imperative approach in this headline, "If you don't plan to work forever, you better plan to read this ad."
AT&T asks: "Are you spending too much time on hold?"

The illustration in an advertisement serves several important functions. In addition to attracting attention, it speeds communication, sets a mood, or conveys an atmosphere. Chapter 9 discusses in detail the uses of original art or photographs as illustrative materials.

The radio writer does not have the advantage of illustration to attract attention or to convey mood or feeling. In place of this, music and/or sound effects are employed. TV can combine pictures, sound effects, and music in order to attract attention.

Supporting the Headline: The Body. The body copy of the ad supports the headline idea and performs the function of stimulating interest, arousing desire, and providing conviction or proof that what is promised is attainable by the reader, listener, or viewer.

One of television's great advertising advantages is its ability to demonstrate product features and advantages. Sears has been using demonstrations to show the superiority of its Diehard batteries. The Ford Motor Company has used this approach to give evidence of product features, as have other automobile manufacturers.

Action: The Closing. As every ad starts out with a purpose, it should close with an appeal for an action consistent with the purpose. Some closings are very outspoken and direct while others are subtle and hardly whispered. Retail ads reflect the request for immediate and direct response. They close with; "Hurry, while limited quantities last!", "Sale Friday and Saturday Only!", "Come in and see the new models now, open tonight until 9." In magazines, a coupon may be included or an offer of additional information made in some other way. Accompanying an ad may be a list of dealers in the area or a number to call for that information. On the quiet and subtle side of asking for action, we find such expressions as, "You ought to be in Mink and Pearls," says Jovan, or Waterman's "You'll find them wherever truly fine gifts are sold."

The Design of the Ad. The design of an ad is a medium, a carrier of the message. It should be there, but not seen. The typography should be readable, but not distracting. All parts must fit together in a system to present the message and accomplish the stated objectives. The design is subject to limitations such as the amount of time or space available which, in turn, may be determined by the budget rather than by the message content. A rule of thumb for the number of spoken words on radio or television is two per second. A 30-second announcement, devoid of music or sound effects, would allow for only 60 words of message. In this short time span only one major idea can be presented. A one-minute, full-production (song, dance, big-name talent, elaborate set, etc.) commercial can cost well over a hundred thousand dollars. Most television commercials today are 30 seconds long and the trend is toward lower cost, less elaborate presentations. In the next few paragraphs, we shall examine the design process and see how the ad is put together.

Layout. A layout, a storyboard, a dummy, and a rough script are all tools used in the process of bringing together the ideas and elements of an ad in some tangible or physical sense. As the advertisement is the product of various ideas incorporated into one presentation, these tangible devices are very necessary so that all who are participating, and those who must approve the final effort, can see in a real sense what the final product will resemble.

Using print as an example, the layout serves several very important functions:

1. It allows the designer to change or modify all of the elements of the ad until satisfied with the arrangement. This is done on paper and without any cost other than the time consumed.
2. It permits others involved to see approximately what the finished product will look like and allows changes for improvement.
3. It provides the client with hard copy to examine and approve before actual work and expense are incurred.
4. It serves as a blueprint or guide for those who will participate in producing the ad. The layout also allows for obtaining cost estimates for production.

The designer, working with the copywriter and other members of the team, must first determine what is going to be needed in the ad. From this decision, a series of proportionate thumbnail or thought sketches are developed. These ideas are next drawn full size but in rough form. This stage permits making visual space adjustments and gaining a better grasp of what the finished product will look like. For most retail newspaper ads, the rough stage is as far as the designer will have to go. From the rough, a finished layout or a comprehensive design may be produced. The degree of finishing will depend on such factors as the cost of space, how the ad will be used, the cost of preparation, and the ability and desire of the client to understand the content before giving approval. Figure 17–8 shows the progression of an ad through the thumbnail, rough, and finished stages. The actual ad as it ran is shown for comparison.

Radio copy is prepared in script form and read through for timing and effect. A rough tape may be produced and presented to the client for approval prior to the actual production. The script should contain all information needed to produce the announcement including cues, music, sound, and the nature of the voice or voices to be used.

The television storyboard is a combination of the print layout, showing a frame at a time, and the script used in radio. A sequence of frames is developed that will give the viewer an idea of the video action taking place. The audio cues and copy go along with the pictures. The number of frames required will depend on the complexity of the idea. Usually all that is needed are changes of action or settings. This gives the people working with the commercial an idea of what is expected. Figure 17–9 will give you an idea of how the storyboard is created.

a). Thought sketch

b). Rough layout

c). Finished layout

Figure 17–8 Progression of a layout to finished ad. (By permission: *Fortune* and Young & Rubicam, Inc.)

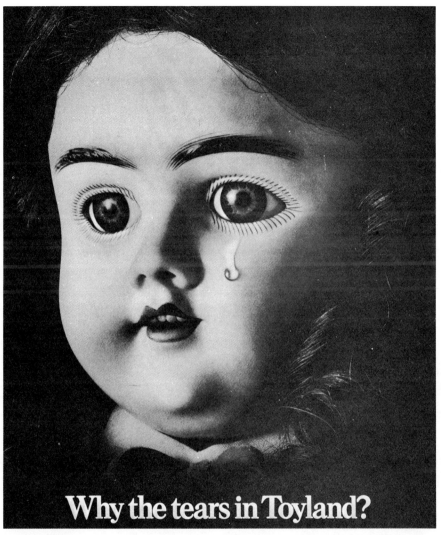

Why the tears in Toyland?

Pity the poor toymaker.

His profits are low. Competition is dog-eat-dog. And now, consumerism has come to Toyland.

About the only friends the toymakers seem to have left are the kids. The $2 billion toy industry is under attack by fed-up parents, consumerist crusaders, Congress, and the regulatory agencies —and not without reason.

This month, Fortune Magazine journeys through beleaguered Toyland in the second of a continuing series of articles on consumerism. Read it, whatever business you're in. Because sooner or later, the long shadow of consumerism is going to fall across you. It's not going to go away!

Fortune's series on consumerism is cool and rational, because a counterweight to rhetoric, emotionalism, and shoot-from-the-hipism is desperately needed. Quickie solutions are turning out worse than no solutions at all.

For example, when Congress passed an unwieldy Child Protection and Toy Safety Act, statistics like this were quoted at the hearings: "15,000 children under fifteen years of age are killed by accident in handling unsafe toys each year." The truth? The figure referred to *all* accidental deaths, whatever the cause. The number that clearly involved toys was 72.

In this important series, Fortune undertakes to cut through the fogs of ideology, supposition, and accusation that surround consumerism. It's a study not in blacks and whites but in the greys that color real life. (Last month, detergents. In coming months, appliances, food additives, auto safety, packaging and other embattled consumer areas.)

Depth. Clarity. Objectivity. Balance. They're why the men who make America's business decisions rely on Fortune more than any other business publication.

Rely on it—as reader or advertiser, you'll profit from Fortune. Because the real, strong stuff about business is... **ONLY IN FORTUNE**

Figure 17–8 (cont.) The advertisement as it actually appeared in *Fortune* magazine.

vlasic

America's largest selling pickle

TWO OF AMERICA'S FAVORITE PICKLE COMMERCIALS, RUNNING IN HEAVY PRIME TIME
NETWORK AND SPOT SCHEDULES, CONTINUE TO PAMPER VLASIC'S CONSUMER FRANCHISE.

Girl and dog	Girl: Daddy, can I have a dog? Man: No, Elinor. You can't have a dog. Girl: You had a dog when you were little. Man: Things were different then.	Girl: Aren't things different now? Man: No, they're the same. Girl: Then, can I have a dog? Man: No, Elinor. You can't have a dog!	Girl: (Softly) Daddy, I already have a dog. Man: You already have ... CRUNCH ... dog?

Man: You can't, NO DOGS ... CRUNCH ... Man: Dog? I had a nice, big dog once.

V/O: Vlasic pampers pickles to pamper people. For whatever pampering needs to be done.

Boy: Hey, Dad. Can I have a horse?

Man: Give me another Vlasic pickle.

4 O'Clock Pickle	Guy: Wake up, sweetie. It's time for your 4 o'clock pickle. Gal: (HALF ASLEEP) Ohhhhhhh.	Guy: You know what the doctor said.	Gal: Oh, yes ... bring me a ... ummmm ... Vlasic Kosher Dill.

Guy: Honey, would y' mind having a Vlasic no garlic dill? Gal: But I crave a garlic dill.

Guy: Well ... aahh ... can't you just eat them during the daytime maybe ... Gal: (SNIFF) ... ummmm ... All right.

Guy: Honey ... SFX: KISS you've really been a brick through this whole thing.

ANNCR V/O: Vlasic Pickles. For whatever pampering needs to be done.

HUNWAULT COLOR CORP., 11 RICHMOND ST. CLIFTON, N.J.

Figure 17–9 TV storyboard. (Case history by S. M. "Skip" Roberts, Executive Vice President, W.B. Doner and Company)

public relations:
good will through communication

As the U.S. entered the decade of the 1980s, pessimistic statements marked the 32nd National Conference of the Public Relations Society of America, November 1979, in St. Louis. Heard were statements as, "the people have become more disenchanted with, more distrustful of, more alienated from the very institutions designed to save them," and "We can't get a fix on our morality or our own ethics, and we aren't sure of the roles we want our established institutions to play."

This uncertainty was accelerated by such events as the Three Mile Island nuclear reactor accident, the crash and loss of life when the engine of a huge DC-10 fell off shortly after take-off from O'Hare Airport in Chicago, and the third largest automaker in the U.S. asking the federal government to guarantee a loan for them to prevent bankruptcy. Incidents such as these demand skillful communication by those involved in presenting their views of the story—or they risk damages to image and prestige caused by inaccurate or exaggerated press coverage or by rumor flow. This sometimes very difficult job is the function of public relations specialists.[10]

Public relations (PR) is the development and maintenance of good will in the various publics of an organization through their involvement and participation in company activities. Public relations is based on two-way communication.[11]

To understand public relations better, let's use ourselves as examples. You, as an individual, want to be liked and accepted by your friends, associates, and family. These are some of your publics, and you practice PR on them at all times! You try to be helpful in various ways; you try to be a good neighbor; you want people to think kindly of you so they will be happy to have you around. You are communicating with your public all the time. In your various PR activities you use different communications techniques—a smile, a letter, a call. In the business world it is not quite this simple, but the end result is not too different.

_____ Definitions and Objectives

Public relations is defined in _Webster's New Collegiate Dictionary_ as, "The activities of a corporation, union, government or other organization in building and maintaining sound and productive relations with special publics such as customers, employees or stockholders and with the

---

[10]Leo Northart, "Public Relations and the Decade Ahead," _Public Relations Journal_, Dec. 1979, pp. 8–9.

[11]Bertrand R. Canfield and H. Frazier Moore, _Public Relations: Principles, Cases and Problems._ Homewood, Ill.: Richard D. Irwin, 1973, p. 9.

public at large, so as to adapt itself to its environment and interpret itself to society."[12]

The importance of public relations to the modern business firm is recognized on the organization chart. In many major corporations, this staff function reports directly to the president. PR people serve as consultants to key personnel and on the executive planning boards and committees for their knowledge of public opinion and to analyze public-related decisions. The importance of public relations today can be further seen in some of the major PR objectives:

1. To interpret the firm's policies, practices, and nature of business operations to its publics.
2. To interpret to management the opinions and attitudes of the public about the company.
3. To discover and prevent internal people-oriented problems that could cause business problems.
4. To obtain customer acceptance of products, increase sales, and gain other concessions by winning customer friendships.
5. To guide management in making decisions.
6. To personalize the company.
7. To focus on service.

Because of their role in fact-finding and interpreting the opinions and attitudes of the various publics, the advice and comments of public relations personnel often make the difference between the success and failure of a company decision.

_____ Historical Background

Public relations of some sort, in some form, and under some guise has probably been going on as long as man has been around. Canfield and Moore write that, "The rise of democracy and the actual beginnings of our concept of public relations, however, can be traced in America to the presidency of Andrew Jackson."[13] It was at this time, the late 1820s and early 1830s, when the common man won the ballot and gained political power, becoming more interested in the issues and events surrounding him.

Unfortunately, many people today see public relations as it was in the heyday of the early publicity agents. Some consider PR as an outgrowth of the publicists of the nineteenth century. Phineas Taylor (P.T.) Barnum was one of the most famous of the early showmen and publicity agents. He had an uncanny ability to exploit controversial issues, fantasy, and the news. Like others to follow, P.T. secured columns of newspaper coverage for faked and staged events. It is this early image that persists today and has resulted in a misunderstood and erroneous conception of a public relations practitioner.

---

[12]Canfield and Moore, p. 11.
[13]Canfield and Moore, p. 12.

The last quarter of the nineteenth century was one in which emerging and powerful businessmen cared little for the public. This attitude and environment paved the way for men like Ivy Lee and others to repair and rebuild the image of business and practice PR as we know it today.

As the twentieth century comes to a close, a whole new set of problems confronts business and the public relations industry. Business must reconcile itself and its publics to such issues as environmental conditions, pollution, resource depletion, inflation, unemployment, equal opportunities, excessive and "windfall" profits, galloping technology, quality of life, and other key issues. Luther Hodges, Jr., sees the erosion of confidence in the capitalistic system as one of the greatest opportunities and heaviest obligations for the public relations people in the future. He cited a study conducted in 1975 in which college students were asked to rate the honesty and ethical standards of people in fifteen areas of activity. Business was rated ninth below labor unions and building contractors and just ahead of public officials.[14]

It seems safe to say that with our growing population, our rapidly moving and changing society, our complicated interdependence, and our ever-increasing need to communicate, the public relations role must expand in order to meet the challenges.

the public relations process

While the casual observer may think public relations "just happens," this is not true. Certain aspects of day-to-day, routine PR may seem automatic, but this is merely because the procedures were so well handled originally. In addition to the normal public relations practices, there will be special situations that arise—some on a "crash" basis. All of these events require the same careful handling by PR people. Whether a communication deals with a minor change in billing procedures or a major expansion into new territory, careful attention to detail is important. Cutlip and Center discuss the PR process under these headings: fact-finding, planning, communicating and evaluating.[15]

Fact-Finding. Correctly identifying the problem enables the real problem to be solved rather than symptoms treated. Fact-finding is the probing of opinions, attitudes, and reactions of people concerned with the business firm. Facts about the organization must also be ascertained and then the inflow be evaluated in light of the actual operation.

---

[14]Luther H. Hodges, Jr. "The New Challenge for Public Relations," *Public Relations Journal.* August 1975, p. 8.

[15]Scott M. Cutlip and Allen H. Center, *Effective Public Relations.* Englewood Cliffs, N.J.: Prentice-Hall, 1964, pp. 108–179.

Planning.   Once the facts are gathered and evaluated, a plan of action should be implemented. The ideas, opinions, and attitudes should be brought to bear upon the organization in an effort to correct or change policies and actions that affect good will.

Communicating.   This step involves explaining and dramatizing what is being planned and what is being done to all of those affected, and in doing so, secure their support in the effort.

Evaluating.   Feedback is the means by which we evaluate our communication progress. In this step we seek out how well we are doing in attaining our objectives and what could be done to improve our performance. It answers the question, "How well did we do?"

Public relations is a continuous process. Research and fact-finding are at the heart of the process, and in fact, distinguish public relations from straight publicity. Information is constantly sought and serves as stimulus for communication to the various publics in an effort to maintain balance between the firm and its environment.

The Business Publics

The most important publics of a business are: employees, customers, stockholders, suppliers, distributors, community neighbors, government, educators, and the general public. Each of these has a different interest in the firm and specific public relations programs must be designed for each interest group.

Communication Tools

People engaged in public relations work send their messages by means of written, spoken, and visual communication or by combinations of them. The particular communication tool will be determined by the message and the public to be reached.

Some of the more common public relations communication tools are: house organs or internal publications, bulletin boards, billboards, conferences, meetings, speeches, news releases, films, audio systems, radio, television, advertising, and the annual report.

Example: A Successful PR Campaign

In 1974 the multimillion dollar industrial firm, TRW, was told by a public relations organization that it had an "identity void." This meant that nobody hates you . . . nobody loves you . . . NOBODY KNOWS YOU!

From 1964 to 1974, TRW had a relatively low advertising budget in the low hundred-thousands. Magazines were the medium they used in order to reach their target audience, defined as investors and investment-minded people. In order to overcome their "identity void," television was recommended to reach the powers in the investment world. From 1974 to 1976, their public relations firm ran a campaign using the theme, "A Company Called TRW," on spot television in ten major U.S. markets. The success was dramatic. In one of the markets in which the campaign ran, Washington, D.C., nine out of every ten people earning $30,000 a year or more had a favorable opinion of TRW and said they would consider stock in the company to be a good investment. Similar results were found in other markets.

Television spots were run on late evening news telling of products manufactured by TRW. Radio announcements were run on business and news programs and weather reports. Late evening news and morning drive-time, 6:30 to 9:00 A.M., were the favored periods. Magazine advertising was continued in such publications as *Business Week*, *Forbes*, and *Fortune*.

After reviewing the results in 1976, it was decided to move from spot television in ten major markets to national TV covering the entire United States. By 1978, the advertising budget had grown to over $3 million per year, and TRW's success continued. Sales and profit more than doubled between 1974 and 1978 to over $3.8 billion in sales and $174.2 million in profits. Favorable recognition grew from 20 to 60 percent of the target market during this period. From a company with an "identity void," a company called TRW became a very visible and viable one through carefully planned and administered public relations.[16]

the future of public relations

Public relations as an area of work and as a profession has had phenomenal growth in the past quarter century. The Public Relations Society of America was formed in 1948 and established a Code of Ethics in 1954. It has an accreditation process for membership acceptance that calls for experience in the field and passing a written and oral examination covering the history, theory, fundamentals, techniques and ethics of public relations. These efforts have raised the professional standards and have improved the status of the profession.

Growth should continue for the PR field as a whole, and for business in particular. Some of the reasons for this are: the increase of government regulation of business; the growing complexity of business; the continued centraliza-

---

[16]"The TRW Story," *Public Relations Journal*, Nov. 1979, pp. 28–31.

tion of business into the hands of fewer firms; the application of new technology; and the concern with environmental and social problems.

Summary

Business and mass communications go hand-in-hand. The billions of dollars spent annually for advertising pay all of the costs of commercial radio and television. Advertising revenue is the principal means of income for newspapers and magazines as well. In addition to reaching audiences through advertising, the public relations function produces newsletters, magazines, films, publicity and news releases, and organizes and writes speeches to reach the many internal and external publics of the firm.

Mass communication is differentiated from interpersonal communication in several ways; rather than direct communications with one or more, mass media can reach millions of people simultaneously with little or no immediate feedback. The individuals within the mass audience interact with one another in the same or different groups. At any given time, a mass media audience is bombarded with many messages, often of a conflicting nature.

Although an audience is large, it is no longer thought of as a homogeneous glob subject to the effects of the all-powerful medium. Modern theorists see an audience made up of individuals with selective preferences for those messages affecting their well-being. The audience is also viewed as individuals with certain characteristics that suggest subgroups with similar folkways and behavior patterns. Group opinion leaders are now recognized as being very important to the overall mass communication process.

A cultural norm approach to understanding mass communication and persuasion implies that the media can reinforce, create, or change existing convictions and cultural patterns. As media tends to be conservative, this has not been a problem. Advertising uses cultural norms and the theory of "selective differences" in encoding persuasive messages. If people believe a product to be socially accepted and desired—a cultural process—then it is all right to purchase and consume that good. The selected preference approach is seen in the appeals of ads for self-satisfaction and gratification.

Advertising in one form or another has been around as long as man has bought and sold goods and services. It has reached its highest form in the United States where over $50 billion are spent annually by business firms to promote the immediate and long-run sales of their products. Advertising is a function of marketing, and, because it is the voice of the business firm, it has become the best-known and most often criticized function.

Businesses of all sizes and scope, as well as nonprofit organizations, send out their persuasive messages via newspapers, television, magazines, radio, outdoor posters, direct mail, and other ways. Specialized organizations such as advertising agencies serve to aid and assist businesses in the encoding and production of these advertising messages.

Regardless of medium or audience, the basic approach to advertising is much the same. The problem must be defined, information gathered to help determine the best possible selling appeal, testing the premise, modifying if necessary, and then evaluating the results.

An ad must first attract attention. This is done with the headline and/or illustration in print media. The first few words of the radio or TV announcement serve the same purpose. The body of the copy attempts to stimulate interest, arouse desire, provide conviction, and in the closing, ask for the desired action.

The creative people responsible for the encoding of ads have many styles and approaches available to them. Ads may be straightforward and highly informational or they may be just the opposite, humorous or emotional and very entertaining. Many other possibilities exist in-between. There is a great deal of variety possible, but in the long-run the test of any advertising rests in its ability to accomplish objectives set forth initially.

Public relations is the development and maintenance of good will in the various publics of an organization through their involvement and participation in company activities.

Most organizations have several publics (groups of people with special and similar interests) ranging from employees to the general public. These are the groups toward which public relations activities are directed.

The public relations process is composed of four major steps: fact-finding, planning, communicating, and evaluating. Communicating, the area we are mainly concerned with in this book, is accomplished through all forms of spoken, written, and visual means.

The complexity of modern business and the problems of society will call for increased dialogue between the firm and its publics. PR has come a long way from the activities of showman-like publicists to a very responsible and respectable profession with all signs pointing toward still more important future activity.

Discussion Questions

1. Explain, with examples, how mass communication differs from other forms of communication.
2. Discuss some of the different ways a business firm would employ internal and external mass communication.
3. How does receiver interaction affect message perception?
4. Why has the "bullet" theory of mass communication been discarded?
5. Explain the role played by the "opinion leader" in the mass communication process.
6. Why do you think TV and radio are best suited as media for sharpening opinions?
7. Why are people often so critical of advertising?

8. Discuss some of the ways nonprofit organizations employ advertising to attain their goals.

9. If you had a product to sell to teenagers, what medium would you employ to reach this market?

10. Why is copy thinking the most important step in the creating of an ad?

11. What kind of headlines or openers seem to attract the most attention and why?

12. "Public relations is communications." Explain.

13. What public relations practices do you engage in?

14. What are the four steps in the PR process? What additional details would you list under these steps in addition to the ones mentioned in the chapter?

15. Comment on what you think the future of PR is likely to be.

Problems and Projects

1. You are to assume the role of Employee Communication Manager of the Big Town Utility Company. Your immediate superior, the personnel director, has just returned from a high-level management meeting and one of the topics discussed was employee morale.

   It appears that productivity is down and customer complaints are up. The employees seem to be apathetic and lack identification with the firm. You are asked to develop a campaign to improve morale and to be prepared to present your plan to the operating committee in three weeks.

   Develop an outline of what you propose to do.

2. Brainstorm by yourself, or in a group, all of the possible styles or means of presenting a 30-second TV commercial for a chewing gum manufacturer (or product or service of your choice).

3. Thumb through a newspaper or magazine and select an ad you think is particularly bad. Redesign it and write new and better copy for it.

4. Select a small, independent neighborhood store and plan a public relations campaign for it.

5. Visit a local firm having a public relations department and request a statement of objectives for that department. How does the statement compare with discussion in this chapter?

Additional Reading

Burton, **Philip Ward,** *Advertising Copywriting,* 3rd ed. Columbus, Ohio: Grid, 1974.

Canfield, **Bertrand R.,** and **H. Frazier Moore,** *Public Relations, Principles, Cases and Problems,* 6th ed. Homewood, Ill.: Richard D. Irwin, 1973.

Cutlip, **Scott M. and Allen A. Center,** *Effective Public Relations,* 5th ed. Englewood Cliffs, N.J.: Prentice-Hall, 1978.

De Fleur, **Melvin L.,** *Theories of Mass Communication,* 2nd ed. New York: David McKay, 1970.

De Vito, Joseph A., ed., *Communication: Concepts and Processes*. Englewood Cliffs, N.J.: Prentice-Hall, 1971.

Fitz-Gibbon, Bernice, Macy's, Gimbels, and Me. New York: Simon and Schuster, 1967.

Hayakawa, S.I., Language in Thought and Action. New York: Harcourt, Brace, Jovanovich, 1957

How to Tell Your Story. **Washington, D.C.: Consumer Finance Association, 1975.**

Lesly, Philip, ed., *Lesly's Public Relations Handbook*. Englewood Cliffs, N.J.: Prentice-Hall, 1971.

Mandell, Maurice I., Advertising, 3rd ed. Englewood Cliffs, N.J.: Prentice-Hall, 1980.

Marston, John, The Nature of Public Relations. New York: McGraw-Hill, 1963.

McGarry, K.T., ed., *Mass Communications*. London and Hamden, Conn.: Clive Bingley Ltd., and Linnet Books, 1972.

Nelson, Roy Paul, The Design of Advertising. Dubuque, Iowa: William C. Brown, *Public Relations Guide*. Cincinnati: Procter & Gamble Educational Services, 1977.

Reeves, Rosser, Reality in Advertising. New York: Alfred A. Knopf, 1961.

Schramm, Wilbur, ed., *The Process and Effects of Mass Communication*. Urbana, Ill.: University of Illinois Press, 1965: 2nd ed., 1971.

Wärneryd, Karl-Erik and Kjell Nowak, Mass Communication and Advertising. Stockholm, Sweden: AB Svenska Telegrambyran STB, 1967.

Some Periodicals to Read:

Advertising Age
Ad Direction and Commercial Art
Journal of Advertising
Journal of Communication
Journal of Personality and Social Psychology
Journalism Quarterly
Media Decisions
Public Opinion Quarterly
Public Relations Journal
Public Relations Quarterly

Appendix:
communication
and
your
career

appendix a: looking for employment

—————————— Planning the Campaign

Job hunting is an exciting and challenging experience in which most people engage sooner or later. Whether it be the first job after college graduation or a change of scene later in life, looking for employment requires careful thought and planning on the part of the job seeker.

Having decided that it is time to begin the search for employment, you should approach the project with the same thoroughness and determination with which sales personnel plan sales campaigns or with which military people prepare for a major battle. You must decide upon companies which interest you and then prepare letters, data sheets, and a plan of "attack" (including a timetable). While it is obvious that you are looking for a means of making money to buy food and shelter, you are also looking for a situation which will enable you to use your talents in the attainment of personal goals.

Study Yourself. What do you have to offer a prospective employer? What have you accomplished in your lifetime that makes you worth employing? How can you help a particular company meet its objectives?

Study and analyze yourself and think about the things you have done which make you a potentially valuable employee. Concentrate on listing on paper your achievements to date. Be sure to list everything regardless of how insignificant it may seem to you. Some of the areas you should include are: education (academic and extra-curricular achievements), work experience (full-time and part-time), organizations to which you belong (and leadership activities in these groups), military experience; special training, short courses, or any other continuing education instruction you may have had; perhaps list hobbies, travels, and other special interests which may indicate a broad background of activities and interests.

The objective of this self-study procedure is to compile the information for your data sheet, to determine how you can benefit a particular employer, and to prepare for the interview itself.

Study the Employment Market.   You should consider your life's work as more than just a means of making money. Along with the money, you need work which interests you and which satisfies your need for accomplishment and self-fulfillment. Having selected the occupation which appeals to you, you should list the names of companies in which you are interested where your particular specialty is employed.

Investigate thoroughly the companies in which you are interested. You are investing your time and energy, so use them wisely! Read about the companies in business periodicals and newspapers. Check the rating of the companies in Standard and Poor's and in Dun and Bradstreet publications. Talk with friends and relatives who are employed, or who have been employed, by the companies. If possible, use the products or services of the companies to see whether you like them and whether you would be willing to promote them.

Be careful and thorough in your analysis and final selection(s) of prospective companies. The process is not one-sided. While it is true that the company would be paying out money for your services as an employee, it is possible that you are deciding where you will spend all the working years of your life. This is indeed an important decision and one which should be based on sound information!

You should also find it helpful to study the employment situation in general. It is frequently beneficial to know what the competition is doing. Which industries are growing? Which companies are expanding? What types of jobs are most plentiful? What types of jobs are least plentiful? What is the salary range for beginning college graduates in your line of work? How does the future look for the industry?

In other words, spend some time *decoding;* read about the economy, listen to business people, and observe the business world in general and the companies which especially interest you in particular before you make this important career decision.

Select Prospective Employers.   Since a person cannot safely assume that he or she will be hired by the company which is the first choice, you should select several companies to be contacted in your campaign. You will, of course, decide upon these companies as a result of the facts you uncover in your study of the business world.

Having decided upon those companies which you believe to be "on the way up," decide how your talents can be used to help these companies climb. There will be some companies with which you can identify more than others; using "you attitude" (see Chapter 14) in your approach, prepare to tell the personnel managers of these companies why you are worth hiring, show how your qualifications will help the company attain its objectives. Please notice that you should personalize in some way your letter to each company. Do not use the same approach with all companies.

The Employment Application Letter

Although the bulk of the facts concerning an applicant's qualifications for employment should appear on the data sheet, it is customary to send with the data sheet a cover letter in which the writer: (1) expresses interest in the company, (2) makes clear he or she would like to work for the company and how the writer can be an asset to the company, and (3) requests an interview. Many of the areas discussed in the chapter on business letters apply to the employment application letter, so you should review Chapter 14.

Metacommunication. The appearance of your letter is extremely important because this is your first contact with the company. It may be your only contact with the organization if the letter makes a bad impression on the personnel staff.

Be sure that the letter is neatly typed. If you cannot do a good job yourself, hire a typist to do it. Has a correct, consistent letter style been used? Proofread the work carefully and have others read it for you. Check closely on such matters as spelling, grammar, punctuation, and syllabication.

Prove to your reader that you are a person who is aware of details and how to handle them. Careful handling of the metacommunication aspects of your letter is the first step to reader acceptance and an interview.

A Sales Letter. As you write your employment application letter, think of it as a sales letter—you are selling your experience and talents to some business organization. Remembering that people purchase a given product for what it will do for them, tell the reader how the company can expect to benefit because you are on the payroll.

This letter must "sound like you on paper." Since your objective in writing the letter is to obtain an interview, you should try to make the same favorable impression in the letter that you expect to make in the interview. Although you should not become "folksy" in your letter-writing style, neither should you become stiff and formal; try to be relaxed and natural and achieve a good middle-ground style of writing.

A good way to begin this letter is with some expression of interest in the company and/or how you happen to be writing the letter. For example, you have read about the company, or you have friends who work there, or you have used the products they manufacture. Having personalized your approach in some manner, you should make it clear in the letter that you would like to be associated with the organization.

The last paragraph of your letter should be a request for an interview. Since you will have favorably impressed your reader with your qualifications by this time, you need to leave him or her with a clear understanding of "what happens next."

The middle part of your letter is the place to use "you attitude" to impress upon your reader how certain of your accomplishments and qualities will benefit the company. Select three or four facts from your data sheet and tell how these will benefit the company. Even though you may not have had any actual business experience in the line of work for which you are applying, make the most of what you have to offer (positive approach). If you have worked on highway crews or cut grass during the summer months to earn college expenses, this shows that you have ambition and initiative and are not afraid of work. Your part-time jobs and your extracurricular activities have given you additional experience in working with people. In other words, the employment application letter is the place to show how a few of your major accomplishments make you worth hiring by a specific company.

A Masterpiece.   Your employment application letter and data sheet should be the very best work which you are capable of doing. In many cases, this will be your first contact with the company; therefore, it is important that the letter and data sheet be well done. Your reader has no way to tell that you can do any better than the letter he or she has in hand, and so you may be judged on this one effort alone. You have only one chance.

Rely on a well-written message to get and hold your reader's attention. Do not use colored stationery or scented stationery in order to stand out in the crowd. The message is the important thing throughout communication attempts—a properly composed message which is beautifully typed on a sheet of plain white 8½ × 11 paper is your best ambassador.

The Data Sheet

A data sheet is a concise and orderly listing of personal details and major accomplishments in your life. It enables your reader to learn the high points in your life very quickly.

Notice that we have said the "high points in your life." When you are making your first contact with a company with the objective of getting an interview, you need not account for every day of your life—list only significant events or achievements. There is nothing dishonest in this approach because your complete story will be revealed either in the interview or on the company's employment application blank which you will be asked to fill out.

In order to prepare an effective data sheet, there are a few important points you need to remember. The first of these is mechanics of constructing the data sheet.

Mechanics.   Since in your data sheet you are attempting to tell a lot about yourself in a relatively small amount of space and in a form which is quickly and easily read, you need to observe a few basic rules of mechanics.

Use parallel construction. This means that similar or comparable parts of the data sheet must follow the same construction. If, for example, under work experience you list your job title first in the entry for your present employment, you must list job title first in all entries under work experience. You will see this and other pointers on data sheet construction illustrated in the sample data sheet in Appendix C.

Use marginal and/or center heads. The use of headings such as you see in this book and such as are recommended for use in reports helps you to organize your data properly and helps your reader to locate quickly the information he wants. The headings also improve readability by breaking up the page into smaller sections.

Use telegraphic style. Write briefly and concisely and use a clipped telegraphic style of writing. Do not use the first person in your data sheet; by eliminating the pronoun "I" you are helped to achieve this style. For example, "I mowed lawns" becomes "Mowed lawns."

List latest events first. Under headings such as education and work experience, where a time sequence is involved, it is desirable to list the most recent event first—that is, the college from which you are graduated or the job you presently hold.

Use a page heading. Even though it is rather obvious that your data sheet is a data sheet, the words "data sheet," "qualifications of," or some other appropriate heading should appear at the top of the page. However, some people prefer to put only their name at the top of the page, feeling that the rest is obvious. It is *very important* that your name, mailing address, and perhaps your telephone number appear on the page. Even though this information appears in the cover letter, it should also be in the data sheet in case the two documents become separated.

Use variety in format. By placing data in one section in long lines which run entirely across the page, and by presenting data under another head in two columns, you eliminate the monotony of long lines throughout the data sheet. Also, you encourage the reading of your data sheet because it is not dull looking and because the reader is able to find the information he wants very quickly.

Parts of the Data Sheet.   It is usually possible to list the major points about yourself under four or five major headings. It is a good idea to use as few divisions as possible so that the data sheet will not appear too "busy."

These divisions are almost always used on the data sheet: personal, education, work experience, and references (although you may prefer to say "available on request" rather than to list names). Some other possible divisions are: memberships, military experience, travel, and hobbies. These are only suggestions; each individual should be the best judge of how he wants to organize his own presentation. A little creativity is a good idea.

You may change the wording in these headings to fit your needs; for example, you may wish to say "Record of Employment" instead of "Work Experience." Also, there is no particular order in which these categories must appear. If you wish to emphasize your education and training, you might want to list that section first. Your references should probably be listed last because this section is least important. (After all, you aren't going to ask someone to serve as a reference if you think this person will say anything unfavorable about you, are you?)

The type of information which should appear under these various headings is rather obvious; however, it should be noted that the "personal" heading is sometimes used as a "catch-all" by some people. It is customary to place under "personal" such details as height, weight, birthdate, birthplace, and physical condition. Some applicants, however, will include such other bits of information as military experience, travel, hobbies, and memberships. Be careful not to clutter your data sheet or you will defeat its prime objective—to present a lot of information about yourself in an orderly manner and in a relatively small space (one page if possible).

The Interview

Although the purpose of this appendix is to acquaint you with vital information about the employment application letter and data sheet, it is proper that you be reminded of the importance of adequate preparation for your interview.

Do not think of the interview as just "a talk" or as merely "a chance for personnel to look you over." After all, to secure an interview has been your objective throughout this detailed and rather time-consuming campaign we've discussed.

If you have handled your employment campaign as thoroughly and carefully as has been recommended here, you should be acquainted with important facts about yourself, about the employment picture in general, and about the specific companies with which you will interview. You must be prepared for the interview, and this means that you have fresh in your mind facts and details in all these areas. *Be prepared!*

By this time you should know the importance of being well-groomed and appropriately dressed for the interview (nonverbal communication). Don't defeat your purpose because of carelessness in your appearance.

1234 Fifth Street
Small City, Texas
March 15, 19--

Personnel Manager
Acme Company
1500 Office Building
Metropolis, New York 10000

Dear Sir:

The outstanding management training program conducted by your company
has been the subject of much discussion in my college management classes.
I'd like to be associated with your company because I believe the
excellent experience I've acquired already, augmented by your fine training program, would make me a valuable asset to your company.

While earning my B.B.A. degree at Collegiate University, I earned fifty
percent of my expense money working at various jobs. You'll find this
and other information on the enclosed data sheet. My business experience
taught me the importance of using time wisely, and it gave me the chance
to associate with all types of people.

I've especially enjoyed my present job as manager of an apartment complex
because of the opportunity to work with the same people on a day-in, day-out
basis. Trying to keep 200 people reasonably happy is not an easy assignment.
This job has been extremely valuable because it has given me the opportunity
to practice my management theory--additional experience I'd bring to your
company. I think you'll find my combination of education, experience, and
common sense very helpful in your organization.

After you've studied my qualifications and contacted my references, will
you please write to me and suggest a time when I may come to your office
for an interview.

Sincerely,

John Doe
Enc.

APPENDIX B: AN EMPLOYMENT APPLICATION LETTER

```
                    QUALIFICATIONS OF

                        John Doe
                    1234 Fifth Street
                    Small City, Texas
                      (123) 456-7890


Personal

Weight:  165 lbs.
Height:  6' 2"
Birthdate:  January 15, 19--
Birthplace:  Center City, Oklahoma
Health:  Excellent

Education

Graduated, Collegiate University, Centerville, Texas, B.B.A. degree with
   major in management, June, 19--
Attended, Midville College, Midville, Texas, majored in business adminis-
   tration, September, 10-- to May, 19--
Graduated, Small High School, Small City, Texas, May, 19--

Work Experience

September, 19-- to Present     Manager, River View Apartments
                               Centerville, Texas
                               Cared for property, collected rents

Summer, 19--                   Assistant Manager, Hamburger Heaven
                               Small City, Texas
                               Kept records, waited on customers, did some
                               cooking

Summer, 19--                   Gardener, Self-employed
                               Small City, Texas
                               Mowed lawns, did general lawn and garden
                               work

Memberships

Alpha Omega Alpha Omega (honorary fraternity)
Amateur Gardeners League
Apartment Managers of America
Dean's List (six semesters)



References

Dr. John Blank          Mr. Ralph Roe          Dr. John Smith
College of Commerce     657 Broadway           Medical Clinic
Collegiate University   Small City, Texas      Small City, Texas
Centerville, Texas      (Insurance Agent)      (Family Physician)
(Professor)
```

APPENDIX C: A RESUME

Seeking employment is not only an essential activity in which most of us engage at some time but also an exciting and interesting experience. By knowing yourself and the job market as well as possible, you will be better able to engage in the job-hunting activity and to recognize and grasp the best career opportunity when it appears.

While a well-written employment application letter and a well-structured data sheet will not guarantee you a job, they are certainly very important parts in the total employment picture. The research that goes into their preparation is also of great help in preparing you for the interview itself. The interview is the culmination of your employment campaign. Sell yourself there, and the job is yours!

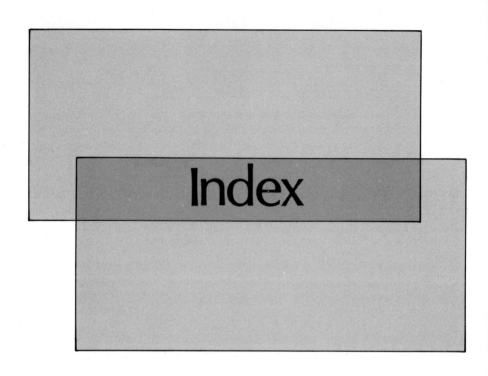

Index